Endorsements for
DANGERS TO THE FAITH

"The great need today is to love our enemies into the saving power of Jesus Christ. How can we do that unless we know who they are? Many thanks to Al Kresta for showing us the field of our love with *Dangers to the Faith*. He treats mainly of ideas, but it is people who hold these ideas. Some of these may even have taken a small root in our own hearts. Let us allow Christ's love to root them out and then help us be a sign of salvation to our whole world."

BISHOP EARL BOYEA, DIOCESE OF LANSING, MICHIGAN

"Al Kresta is like a powerful satellite for Catholics in this country. He picks up the signals of cultural trends and he beams us the message we need to take home. He's open-minded yet discriminating, culturally fluent yet profoundly Catholic. This book is a useful tool for those who are called to the New Evangelization — and that means all of us."

SCOTT HAHN, FATHER MICHAEL SCANLAN CHAIR OF BIBLICAL THEOLOGY AND THE NEW EVANGELIZATION AT FRANCISCAN UNIVERSITY OF STEUBENVILLE

"In this primer on the intellectual potholes in our increasingly bizarre culture, Al Kresta helpfully scouts some of the roughest terrain on which the New Evangelization must contend for the soul of the West. Fasten your seat belt for a bumpy — but essential — ride through the wastelands."

GEORGE WEIGEL, AUTHOR OF *EVANGELICAL CATHOLICISM: DEEP REFORM IN THE 21ST-CENTURY CHURCH*

"Al Kresta has saved you about 10,000 hours of study and research with this book. Read it. It is incredibly informative and will awaken you to the work we have to do if we are to awaken the people of our times to the genius of Catholicism."

MATTHEW KELLY, FOUNDER OF DYNAMICCATHOLIC.COM AND AUTHOR OF *REDISCOVER CATHOLICISM*

"As intense as his research is in detailing the worldview of those who mean the Church harm, Al Kresta never forgets that we are called by Christ to love them, pray for them, and even give our lives in proclaiming the truth to them. That may be the most powerful lesson of this wonderful book."

MATTHEW BUNSON, AUTHOR OF *POPE FRANCIS* AND GENERAL EDITOR OF THE *CATHOLIC ALMANAC*

"Al Kresta's new book is studded with delightful sections on Oprah, Carl Sagan, evolutionists, reincarnationists, and other popular gurus. It offers a quick tour through today's pretenders to spiritual superiority over Jesus Christ. An informal, cheerful guide to our enemies, by a warrior who takes our age as a wonderful time to be alive."

MICHAEL NOVAK, FORMER GEORGE FREDERICK JEWETT SCHOLAR
IN RELIGION, PHILOSOPHY, AND PUBLIC POLICY
AT THE AMERICAN ENTERPRISE INSTITUTE

"Al Kresta has answered 'How do we stand up against the constant attacks on Catholicism?' brilliantly in *Dangers to the Faith*. This book should be right next to your Bible and *Catechism*, as it helps us clearly identify those challenges and attacks and then lays out clear, concise, and loving responses for a world so desperately in need of Jesus and the teachings of His Church."

TERESA TOMEO, BEST-SELLING CATHOLIC AUTHOR
AND SYNDICATED TALK SHOW HOST

"*Dangers to the Faith* is for our century what Chesterton's *Heretics* and Belloc's *Great Heresies* were for the last century. It is a damning indictment and demonstrative demolition of the major errors of our age. Al Kresta shows us what's wrong with the world and that the Catholic Church is the only thing that can put it right."

JOSEPH PEARCE, LITERARY BIOGRAPHER AND
WRITER-IN-RESIDENCE AT THOMAS MORE COLLEGE

"This is an extremely interesting book — compelling, thoughtful, insightful, respectful, charitable, measured, bold, and unafraid. Al Kresta is as fearless as he is comprehensive, covering everything from Islam to New Age, from reincarnation to relativism to consumerism, from evolution to the Catholic Church's misunderstood yet seamless integration of faith and reason. Through it all, Al Kresta remains . . . well, orthodox. When I tune in to Al's show on the radio, I'm pleased to occasionally catch a 'Best of Kresta.' Well, this book may be the ultimate Best of Kresta."

PAUL KENGOR, PH.D., PROFESSOR OF POLITICAL SCIENCE
AT GROVE CITY COLLEGE

DANGERS TO THE FAITH

Recognizing Catholicism's 21st-Century Opponents

Al Kresta

Our Sunday Visitor Publishing Division
Our Sunday Visitor, Inc.
Huntington, Indiana 46750

Nihil Obstat
Msgr. Michael Heintz, Ph.D.
Censor Librorum

Imprimatur
✠ Kevin C. Rhoades
Bishop of Fort Wayne-South Bend
January 21, 2013

The *Nihil Obstat* and *Imprimatur* are official declarations that a book is free from doctrinal or moral error. It is not implied that those who have granted the *Nihil Obstat* and *Imprimatur* agree with the contents, opinions, or statements expressed.

ISBN: 978-1-59276-725-0 (Inventory No. T1046)
eISBN: 978-1-61278-325-3
LCCN: 2013933894

Cover design: Rebecca J. Heaston
Cover art: Shutterstock
Interior design: Sherri L. Hoffman

PRINTED IN THE UNITED STATES OF AMERICA

This book is dedicated to Sally Morris Kresta, my beloved partner in mission for 36 years. Her eager expectation, her innumerable suggestions, and, finally, her graceful application of pressure to get my thoughts straight, my words out, and the book done testify to her immense worth, which extends far beyond the great pleasure of her company.

May this book afford her a flash of the light and joy with which she has blessed our home, her domestic church. Through her brood — Alexis Lynne, Nicholas Joseph, James Logan, Albert Evan, and David Sterling, their wonderfully game and enjoyable spouses and offspring — may we continue to glimpse Christ's Kingdom in some small, mustard seed-like way.

"At any given moment, there is an orthodoxy, a body of ideas, which it is assumed that all right-thinking people will accept without question. It is not exactly forbidden to say this, that or the other, but it is 'not done'. . . . Anyone who challenges the prevailing orthodoxy finds himself silenced with surprising effectiveness. A genuinely unfashionable opinion is almost never given a fair hearing, whether in the popular press or in the highbrow periodicals."

— GEORGE ORWELL[1]

"The hostility toward religion among American intellectuals arises from a clear awareness that it was against a publicly religious culture that their own culture rebelled. Now that rebellion is completely successful in terms of capturing control of all the public instruments of transmission of culture — the universities, the media, and the literature and art — but it has become such a shibboleth of intellectual life to snipe at religion that, like the aging 'revolutionaries' of the old Soviet Union, they mindlessly continue to 'rebel' in order to defend their tight grip on the establishment. Indeed, those intellectuals are the establishment. And what was once a daring and rebellious stance is now just another example of lockstep conformists mindlessly echoing ideas that they haven't examined."

— ORSON SCOTT CARD[2]

Contents

Acknowledgments

Like bringing forth a child, this book was far easier in the conception than in the delivery. Many shouldered the burden but in many very different ways. I owe many thanks, first of all, to my family. My sons David and Evan lived at home while I was preoccupied with writing and was less available for fun and frolic. My entire extended family, however, was patient in tolerating my absence from various dinners, movies, and day trips.

My team at Ave Maria Communications juggled schedules and tossed out criticisms and suggestions. Even if they are paid to put up with me, their good humor and faithfulness showed them to be truly co-laborers in Christ and no mere employees.

My editor and friend Bert Ghezzi suggested the idea for this book. He corrected me as a brother and challenged me like a coach. The book is vastly better for his patience and suggestions.

Two organizations deserve recognition. No one has done more to increase the visibility of contemporary Catholic apologetics than my friend Karl Keating and his team at Catholic Answers. I didn't consult with Karl on this book, so he bears absolutely no responsibility for its shortcomings. He does deserve credit, however, for helping to create an intellectual climate in which a publisher would even find a work like this worthy of distribution.

Similarly, when the history of 20th-century American Catholicism is written, the influence of Mother Angelica and Eternal Word Television Network (EWTN) will finally be laid out for all to see. Without her commitment to the work of "remedial catechesis," far fewer Catholics would be interested in books of this sort. I must also thank Doug Keck and Michael Warsaw at EWTN for their steady leadership and for selecting *Kresta in the Afternoon* for distribution to their 200-plus radio affiliates, a number which is growing monthly.

Two features of this book must be acknowledged: one is an absence, the other a presence. First, the absence. The book lacks separate chapters on the "life" issues, disordered sexual behavior, and the stunning fact that roughly half the human race lives in poverty. Though our opponents advance an agenda through these problems, these topics have been so well treated by so many others that I chose not to include them as separate chapters. Books can only be so long.

Second, the presence, even the excess, of so many endnotes is deliberate and not just for purposes of citation but to aid in further reading and research. Not everybody pays much attention to endnotes but those who do will, I trust, find them packed with many future possibilities for study. I should mention — but, I hope, needn't justify — the inclusion of many works with which I greatly disagree. This is a work about opponents to the Catholic faith. We owe it to them, as a mark of decency and common humanity, to represent their positions in ways that they would recognize as fair and accurate. To that end, we should have some acquaintance with their writings and teachings. While I wouldn't expect priests and deacons or RCIA directors to recommend many of these works in their catechetical work, I do think the aspiring apologist/evangelist must have firsthand familiarity with the worldviews of our various opponents. That requires reading their books, hearing their lectures or engaging them in direct conversation.

INTRODUCTION

We Have Enemies to Love and Challenge

"He who does not bellow the truth when he knows truth makes himself the accomplice of liars and forgers."
— CHARLES PÉGUY (*Provincial Letter, Basic Verities*)

"Christ as the light of the world, as light on the world, makes the believer see things differently, even contrarily."
— GEORGE H. NIEDERAUER (Archbishop of San Francisco, 2007)

WE HAVE EYES TO SEE

Most of us know Vincent van Gogh (1853-1890) as the half crazed, earless, suicidal painter of *Sunflowers* or *Starry Night* or as the touched and touching subject of Don MacLean's 1970 pop ballad "Vincent" ("Starry, Starry Night"). Few realize that Van Gogh spent the early years of his adult life as a missionary evangelist, radically committed to Jesus Christ, as he saw him in the coal miners working the dreary mines of Borinage, Belgium. Van Gogh identified himself with the poor and gave away his food, clothing, and possessions as the natural overflow of sharing the gospel. "Those who walk in the darkness, in the centre of the earth like the miners," are more "impressed by the words of the Gospel" than those who do not face such dark conditions.[1]

Not only did Van Gogh, the artist, see and paint the world differently, but he saw people differently.[2] He did not see people as they were but rather as they might be. "I prefer painting people's eyes rather than cathedrals, for there is something in the eyes that is not in the cathedral — a human soul, be it that of a poor beggar or of a street walker."[3]

C. S. Lewis said something similar: "There are no ordinary people. You have never talked to a mere mortal. . . . Next to the Blessed

11

Sacrament itself, your neighbor is the holiest object presented to your senses."[4] Artists and evangelists/missionaries see splendor in the ordinary, called, as they are, to be artists of the soul, "to see in every human being, no matter how ruined and desolate, the glorious possibility of restoration through Christ's love. Total restoration will not be complete until Christ's return. But the beautiful beginnings of a masterpiece are evident in every believer."[5] We are like a Van Gogh masterpiece that has been vandalized or like a magnificent medieval castle that has fallen into disrepair. These artifacts are very good, but in need of restoration. Christ does this work of restoration in our lives. Van Gogh knew this: "Christ is more of an artist than the artists; he works in the living spirit and the living flesh, he makes men instead of statues."[6]

This book doesn't do statues, but I do take a few icons and try to see them as men and women made to image God, unfulfilled until they do. I tell stories that reveal something about the spiritual dynamic of an Oprah, Steve Jobs, Tiger Woods, Christopher Hitchens, and others. With a few facts about their own spiritual "conversation," the reader is enabled to pivot and, when appropriate, turn conversations away from celebrity gossip and instead toward the direction of something more edifying and consequential.

We Have Enemies to Love

For us, Mother Teresa modeled how to see "Christ in his most distressing disguise" in those dying on Calcutta's streets. We have fewer examples of those who love their enemies, those who sustain love toward those who mock, harass, and, ultimately, continue their crucifixion of Jesus by persecuting his followers, his body, the Church.[7]

Paul puts a high premium on Christians behaving constructively: "If possible . . . live peaceably with all."[8] But most of us suffer not from an excess of zeal. More likely, we are afraid or, worse, apathetic. We needn't be. This book will show that the Catholic faith is a blessing to the world because it tells the truth about reality. Many people don't want to talk religion, but they will follow a conversation they think is reality based. Catholic teaching best corresponds to life as we experience it. It best explains human aspirations for love, life, significance, and meaning, the appearance of design in the cosmos, the function of conscience, the rise of modern science, the persistence of the Jews and the papacy, the rise of the Christian Church and a God who reveals himself as Love, is Infinite and Personal, who is both one and many, and who we are called upon to image. Are we convinced of that?

WE KNOW OUR OPPOSITION

We have radically different, competing conceptions of human origin and destiny, of morality and the good life, even the nature of truth. This book gives you tools to deal with the competing visions of secularity, Islam, New Age, Eastern thought, and so on in popular conversation. These opponents take many forms and recur in different contexts throughout the book:

- Some are blatantly false ideas in the hands of influential and wealthy philanthropists and foundations.
- Some are outrageous journalistic abuses of the great goods of science, reason, and spirituality.
- Some engage the shadow world of spiritual warfare.
- Some are governmental and political players seeking to create a thoroughly secular society in which we are reduced to a freedom from religion rather than freedom of religion.
- Some are competing religious groups who distort and twist the doctrine and history of the Church.
- Some are activist groups bent upon marginalizing Catholic cultural influence in the world of entertainment, politics, business, education, international affairs, and even health care and ministry to the poor and orphans.
- Some are brilliant futurists who seek to remake human nature. Others want to diminish humanity's status and elevate the "lower" animals. Both deny human exceptionalism.

Obviously, topics this broad can't be dealt with exhaustively. They can, however, be dealt with accurately and suggestively — i.e., in a popular enough way to pick up a few conversational gambits and responses.

WE ARE ALL MISSIONARIES

Baptism identifies every Catholic with the mission of Christ. The question isn't whether or not we are involved in the mission of the Church. Baptism has already involved us. The question is whether or not we will embrace that call and receive the gifts God has prepared to help us build up the body of Christ.

First of all, we must know and love the faith. Never have there been so many excellent catechetical tools available on the Internet, in parishes, Catholic bookstores, and Catholic television and radio. Social media allows us to pool the intellectual resources of all our friends with virtually no effort. There is no excuse for a Catholic adult to say he doesn't know what the Church actually teaches, even if he is illiterate. Loving the faith, of course, also means living it — but this is only a book, not a retreat. So I'll leave it to others to strengthen the link between belief and behavior.

WE ARE A MINORITY

Secondly, we must love our mission field. We are missionaries in a land where we have enemies that we must learn to love. Many of us haven't yet come to grips with the fact that, as observant Catholics, we are a bona fide minority. As a minority, we are prone to the spiritual temptations of anger, resentment, bitterness, and vindictiveness. These assault minorities because they feel the dominant culture exercises undue power over them. Those things that matter most to us are often the object of mockery. We are easily caricatured. Our leaders are trivialized. Our doctrines are misstated and then called ridiculous. And yet, we know our worldview is rational — even, in some aspects, self-evident. But the mission field we are working doesn't see that mothers must protect, not abort, their offspring; or that marriage is not in need of redefinition. Even our government has recently refused to any longer work with us in key areas of service. (More to follow.) Yes, observant Catholics are a clear minority, and we share a similar problem with the apostolic Church: the pressure to let the dominant culture define us and then conform and accommodate evils that will prevent human flourishing.

How bad is it? You tell me. The Catholic Church is accused of:

- Mythmaking in an age of science.
- Sexual repression in an age of erotic emancipation.
- Rigid hierarchy in an egalitarian society.
- Patriarchal authority in an age of feminized religion.
- Monarchical tendencies in a democratic age.
- Insisting on accommodation to religion in a secular age.
- Calling for a universal voluntary sharing of goods in an age celebrating personal acquisition and private property as absolute.
- Highlighting the futility of violence in an age stabilized and entertained by perpetual small wars.
- Talking about corporate personality and communitarian ethics in an age of individualism.
- Believing in a universe of design and purpose in an age that believes in purely naturalistic forces acting with no prevision of the end they are achieving.
- Urging the priority of the personal in an age of bureaucratization.
- Insisting on prudence in a world impressed with flamboyance.

Yes, we are getting it from all sides. But if the left complains and the right complains, we might be doing something right.

Joseph Ratzinger, in his *Introduction to Christianity*, tells the story of a traveling circus in Denmark that catches fire. The clown, already made up and dressed for performance, speeds into the neighboring town to fetch help and warn the inhabitants. As he is calling "Fire," the townspeople take his pleas as an excellent bit of advertising intended to lure them to the circus. They begin laughing, and as his agitation grows, their humor rises until they are tearing up, applauding the clown on his performance. The clown is also in tears, but weeping for his inability to communicate effectively, and this amuses them all the more. He can't get them to take him seriously because he is, after all, such a clown. Finally, as the flames begin to catch their fields on fire, they realize that the clown's message was authentic, but now the circus and the town burn to the ground.

Do we feel like the clown? People think they know us and what we are up to. They've heard the message before, and they think we are trying to lure them into our show. We amuse them. To make matters worse, none of us knows our message as clearly as the clown knew his. Nor is our intended audience so blatantly ignorant as the townspeople. Our audience is not without some legitimate truths of their own that we may not quite comprehend. So we still look the clown, but without the clown's clarity and without his audience's absolute ignorance.[9]

We Don't Take the Credit, and We Won't Take the Blame

Take heart! We also have some advantages. First, the Holy Spirit is already at work in people's lives throughout the world. Second, human beings were made for God. They are hungry and restless. Third, even the rich and powerful have inner struggle and dialogue about spiritual things. Fourth, there are more of us strategically placed than we realize.

Above all, the Holy Spirit has already gone before us and is operative in the lives of people long before we open our mouths. Jesus said that we would have tribulation, but be of good cheer for he has overcome the world. Our aim is not separation from the world or accommodation to the world, but rather, to the degree that God gives us the grace, transformation of the world to resemble the Kingdom. Wherever God's will is done, we glimpse the Kingdom. Our relationship to the world is complex. We are set apart from the world, taking our cues from a Kingdom not of this world, and yet we are sent into the world in imitation of the Incarnate Christ. Throughout the world, we have allies as well as enemies. Get serious about missions, and live in expectation of expanding your circle of co-workers and friends.

Unknown, at this very moment, serious Catholics and other Christians are in our place of employment, school, extended family, and electoral district. These Catholics are not sneaking around subverting the work they were hired to do. Rather, they are engaging in elevating and perfecting those works. I write here of what I know and have seen firsthand. Because of a Catholic professional working within Oprah's organization, Oprah more effectively used her influence to establish programs to elevate and protect untold children's lives. Because of an evangelical Christian working quietly behind the scenes in Washington, DC, years ago, President Richard Nixon's hatchet man, the late Chuck Colson, was accepted into Christian service after prison and went on to organize Prison and Justice Fellowship, transforming inmates by the thousands. We are not alone.

Behind the scenes, Christ's Spirit is already at work and is no respecter of persons. He strives with all because he desires that all would be saved. This is as true today as when Emperor Constantine; the youthful Perpetua and Felicity; the British abolitionist William Wilberforce; the young, urban lawyer Augustine; the wounded soldier Ignatius; or the young son of an Assisi cloth merchant, Francis, found conversion. In all these cases, the world was unaware of the interior dialogue going on in their minds. Jesus gets into your head. That's my prayer for this book.

PART ONE

Abusers of Spirituality and Revelation

From New Age to the New Self-Styled Spirituality of Oprah

"The Christ 'is the God in us all . . . the Christ or God in us is the same that was in Jesus, only in greater degree in Him.' "

— ROBERT FULLER (commenting on Phineas Parkhurst Quimby's Christ)[1]

"Most New Agers are very positively inclined towards Jesus. When he is mentioned, it is almost without exception as a supreme example of spiritual wisdom: a 'fully realized being,' 'great Master,' or accomplished mystic or Gnostic."

— WOUTER J. HANEGRAAF[2]

THE ODD COUPLE

In November of 2010, the *Oprah Winfrey Show* was featuring unconventional marriages. What did viewers expect? Same-sex so-called marriage? "Open" marriages with "swinging" partners? Polygamous marriages among renegade Mormons? Maybe women who marry penitent axe murderers and then sport T-shirts that read: "Axe me about my man." But Oprah is no Jerry Springer, so I was sure she would stay away from prostitutes who marry their pimps.

What I didn't imagine was that I would see Oprah's crew show up at my parish, Christ the King, Ann Arbor, Michigan, to watch several of the Sisters of Mary, Mother of the Eucharist — a new Dominican community of over 100 women, average age 26 — profess their vows and "marry" Christ Jesus. Unconventional marriage, indeed.

The sisters bore beautiful witness to a spiritual reality few people, including Oprah (b. 1954), ever consider: the Wedding Supper of the Lamb, the final union of Christ with his Bride, the Church.[3] By bearing visible witness to the life of the age to come, they made it tangible, plausible, believable. Thanks to the openness of Oprah's team, including at least one mission-minded Catholic, the nation would witness a truly unconventional nuptial union among, biblically speaking, a "peculiar people."

"NEW AGE" OR "NEW SELF-STYLED" SPIRITUALITY?

Oprah had featured the Sisters of Mary once before, and true to her reputation she treated them with grace, fondness, and even a bit of respectful perplexity.[4] Oprah respects Christian commitment. During her final episode, she credited her "team and Jesus" for her success and closed with a "Glory to God." She's never denied the Name, though she has denied being a "New Ager." Spirits in the trees and rooms full of crystals aren't her cup of tea. Oprah does, however, model a "new self-styled" spirituality, which is a more expansive term for "New Age" spirituality without the off-putting weirdness. *O, The Oprah Magazine* describes the spiritual smorgasbord that is Oprah's banquet: "We're browsing the spiritual marketplace, dropping new ideas and philosophies into our carts — a smidgen of Buddhism, some New Testament, maybe a little tai chi tossed in."[5] Mixing and matching, it is a do-it-yourself religion. Elizabeth Gilbert (b. 1969), an Oprah alum, author of *Eat, Pray, Love* (2007), says it best: "You have every right to cherry-pick when it comes to moving your spirit and finding peace in God. . . . You take whatever works from wherever you can find it, and you keep moving toward the light."[6]

Oprah cheerleads this individualistic, eclectic spirituality that challenges and, for many, replaces the more traditional denominations. Thirty-three percent of people polled say Oprah has "a more profound impact" on their spirituality than their pastors.[7] But even Oprah's pastoral influence is outshone by the bright constellation of those she has hosted, championed, and practically commissioned. She devoted two episodes to Elizabeth Gilbert and helped launch — or in some cases, breathed new life into — teachers like Rhonda Byrne, Eckhart Tolle, Deepak Chopra, Miguel Ruiz, Wayne Dyer, Marianne Williamson, Barbara DeAngelis, Marilyn Ferguson, and psychic mediums John Edwards and James Van Praagh.

"New Age" has been so often parodied that bookstores often substitute "Metaphysical" or even the older "Occult" to head those sections. Books in these fields, however, compete quite well against Christian titles. In December 2010, I measured the shelf space devoted to spiritual/religious reading at Barnes & Noble and now the tragically extinct Borders Books. These stores devoted roughly 1,200 feet of shelf space to various religious/spiritual books. Christianity took up 750 feet. "New Age/Metaphysical/Occult" (astrology, channeling, divination, magic, mental healing, reincarnation, tarot, Theosophy, Urantia, UFOs, etc.) covered 350 feet. It looks as though Christianity still more than doubles New Age. But this isn't as impressive as it sounds. The commercial relationship of Christian to New Age is only slightly stronger than the relationship between sales of Coca Cola to Pepsi.[8] Does anyone think Pepsi is not a serious competitor to Coke?

Fascination with things New Age peaked in January 1987, when Oscar-winning Shirley MacLaine (b. 1934) portrayed herself in *Out on a Limb*, an autobiographical miniseries rich with illicit romance, past-life regressions, extraterrestrials, astral projection, and the discovery of her own divinity — all in six hours of ABC's prime time.

Twenty years after MacLaine led us out on a limb, Elizabeth Gilbert's *Eat, Pray, Love* led us on a spiritual travelogue to Italy, India, and Indonesia, in which she manages to match MacLaine's *Limb* for "unconventional experiences." Gilbert hears her own voice as the Voice of God and wildly abandons her marriage, embraces prophecies from a "ninth-generation Balinese medicine man,"[9] gets "pulled through the wormhole of the Absolute,"[10] precipitates a miracle through an eccentric invocation of the saints (who include Bill and Hillary Clinton, Mahatma Gandhi, Nelson Mandela, Francis of Assisi, and the Dalai Lama), and reveals an almost preternatural self-preoccupation[11] as she stars winsomely in her I-centered pilgrimage toward self-understanding.

Gilbert's "new self-styled spirituality" tops even MacLaine's "New Age spirituality" for idiosyncrasies. Nevertheless, they share much common ground, including a cavalier dismissal of 2,000 years of Catholic spirituality[12] and an embrace of one's own divinity as the *sine qua non* of authentic spirituality. Because MacLaine is even less "self-styled" than Gilbert, let's go fondly back to 1987 and *Out on a Limb* with Shirley. Don't feel guilty if you swell with nostalgia. Just remember the good old days weren't all that good and, in this case, not really all that old.

ABC Goes *Out on a Limb* (1987)

Middle-aged David Manning (John Heard) and Shirley MacLaine sit idyllically on the beach:

> DAVID: "Don't you ever get frustrated when you feel that you are not really being yourself?"
>
> SHIRLEY: "Yes, all the time. Right."
>
> DAVID: "That's what all the Masters have tried to help us with."
>
> SHIRLEY: "What masters?"
>
> DAVID: "You know Christ, Buddha, the Indian avatars. They . . . went right to the root of the problems in society: *The individual* . . . [If] everybody believed that he was a part of God, the Kingdom of heaven was within, and that if we took responsibility for that then we wouldn't get so frustrated . . . with ourselves and with everybody else — . . . it seems like it takes multiple lifetimes to come to that simple realization."
>
> SHIRLEY: "Why isn't reincarnation in the Bible? Why isn't it taught in Christianity?"

David, a composite character, represents MacLaine's spiritual mentors. Knowingly, he blames Emperor Justinian for dominating the Second Council of Constantinople in A.D. 553 and forcing it to condemn reincarnation in spite of the frequent approval of the Church Fathers.[13] He is *pathetically wrong* on all the particulars.

Innocent and now indignant, Shirley asks, "How could the Church go along with such a thing?"

David thinly disguises his arrogance by a winsome and gentle manner. He shows no reluctance attributing the most sinister motives to Church leaders 1,500 years removed from his acquaintance. David would never want to be caught judging. Yet he can't resist posing as though he was intimately familiar with the cravenness and ungodly ambition of those old boys. Those Church leaders, he judges, "went along with it because they just didn't want people to assume responsibility for their own karmic destiny." Our culture's disregard for history and organized religion grants people no resistance to inventing lies about institutional religion's past.

Shirley, rendered mute by David's apparent mastery of Church history, muses: "Karmic destiny. . . . Boy, you know if I really believed that I lived before and was going to live again and that everything I put out there would come back, there would be no doubt in my mind that I'd be completely responsible for everything that happened in my life. . . ." Why does reincarnation, rather than the *Dies Irae*, the Day of Judgment, awaken Shirley's moral accountability?

Sensing her vulnerability, David nudges her toward the God within. "Just stand up and hold your arms out like this and say, 'The Kingdom of heaven is within. I love myself.'"

Uncertainly she repeats: "The kingdom of heaven is within. . . . I love myself."

David ups the ante. "Better than that, say 'I and God are one.' No, wait, wait, wait, wait. I've got the best one. Just say 'I am God.'"

Raised Baptist, residue from the prohibition against worshiping other gods won't yield so easily. "David, I can't say that."

He gently reprimands: "See how little you think of yourself; you can't even say the words." Mr. Mentor shames her for refusing to attribute to herself the highest name in our vocabulary.

Then, proving how little she really does think of herself, she conforms to his expectations and speaks what a moment earlier she had thought unspeakable: "I am God . . . I am God."

But Shirley is not yet bereft of all logic. She pauses from affirming her own divinity for a moment of reflection. "David, if I'm God, what does that make you?"

David rises, faces her, and with a Zen-like economy of words skirts basic logic and with guru-like earnestness pronounces: "We always see in others what we see in ourselves. . . . I am God."

They repeat the "mantra" antiphonally to each other and then, turning toward the sea, join hands and repeat "I am God" to the fish of the sea and the gulls of the air, their voices rising in volume until a giggling Shirley shoves David to the sand. Falling over him, she teases, "I am God, not you."

Love all around.

Do We Need a New Age Attitude Adjustment?

By 1992, the fuzz was clearly wearing off this New Age peach, and the press had begun putting it in quotes.[14] Oprah, however, avoided parody. Her generosity of spirit, mission to alleviate personal suffering, skillful communication, openness to others, and her carefully crafted image established her as the visible sign of unity for modern American spirituality.

When terrorists destroyed the World Trade Center, America's mayor, Rudy Giuliani, gathered representative clergy to pray at a Yankee Stadium inspirational service for 20,000 mourners. Thirty years ago, Billy Graham, advisor to six presidents, one of the most admired men in America, would have emceed. But in 2001, Oprah, entertainer and social entrepreneur, got the nod.

In America, We Did It Our Way

America's colorful and innovative religious history shows a "democratization of religious authority" and an "individualization of conscience." Over three centuries, new and creative religious leaders have claimed special authority based on personal experiences and, for better or worse, gathered followers.[15]

Transcendentalism, America's first philosophical movement, flourished in the 1830s and '40s. Ralph Waldo Emerson, Henry David Thoreau, Bronson Alcott, and Margaret Fuller rejected Christian orthodoxy, introduced Southeast Asian religious texts, and forecast the imminent dawning of a new age. What spiritual movement would embody this new age? Spiritualism[16] (1848-1920s), Theosophy (1875-present day), the Mind Science groups emanating from Phineas Parkhurst Quimby (1802-1866)?[17] People disagreed, but all of these elite leaders believed they had transcended historic

Christianity. They even congratulated themselves for rescuing the Nazarene's reputation and freeing him from dusty texts, empty rituals, and petty theological disagreements.

America applauds the unorthodox. By toasting the individualistic, democratic, and egalitarian, we became "a nation of heretics"[18] — not a nation of unbelievers, since American spirituality exceeds that of Europe. Many of these "once Christians" have chosen to fashion their own version and discard Christian orthodoxy while retaining what works for them from the Christian tradition.[19] These were often Catholics, sacramentalized but not evangelized;[20] they became and remain Oprah's audience.

What's the appeal? Like Fulton Sheen, America's pioneer Catholic broadcaster, Oprah knows: *"Life Is Worth Living."* She confessed to producing some "trash TV" in the early '90s. Confronted by critics, though, she determined to "use television to transform people's lives . . . I am talking about each individual coming to the awareness that, 'I am Creation's son, I am Creation's daughter. I am more than my physical self, . . . but ultimately I am Spirit come from the greatest Spirit.'"[21] "Seekers," like Oprah, don't necessarily hate the Catholic Church. Filled with misconceptions about the faith, she just thinks she found something better and wants to share it. Let's face it. Many Americans prefer Oprah's way of doing it to our way of not doing it.

Oprah's Jesus Was Made in America

World religions are built on theological propositions or philosophical ideologies. Christianity, however, builds on the identity of its founder. "'Who do you say that I am?' . . . 'You are the Christ, the Son of the living God.'"[22] Jesus and Paul warned against false Christs,[23] yet America fashions many Jesuses, functionally displacing the Jesus of Christian orthodoxy.[24] For instance:

- The Jesus of Christian Science is a divine idea or principle — not a person.
- The Jesus of Jehovah's Witnesses is the first and greatest creation of Jehovah God — not himself divine.

- The Jesus of the Unification Church is a messiah whose work was frustrated by human evil and remains to be fulfilled — not God's full Word to humanity.
- The Jesus of the "I Am" movement is an Ascended Master of the sixth sphere of consciousness — not the unique Son of God.
- The Jesus of John Allegro is consumed as a sacred mushroom[25] — rather than the Bread of Life. At least we agree that you are what you eat.

The 1970s and '80s fashioned Jesus images throughout pop culture — some good, many twisted. Remember the hippie Jesus in *Godspell* and *Jesus Christ Superstar*; Monty Python's *Life of Brian*; Edwina Sandys' bare-breasted cruciform Jesus, sculpted to commemorate the United Nations' Decade of the Woman; James Cone's black Jesus of *Black Theology and Black Power*; Hebrew scholar Geza Vermes' *Jesus the Jew*; the non-Jewish, cynic philosopher Jesus of Robert Funk's Jesus Seminar; Martin Scorsese's sexually vulnerable Jesus in *The Last Temptation of Christ*; the robustly cheerful "Laughing Jesus" in *Ligourian*;[26] or the Jesus of St. Faustina's Divine Mercy Chaplet, popularized on Mother Angelica's Eternal Word Television Network (EWTN).

Young Oprah's image of Jesus was forming when her pastor preached on "the jealous God." She didn't buy it and decided "that there are certainly many more paths to God other than Christianity."[27] Enter Eric Butterworth (1917-2003), a legend within the Unity/New Thought movement.[28] He taught a different Jesus, no longer the Divine Savior who made atonement for sin but the way-shower[29] who showed us how to enter the Christ consciousness. History is important here.

JESUS AND CHRIST, GOD AND MAN

The Unity Church emerged with the 19th-century New Thought movement. Like Mary Baker Eddy's Christian Science, its "theology" flowed from mesmerist healer Phineas Parkhurst Quimby. Quimby, and later Eddy, blamed wrong thinking and false beliefs for humanity's many ills. Right thinking and true beliefs resided in the impersonal, universal mind-principle: "the Christ." Christ, the divine consciousness, was not Jesus of Nazareth. Jesus had to, like the rest of us, discover this Christ principle within. He wasn't the Christ by nature. Once he learned it, he showed us the path to Christ consciousness.[30]

"Jesus' great discovery," according to Butterworth, was "the full realization of his unity with God . . . the breaking down of the 'wall' between man and God.[31] . . . *Yet he attained no more than what is expected of every one of us.*"[32] All must encounter their true self as God and God as their true self. The ancient heresy of Gnosticism that Elaine Pagels claims to have rediscovered in the "lost gospels" of early Christianity sounds just like this: "Self-knowledge is knowledge of God."[33]

Gnosticism sees the material world as evil or obstructive or burdensome. Catholics and other Christians note that Gnostics, old and new, must deny that God **could** come *in the flesh*, stooping to restore the friendship we aborted in Paradise. Rather, Gnosticism beckons us to *escape* our flesh and discover that we are the divinity we have been seeking.[34]

Hopefully, these contrasts will clarify:

- For the Christian, God is in Christ, redeeming or saving him.
- For the Gnostic, God is spiritually within, awaiting the soul's awakening to its own divinity.

- The Christian struggles against sin and death.
- The Gnostic struggles against sleep and illusion.

But why asleep? Why isn't our divinity self-evident? H. Emilie Cady (1848-1941), whose *Lessons in Truth* laid the foundation for the Unity Church, tells us: Humanity "originally lived consciously in the spiritual part of himself. He descended, fell in his consciousness to the external or more material part of himself."[35] Cady's fall into physical matter blinded her to her own divinity. For Cady, embodiment was a bondage to be escaped, rather than an original blessing for which we should give thanks.[36] Did she forget that God liked matter? It was his idea.

So we have another contrast that clarifies:

- For Gnosticism, the Fall is a metaphysical problem. Being embedded in matter, we are blinded to our true identity. We must get out to rediscover our divinity.
- For Catholicism, the Fall is a moral problem. Relationships are broken by sin and rebellion. We need someone to reconcile the alienated parties.

JESUS: REDEEMER OR WAYSHOWER?

In Unity, redemption is unnecessary. Once we recover from our spiritual amnesia, we will know that we were always the Divine, Christ consciousness. For the moment, however, we are blinded by illusion, not sin. Self-knowledge, not sacrificial atonement, lifts the illusion. It's no surprise, then, that Unity teaches that Christ DID NOT DIE for our sins in accordance with the Scriptures.[37] *The Way to Salvation* clarifies: "Jesus Christ was not meant to be slain as a substitute for man; that is, to atone vicariously for him. Each person must achieve at-one-ment with God, by letting the Christ Spirit within him resurrect his soul into Christ perfection."[38]

How? Right thinking, positive attitude, harmonious feelings, spiritual study, affirmations and meditations. Above all, I must "Be still and know that I Am God." When my consciousness becomes one with the divine consciousness, I have at-one-ment. Jesus is the Wayshower to the attainment of that Christ consciousness. During a program, Oprah told a Margy: "I was like you . . . I thought . . . that Jesus' being here was about his death and dying on the cross — when it really was about coming to show us how to do it, how to be, to show us the Christ consciousness that he had and that that consciousness abides with all of us."[39]

When confused about what road to take, Christ as Wayshower would be just fine. But we are not merely confused; we are broken and disabled. Weakness, illness, resentment, rebellion, broken relationships, depression, murder, terrorism, poverty, injustice, oppression, anxiety, addictions, fear, and a few other compelling matters like guilt and death afflict us. These problems don't yield to street signs, road maps, or wayshowers. We need an ambulance, a driver, an emergency room, an operating theater, a community of spiritual surgeons, healers, grace, mercy, forgiveness, love, acceptance, reconciliation, and, yes, a wayshower would be nice. But bondage to sin, requires a redeemer, not merely a wayshower.

LEARNING TO WORSHIP YOURSELF IS THE GREATEST WORSHIP OF ALL

How will the "discovery of my divine self" alter the proper act and object of worship? Isn't it an absurdity to now worship my Self as the divine one? Shockingly, Butterworth rejects worship of Jesus as an obstacle to "our own self-realization and self-unfoldment."[40] This strains credulity. Can it really be that for two millennia Catholics and other Christians have totally misidentified the proper object of worship?

By definition, *worship declares the worth of an other.* In the Anglican marriage rite, we hear, "With my body, I thee worship,"[41] as the husband pledges his body as a declaration of his bride's worth. At Mass, we present our bodies as living sacrifices, declaring the worth of the God revealed to us in Christ and who offers himself to us under the appearance of bread and wine. Worship is always directed toward an other. If so, then once I have discovered my own divinity, does it turn out that I am the One worthy of worship and for whom I have been waiting? Do I cease worshiping? Perhaps, as in Marx and Feuerbach, worship signals that one is alienated from his true self and work? Consequently, the integrated, mature man ceases to worship.

But this invites a *reductio ad absurdum.* When we blur or dismiss the Creator/creature distinction (he is God, we are not), we must respectfully push the language back toward clarity or forward toward absurdity. When doubting Thomas confessed Jesus as "My Lord and my God,"[42] could he have just as legitimately uttered those words while gazing into a mirror? "You shall worship the Lord your God, and him only shall you serve," says Jesus (Lk 4:8), citing Deuteronomy 6:13. Couldn't Jesus have been less restrictive in his language in order to accommodate Eric Butterworth's theology?

Aren't humans created to image God, not be God? Get this wrong and the good news turns into a proclamation about me, not God! It becomes "Look. I've gotten over my divine amnesia. You can too. Glory to me."

Della Reese, the wise, tough-love, top angel Tess, in *Touched By an Angel*, is Oprah's friend and pastor of New Thought's "Understanding Principles for Better Living" Church. What is Della's gospel? "We are Divine through the Christ within, the individualization of God in us."

Isn't this Oprah's gospel of ME: "God wants you to love yourself. It starts with you." Reese proclaims, "Discover, embrace and nurture yourself . . . celebrate and honor you!" The lyrics of George Benson's and, later, Whitney Houston's ballad, *Learning to Love Yourself Is the Greatest Love of All*, is meant to be an inspired tune. It invites caricature, however, by its over-the-top lyrics. Given this new theology, should we rewrite the lyrics, retitling the song, *Learning to Worship Yourself is the Greatest Worship of All*?

I/THOU, KNOWING GOD, KNOWING SELF

The comeback might be, "Yes, I know the logic sounds ludicrous. The language sounds clunky. But the spiritual experiences are undeniable. As the old Pentecostal preacher used to say, 'It's better felt than telt!'"

Indeed, Elizabeth Gilbert writes vividly of "the sense of an overwhelming divine love, like a 'lion roaring from within my chest'; the sense of a God who 'plays in my bloodstream the way sunlight amuses itself on water.'"[43] But those beautiful words simply don't square with "God dwells within you as you . . ." or "the Soul of God is my own soul."[44] Is ultimate reality two or one? Her words still hint at a God who "plays in my blood stream." That is two, not just one!

Jewish philosopher Martin Buber (1878-1965) introduced a key distinction between I and Thou.[45] *Is there or is there not a self that persists in an "I/Thou" relationship to God; distinct from God yet in union with him and others?* Gilbert speaks both ways. At times, all is One. Yet, other times she loves and is also the beloved. She would be blessed by consulting Catholic spirituality with all its multiplicity of styles and forms — Carmelite, Franciscan, Ignatian, Dominican, Benedictine, Augustinian, Desert, Charismatic, Servite, Montfortian, and so on. Whatever can be thought, felt, or experienced probably has been thought, felt, or experienced in some Catholic monastery, convent, cell, or cave over the last 2,000 years of prayer and contemplation. The late Trappist monk and hermit Thomas Merton (1915-1968) wrote of knowing God, self, and others without dissolving one into the other:

> Our knowledge of God is paradoxically not of him as the object of our scrutiny, but of ourselves as utterly dependent on his saving and merciful knowledge of us. It is in proportion, as we are known to him, that we find our real being and identity in Christ. We know him in and through ourselves in so far as his truth is the source of our being and his merciful love is the very heart of our life and existence.[46]

Merton knows that Christ doesn't practice existential imperialism. When he calls us to union, it isn't to consume us but strengthen us and lead us to imitation. It resembles the way a mother's hand cups the smaller hand of the daughter learning to write. She doesn't write it herself or so control the hand that it lacks freedom. The two can be one without eliminating one or the other. Since he created the human to image him, he cannot be jealous when we do. Why would he long to extinguish what he created to shine?

Nuptial Spirituality Is Zealous, Not Jealous

A young Oprah, scandalized by "the jealous God," needn't have walked away from historic Christianity. It was a misunderstanding over language. "Jealous" in Old Testament Hebrew doesn't mean what it does in English. "Zealous" comes closer and lacks the pettiness and insecurity that goes with "jealous." God is "zealous" to win the promiscuous over to faithful, covenantal love.[47] Our heavenly Father zealously pursues us, even as we look for love in all the wrong places.

Back to Oprah's unconventional Ann Arbor wedding. When those vowed Sisters of Mary gave themselves to Jesus, he didn't arrest their spiritual formation. They will continue to reflect Christ, not by displacing him, but by giving themselves to him and receiving his divine life in dynamic thanksgiving. Eucharist, Holy Communion, is a sacred exchange between two, not merely an assertion by one.

In the sacrament of marriage, the two become one — not by eliminating one party but by mystically uniting the two. If, rather than enter nuptial union with their Creator and Redeemer, the Sisters of Mary pledged before the gathered assembly the words of Shirley MacLaine, "I am God, I am God," the grotesque character of this charade would have been immediately evident.

We aren't made to marry ourselves, or throw ourselves birthday parties, or clone ourselves, or pray to ourselves, or feel jealous for ourselves. We are made for an Other; it is I and Thou. The spiritual relationship between I and Thou is pregnant with possibilities. We don't know exactly what we will birth, what form our spiritual maternity or offspring will take. We do know, however, that it is *cooperative*, open to the influence of an other and definitely not self-styled.

The Dark Side of the Bright New Age Movement[1]

"Since I realized I created my own reality in every way, I must therefore admit that, in essence, I was the only person alive in my universe."
— SHIRLEY MACLAINE (*It's All in the Playing*, 1987)[2]

"Mind becomes a creative factor not only in image-forming but also in the active transformation of outer reality."
— ERIC JANTSCH (*The Self-Organizing Universe*, 1980)[3]

STEVE JOBS, LITTLE DID WE KNOW YOU

In October 2003, Apple's Steve Jobs (1955-2011) — tough, charismatic pioneer of the digital revolution — learned that he had pancreatic cancer. Immediately, he phoned Larry Brilliant, his longtime friend, meditation partner, and director of Google's philanthropy.[4] While teenagers, they studied Zen Buddhism, sought a guru, and lived ascetically at an ashram in India. They strove for expanded perception, altered states, and nirvana by any means necessary. "I came of age at a magical time. Our consciousness was raised by Zen, and also by LSD."[5] At least the yen for Zen persisted through adulthood.[6]

"Do you still believe in God?" he asked Brilliant. Yes, and they recalled Hindu guru Neem Karoli Baba's many paths to God. For Jobs, all religions were essentially one. "I think different religions are different doors to the same house. Sometimes I think the house exists, and sometimes I don't. It's the great mystery."[7] For a man who charged us to "Think Different," this was disappointing, a lazy conformity to a culturally dominant cliché. It is a statement as preposterous as claiming the interchangeability of all operating systems just because they have some surface similarities and perform similar tasks. Rightly or wrongly, it's common to hear that Beach

Boy savant songwriter Brian Wilson was a genius musician and an amateur human being. Jobs was a genius entrepreneur and an amateur spiritual disciple. On spirituality, he was a child of his age.

And when cancer ate its way into his life, he turned to the only spirituality he had ever earnestly practiced. Rejecting traditional medicine, he kept to a strict vegan diet, and he added acupuncture, herbal remedies, and other treatments he found on the Internet. He consulted with many people, including a psychic.[8]

He had just turned 50. The cancer was rare and, thankfully, slow growing. Surgery looked promising. To the horror of his wife and friends, however, he refused, or at least indefinitely postponed, the only accepted medical approach. Nine months later, the tumor had grown. The doctors operated — but it was too little, too late. Jobs fought on until October 5, 2011, when he reached the end of his earthly course. His beloved family lost a husband and father. An admiring public lost a visionary, pioneer, and genius, who, with no formal engineering study, is listed as inventor on more than 200 U.S. patents; a man who revolutionized at least six industries, and who may have changed our way of living on a par with Bell, Morse, Edison, and Ford.[9] He was only 56 years old and at the height of his influence. Harvard researcher Dr. Ramzi Amir lamented the alternative New Age-style treatment that "led to an unnecessarily early death."[10] This "most powerful person in business,"[11] known for his flamboyant presentations and brilliant marketing, was laid low by a quiet, opportunistic cancer that burrowed its way into the soil of erroneous spiritual assumptions. What Steve Jobs believed had profound consequences for not only how he lived but for how he died.

Every year since a teenager, he had pored over the classic *Autobiography of a Yogi* (1946)[12] by Paramahansa Yogananda (1893-1952). The yogi's Vedic[13] philosophy taught that all is One, all is God, "I am" God. Yogananda's Kriya Yoga[14] engineers consciousness through breathing exercises, quieting the action of the lungs and heart, and supposedly arresting growing mutations and neutralizing the body's decay.[15] As if presenting Exhibit A, the *Autobiography* reproduces an intriguing affidavit from Forest Lawn Memorial Park Cemetery confirming that Yogananda's corpse did not deteriorate for twenty days after his death.[16] This annual reading must have influenced Jobs' expectation of healing.

Not shy when trumpeting his technological innovations, Jobs did not go "out on a limb" aping Shirley MacLaine, as he lived his experiments in spirituality. He would not bristle with New Age rage nor mellow into a New Age sage. His introduction of Apple II, "The Dawn of a New Age," was for marketing, not metaphysical, purposes. Nevertheless, he gave "new consciousness" spirituality enough weight to drag him into an early grave. His story forces us to consider the dangerous mental and spiritual habits, the dark side, of New Age thought and practice.

New Age — Vast and Varied, Sober and Silly

Though Jobs neglected meditation in later years, his pursuit of Eastern spirituality seemed earnest enough.[17] Others draw up astrological charts, or uncover past lives through hypnosis, or find the "heroic" in men's-only sweat lodges or in Joseph Campbell's works on mythology.[18] Some seek love and forgiveness in Marianne Williamson's application of *Course in Miracles*[19] or serenity in Thomas Keating's centering prayer.[20] Many, in the tradition of American consumerism, just shop, spiritually restless, purchasing cosmic peace through inner goddess oils, Tibetan Obsidian protective crystals, or the glowing rainbow moonstone pendant. For some, New Age spirituality is a rigorous daily effort at Yoga or vegetarianism, or in manipulating ectoplasm, living eco-communalism, or repeatedly trying to understand Ken Wilber's *A Brief History of Everything*. For others, it's not much more than an annual trip to the International New Age Trade Show West after combing through the *Aura* catalog.[21]

The Secret, the Law of Attraction, the Spiritual Laws of Success, The Power of Positive Thinking

In the 1991 movie *City Slickers*, three men in mid-life crisis take up a dude ranch cattle drive, hoping to reignite their masculine confidence. The tough-as-nails trail boss Curly plays guru, cryptically advising the city slickers to focus on the "one thing" that is most important in life. What is it? That is for each to discover. Not so with New Age spirituality. The one thing necessary is learning the Law of Attraction, the power of possibility thinking, or similar phrases.

The most culturally acceptable and lucrative products in the New Age catalog are those on the human potential, self-improvement, and success motivation pages.[22] For instance, Deepak Chopra (b. 1946)[23] presents *Seven Spiritual Laws of Success* as deep Indian philosophy. But strip off the pretentious metaphysical giftwrap and Sanskrit bows and what you are left with is some nice alliteration and Norman Vincent Peale's (1898-1993) *Power of Positive Thinking* (1952). Chopra's book was dwarfed by Australian TV producer Rhonda Byrne's *The Secret* (2006), *The Power* (2010), and *The Magic* (2012). *The Secret*, alone, sold four million books and two million DVDs the first month after its release.

Byrne alleges she discovered "the single greatest force in our Universe." This is "The Secret" — i.e., "the Law of Attraction." But it is the secret that was not. *Newsweek's* Jerry Adler reports her reliance on New Thought's Wallace Wattles' (1860-1911) *The Science of Getting Rich* (1910) and Hindu maven[24] William Walker Atkinson's (1862-1932) *Thought Vibration or the Law of Attraction in the Thought World* (1906).[25] These books have never been out of print! In fact, the Law of Attraction is one of the most repeated and commonly taught principles by Theosophical, Mind Science, and religious science groups from the late-19th century to the present day.[26] The only secret is why people continue to think it's a secret . . . or is that the real mystery?

THE SCIENCE OF THE SECRET

Physicists, neuroscientists, as well as Christian and Jewish theologians, find no "law of attraction" hidden in the cosmos, the brain, or the Bible. Nevertheless, New Age and Mind Science teachers like to cast a scientific aura around their claims, hoping to co-opt science's unrivaled cultural prestige. So books are given titles like *Science and Health with Key to the Scriptures*,[27] *Scientific Healing Affirmations*,[28] *The Law of Manifestation*, *The Science of Power*,[29] and *The Science of Deliberate Creation*.

With the Law of Attraction, the mind is presented as a receiver and transmitter of thought vibrations or, similarly, the mind is a magnet attracting thoughts of like frequency. These might be striking and helpful metaphors for spiritual "truths."[30] But are they science?

Can the human mind receive and transmit vibrations? Many 19th-century scientists, politicians, poets, and clergy thought so. They were fascinated by the quasi-scientific claims of mesmerism, Spiritualism, and animal magnetism. Since, then, experimental work has given us no reason to believe that the human mind receives or transmits vibrations that can in any way influence the external environment. Nevertheless, *The Secret* claims the support of science:[31]

- "It has been proven scientifically that an affirmative thought is hundreds of times more powerful than a negative thought."[32] No, our brain waves are so weak that we need electrodes attached to our brain to even find them. I also know that my radio listeners are more apt to communicate when they are negative and angry than when they are positive and appreciative.
- "Our physiology creates disease to give us feedback, to let us know we have an imbalanced perspective and we're not loving and we're not grateful."[33] Even if true, this is not science. Science cannot establish the meaning of phenomena. It can't say you are sick because you are an ingrate. Wisdom might draw those connections, but it's outside science, strictly speaking.
- "Even under a microscope you're an energy field."[34] No. You don't see energy fields under microscopes. You see matter. Can matter be transmuted into energy? Yes, under extreme conditions, such as those that exist in the sun, not in your brain.

The Law of Attraction takes striking metaphors and turns them into impossible metaphysics. I have it on good authority, however, that on the way to the bank, many of these teachers have very positive thoughts. The Law of Attraction surely works for them.

THE LAW OF ATTRACTION: HOW DOES IT WORK?

"Everything coming into your life is the result of what you have been attracting to your life. Our lives are magnets, which draw events *into* our lives — both good and bad."[35] The Law of Attraction is based on absolute, inflexible reciprocity, a transaction between your thoughts and this hidden, impersonal law of the universe.[36] The brain frequency of anger attracts anger; greed draws greed to itself.[37] It is no respecter of intentions:

> When you focus on the things that you don't want, *"I don't want to be late, I don't want to be late,"* you really are calling *that* [lateness] into existence. . . . The law of attraction is always working. . . . You don't press pause, you don't press stop. It is forever in action, as your thoughts are.[38]

The Law is mastered by clearly conceiving one's desire: visualizing it and then commanding it with great feeling. The stuff of the universe will respond. *What you conceive and believe, you will achieve and receive. If you decree it, you will receive it.*

ATTITUDES TOWARD OTHER PEOPLE

New Age adherents are often better people than they are thinkers. If you follow the logic of the Law of Attraction, you will tend to shun the weak and blame the victim: "If you see people who are overweight, do not observe them, but immediately switch your mind to the picture of you in your perfect body. . . ."[39] Since the rape victim attracted her perpetrator by her negativity, we must shun her for our own good. We can't risk her negativity attracting the same thing to us. And, certainly do not hug a leper! Madame Blavatsky (1831-1891), the foundress of Theosophy, tells us we all get what we deserve: "There is not a mental or physical suffering in the life of a mortal which is not the direct fruit and consequence of some sin."[40]

The Law of Attraction also exaggerates our control over life. Byrne calls us "omnipotent," "all powerful," and "creators of our own reality." Placing ourselves at the center of the universe is normally what parents train out of their toddlers. Yet the Law of Attraction bids us to adopt, not the humility of little children, but their illusion that the world revolves around them. Scripture presents a very different sovereign: "Many are the plans in the mind of a man, but it is the purpose of the Lord that will be established."[41]

ATTITUDES TOWARD PRAYER AND GOD

The Law of Attraction redefines God and prayer:

- The Law commands. Prayer petitions.
- The Law requires "Just you!" Prayer needs two for real communication.
- The Law works impersonal cosmic laws. Prayer resonates in God, the personal Creator of cosmic laws.
- The Law admits no will but your own. Prayer is always according to the will of God.

For Byrne, *The Secret* is the proverbial Genie: "Your wish is my command."[42] How do genies relate to God, the Father? "Our Father . . . *Give* us this day our daily bread" becomes "O Genie, is my wish really your command?" When Jesus seeks solace and strength in Gethsemane, he doesn't isolate himself to meditate on the God within or to magically stroke some talisman or chant some affirmation. He prays to a loving Father who is to be obeyed and not commanded like an impersonal reservoir of energy. "Is God a being with whom we have a relationship or something to be used, a force to be harnessed?"[43]

ATTITUDES TOWARD HEALTH AND WEALTH

Rhonda Byrne on aging and health: "Don't cover your cake with sixty candles, unless you want to summon aging to you . . . in reality there is no such thing."[44] I didn't realize aging was optional. Magical thinking strengthens denial and encourages us to ignore illness, for if illness enters our thoughts we are attracting illness to ourselves. Staying positive replaces the unpleasantness of diet, exercise, and doctor visits.

Lisa Nichols on money: "When you want to change your circumstances, you must first change your thinking. Every time you look inside your mail expecting to see a bill, guess what? It will be there. You're expecting debt, so debt must show up. . . . Debt is there because of the Law of Attraction. Do yourself a favor: Expect a check!"[45]

Expect these prosperity teachers to quip that thrift is no more a virtue than poverty. Classically, thrift is the virtue of prudence applied to money. It is necessary, because the first law of economics is **scarcity**. The first law of prosperity teachers, however, is to **deny** the first law of economics.[46]

Injustice, inequality, oppression, and all social factors contributing to poverty are irrelevant since "*You* are the *only* one who creates your reality — for *you* are the attractor of your experience. It is *only you*, every bit of it *you*. *Just you!*"[47] Perhaps Mother Teresa missed the mark. How would *The Secret* sound in Calcutta's open-air meetings?[48]

ATTITUDE TOWARD ONE'S SELF

The Law of Attraction inflames desire for limitless wealth to be used by a limitless Self. Book titles are revelations:

- *Think and Grow Rich*
- *Money and the Law of Attraction: Learning to Attract Wealth, Health, and Happiness*
- *The Method — How To Apply The Law Of Attraction & Get Everything You Want Out Of Life*
- *Mind Over Money: How to Program Your Mind for Wealth*

St. Paul taught that the desire for riches leads us into all kinds of mischief.[49] These teachers have, apparently, improved on Jesus' and Paul's alarmism.[50] They have discovered that you can in fact gain the whole world and keep your soul.[51] There is no jeopardy in riches after all. In their world, a man's self-worth is measured by his net worth, and his spiritual standing by his social status.

THE GOD WITHIN: FANTASY AND REALITY

Spirituality and psychology deal with the inner life. Law of Attraction teachers, on the other hand, urge us to "discover our own divinity."[52] Psychologists want us to get mentally healthy. But the search for the divine self rarely considers defense mechanisms, denial, stages of grief, anger triggers, symptoms of clinical depression, or anxiety disorders. The "power of positive thinking" offers no "positive psychology."[53]

Prior to his death, atheist Albert Ellis (1913-2007), founder of Rational Emotive Behavior Therapy (1955), was deemed the greatest living psychologist in Canada and America.[54] Earlier in his career, he documented mental health breakdowns among those employing the deceptive mental habits of Norman Vincent Peale's *Power of Positive Thinking* (1952). "Denial," he pointed out, leads to procrastination. We prefer feeding our fantasy to facing our reality. Thus, we set ourselves up for future disillusionments. Reality testing and sober self-assessment are difficult through the constant refrain of positive affirmations. Furthermore, the constant assertion of one's well-being "prejudices one against effective therapy."[55]

Catholic spirituality rests on a foundation of mature humanity. Discovering one's divinity before becoming a good, self-aware person is dangerous. G. K. Chesterton's wit sugars a wicked truth: "Of all horrible religions the most horrible is the worship of the god within . . . that Jones shall worship the god within turns out ultimately to mean that Jones shall worship Jones."[56] What's so dangerous? The "god within" is a self with no boundaries, a self who will deceive himself about the nature of reality because he recognizes no limits.

Art Levinson, Apple board member and close friend of Steve Jobs, observed: "I think Steve has such a strong desire for the world to be a certain way that he wills it to be that way."[57] In the past, Jobs had been rewarded for what his wife called his "magical thinking" — his assumption that he could will things to be as he wanted. It was his undoing. The Law of Attraction is magical thinking on steroids.[58]

I Am God: New Age or Old Lie?

God created us for friendship with him. *Each human soul is a single, concrete act of God's creative love.* This love holds us to the Father. In Paradise, however, we sabotaged our friendship with God. Refusing to trust, imagining he was withholding good from us, our suspicions dissolved the truth that our Creator only desired our good.[59]

New Age thought embodies the primal Edenic lie:

- *There is no death.*
- *Man is God.*
- *Knowledge of self is salvation and power.*[60]

In the Garden of Eden, what did it mean to "discover your own divinity"?

- It meant eating from the tree of the knowledge of good and evil.
- It meant defining moral truth apart from the revelation of God.
- It meant refusing to accept the limits appropriate to a creature.

The Law of Attraction, if taken as a "law" — and not just as an exhortation to decently steward our thoughts away from despair, self-pity, hatred, anger, etc. — is a satanic inducement to break our friendship with God. We act unilaterally and create our own rules. We create our own reality, which is plastic to our will and recognizes no limits to our desire. The Law of Attraction encourages magical thinking, narcissism, and an adversarial relationship with those who pose obstacles to the fulfillment of our decrees. *Should anyone be surprised that when we define our own reality, we discover our own divinity?*

OUR FATHER DOESN'T ABSORB US INTO HIMSELF

New Age spirituality prizes altered states of consciousness. John Lilly's memoir *Center of the Cyclone* vividly describes such a state:[61]

> Central to cosmic consciousness is the unitary experience: *first*, the experience of perceiving the wholeness of the cosmos; *second*, the experience of becoming one with the whole cosmos; and *finally*, the experience of going beyond even that oneness with the cosmos to recognize that the self is the generator of all reality and in that sense is both the cosmos and the cosmos maker.[62]

Shirley MacLaine puts it bluntly: "Know that you are God; know that you are the universe."[63] Other New Age theorists strain for appropriate language: "Cosmic Consciousness," "Mind at Large,"[64] "Separate reality,"[65] "God-consciousness,"[66] "Universal Mind."[67] These describe the absorption of the personal self into the One Universal Consciousness where Creator and creature, individual selves, and cosmic consciousness become the One.

In contrast, the Beatific Vision,[68] the goal of our life on earth, is the state where "we shall see God 'face to face'" for "we shall be like him, for we shall see him as he is."[69] Our personality is preserved in union with God, who is Being itself. What is the nature of this union? Friendship. Friendship is not code for self-discovery. When Jesus prays for union — i.e., for the oneness of his disciples with him and the Father — he calls them "friends."[70] *Whatever "oneness" means, it clearly doesn't entail the abolition of the very selves that are necessary for friendship.*

CHRIST IN US DOES NOT DISPLACE US

"Do you have a personal relationship with Jesus Christ?" the young evangelist asked Fr. Dave Meconi. She registered clear alarm when he impishly said that *he didn't want a relationship with Jesus.* "With Mother Mary and with you and with all the saints I want a relationship, but with Jesus I want union. I do not want to be simply face to face with Jesus, or side to side. I want his face to become my face, his heart to beat in perfect harmony with mine. With St. Paul, I want to be able to say that it is no longer I who live but Christ who lives in me.[71] I want divine union." She fled. Fr. Meconi wrote *Union with God.*[72]

This union involves a plurality. "I can do all things through Christ who strengthens me."[73] For Christians, it is not me vs. Christ, but Christ in me, the hope of glory. The source of our strength comes from another. He indwells us, but doesn't displace us. Catholics should love the phrase *E pluribus unum* ("out of many, one"). New Age thinkers emphasize the *"unum"* at the expense of the *"pluribus."* Atheists emphasize the *"pluribus"* and don't believe in the *"unum."* But Catholics, just like Goldilocks, get it just right.

WHAT IF?

Steve Jobs, then age 13, brandished the July 19, 1968, issue of *Life* magazine to his Lutheran pastor. Two emaciated, unwashed, Biafran children stared out, accusingly, from the cover. One million would face murder and starvation over the two-and-a-half-year Biafran-Nigerian civil war. "Does God know about this and what's going to happen to those children?" His pastor said yes. Jobs never returned. Five years later, Eastern spirituality got a hold on him.

Jobs couldn't have known that Christ was already ministering to these children. Almost singlehandedly, Vatican City provided support to the Biafran people over the objections of the United States and the Soviet Union. The Holy Ghost Fathers of Ireland, Caritas International, and U.S. Catholic Relief Services were right there saving those children on *Life's* cover. Jobs, the rebel, would have enjoyed such humane defiance.

Had he witnessed Christ's mystical body mercifully ministering to the children who had moved his heart, would he have opened that heart to a spiritual autobiography other than Yogananda's? Perhaps those of the Carmelite mystics — *Story of a Soul: The Autobiography of St. Thérèse of Lisieux* or *The Life of St. Teresa of Jesus*? Later, John Paul II would challenge seekers like Jobs, noting that "*Carmelite mysticism begins at the point where the reflections of Buddha end.*"[74]

As Jobs walked away from the Lutheran Church, Mother Teresa (1910-1997) was finishing 20 years serving the poorest of the poor in Yogananda's hometown of Calcutta.[75] At the very moment evil seized Jobs' young eyes, British journalist Malcolm Muggeridge was aiming to grace the world's eyes with *Something Beautiful for God*, the documentary that lifted Mother's work to worldwide prominence and, ten years later, the Nobel Peace Prize.[76]

Moral outrage over those traumatized Biafran children opened Jobs to a winsome yogi from Calcutta. Ironically, though, Yogananda had neglected to do in Calcutta what Jobs insisted God and man do in Nigeria. Would that have disqualified his spirituality in Jobs' eyes? Would Jobs have recognized in Mother Teresa's Calcutta ministry what he accused God and man of neglecting in Nigeria?

Here is another odd parallel.[77] Both Christ and the yogi had lain in a "mortuary" incorrupt: Yogananda, remarkably, for 20 days; Christ for only three days, because, unlike Yogananda, he, miraculously, left his tomb empty, raised by the power of God to a higher level, never to die again. Christ also had his post-mortem affidavits: eleven apostles, Paul, and more than 500 fellow Christians.[78]

"You do not give me up to Sheol [the grave], or let your godly one see the Pit [corruption],"[79] predicted the singer/songwriter David, as he meditated on the promised Messiah a thousand years before the new humanity was recreated in Christ's cross and resurrection. Steve Jobs always wanted to make a new beginning, to fashion a new history, to just do it better. He now knows that Christ has. May God show Steve Jobs mercy. May we turn our gratitude for his genius into prayer for his glorification.

The East in the West:
The Case of Reincarnation

"The sharp edge of a razor is difficult to pass over; thus the wise say the path to Self is difficult to traverse."

— From the *Kata Upanishad,* used by Somerset Maugham
in *The Razor's Edge* (1944)

TIGER WOODS, WOMEN, BUDDHISM, AND BRIT HUME

Through the 2000s, Tiger Woods dominated golf and was among the world's most admired and marketable athletes. He was the first sportsman to earn over a billion dollars. Among African-Americans, only Oprah topped the Tiger in net worth. Elin Norde-gren, a stunningly beautiful Swedish model, bore him two children in four years of marriage. It wasn't enough to hold that Tiger.

On November 25, 2009, *The National Enquirer* revealed Woods as a philandering, unfaithful husband. Several women came forward, and before our eyes, the well-crafted image of a most admired man morphed into a sexually driven serial adulterer. He quickly entered a 45-day therapy program, was quickly divorced by August, and quickly fell to number 58 as a golfer.[1] Truly, bad karma.

Years before, he confessed, "I believe in Buddhism. Not every aspect, but most of it, so I take bits and pieces. I don't believe that human beings can achieve ultimate enlightenment, because humans have flaws."[2]

Was Tiger sinful or merely flawed? On January 10, during *Fox News Sunday*, political analyst Brit Hume (b. 1943) commented that Woods would recover as a golfer but "the extent to which he can recover [as a person] — seems to me to depend on his faith. He's said to be a Buddhist; I don't think that faith offers the kind of forgiveness and redemption that is offered by the Christian faith. . . . 'Tiger, turn to the Christian faith and you can make a total recovery and be a great example to the world.'"

That Buddhists weren't happy, I understand. But the "nonjudgmental" mainstream press, without a dog in this fight, turned so catty that I thought Hume had threatened to forcibly baptize Tiger's children. "Ridiculous" . . . "Denigrating" . . . "Arrogant bluster" . . . "Proselytization" — Hume was, apparently, a genuine threat to the stability of the Republic.[3] Unsatisfied with secularized government, the press apparently expects Christians to secularize their public discourse. Tolerating other faiths must mean that you should not publicly share your own.[4]

Does Christianity have resources that Buddhism doesn't? That was the serious follow-up question. A good journalist would have helped his reader gain conceptual tools, authoritative references, and appropriate vocabulary to deal with these deep differences. Hume's lay theological instincts were right.[5] John Paul II, a theologian in his day job, dared to write: "The doctrines of salvation in Buddhism and Christianity are opposed. . . . *Carmelite mysticism begins at the point where the reflections of Buddha end. . . .*"[6]

Christianity offers forgiveness from sin and union with the infinite, personal God who is love and who created a good world that we must steward and develop. Buddhism offers an impersonal *nirvana*, gained after repeated reincarnations, as one seeks perfect detachment from the world, whence comes suffering and evil. The Christian experiences forgiveness, redemption, and union. The Buddhist experiences karma, reincarnation, and the self's absorption into ultimate being.[7] Even comparative religions scholar Stephen Prothero snidely agreed with Hume: "You have the law of karma, so . . . Woods . . . is going to have to pay for whatever wrongs he's done. There's no accountant in the sky wiping sins off your balance sheet, like there is in Christianity."[8] In Asian religious philosophy, karmic doctrine threads all the odd-shaped, colored beads we call Buddhism, Hinduism, Jainism, Sikhism, Taoism, etc.[9] "*It would be no exaggeration to say that the one concept which distinguishes Indian philosophy from European philosophy is the concept of karma. . . .*"[10]

KARMA, SAMSARA, MOKSHA: THE DYNAMIC OF EASTERN SPIRITUALITY

Westerners have embraced two forms of Indian philosophy: Vedanta and Yoga.[11] Vedanta relates the self to ultimate reality.[12]

Yoga teaches the physical, mental, and spiritual disciplines necessary to realize ultimate reality.[13] Key principles adapted for Western audiences include:

1. Ultimate Reality is both transcendent and immanent, personal and impersonal.[14]
2. The infinite, the divine, transcends words, yet we must speak of Brahman, God, Lord, Allah, etc. *"Truth is one, the wise call it by many names"* (Rig Veda).
3. The true self is identical with Ultimate Being. *"Atman is Brahman."*
4. Our divine identity is obscured by ignorance and false attachments.
5. Liberation, awakening, or enlightenment is available through a multitude of paths, techniques, and methods.[15]
6. We progress or evolve through stages and acquire virtues as we go on.
7. Realizing one's true nature brings an end to suffering and results in liberation or enlightenment called *moksha*.[16]

Eastern thought presents life as a long series of births, deaths, and rebirths — an aimless wandering called *samsara*. *Karma* (action, deed) lends direction to *samsara* by generating cosmic reaction to our deeds. Good deeds result in a higher place in rebirth — bad deeds, the opposite. When one ceases generating karma, through detachment or elimination of desire, he finds release, moksha, from samsara, ending the cycle of birth, death, and rebirth.

REINCARNATION MEANS NEVER HAVING TO SAY YOU'RE DEAD

Eastern thought is many faceted. It offers meditation, monism, polytheism, nonviolence (*ahimsa*), a caste system, and so on. For space considerations, I'll drill down on reincarnation because 25 percent of Americans, including Christians, accept it. Further, reincarnation directly opposes Catholic teaching, making it easier to address it unambiguously. Lastly, although they don't do it very well, and one is surprised to find it done at all, many try to twist Scripture to teach reincarnation.

The *Catechism of the Catholic Church* orients us:

> Death is the end of man's earthly pilgrimage, of the time of grace and mercy which God offers him so as to work out his earthly life in keeping with the divine plan, and to decide his ultimate destiny. When "the single course of our earthly life" is completed, we shall not return to other earthly lives. "It is appointed for men to die once." There is no "reincarnation" after death.[17]

Eastern and Western Differences on Reincarnation

In Eastern philosophy, reincarnation into a nonhuman form is possible. Karma doesn't respect any created boundaries. Christianity, on the other hand, teaches that angels remain angels, animals remain animals, and humans remain humans.[18]

Another difference between East and West concerns reincarnation's desirability. In the East, rebirth represents futile repetition — i.e., doing the same thing over and over again. The Vietnamese Buddhist monk Thich Nhat Hanh challenges Western expectations: "You may be surprised to know that people in Buddhist Asia are not fond of reincarnation. They want the circle of birth and death to end, because they know it represents suffering without end."[19] Easterners want out.

In the West, though, reincarnation represents an opportunity to make spiritual progress: a second, third, fourth, fifth, hundredth, thousandth chance at self-perfection. As Boston University religion scholar Stephen Prothero quips: "Reincarnation means never having to say you're dead."[20] Westerners want in.

What's the Appeal?

Philosophical and Personal

Why do the wicked prosper and the righteous suffer? "The reincarnationist has a ready answer: we are seeing in this life only a fragment of a long story. . . . [T]he rest of the story . . . will unfold a much richer pattern in which the punishment of the wicked and the vindication of the righteous will be brought to light. Death is but the end of a chapter; it is not . . . the end of the story."[21]

Reincarnation also denies hell. "One of the most attractive aspects of reincarnation is that it removes entirely the possibility of damnation."[22] Reincarnation forever postpones final judgment. Gadadhara Pandit Dasa, Columbia University's first Hindu chaplain, calls reincarnation a " re-do," like a test you get to take over. Life is a series of endless auditions. After an unspecified number of tries, the eternal soul finally achieves perfection and goes to live with God. Evolution is a long process with much trial and error. What is a series of past lives but the evolution of a soul?[23]

Experiential, Empirical

Family resemblances, illnesses, child prodigies, and love at first sight used to be presented as evidences of reincarnation. Genetics and heredity now explain many of those features. Many still claim that empirical evidence exists in past-life memories, intuitive recall, and déjà vu. Many of these memories are induced by hypnotic regression techniques, which deeply concerned Dr. Ian Stevenson.

For 40 years, the late Dr. Ian Stevenson (1918-2007) investigated 3,000 childhood cases of past-life recall. Though his work is judged as pseudoscience by critics, others defend his research methods as rigorous.[24] All agree it is the most serious empirical study of reincarnation. Stevenson, however, rejected stories of hypnotic past-life regression and even published a statement on his website distancing himself from them. They polluted the data. "Nearly all such hypnotically evoked 'previous personalities' are entirely imaginary, just as are the contents of most dreams."[25]

Nevertheless, Dr. Raymond Moody, famed for popularizing near-death experiences, claims to have experienced memories of nine past lives through hypnosis and wants to popularize past-life exploration, as he had near-death experiences.[26] Other psychiatrists and psychologists give a scientific gloss to reincarnation. Dr. Brian Weiss, with an Ivy League pedigree, was censured by his professional association in 1988 after he published *Many Mansions, Many Masters.*[27]

Let's evaluate these reasons advanced for adopting a belief in reincarnation.

Examining the Claims of Reincarnation Advocates

From the start, we have a methodological problem. How is karma calculated and transferred? How is it eliminated? What is the relation between individual, familial, national, and global karma? To what degree do individual "sins" produce collective suffering as well as individual karma? Not knowing how karma is administered means not knowing if it presents a satisfactory account of human suffering.

Do We Really Get What We Deserve?

When a horse kicks the head of a fallen nine-year-old rider, do I tell her parents that in a previous life she must have mistreated mares? A good father would wrap the nearest horseshoe around my neck. Reformed theologian Jurgen Moltmann charges a cruel consistency: "Trying to explain massive suffering by pointing to the law of karma seems to me — and here you must pardon me — to be nothing short of an obscene insult to the victims."[28]

In practice, many Buddhists seek to imitate "the compassionate Buddha."[29] The Dalai Lama begins his talks by stressing the universal presence of suffering and our responsibility to not only escape our own suffering but to relieve the suffering of others. Buddhist monk Thich Nhat Hanh says that "we invented 'engaged Buddhism' so that we could continue our contemplative life while in the midst of helping the victims of war."[30] Buddha's entire career is said to have been launched by his compassion and his search to end suffering.

This is true. But sensitivity to suffering, seeking to relieve suffering, doesn't resolve the philosophical problem of unjust suffering, which many claim was their reason for adopting reincarnation:

- Karma offers no explanation for how actions produce consequences from one life to the next or even within one life.
- The claim that unjust suffering doesn't exist, since all sufferers receive their deserved karma, is a morally repugnant way of blaming the victim. India accepted the caste system, and the ostracism of the untouchables seems evidence that this belief carries significant social baggage.

Reincarnation Doesn't Deliver Spiritual Progress

With rare exception, reincarnationists don't remember past lives. Without memories of past tests, there can be no progress. Each test is as the first. Without memory, one doesn't have a million lives; one has a single life a million times over, each one walled off from the other. How is one to learn from experience if those experiences aren't remembered? The reincarnationist, then, has no advantage over the Christian, who lives as though he has but one life to live.

A Look at the Empirical Data

Reincarnation advocates often claim that karma is a law of the cosmos that can be studied and investigated, like gravity or relativity, with the right tools.

But even the Dalai Lama questions this claim: "Science, as we know it, involves investigation of something that can be measured or calculated. *The concept of mind or the concept of self itself cannot be measured.*"[31] In response to a question from Carl Sagan, the Dalai Lama acknowledged that if science could disprove reincarnation, he would give it up. But he thought it would be awfully difficult to disprove reincarnation.

One of the most celebrated reincarnation cases is that of Jenny Cockell. Her *Across Time and Death: A Mother's Search for Her Past Life Children* (1993) describes dream-memories in which Cockell is an Irishwoman, Mary Sutton, who died more than 20 years before Cockell's birth. Hypnosis was employed to stimulate these childhood memories. How good is the evidence?

First of all, there isn't much. Unknown were Mary's surname, either maiden or married, the names of her husband and children, the name of the village, and even its location. Cockell was ignorant of dates as well, including Mary's birth date. And so, on and on. This all gets filled in as she investigates.

Secondly, Cockell's method of inquiry permits her to get the results she desired. She sent out queries asking about a village with certain sketchy requirements. Lo and behold, when such a village was discovered, she adopted it as the one she was looking for. This amounts to drawing a target around an arrow once it has struck something.

Thirdly, she retrofitted the facts. After a hypnosis session, she sketched a church that was compared with a photo of the actual village church, St. Andrew's. The sketch showed only a gabled end. It ignored the larger architecture and the distinctive details, even the massive Gothic window that is the central feature of the church's gabled end. It was further learned that Mary Sutton had not actually attended St. Andrew's but would have merely walked by it.

No wonder the Dalai Lama was so circumspect when asked whether or not he had memories of previous lives. With transparency and good humor, he replied: "Sometimes it is difficult to remember what happened this morning! However, when I was small — say, two to three years old — my mother and some close friends noticed that I expressed some memories of my past life. That is possible! But if you are asking me for a definite memory, I must say it remains somewhat unclear."[32] One appreciates the refusal to overpromise.

REINCARNATION, SCRIPTURE, AND THE CHURCH

Scriptural Evidence

No biblical passage supports reincarnation. Geddes MacGregor, in *Reincarnation in Christianity*, tries hard to create a hybrid form of reincarnation and Christianity but is forced to admit, "[T]he Bible does not explicitly teach reincarnation."[33] Not satisfied, he then argues that the Trinity also has no direct biblical warrant: "There is no reason at all why the doctrine of reincarnation *might* not be in a similar case."[34]

Nonsense. Scripture never denies the Trinity; it explicitly denies reincarnation. "It is appointed for men to die once, and after that comes judgment."[35] Further, passages do refer to Father, Son, and Holy Spirit as somehow a divine threesome. Even further, bodily resurrection, not reincarnation, climaxes Jesus' earthly life. In both Scripture and the early creeds, Jesus' followers await resurrection not reincarnation. "We await a Savior, the Lord Jesus Christ, who will change our lowly body to be like his glorious body."[36]

Born Again

"Truly, truly, I say to you, unless one is born anew, he cannot see the kingdom of God" (Jn 3:3). Reincarnationists interpret "born anew" as receiving another physical body on earth after you die. They repeat Nicodemus' mistake. Jesus prescribed the baptismal rebirth of water and the Spirit, not physical procreation: "Truly, truly, I say to you, unless one is born of water and the Spirit, he cannot enter the kingdom of God" (Jn 3:5). One must be born again to enter the Kingdom — not born again, again, again, and again!

John the Baptist and Elijah

Was John the Baptist a reincarnated Elijah? No. Three New Testament passages (Mt 11:14; 17:12-13; Mk 9:13) describe John the Baptist's relationship to Elijah.

Malachi prophesied, "I send my messenger to prepare the way before me. . . . Behold, I will send you Elijah the prophet before the great and terrible day of the Lord."[37] In the New Testament, the angel announced the birth of John the Baptist to his father: "And he will go before him *in the spirit and power of Elijah*" — not as Elijah reincarnate.[38]

Furthermore, reincarnation requires one's death before rebirth, yet Elijah never died.[39] "Elijah's end is not death and burial but translation to heaven."[40] Centuries later Elijah appeared with Jesus and Moses on the Mount of Transfiguration. Peter, James, and John were not confused. Nobody said, "Whoa, that's not Elijah; that's John the Baptist."[41]

The Man Born Blind

" 'Rabbi, who sinned, this man or his parents, that he was born blind?' Jesus answered, 'It was not that this man sinned, or his parents, but that the works of God might be made manifest in him.' "[42] Ananda Coomaraswamy (1877-1947), an influential Ceylonese philosopher who introduced Indian art to the West, answers differently: "The Indian theory replies, without hesitation, *this man*."[43] But the man born blind cannot be interpreted as New Testament evidence for reincarnation.

Reincarnation wasn't debated in Palestinian Judaism. Why then did the apostles even bring up the possibility that this man was born blind because of his sin or his parents'? Some rabbis entertained the idea that an infant might sin while still in the womb. When a pregnant woman worshiped in a heathen temple, the fetus committed idolatry as well.[44]

So how could the parents' sin cause the son's blindness? This principle is much more familiar to us than karma and reincarnation. "I, the Lord your God, am a jealous God, visiting the iniquity of the fathers upon the children to the third and fourth generation."[45]

Jesus, however, challenges the fundamental assumption behind the disciples' question: Forget trying to determine causation, and work the redemptive healing opportunity before you. The issue was "neither" parental nor prenatal sin, nor sin from a previous life. This man was born blind that the glory of God might be revealed through his ailment.

A New Myth of Christian Origins

One of the Catholic Church's 21st-century opponents is ignorant and often hostile myth-making about her past. S. L. Cranston's very influential book teaches: "In the sixth and later centuries, when the present bible was decided on, a number of differing gospels existed. Those deemed unacceptable were destroyed. By this time there was a strong anti-reincarnationalist sentiment in the Church, and it would be surprising if anything on reincarnation managed to survive."[46]

Almost everything in this statement is false. The Scriptural canon of both the Old and New Testaments was formalized in the fourth century, long before the "sixth and later centuries." Even in the fourth century, Christians were formalizing a canon that had been largely settled since the second century. There is no evidence that any texts dealing with reincarnation were ever considered inspired or used in the liturgy. No ecumenical councils dealt with reincarnation, although at least one did condemn the doctrine of the preexistence of the soul.[47] Sometimes it is claimed that the Church Fathers taught reincarnation based on the New Testament. Again, nonsense.[48] Some claim that reincarnation may be found in some later non-canonical writings.[49] Yes, that is one reason they were non-canonical. The "lost gospels" lost out because they had no claim to be an authentic witness to Christ or the apostles. What about the Fathers?

Early Christian Teaching

Where reincarnation is mentioned or implied, it is rejected as outside the canonical tradition. Justin Martyr (c. 100-c. 165) in a passing reference, rejected it clearly.[50] Irenaeus of Lyons (c. 130-c. 200) criticized Carpocrates' doctrine of the transmigration of souls, as did Hipploytus (c. 176- c. 236).[51] Clement of Alexandria (c. 150-c.215) regarded reincarnation as an unacceptable falsehood.[52] Origen (c. 185-c. 254) believed in the preexistence of the soul (not reincarnation), but even this was condemned by later Church councils.[53] Tertullian (c. 160-c. 225) attacked both Plato's doctrine of the preexistence of the soul as well as Pythagoras' transmigration doctrine.[54] All this scratches the surface. Minucius Felix, Ambrose, Augustine, John Chrysostom, Gregory of Nyssa, and Basil the Great all rejected reincarnation because they were awaiting the resurrection.[55]

Conclusion

Reincarnation contradicts the entire tenor of the most influential spiritual leader to walk the earth, as well as the mission and teaching of his chosen delegates and their successors. Reincarnation directly contradicts the Christian hope of the resurrection of the body. It renders purgatory meaningless and plays havoc with the communion of saints. "For the reincarnationist the soul is its own saviour by its own efforts."[56] In contrast, we live in hope, not the hope of balancing the karmic scales but the hope of grace as the means to the ultimate regeneration — the resurrection, not the elimination, of the body and the life of the age to come, in which "death shall be no more, neither shall there be mourning nor crying nor pain any more" (Rev 21:4).

The greatest problem with reincarnation is that it leaves us as our own saviors. Christ is unnecessary. The entire story of salvation is meaningless. If the worldview assumed by reincarnation was true, what could this following text mean? "This was his will and pleasure in order that the glory of his gracious gift, so graciously conferred on us in his Beloved, might resound to his praise. In Christ our release is secured and our sins forgiven through the shedding of his blood. In the richness of his grace God has lavished on us all wisdom and insight."[57] The whole doctrine concerning Church, sacraments, and grace stands or falls on this central point.[58]

We are much better off treasuring the life we live on earth as a unique opportunity rather than an audition we can return to as many times as we'd like. Each person's life is a unique and unrepeatable moment in the grand sweep of God's cosmos. He creates only originals, never replicas, and calls us by name counting every hair of our heads (see Is 43:1; Mt 10:28-31). In the grand scheme of reincarnation, what personality of the hundreds or thousands one may have had is the recipient of God's creative and redeeming love? Does that mean those former personalities are just discards, lacking enduring personal reality?[59]

Reincarnation fails to answer why some are born better off than others. Why is there undeserved suffering? The Christian answer is that God permits evil because a greater good will ultimately be achieved as a result of evil's possibility. But that is merely a philosophical answer. We want to know that God has some skin in the game. And indeed he does. It's called the Incarnation, the Word become flesh.

In Christ, God demonstrates to us that he is most intimately involved in and aware of our suffering. Christ submitted himself to the same historical process of suffering and victimization that we endure. He also vindicates that process by rising from the dead, showing us that all the suffering is worth it. The painful toil will have been fruitful. And he is there with us every step of the way. We don't suffer alone for he is Emmanuel, God with us. He is not distant or removed from us or exempt from "investment" in our griefs, losses, pains, abandonments, false accusations, impaired health, miserable failures, and sins. God is not willing that any should perish, and he shows that by taking on our human condition and saying, "Follow me."

The historical evidence for the empty tomb and the Resurrection of Christ is compelling and quite worth arguing over in the university classroom as much as the local bar.[60] Other truths of revelation aren't as amenable to empirical investigation. They are believed on the authority of God's revelation. When the end comes, or my end comes, then I will have empirical verification, for, by God's grace in Christ, I will see him face to face.

Islam: A Competing Kingdom on Earth

"The religiosity of Muslims deserves respect. It is impossible not to admire, for example, their fidelity to prayer. The image of believers in Allah who, without caring about time or place, fall to their knees and immerse themselves in prayer remains a model for all those who invoke the true God, in particular for those Christians who, having deserted their magnificent cathedrals, pray only a little or not at all."

— JOHN PAUL II (*Crossing the Threshold of Hope*, 1994)[1]

BEST OF INTENTIONS

During the Day of Prayer and Remembrance, the memorial service held in the National Cathedral shortly after the attacks of 9/11, one of the ministers opened his prayer, "God of Abraham, God of Mo—", philosopher William Lane Craig recalls: "I thought he was going to say God of Moses — but those weren't the words that came out of his mouth — 'God of Abraham , God of Mohammed, Father of Jesus Christ.'"[2]

Craig then asks the question that sets up the central conflict between Islam and Christianity: "Is that correct? Is the God of Mohammed, the Father of Jesus Christ? Anybody who knows anything about Islam knows that these two descriptions are incompatible with each other. Like oil and water, they cannot be mixed."[3] Most of us, however, don't know anything about Islam. How do we find out?

ISLAM: GOD IS NO FATHER, AND HE HAS NO SON

The first rule of both interreligious dialogue and missionary proclamation is: **Listen.** Listening is the beginning of loving. Who says the God and Father of Jesus Christ is not the God of Muhammad? Muslims do. While Catholics like to begin with our common belief in a Creator God,[4] the Qur'an, the highest authority for Muslims, says: "No, Allah has no son." In fact, Islam sees its primary task to declare God's unique oneness. Correlated with that, it sees its primary negative contribution to insist that God is no Father and he has no son. "*God is but one God. God forbid that he should have a son.*"[5] Those who say that God has begotten a son have uttered "*a monstrous blasphemy.*"[6] "*God forgives not [those] joining other gods with Him . . . one who joins other gods with God has strayed far, far away. . . .*"[7] Those who do are destined for hell and everlasting fire.[8] It is Islam's unforgiveable sin, a crumbling of the first of Islam's Five Pillars.[9]

The first of the Five Pillars of Islam is called "bearing witness." To what does the Muslim witness? "*There is no God but Allah, and Muhammad is the Prophet of God.*"[10] When people make this declaration, called the *Shahada*, they have become a Muslim, meaning "one who submits." For new Muslims, the "first act is to declare the faith publicly in front of two witnesses. From that moment of public witness, they are Muslims.[11]"

Your average converts have little idea of the many obligations that they have inherited with their profession of faith. For instance, *serious* Muslims are expected to learn Arabic. One of the most influential teachers, Ibn Taymiyyah (1263-1328) has declared: "*The Arabic language itself is part of Islam.* . . . If it is a duty to understand the Qur'an and Sunnah (Muhammad's Tradition), and they cannot be understood without knowing Arabic, then the means that is needed to fulfill the duty is also obligatory."[12]

Christianity's "science" is theology; Islam's is law. Four different schools of Islamic jurisprudence govern everything from prayer postures to treatment of the Jews to sexual intercourse. While Catholics believe that "canon" law helps organize our communal life — and that laws and rules sometimes burden the immature, who need counsel, not commandment — yet Catholicism's central emphasis is love, not law.

Notice the legal character of the remaining Pillars of Islam:

- Prescribed *Prayer, Worship* (*Salat*), at least five times a day, after ablutions and in a swept place. The day of public worship is on Friday, when all the adult males gather together at the mosque.[13]

- The mandated *Religious Tax* (*Zakat*) for the poor is minimally a 2.5 percent levy and is not considered charity.
- Set *Fasting* (*Sawm*) from dawn to dusk, followed by feasting during the ninth month of the Muslim year, Ramadan.
- The compulsory pilgrimage (*Hajj*) to Mecca, the "Mother-town" of Islam, at least once, if health permits.[14]

While Catholics are obliged to pray, fast, give alms, and do pilgrimage, these are not, first of all, legalistic obligations. Ideally, they extend the thanksgiving that is the Eucharist. Muslim manuals, on the other hand, emphasize the legal obligation.

While I stress the average Muslim's legalistic motive, I am aware that when it comes to motives, we are trespassing on slippery ground. Only God knows and can judge the authentic stirrings of grace in our hearts. Sufi Muslim writers, for instance, often write believably about their response to Allah's mercy.[15] They represent the Islamic mystical tradition, however, and are frequently suspected of undermining obedience to *Sharia*.[16] Some scholars believe that during the Muslim conquests of Syria and Egypt, vast numbers of hermits and monks came to spiritually influence their conqueror.[17]

The Oneness of God

Proclaiming the "utter uniqueness" of God: That is Islam's reason for existence. Remove this, and Islam disappears. The verse called Surah 112 is "held to be worth a third of the whole Qur'an, and the seven heavens and the seven earths are founded upon it. To confess this verse is to shed one's sins as a man might strip a tree in autumn of its leaves."[18]

> Say: He is Allah
> The One and Only,
> Allah, the Eternal Absolute;
> He begetteth not,
> Nor is He begotten;
> And there is none
> Like unto Him.[19]

Denying Jesus as *God's only begotten Son* simply defends the oneness of God. "[Christians] say, *'Allah hath begotten a son:'* Glory be to Him — **Nay**, to Him belongs all that is in the heavens and on earth: everything renders worship to Him."[20]

THE FATHER AND THE SON

Muslims take moral offense at Christ's Sonship. Yusuf Ali's (1872-1951) translation of the Qur'an, with commentary, is the most used among English speakers. "It is a derogation from the glory of Allah — in fact it is blasphemy — to say that Allah begets sons like a man or an animal."[21] Similarly, Islamic missionary Ahmed Deedat (1918-2005), recipient of the prestigious King Faisal International Prize, taught: "[God] does not beget because begetting is an animal act. It belongs to the lower animal act of sex. We do not attribute such an act to God."[22] For centuries, Christians have protested: "Good heavens, listen! Neither do we." I'm reluctant to put it so baldly, but Muslims have believed a lie. The *Catechism of the Catholic Church* affirms that "He [God] also transcends human fatherhood and motherhood, although he is their origin and standard: no one is father as God is Father."[23] Why do Muslims insist "Sonship" requires biological procreation in spite of centuries of unambiguous denials by Christians? We speak of the "Eternal generation of the Son," and virtually all Christian theologians and traditions echo the doctrine. Yet absolutely nothing in that definition even permits a genital begetting of a son.[24] Nevertheless, Christ's relationship to the Father is at the heart of Christian self-understanding.

When Jesus called God his Father, Jewish leaders concluded that he was grasping at equality with God (Jn 5:18). Hebrew culture considers a son equal in stature to his father. So when Jesus presents himself as "Son of God" or refers to God as his Father, the Jewish leaders charge "blasphemy," just as the Muslims do. The objection of the Jews, however, is that Jesus usurped God's authority. Sexual reproduction doesn't even come up.

Addressing God as Father was not common in Israel's history.[25] Occasionally, however, individuals address God as Father in prayer.[26] With Jesus, however, a new age emerges. The late Fr. Louis Bouyer (1913-2004) builds a case: "Father" is his (Jesus') most frequent term for God[27] entirely disproportionate to what we find in all other Jewish literature. He even teaches his disciples to pray, "*Our Father*." This "is not simply a feasible extension of this privilege to all men, but the deepening of the concept of the fatherhood of God itself. This no longer appears as merely a possible aspect of God's relationship with his creatures, but rather as the most intimate revelation of the very nature of God."[28]

Muslims unequivocally deny the Fatherhood of God and the Sonship of the Christ.[29] So why did that poor minister in the National Cathedral, so anxious to please, end up offending Christians and Muslims alike? Because he patronized Muslims instead of listening to them. Because he assumed they thought like he did or that he thought like they did. Any Muslim would have told him that Allah regards Father-God talk as *shirk*, the unforgivable blasphemous sin of associating anything with God. This is nonnegotiable.

Shirk comes from an Arabic word meaning "to share." God has no partners, no kin. He shares himself with nobody. He cannot be likened to anything. Nor can anything be likened unto him. Alhaj A. D. Ajijola, former attorney general, serves on the Supreme Council of Islamic Affairs in Nigeria and writes: "The Unity of Allah is the distinguishing characteristic of Islam. This is the purest form of monotheism: the worship of Allah Who was neither begotten nor begets nor had any associates with Him in His godhead. Islam teaches this in the most unequivocal terms."[30] Since God in Islamic theology is conceived to be incomparable, it follows that he cannot have a Son. I have repeated myself on this point deliberately because *if you want to know Islam, get this: nothing is like God*. Of this, Muslims are proud. The *Shahada* is their contribution to human history. "The greatest service Islam rendered to humanity was the exaltation and purification of the concept of God. Islam strove to deliver humanity from a multiplicity of gods on the one hand *and from incarnationism* on the other and to bring man back to the Unseen God!" (emphasis added).[31]

THE DIFFERENCE: DOES GOD SHARE HIS LIFE WITH HIS CREATURES? CAN GOD EVER BE IMAGED?

Does anything resemble God? Are human beings made in his image and likeness? Does he establish covenants or family relationships with human beings? Can God indwell us? Does God share his life with us? Can God take on human flesh? Christians answer a qualified yes; Muslims answer an absolute no. All subsequent differences proceed from this foundational difference. Even our art is an exercise in contrasts. Christian art is rich with concrete images, while Islam relies on abstract calligraphy and forbids (remember the 2005 Muhammad cartoon controversy in the Netherlands) imaging even the human Muhammad. For Christians, however, the Incarnation itself was an imaging exercise. Because Christ images the Father, Christians feel they must portray Jesus in art. Muslim theology is pre-Incarnational and similar to the Jews on this point.[32]

Islam is right in what it affirms about God but wrong in what it denies. Since 1962, Baptist missionary Phil Parshall has been asking Muslim converts to Christ: "When you became a Christian, did you, cognitively or emotionally, think of yourself as commencing worship of a different God from that who you worshiped as a Muslim?" Without exception, the answer has been no.[33] This shouldn't surprise us. The Second Vatican Council teaches that "the Muslims . . . worship one God, living and subsistent, merciful and omnipotent, the Creator of heaven and earth."[34] As far as it goes, all three "Abrahamic" religions are strictly monotheistic. Christians, however, are not solitary monotheists. We affirm that there is a plurality within the divine oneness, a triunity of God. Islam denies this vociferously. Islam rightly affirms God's oneness; they wrongly deny his triunity.[35]

CHARACTER OF GOD

This difference reveals itself in the character of God. "Christians and Muslims agree that God loves. . . . But for Christians it is not enough to say that God loves. We insist that God *is* love. The difference seems small, but the whole character of the Christian faith depends on it" (emphasis added).[36] Love is inherent in his nature. It isn't just a possibility for action. The Christian message is "God is love." The Muslim message is "God is uniquely alone." For the Christian, love radiates from within the very being of God because he exists as a triune "society" of love and communion. The solitude of Allah, however, has no object within himself to love. He cannot love until he decides to create. Active love is, therefore, not within his nature.[37]

RELATION TO THE WORLD

This difference, also, manifests itself in the relation of God to the world. The Father of Jesus walks in the cool of the day with "friends."[38] But Eve grows suspicious, and Adam conspires. They act on their mistrust. The friendship is shattered. Immediately, fear, shame, alienation, and guilt enter their experience, and just as immediately God begins a program of reconciliation. Alienated from us, he draws closer and closer over time through covenants he establishes with Abraham, Moses, and David. Later, Jeremiah the prophet will promise a better, more expansive, more effective "New Covenant." The friendship will be restored, and with a higher degree of intimacy. God himself will take on human flesh — Emmanuel, God with us.

What's new about the New Covenant is that both parties will keep it. Jesus, the Last Adam, in our human stead keeps the terms of the covenant. Jesus, the New Man, is the first of the new humanity and leads us as he ascends to his Father and our Father. He opens the family circle to us, provided that we, by faith and baptism, are reborn into this family and reconciled as "friends" and "brothers." In becoming children of God, we receive God's spirit of adoption. Sonship leads to family likeness and inheritance. We become heirs of Christ's Father, our Father. The Holy Spirit comes to indwell us and, through his body, the Church. And Christ offers us his body and blood in the Eucharist so that he might share his life with us. He will now live within us, and we will live within him as we prepare for the final state of perfect union between God and his perfected creation.[39]

Allah, in contrast, creates humanity in a condition of absolute dependence. Human beings are NOT made in his image and

likeness because nothing can image Allah. He establishes no covenants with human beings because covenants extend kinship through
the swearing of oaths and acceptance of stipulations or conditions.[40]
While Muslims can "pledge," Allah is not bound by covenant to
share anything. Allah is the absolute sovereign, the absolute ruler,
absolute justice, absolute mercy, and the absolute one who is absolutely unknowable.[41]

ALLAH AND LOVE

Sometimes Christians overstate this very real difference by saying that Allah does not love. In Allah's 99 names, he is the merciful
and compassionate, even loving One.[42] He is quick to forgive and
as close to the believer as one's jugular vein.[43] *However, there is no*
reciprocity or mutuality between Allah and the human. We cannot
speak of a "self-communication" or "an incarnation" of God.[44] Allah
doesn't disclose or offer himself. He reveals a law for man to follow,
not a love to share. Isma'il Raji al-Faruqi (1921-1986), a Palestinian-
American philosopher, from Islam's most prestigious institute of
higher education, Al-Azhar University in Cairo, and later Temple
University in Philadelphia, confirms this point: "He [God] does not
reveal Himself to anyone in any way. God reveals only His will. . . .
'No, it is not possible for Me to reveal Myself to anyone.' This is
God's will and that is all we have, and we have it in perfection in the
Qur'an."[45] Allah is lawgiver, not lover; master, not friend. Muslims
are servants, not children. As Franciscan University of Steubenville,
New Testament scholar Scott Hahn has memorably put it: *Is God*
Allah or Abba?[46]

This absence of personal relationship drives former Muslims to
seek Christ. For instance, Ilyas Khan, a merchant banker and the
owner of the Accrington Stanley soccer team, chairs the largest
organization in the world helping the disabled. "Remember, I was
raised a Muslim, and I have been to Medina and Mecca," he said.
"[T]he difference between the two religions, is vast. So while there
are similarities, and I can see them, they don't count really for very
much. . . . I celebrate the fact that Jesus Christ *is* love. It's a simple
statement. It is the defining difference. . . . [T]he thing we call

'love,' that we as Christians concern ourselves (with) at the heart of our faith, is a living, real and tangible quality. Jesus is actually with us. . . . We are blessed by the Holy Sacrament and nourished by the direct intercession of Our Lord through his sacrifice."[47]

Fuller Theological Seminary's School of World Mission questioned some 600 Christian converts from very different Muslim backgrounds. "They have . . . been drawn to the God-man Jesus Christ. And for their spiritual direction, they have found one book that stands out above all others: the Bible. And more than any other portion of scripture, these believers are attracted to the Sermon on the Mount." They sought the love of a close, caring, loving, and forgiving God who could fathom their needs and feelings.[48]

A Few Thoughts on the Qur'an

Because love is who God is, Christianity prizes personal relationships. Even the Supreme Revelation of God is a person. ***What Jesus is to Christians, the Qur'an is to Muslims.*** For Christians, Christ Jesus, the Logos, a person, is the Supreme Revelation. For Muslims, however, the supreme revelation is an impersonal book, the inscripturated Word, the Qur'an.

For Catholics, to regard the Qur'an as revelation is to descend from the richness of a person to a résumé of propositions.[49] Why would human beings who create books regard a book of words as superior to a revelation in the form of a person who we can't make or create. We beget bodies; we make books; but only God creates a person. How appropriate that God's Supreme Revelation would come through what only he can produce, personhood, which is supreme in our experience, and which we share with the Godhead.[50]

Knowing God as Father

The most popular Muslim conversion story among evangelical Protestants is Bilquis Sheikh's *I Dared to Call Him Father*, published in 1978. With 300,000 copies in print, it emphasizes the personal dimension of the faith. An upper-class Muslim Pakistani woman, Bilquis, 54, is challenged by Christian missionaries to relate to God as Father. "No Muslim, I felt certain, ever thought of God as his

father," she said. "Since childhood I had been told that the surest
way to know about Allah was to pray five times a day and study and
think on the Qur'an. Yet Dr. Santiago's words came to me again.
'Talk to God. Talk to Him as if he were your father.'" On December
24, 1966, "alone in my room, I got down on my knees and tried to
call him 'Father.' But it was a useless effort and I straightened in
dismay. It was ridiculous. Wouldn't it be sinful to try to bring the
Great One down to our own level?"

Note well: Muslims believe that a God who reaches down to
save us violates the divine majesty. Where we see overwhelming
love, they see weakness and triviality.

Her earthly father, a high government official, held a regal bearing. But he was also easy to approach. He would speak endearing
words to her, even fulfill her requests. If her majestic earthly father
would put everything aside to listen to her, then maybe so would
her heavenly father. She tries again, and this time God speaks to
her as Father, amidst tears of joy.

"'I am confused, Father,' she said. . . . She picked up her Qur'an
and Bible and lifted them, one in each hand. . . . 'Which is your
book?' Then a remarkable thing happened. Nothing like it had ever
occurred in my life in quite this way. For I heard a voice inside my
being, a voice that spoke to me as clearly as if I were repeating words
in my inner mind. They were fresh, full of kindness, yet at the same
time, full of authority. *In which book do you meet me as Father?*' I
found myself answering, 'In the Bible.' That's all it took."

THE VOCABULARY OF RELIGIOUS EXPERIENCE

Catholics may describe this experience of God as a "word of
knowledge," "word of wisdom," "private revelation," "an actual
grace," "illumination," "hearing God's voice" — which illustrates
again how rich is the Catholic communion with God. Vocabulary,
generally, grows in proportion to the frequency, importance, and
public recognition of a phenomenon. The more common the experience, the richer the vocabulary to describe it. How many ways can I
say, "I love you." Let me count the ways. In contrast, "It is even difficult to find an appropriate Arabic or Persian expression for 'expe-

rience of God' without running the risk of encroaching upon the absolute transcendence of the God of Islam, of anthropomorphizing him."[51] To Muslims, a God who shares himself with his creatures, who speaks personally, is blasphemous.[52]

Even a study of prayers in the Qur'an reflects the impersonality of the God-human relationship. Qur'anic prayers are primarily supplications, a vassal to a lord, to meet particular needs. Prayers of affirmative praise are much rarer, and there are hardly any prayers of thanksgiving. In contrast, at the heart of Catholicism is the Thanksgiving, the Eucharist, the "source and summit of the Christian life."[53] The novelist Anne Lamott recently published a book on prayer with the vivid title, *Help, Thanks, Wow: The Three Essential Prayers*. Using her schema, Qur'anic prayers are primarily *Help. Wow* is much rarer, and *Thanks* hardly at all.[54] This human experience of God is neglected in mainstream Islamic thought.[55]

MARY AND THE MUSLIMS

Many Catholics have pored over the challenge of Islam. A few curious, non-dogmatic but, you might say, sanctified speculations are worthy of mention. Islam is the only major post-Christian world religion. The Catholic writer Hilaire Belloc (1870-1953) called it the last great Christian heresy.[56] If so, it is the only one to increase over time. Islam often distorts Christian and Jewish elements, yet the Mother of Jesus is honored in her Immaculate and his Virginal Conceptions. She is even called greatest among women. Muhammad wrote, after the death of his daughter, Fatima: "You shall be the most blessed of all the women in Paradise, *after Mary*." Is Our Lady of Fatima inviting Muslims to show their honor to the Mother by heeding her when she says to "Do whatever he [the Son] tells you"?[57]

A young Muslim woman, by the name of Fatima, did just that. When her people, including her chieftain father, were driven out of Portugal, she stayed behind to marry a Catholic boy and to embrace Christ. After her death, the young husband changed the name of their town to Fatima, in her honor. Archbishop Fulton Sheen observes: "Thus the very place where Our Lady appeared in 1917

bears a historical connection to Fatima the daughter of Mohammed."[58] Other tantalizing connections between the Blessed Mother
and the Muslim people may stimulate hope. Muslims and Christians are gathering at Mary's alleged last dwelling place on earth, a
house in Ephesus.[59] The Coptic Orthodox Church approved appa-
ritions of the Blessed Mother, Our Lady of Zeitoun, from 1968 to
1971, at a Coptic church in Cairo, which attracted great attention
from Muslims as well as Christians.[60]

CONCLUSION

Muslims regard our recitation of the Nicene Creed as blasphemous. And yet, Christ's Church acknowledges that the Muslims
"adore the one God, living and subsisting in Himself; merciful and
all-powerful, the Creator of heaven and earth, who has spoken to
men; they take pains to submit wholeheartedly to even His inscru-
table decrees, just as Abraham, with whom the faith of Islam takes
pleasure in linking itself, submitted to God."[61]

John Paul II even adds: "As a result of their monotheism, believers in Allah are particularly close to us."[62] Two pages later, however,
he acknowledges that the God of the Qur'an is "ultimately a god
outside of the world, a God who is only *Majesty, never Emmanuel,
God with us*. . . . There is no room for the Cross[63] and Resurrection.
Jesus is mentioned, but only as prophet who prepares for the last
prophet, Muhammad. There is also mention of Mary, His virgin
Mother, but the tragedy of redemption is completely absent. For this
reason not only the theology but also the anthropology of Islam is
very distinct from Christianity."[64] This is why *it is impossible to identify the God of Muhammad with the Father of Jesus Christ.*

Some may think this relieves Catholics of the obligation to reach
out. If one is so tempted, hear Benedict XVI in a Wednesday audience in January, 2010:

> In 1219 Francis obtained permission to go to speak with the
> Muslim Sultan Melek-el-Kamel in Egypt, and also to preach
> the Gospel of Jesus there. I want to underline this episode of
> the life of St. Francis, which is very timely. At a time in which

there was under way a clash between Christianity and Islam, Francis, armed deliberately only with his faith and his personal meekness, pursued with efficacy the way of dialogue. The chronicles tell us of a benevolent and cordial reception by the Muslim Sultan. It is a model that also today should inspire relations between Christians and Muslims: to promote a dialogue in truth, in reciprocal respect and in mutual understanding.[65]

May we imitate St. Francis in courage, gentleness, and honesty.[66]

PART TWO

Abusers of Science
and Reason

Science and Warfare With Religion

"Science is today the greatest authority in our lives- greater than any political or religious ideal, any cultural tradition, any legal system. We depend on science and defer to it as we do to nothing else."

— ANTHONY KRONMAN (*Education's End: Why Our Colleges and Universities Have Given Up on the Meaning of Life*, 2007)[1]

"When you encounter a conflict between science and religion, you're either dealing with a bad scientist or a bad theologian."

— FR. THEODORE HESBURGH (*Believing Scholars*, 2005)[2]

"Science without religion is lame, religion without science is blind."

— ALBERT EINSTEIN ("Science, Philosophy and Religion," 1940)[3]

SCIENCE, GOD, AND OBSOLESCENCE

Do advancements in science make belief in God obsolete? The Templeton Foundation asked the question and produced a little booklet.[4] The Science Network asked and convened a symposium.[5] My wife didn't think so, but she asked him this morning and guess what? He's doing fine. Not at all threatened. Glib? Yes, but it forces the foundational question: "*Does God exist?*" Is he objectively there, and has he communicated with us? "More consequences for thought and action follow the affirmation or denial of God than from answering any other basic question."[6]

Everyone tries to answer it — sometimes very simply, sometimes most profoundly. Sometimes an answered prayer, an inexplicable healing, or a stunning synchronicity is all it takes to settle the matter. Everyone walks his own way. Philosophical arguments for God's existence persuade some.[7] Still others may be moved by the clear evidence of design behind the cosmological constants and the appearance of Earth as a "privileged planet."[8] Sometimes it is a firm intuition like that of physicist Paul Davies: "I cannot believe that our existence in this universe is a mere quirk of fate, an accident of history, an incidental blip in the great cosmic drama. Our involvement is too intimate. . . . We are truly meant to be here."[9] Still others encounter a presence of love, wisdom, or power that feels like it transcends this world.[10] The promise is that all who seek shall find. We must, however, develop what we discover. When we do, God's existence becomes the properly basic presupposition of all we do and are. God obsolete? About as much as oxygen or sunlight. God isn't our crutch; he's our iron lung. A husband in loving communion with his wife of 35 years doesn't worry that science will render love or his wife obsolete. Whatever science discovers about oxytocin and the biochemistry of infatuation, the communicability of sex pheromes, or the mating rituals of gazelles will enhance, not negate, his experience of love.

Science vs. Religion: The Bogus Tale of Warfare

The religio-political violence of 9/11 drove the late Christopher Hitchens, Richard Dawkins, Daniel Dennett, Sam Harris, and a host of others, including magicians Penn and Teller,[11] to charge that religion is dangerously unstable and unnecessary. "Science has buried religion," therefore we should no longer show it respect. In 2010, the famed physicist Stephen Hawking got into the act. In September of 2010, Hawking's *The Grand Design* (2010) declared God unnecessary, irrelevant, and obsolete.[12] Celebrity atheist Dawkins crowed: "Darwin kicked [God] out of biology but physics remained more uncertain. Hawking is now administering the *coup de grace*."[13]

According to their storyline, God is steadily receding after each new scientific discovery, hiding in the shrinking shadows of our ignorance. Novelist John Updike (1932-2009) charts it in *Roger's Version* (1986): "In the sixteenth century astronomy, in the seventeenth century microbiology, in the eighteenth geology and paleontology, in the nineteenth Darwin's biology all grotesquely extended the world-frame and sent churchmen scurrying for cover in ever smaller, shadowy nooks, little gloomy ambiguous caves in the psyche where even now neurology is cruelly harrying them, gouging them out of the multifolded brain like wood lice from under a lumber pile."[14] I should point out, however, that Updike lived and died as a Christian.[15]

Let's get some things straight:

- God is not the excuse we summon when science can't explain something.
- We discover God in what we know, not in what we don't.[16]
- God produces the whole play, not just the intermissions.
- No discovery in astronomy, biology, or neuroscience threatens the faith.
- Rigorous scientific discovery is perfectly compatible with robust faith. For many, science is a spur to faith and vice versa.[17]
- The universe appears to be designed as both Dawkins and Hawking are forced to admit before they try to explain design away.[18] Try as they might, they can't deliver the *coup de grace*.

The late paleontologist Stephen J. Gould knew that science and religion don't ask or answer the same questions. Their different domains of inquiry and authority make them "non-overlapping magisteria."[19] Roughly put, science deals with material facts and operations; religion deals with immaterial morality and meaning.[20]

ATHEISM'S SCIENTIFIC PRETENSIONS

Atheism, like cigarette smoking, is an acquired taste. Throughout human experience, an ambiguous but real "God-consciousness" naturally arises in very diverse people: from Plato to Bono, from George to Denzel Washington, from T. S. Eliot to Tim Tebow, from Albertus Magnus to Al Kresta. Competing in the Olympics or *America's Got Talent*, contestants and their spectators just slide into thanking God. Why? Former Oxford researcher, Justin Barrett (b. 1971), founding editor of the *Journal of Cognition & Culture*, proposes an early explanation. In *Born Believers: The Science of Children's Religious Belief* (2012), he argues that from an early age children across the world come to believe that there is *"at least one, intelligent agent, a grand creator and controller that brings order and purpose to the world."* It takes training, he says, to deny such agency.[21] Barrett doesn't quote divine revelation. But St. Paul agrees. We can learn to suppress the truth that God has made evident to us through the external world (creation) and the internal world (conscience).[22] This practical atheism does violence to our existential design and darkens our minds.

Barrett doesn't flash his scientific credentials on behalf of theism. Many atheists, however, are bent on some scientific discovery disproving God's existence. This so irked agnostic mathematician David Berlinski (b. 1942) that he exposed their subterfuge in the ironically titled *The Devil's Delusion: Atheism and Its Scientific Pretensions*.[23] Like insecure adolescents hoping for a celebrity call-out at a concert, Dawkins, Hawkings, Dennett et al. all seek validation for their personal philosophy through the cultural prestige of science. The doors of science, however, swing both ways. Oxford philosopher Richard Swinburne (b. 1934) and the late former atheist analytic philosopher Antony Flew (1923-2010) argue that science most naturally supports theism or deism but certainly not atheism.[24]

Thinking atheists should know that good scientific practice limits itself to explaining material causes. Since science only discovers material causes, they cleverly infer, then there must be no immaterial causes. Hmm. Since good cooking practice limits itself to food that is fit for cooking, does that then prove that food that can't be cooked doesn't exist? Letting the method dictate the conclusion is not an act of wisdom.

WARFARE? SAYS WHO?

The "warfare" between science and religion is a storyline enormously influential through the anti-Catholic *History of the Conflict Between Religion and Science* (1874) and the deeply flawed *A History of the Warfare of Science With Theology in Christendom* (1886), authored by John William Draper (1811-1882), and Andrew Dickson White (1832-1918), respectively. These tomes were toxic in tone, careless in philosophy, and, now we know, burdened with baloney, such as claiming that medieval people taught that the earth was flat.[25] Historian Steve Shapin (b. 1943) targets Draper and White. "In the late Victorian period it was common to write about the 'warfare between science and religion' and to presume that the two bodies of culture must always have been in conflict. However, it is a very long time since these attitudes have been held by historians of science."[26]

Philosopher Alfred North Whitehead (1861-1947) noticed that the "medieval insistence on the rationality of God"[27] birthed rather than aborted modern science. By the 1930s, Oxford's Michael B. Foster (1903-1959) launched a serious reappraisal of the origins of modern science.[28] By the 1970s, my professors at Michigan State University chortled at the mention of Draper and White, and they assigned readings acknowledging Christian influence on modern science.[29]

Et Tu, Brute? Even Our Friends Plunge the Knife

But even those who are sensitive to "spirit" often speak of "science and religion locked in mortal combat." Ken Wilber (b. 1949), dubbed "the Einstein of consciousness," warns us in *The Marriage of Sense and Soul: Integrating Science and Religion:*[30]

> One thing is certain! Starting from whatever date we choose, modern science was, in many important ways . . . deeply antagonistic to established religion . . . dissolving, often beyond recognition, virtually all of its central tenets and dogmas. Within the span of a mere few centuries, intelligent men and women . . . could . . . deny the very existence of Spirit. . . . Orthodox science and orthodox religion deeply distrust and often despise each other . . . a philosophical cold war of global reach.[31]

As the equine Mr. Ed (1958-1966) used to say, "Oh, Wilber!"

1. Were Science and Religion "Antagonistic From the Start"?

Not according to historian J. L. Heilbron (b. 1934). "The Roman Catholic Church gave more financial and social support to the study of astronomy for over six centuries . . . during the late Middle Ages into the Enlightenment, than any other, and, probably, all other, institutions."[32] What about Galileo? Ironically, Galileo was one of the astronomers who benefited from Church support. The mishandled "Galileo affair" was the exception that proved the rule: a

zit on the otherwise beautiful face of Mother Church, and even
that blemish is wildly misdiagnosed.[33] In his history of humanity's
changing vision of the universe, *The Sleepwalkers*, atheist Arthur
Koestler (1905-1983) tries to correct the cartoon version so popular in America: "I believe the idea that Galileo's trial was a kind
of Greek tragedy, a showdown between blind faith and enlight-
ened reason, to be naively erroneous."[34] Historian Gary Ferngren
says, from the historians' "Amen" corner: "The traditional picture
of Galileo as a martyr to intellectual freedom and a victim of the
church's opposition to science has been demonstrated to be little
more than a caricature."[35]

The old warfare imagery is just wrong. Lawrence Principe, professor of History of Science and Technology at Johns Hopkins University, lectures: "[G]iven the widespread public acceptance of the
conflict model, it comes as a surprise to many people to learn that no
historians will support it. Let me be clear: *the idea that scientific and
religious camps have historically been separate and antagonistic is rejected
by all modern historians of science.*"[36] The relationship was complex,
but conflict was the exception, not the rule.[37]

David C. Lindberg, former president of the History of Science
Society, is noted for his level-headedness:

> *There was no warfare between science and the church.* The story
> of science and Christianity in the Middle Ages is not a story of
> suppression nor one of its polar opposite, support and encour-
> agement. What we find is an interaction exhibiting all of the
> variety and complexity that we are familiar with in other realms
> of human endeavor: conflict, compromise, understanding, mis-
> understanding, accommodation, dialogue, alienation, the mak-
> ing of common cause, and the going of separate ways.[38]

2. How Has Science "Dissolved Beyond Recognition" Any Dogma?

Every Sunday we repeat the ancient creeds. Most of the propositions are not subject to scientific testing.[39] "Under Pontius Pilate" is
verified by historical, not scientific, research.

3. Do Scientists "Deny the Very Existence of Spirit"?

Rice University's Elaine Ecklund surveyed 1,700 scientists on religion, atheism, and spirituality. "The 'insurmountable hostility' between science and religion is a caricature, a thought-cliché, perhaps useful as a satire on groupthink, but hardly representative of reality." Nearly 50 percent of those surveyed qualified as "religious."[40]

4. Is There "A Philosophical Cold War Across the Globe"?

If so, someone failed to tell the Nobel committee and lots of others. Those listed below are men and women of faith, primarily Christians:

- JOHN ECCLES (1903-1997), neurophysiologist, was a Nobel laureate (1963) for his work on the synapse.
- ALEXIS CARREL (1873-1944), biologist, was a Nobel laureate (1912) for vascular suturing techniques.
- ALBERT CLAUDE was a Nobel laureate (1974) for study of the cell.
- CARL FERDINAND CORI was a Nobel laureate (1947) for breakdown of glycogen.
- CHARLES TOWNES is a Nobel laureate (1964) for inventing the laser.
- WILLIAM PHILLIPS is a Nobel laureate (1997) for the development of laser cooling.
- FR. MICHAŁ HELLER (b. 1936), cosmologist of the Vatican Observatory, is the recipient of the Templeton Prize (2008).[41]
- CHARLES TAYLOR (b. 1931), Catholic Canadian philosopher, is the recipient of the Templeton Prize (2007).[42]
- FR. GEORGE COYNE, (b. 1933), former Vatican observatory director, is the recipient of the Van Biesbroeck Prize of the American Astronomical Society (2010).[43]
- JENNIFER WISEMAN (b. 1974), then an undergraduate, discovered periodic comet 114P/Wiseman-Skiff and, in time, became chief of the Stellar Astrophysics Laboratory at NASA. She heads up the American Association for the Advancement of Science's Dialogue on Science, Ethics, and Religion.

- FRANCIS COLLINS (b. 1950), geneticist, identified the gene that causes cystic fibrosis. After successfully leading the Human Genome Project to completion, he now directs the National Institutes of Health. In 2009, Benedict XVI appointed him to the Pontifical Academy of Sciences.[44]
- JUSTIN BARRETT (b. 1971) founded the *Journal of Cognition & Culture* and is a pioneering cognitive scientist dealing with the neuroscientific basis of belief.[45]
- HENRY SCHAEFFER (b. 1944), a theoretical chemist, has been nominated five times for the Nobel Prize. His book *Science and Christianity: Conflict or Coherence?* is for students curious about science and faith.
- JOHN LENNOX, Oxford mathematician, debates Stephen Hawking and Richard Dawkins.[46]
- JOHN POLKINGHORNE (b. 1930), particle physicist, discovered quarks. Tiring of that mystery, he took up the Eucharistic one as an Anglican priest.[47]
- IAN HUTCHINSON, professor of Nuclear Science and Engineering at MIT, explores the confinement of plasmas hotter than the sun's center, aiming at producing practical energy from nuclear-fusion reactions.[48]
- BILL NEWSOME, professor of Neurobiology, Stanford, experiments with neuronal mechanisms underlying vision.
- JOSEPH EDWARD MURRAY (b. 1919) performed the first successful human kidney transplant on identical twins. He is a Nobel laureate (1990) for his work on organ and cell transplantation.[49]
- ALLAN SANDAGE (1926-2010) was awarded the Crafoord Prize (astronomy's equivalent of the Nobel) and was Hubble's protégé and successor. One of the 20th century's greatest astronomers, he is best known for discovering quasars and determining the first reasonably accurate value for the Hubble constant and the age of the universe.[50]
- WERNER ARBER (b. 1929), Swiss microbiologist, is the president of the Pontifical Academy of Sciences and is a Nobel laureate (1978) in Physiology/Medicine for the discovery that led to recombinant DNA technology.

- MARTIN NOWAK (b. 1965), Harvard professor of Biology and Mathematics and director of the Program for Evolutionary Dynamics, adds "natural cooperation" to mutation and natural selection to explain evolution.[51]

To sum up, warfare between science and religion is based on a woeful misunderstanding of faith and reason.[52] Dawkins is Exhibit A: "Faith is the great cop-out, the great excuse to evade the need to think and evaluate evidence."[53] Really, just think what would happen if these men and women would stop evading the need to think and really learn to evaluate evidence, such as Richard Dawkins who hasn't contributed a thing to science and technology for 25 years because he's been prancing about as a celebrity atheist, taunting men and women who have been discovering the cystic fibrosis gene, the neuroscience of trust in children, recombinant DNA, laser technology, quasars, quarks, the accurate value for the Hubble constant, practical energy applications from nuclear-fusion reactions, comets, and meteors.

Richard, go back to zoology and do something useful. I prefer these Christians' way of doing science to your way of not doing it.

Philosophical cold war . . . only in hell.

THE SCIENCE AND RELIGION HALL OF FAME

There is no final conflict between scientific pursuits and faith in God.[54] The Pontifical Academy of Sciences was founded in 1603, the "first exclusively scientific academy in the world." The Vatican Observatory is one of the oldest astronomical research institutions in the world. St. Albert the Great (c. 1206-1280), renowned for his encyclopedic knowledge of nature and Catholic theology, is a doctor of the Church and patron saint of natural sciences for his advocacy for peaceful co-existence. Jesuits were major contributors to pendulum clocks, barometers, reflecting telescopes, and microscopes. They observed the colored bands on Jupiter's surface, the Andromeda nebula, and Saturn's rings. They theorized about the circulation of the blood, the theoretical possibility of flight, the way the moon affected the tides, and the wave-like nature of light.[55]

Catholics pioneered in their fields, often earning the title "Father
of . . ." in their scientific field:

- Experimental Method, BISHOP ROBERT GROSSETESTE[56]
- Scientific Laws, ROGER BACON[57]
- Mineralogy, GEORGIUS AGRICOLA
- Aurora Borealis, PIERRE GASSENDI
- Infinitesimal Calculus, AUGUSTIN-LOUIS CAUCHY
- Modern Algebra, FRANÇOIS VIÈTE
- Analytic Geometry, RENEE DESCARTES
- Heliocentrism, ARCHDEACON NICOLAUS COPERNICUS
- Modern Observational Astronomy, GALILEO GALILEI
- Modern Anatomy and Physiology, ANDREAS VESALIUS
- Battery, ALESSANDRO GIUSEPPE ANTONIO ANASTASIO
  GEROLAMO UMBERTO VOLTA
- Electromagnetism, ANDRÉ-MARIE AMPÈRE
- Theory of Impetus, JEAN BURIDAN
- Modern Chemistry, ANTOINE LAVOISIER
- Biomechanics, GIOVANNI ALFONSO BORELLI
- Acoustics, FR. MARIN MERSENNE
- Fermat's Last Theorem, PIERRE DE FERMAT
- Coulomb's Law, Electric Charge, CHARLES-AUGUSTIN DE
  COULOMB
- Binet's Formula, JACQUES PHILIPPE MARIE BINET
- Probability Theory and Hydrostatics, BLAISE PASCAL
- Geology, BL. NICOLAS STENO (BISHOP)
- Electrochemistry, LUIGI GALVANI
- Braille Reading System, LOUIS BRAILLE
- Modern Genetics, ABBOT GREGOR MENDEL
- Modern Analysis, KARL WEIERSTRASS
- Microbiology, Rabies Vaccine, Germ Theory of Disease,
  LOUIS PASTEUR
- Casey's Theorem, JOHN CASEY
- Doppler Effect, CHRISTIAN ANDREAS DOPPLER
- Penicillin, ALEXANDER FLEMING
- History of Medieval Science, PIERRE DUHEM

- Big Bang Theory, Fr. George Lemaitre
- And of course, the man without whom I could not have written this book, the Father of Radio, Guglielmo Marconi[58]

These scientists were not necessarily great Catholics. Self-identified as Catholics, however, they found that their faith posed no obstacle to great science.

Should Science Do Away With Religion?[59]

*Science is clearly **not** one of Catholicism's 21st-century opponents.*[60] Yet some atheists want a fight. November, 2006: Some leading practitioners of modern science, some celebrity atheists, gathered in La Jolla, California, for a three-question symposium entitled "Beyond Belief: Science, Religion, Reason and Survival," hosted by the Science Network.

1. *Should science do away with religion?* (Yes.)
2. *What would science put in religion's place?* (Science? Yes, how about science? Yes, of course, science!)
3. *Can we be good without God?* (Absolutely! Although it might be harder to raise as much money for charity.)

Atheist Nobel winner Steven Weinberg: "The world needs to wake up from the long nightmare of religion. Anything we scientists can do to weaken the hold of religion should be done, and may in fact be our greatest contribution to civilization. . . . [Religion is] like a crazy old aunt . . . we may miss her." Weinberg's sentimentalism irked atheist missionary Richard Dawkins: "Scraping the barrel to find something nice to say [about religion], so he comes up with this image of the elderly aunt. I won't miss her at all, not one smidgeon. . . . I am utterly fed up with the respect that even the secularists among us have been brainwashed into bestowing upon religion."

Neil LeGrasse Tyson directs the Hayden Planetarium and sputters when told that 15 percent of the members of the National Academy of Sciences still pray: "How come the number isn't zero?" Tyson apparently needs uniformity. "I don't want the religious person in the lab telling me that God is responsible for what it is they cannot discover."

Oh, come on. Tyson sounds parochial, insular, and churlish, unworthy of the great Hayden Planetarium. How does he think Francis Collins mapped the human genome comprised of 20,000-23,000 genes, one of the great conceptual achievements of modern science?[61] I've interviewed Collins many times, and he describes the hunt for the *single* cystic fibrosis gene and its mutation like "looking for a single burned-out light bulb in the basement of a house somewhere in the United States." Collins sees digging deep into God's creation as a form of worship. In our discoveries, God discloses himself.

"Anything that deserves to exist deserves to be known." That's the agenda of the Christian research scientist, even to counting the holes on the moon. Good heavens, there are more moon craters named for Jesuits than any other collective group. Why? Jesuits like science. And science, thankfully, unlike Tyson, likes Jesuits.

FRIENDS CAN HAVE CONFLICTS[62]

Even good friendships might occasionally have conflicts. For instance, the Church doesn't reject the biological theory of evolution, but she does reject the materialism or philosophic naturalism which certain atheists smuggle in as foundational to it.[63] The Church opposes cloning and embryo-destructive research. Apparently, this steams anti-theist Richard Dawkins. He writes, "[Benedict XVI] is an enemy of science, obstructing vital stem cell research, on grounds not of morality but of pre-scientific superstition." He really needs to pay attention. In October 2012, Dr. John Gurdon, 79, and Dr. Shinya Yamanaka, 50, received the Nobel Prize in medicine for showing how to make the equivalent of embryonic stem cells without any violation of human dignity. Yamanaka's pursuit of the good enabled him to discover the true, and that's beautiful.[64]

Doesn't Dawkins know that there are ethical problems with some research. The Tuskegee experiment in which African-American males were research subjects without their consent failed the Catholic ethical test. Nazi doctor Joseph Mengele's experiments on Auschwitz prisoners failed the Catholic ethical test.[65] Would Dawkins support such research on the grounds of academic freedom or necessary scientific research? If he did oppose it, would it be appropriate to call him "anti-science"? Our opposition to embryonic stem cell research is ethical, not scientific! I'll say it again: "Anything that deserves to exist deserves to be known."[66] Nothing is off-limits for a Catholic except sin, the sin of debasing the human person. The *Catechism of the Catholic Church* declares, "Science and technology . . . require unconditional respect for fundamental moral criteria. They must be at the service of the human person. . . ."[67] This is not anti-science; it is pro-human. "*Human life is sacred* because from its beginning it involves the creative action of God. . . . [N]o one can under any circumstances claim for himself the right directly to destroy an innocent human being."[68] So euthanasia, physician-assisted suicide, abortion, and infanticide are rejected.[69]

Catholic bioethics differs from other approaches by the prizing of human blessedness.[70] For some bioethical schools, the morality of an act is judged by its consequences or outcomes. Does it produce the greatest good for the greatest number? For other bioethical schools, the morality of an act is judged by how it enlarges and protects the extent of human autonomy: What makes for maximum freedom for the individual?[71] Catholic bioethics, however, judges the morality of a human act by the degree it helps or hinders the well-being, virtue, or beatitude of the acting agent, the scientist. Are our acts rendering us more or less fit for the Kingdom of God?[72] Remember Nazi propaganda master Joseph Goebbels, as he watched the newsreel showing the destruction of the Polish people, saying, "Be hard, my heart, be hard." Goebbels' choices and exertions were forming him for hell. Catholic choices and exertions should be forming us for heaven as well as protecting the dignity of other human beings.[73]

The end does not justify the means is another key Catholic bioethics principle. We must not do evil, even in pursuit of a perceived good. An evil action cannot be justified by a good intention.[74] The Church gladly endorses the ethical principles summarized in the Nuremberg Code and the Declaration of Helsinki covering human experimentation.[75]

Artificial intelligence, nanotechnology, genetic engineering, cloning, cyborgs, psychopharmacology, and so on, come bearing promises of bionic or virtual extensions of human life. Each must be considered in terms of its impact on the dignity of the human person, including the dignity of the scientist. The Catholic Church teaches authoritatively, if not exhaustively, in this field.[76] Just because something can be done doesn't mean that it should be done.

CATHOLIC FAITH, FRIEND OF SCIENCE: NO FINAL CONFLICT

The relationship between science and religion is one of _____! People often fill in the blank according to certain assumptions that they hold about life: conflict, combat, concord, congruence, convergence, cooperation, creative tension, compromise, complexity, conversation, coherence, complementarity.[77] All of these have been used to describe the relation between science and religion. The Catholic Church seems to favor complementarity. Galileo's old saw is a pithy summation: "The intention of the Holy Spirit is to teach us how one goes to heaven, not how the heavens go."[78] Discovering how the heavens go is good but subordinated to how to go to heaven. Both tasks, however, have divine favor.

The role of Francis Bacon (1561-1626) in encouraging the West's embrace of the new knowledge is not without some philosophical and political problems for Catholics.[79] However, he frequently drew from broad biblical themes. Atheists try to claim Bacon as one of their own in spite of Bacon's sly essay "On Atheism": "It is true," he writes, "that a little philosophy inclineth man's mind to atheism; but depth in philosophy bringeth men's minds about to religion."[80] Bacon knew that God's dominion mandate to humanity spurred scientific investigation.[81] In this, he shares the view of the *Catechism* that sees technology as "a significant expression of man's dominion over creation."[82] Bacon expanded: "For man by the Fall fell at the same time from his state of innocence and from his dominion over Creation. Both of these losses, however, can even in this life be in some part repaired; the former by religion and faith, the latter by arts and sciences."[83] Like the Catholic Church, Bacon saw the redemptive/salvific value of science. Benedict XVI invokes Albert the Great to teach that "between science and faith there is friendship, and that men of science can undertake, through their vocation to the study of nature, a genuine and fascinating journey of sanctity."[84]

Scripture reveals the mind of God; science uncovers the handiwork of God. If the "book of nature" teaches one thing and the "book of Scripture" teaches the contrary, then we've misread one or the other. Truth is a unity and cannot contradict itself.[85] There is not one truth for science/nature and then another for faith/Scripture. Those who chant, "You have your truth, I've got my truth. Everybody's got their own truth," are sliding into a lazy cop-out. We must not betray our reason and experience. Nor can we betray the Apostolic Tradition. God is One, Truth is One, and there will be *no final conflict*.[86]

Scientism: Science Can Explain Everything

"When we say that scientific knowledge is unlimited, we mean that *there is no question whose answer is in principle unattainable by science.*"

— Rudolf Carnap, Positivist philosopher
(*The Logical Structure of the World*, 1967)[1]

"Scientism is a . . . dogmatic philosophy that can develop from [scientific observation], saying that since this is the only way we can find out about nature, that is all there is."

— Owen Gingerich, Harvard astronomer
(*God's Universe*, 1978)[2]

"The question of God is certainly a factual one, but certainly not a scientific one."

— Keith Ward, Oxford philosophical theologian
(*Why There Almost Certainly Is a God*, 2008)[3]

What Is Science?

Before the mid-19th century, the word "science" simply meant *knowledge*.[4] "Most of the time, today, when people refer to *science* we mean *natural science*, our knowledge of *nature* discovered by experiment and (most convincingly mathematical) theory."[5] Louisiana required that creation science be taught in public schools alongside evolution. The law, eventually rejected as unconstitutional in 1987, was challenged by many including 72 Nobel laureates whose briefs defined science:

- Science offers *naturalistic* explanations for natural phenomena.
- Science seeks to infer the *principles of nature* that best explain the observed phenomena.

- Science is *not equipped to evaluate supernatural explanations* and leaves their consideration to the domain of religious faith.[6]

The late Harvard paleontologist and science writer Stephen Jay Gould (1941-2002) added: "Science works only with testable proposals."[7]

I think I get it!

- If it doesn't deal with the physical world and natural, material causes, it isn't science.
- If it can't be tested, it isn't science.

But is it knowledge? Can "I know" things apart from the "scientific" method?[8] If a yes doesn't come quickly, ask yourself:

- Did science tell you who killed Lincoln? Historical events are not objects of scientific knowledge because they aren't repeatable. Rather, the historical-legal method[9] examines witnesses, artifacts, documents, etc. Does history provide knowledge?
- Did science teach you that "wisdom consists of the anticipation of consequences."[10] How did you learn that? Through proverbs, wisdom literature, the Tao?
- Did science validate stories like the fable of the tortoise and the hare or Steve Jobs' 2005 speech to Stanford graduates, which is filled with personal stories?[11]
- Did science teach you the Golden Rule: "Do unto others as you would have them do unto you?" Is ethics knowledge?
- Did science reveal the Word of the Lord? Is divine revelation knowledge?

The "scientific method" is a great investor in knowledge but is not its sole proprietor.

WHAT ABOUT WISDOM?

T. S. Eliot (1888-1965) famously asked: "Where is the wisdom we have lost in knowledge? Where is the knowledge we have lost in information?"[12] *Scientia* (knowledge) and *sapientia* (wisdom) are two Latin words whose differences seem easier to recognize than to define. Let me try:

- *Scientia* deals with the stage and props of life's drama — e.g., facts, the material setting, the physical environment, and items with quantity, weight, color, texture, and frequency.
- *Sapientia* deals with the storyline and characters of the drama — e.g., meaning, purpose, value, the metaphysically real.[13]

Neither kind of knowledge can be discarded. But in our society "we treat *quantities* as objective knowledge and *qualities* as a matter of subjective preference."[14] Ironically, what we know with greatest certainty is frequently of least consequence. For example, I can absolutely determine the size of the Statue of Liberty. I am less certain of what the statue means. Am I skeptical about the meaning of "liberty"? Of course not. But don't people disagree over abstract concepts like liberty? Yes, but people even disagree about the evidence of their senses. Real knowledge need not be exhaustive. Nor does it require unanimity to be accurate. The inferences we draw from our senses may seem to be most certain. We know intuitively, however, that the truths beyond our five senses are what make life worth living.[15]

What Is Scientism?[16]

"*Scientism* regards science as the absolute . . . only justifiable access to the truth."[17] From the *Oxford English Dictionary*: Scientism is "a belief in the omnipotence of scientific knowledge and techniques." Scientism holds "the view that the methods of study appropriate to physical science can replace those used in other fields such as philosophy and, esp., human behaviour and the social sciences."[18]

In his *Atheist's Guide to Reality: Living without Illusions*, Alexander Rosenberg complains that scientism is a "straw man." But he then states his "conviction that the methods of science are the only reliable ways to secure knowledge *about anything*."[19] Once we claim that ethics, art, theology, human relationships, and so on, yield their truths only through science or when we claim that *science can answer any question, solve any problem, and heal any hurt,* then we certainly have passed from science to scientism.

Scientism is also a form of "intellectual imperialism," advancing its domain by claiming itself a philosophy, religion, or worldview. For example, Newton's mechanics turn into the clockwork universe of deism; Einstein's relativity turns into relativism; Darwin's evolution, a theory explaining the formation and distribution of species, turns into evolutionism, a worldview conveying life's meaning, direction, values, morals, or even a "metanarrative."[20]

Christians know, however, that the fullness of reality exceeds the grasp of science. Essayist Marilynne Robinson writes that science is not "a final statement about reality but a highly fruitful mode of inquiry into it," through which we retain wonder, confident in our capacity to discern material causes, but always open to revision, for we don't know how the universe might surprise us.[21] Science writer Denyse O'Leary knows that "science functions best and teaches best with the knowledge that all scientific hypotheses are provisional, and not a form of dogma or a rule of life."[22] Science services a full-orbed philosophy of life; it doesn't provide one. Science, yes; scientism, no.

WHY SCIENTISM FAILS

Scientism Is Self-Refuting

In the original Star Trek TV series, Captain Kirk must subdue a crazed android, Norman, whose master's name is Harry Mudd. "Remember," Kirk says, "everything Harry tells you is a lie." Mudd then walks up to the android and says, "Now hear this, Norman: I am lying." Within seconds, Norman's brain circuitry starts frying, and he begins stuttering. Unable to reconcile the irreconcilable, Norman shuts down, lifeless.

"I am lying" is a self-refuting statement. Any statement asserting a universal truth must itself be subject to the teaching it advances. Why is scientism self-refuting? Because it teaches that "All valid knowledge is obtained through science." Okay. *"Has that statement been obtained through science?"* No. Scientism is self-refuting.[23]

Scientism Ultimately Rests on Assumptions That Aren't "Scientific"

The scientific method rests on non-scientific assumptions like a belief in the uniformity of natural causes,[24] the value of mental abstraction, and human testimony. Anthony Rizzi calls these assumptions "*The Science Before Science*."[25] We acquire this pre-scientific, "personal knowledge"[26] as people just living in the world.

Likewise, cultures build on particular assumptions about the nature of the world. The "scientific revolution" occurred in Europe because Christianity provided the necessary presuppositions. Other cultures had great cultural achievements. Ming China had its Confucian classics and hydraulic networks. The Taj Mahal is extraordinary architecture by the Mughals, who also produced miniatures of exquisite beauty and precision. The Ottoman Empire's architectural achievements designed by Sina are among the world's most memorable. But Toby E. Huff's *Intellectual Curiosity and the Scientific Revolution: A Global Perspective* (2010) points to the telescope. Though invented in Europe, traders, missionaries, and ambassadors carried it to China, India, and the Ottoman Empire. "'The Discovery Machine' — i.e., the telescope — set Europeans on fire with enthusiasm and curiosity. It failed to ignite the same spark elsewhere. . . . [Why?] The worldview that Europeans brought with them (even before the completion of the scientific revolution) stood at odds with the metaphysical foundations of the other civilizations."[27] Consequently, modern science emerged in the 17th century in Western Europe and nowhere else.[28] What made Europe a science-starter rather than a science-stopper?[29] Two basic assumptions:

1. The world is rational, orderly, and "sensible" because of the God who created it.

Before anyone builds a telescope, he assumes that the cosmos is intelligible, meaningful, and predictable. Nobody plants a pear tree expecting coconuts or waits on mosquitoes to beget acorns. Science is possible because the universe exhibits regularity.

Sociologist Rodney Stark surveyed 52 pioneers of modern science. Sixty percent were personally "devout." All but two held "conventional" religious beliefs.[30] All but two assumed a "rational Creator of all things"[31] who guaranteed a uniformity of natural causes. Alfred North Whitehead (1861-1947),[32] argued that the "medieval insistence on the rationality of God" undergirded modern science.[33] Historian of science Nancy Pearcy (b. 1952) noted: "If you do not expect to find rational laws, you will not even look for them, and science will not get off the ground."[34]

In 1954, Joseph Needham (1900-1995) launched the monumental 24-volume series *Science and Civilization in China*. In ancient Chinese philosophy, he said, "there was no confidence that the code of Nature's laws could be unveiled and read, because there was no assurance that a divine being, even more rational than ourselves, had ever formulated such a code capable of being read."[35]

Former Pontifical Council for Culture member and Oxford physicist Peter E. Hodgson (1928-2008) understood: "Although we seldom recognize it, scientific research requires certain basic beliefs about the order and rationality of matter, and its accessibility to the human mind. . . . [These were developed] through the Judeo-Christian belief in an omnipotent God, creator and sustainer of all things. In such a worldview it becomes sensible to try and understand the world, and this is the fundamental reason science developed as it did in the Middle Ages in Christian Europe, culminating in the brilliant achievements of the seventeenth century."[36] Or as literary historian C. S. Lewis (1898-1963) put it: "Men became scientific because they expected law in nature and they expected law in nature because they believed in a lawgiver."[37]

2. Christianity teaches that our minds are fitted to understand, rule, and develop the world.

"The most incomprehensible thing about the universe is that it is comprehensible."[38] Atheists believe that our brains were randomly produced by blind natural forces. Why should it properly comprehend the world? Pioneer geneticist J. B. S. Haldane (1892-1964) feared that our thoughts were just swirling atoms in our brains. Why, then, believe anything it tells us — including the fact that it is made of atoms? Such a view undermines the very rationality upon which scientific research depends![39]

Cognitive scientist Douglas Hofstadter (b. 1945) describes consciousness as an emergent property of the material brain. "It could be simply an accident of fate that our brains are too weak to understand themselves. Think of the lowly giraffe, for instance, whose brain is obviously far below the level required for self-understanding — yet it is remarkably similar to our brain."[40]

But, thankfully, the Western pioneer scientists assumed the mind's adequacy. God gave us a job to do and equipped us to do it. "We lesser rational beings [must], by virtue of that Godlike rationality, be able to decipher the laws of nature."[41] We must "think God's thoughts after Him," as the first theoretical astrophysicist, Johannes Kepler (1571-1630) memorably put it."[42]

Fill a blank page with letters randomly written. Can you read it? No, it is unintelligible. We can, however, "read" the universe. Even atheist celebrity Richard Dawkins has occasional spells of candor: "Biology is the study of complicated things that give the appearance of having been designed for a purpose."[43] Dawkins hastens to "explain away" the appearance of design. But Antony Flew (1923-2010), one of the 20th century's most influential analytic philosophers, created a major dustup among his atheist fellows when he "came out of the closet," before his death, confessing a divine-like design behind the cosmological constants.[44]

The aging Charles Darwin (1809-1882) felt this problem of ultimate skepticism acutely. Professor William Graham (1839-1911) sent his book *Creed of Science: Religious, Moral, and Social* (1881) to Darwin for review.[45] On July 3, 1881 Darwin acknowledged how much he had enjoyed the book:

> You have expressed my inward conviction . . . that the Universe is not the result of chance. But then with me the horrid doubt always arises whether the convictions of man's mind, which has been developed from the mind of the lower animals, are of any value or at all trustworthy. Would any one trust in the convictions of a monkey's mind, if there are any convictions in such a mind?[46]

Lurking behind Darwin's dark deliberations is that self-defeating skepticism that undermines all human projects. Analytic philosopher Alvin Plantinga of Notre Dame (b. 1932) argues that if both evolution and naturalism are true, then the probability of having reliable cognitive faculties is low. Can we really trust a "monkey's mind"?[47] Because God designed us in his image to have dominion on the earth, however, we would expect our minds to come equipped for the task. Christianity is true to the way things are.

These two assumptions represent the "science before science." When someone claims that the only authentic knowledge is scientific, he's kicked the ladder out from under his feet, and he's toppling toward skepticism.

Scientism Cannot Establish the Dignity of the Human Person

In his documentary *The Ascent of Man*, Jacob Bronowski (1908-1974), agnostic philosopher/scientist, strides into the crematorium ash pond at Auschwitz. Squatting, he scoops up a handful of mud. He recalls his murdered family:

> This is where people were turned into numbers. Into this pond were flushed the ashes of some four million people. And that was not done by gas. It was done by arrogance. It was done by dogmas. It was done by ignorance. When people believe that they have absolute knowledge, *with no test in reality*, this is how they behave. This is what men do when they aspire to the knowledge of the gods.[48]

This most poignant moment serves his lesson that science is provisional and tentative and certainty is dangerous. But Bronowski is aiming at the quasi-religious political ideology of Nazism without sensing the wicked irony that "Nazi barbarism was motivated by an ethic that prided itself on being scientific," not religious.[49] In fact, "Nazism is nothing but applied biology."[50]

For half a century, "racial hygiene" and "scientific racism" had been *tested in reality*. Leading thinkers from America encouraged Germans[51] to produce peer-reviewed literature, write grants, and circulate popular literature, including humor and homilies espousing eugenics and racial hygiene. Support was international, flowing in from Sweden, Japan, Belgium, Canada, Brazil, and Switzerland.[52] To us the Nazis are "monsters"; they saw themselves as the "political expression of biological knowledge." At the turn of the century, German scientists took 50 percent of all scientific Nobel Prizes. Even under Hitler, half the university students were in medical school. Germans discovered the link between smoking and lung cancer, and they banned smoking in public places, overmedication, and the overzealous use of X-rays.[53]

But that magnificent technical, scientific achievement rested on a rotten foundation even before Hitler.[54] The Christian ethic had been sidelined by speculative theories appearing to discredit the historical trustworthiness of Scripture and traditional Christian orthodoxies of Catholicism and the various forms of Protestantism. A new "scientific evolutionary ethic" became regnant. Eminent naturalist, biologist, and philosopher Ernst Haeckel (1834-1919) published *Riddle of the Universe* (*Welträtsel*) in 1899, spreading evolutionary philosophy and ideas of racial hygiene to a popular audience. Pre-Nazi German scientists inflated Darwin's biological theory into a prescription for morality and ethics. Arnold Dodel (1843-1908), a leading German botanist, proclaimed in 1904, "The new worldview actually rests on the theory of evolution. On it we have to construct a new ethics. All values will be revalued."[55] Health replaced virtue. "That which preserves health is moral. Everything that makes one sick or ugly is sin."[56]

In an intellectual sleight of hand, *biological descriptions mutated into moral imperatives*. "If an act contributes to biological decline, it is immoral," wrote Alexander Tille (1866-1912), "even if it fulfills the Christian command of love and compassion."[57] "Honor your parents" became "Honor your child, that it may become fit and accomplish its work in life. [This] teaches ethics on a scientific foundation."[58] The corporal works of mercy, concern for the weak and poor, were despised as unhealthy and lacking survival value. Tille chillingly predicted: "Even the most careful selection of the best can accomplish nothing, if it is not linked with a merciless elimination of the worst people. . . . And *the proclamation of social elimination must there-*

*fore be one of the supreme features of every ethics, which elevates as its ideal **the goal that the theory of evolution has demonstrated**.* . . . Do not spare your neighbor! . . . [T]his means becoming hard against those who are below average. . . . [O]vercome one's own sympathy."[59] That was 1895.

Forty-five years later, Nazi propaganda chief Joseph Goebbels (1897-1945) took Tille's advice. Troubled while watching a newsreel of the German army's wanton destruction of the Poles, he forced himself forward affirming, "Be hard, my heart, be hard."[60] Was this social evolution? Was this moral progress?

Morality can no more be improved upon than the multiplication table. Giving thanks, practicing kindness, and showing solicitude to the weak are not mere social conventions. Where simple politeness exists, we find an implicit recognition that people are ends and never only means. As Rebecca West once put it, "perhaps the sin against the Holy Ghost is to deal with people as though they were things."[61]

The newly emerging German worldview was a "dystopian attempt to fabricate new men and women by erasing or transforming their inherited ethical values,"[62] writes historian Michael Burleigh. "From a modernized and scientized version of pre-Judeo/Christian conduct," Nazi medicine sought to breed a new man. *"Be fruitful and multiply"* turned into *"Be fit before you multiply"* . . . or else. Compulsory sterilization of the "feebleminded" was enforced. The unfit would be eliminated through euthanasia and infanticide. German culture, not just its politics, could not resist what science historian Paul Farber identified as the "temptation of evolutionary ethics."[63]

IS NATURE OUR TEACHER?

Hitler imagined he had mastered the Darwinian lesson.[64] "As in all domains, so also in the area of selection, nature is the best teacher. One could not think up a better design for nature than the advance of organisms . . . only in hard struggle . . . one may not have any pity for people who have been fixed by destiny to perish."[65] Nature had no pity, therefore, Hitler should have no pity.

But did God intend "nature, red in tooth and claw" to form our ethics? Absolutely not. Nature is awesome, but it isn't kind. Annie

Dillard's Pulitzer Prize-winning *Pilgrim at Tinker Creek* (1974) affirms nature's magnificence but won't blink at the cruelty of a water beetle draining and then devouring a frog. The frog's eyes go vacant before his hollowed shiny skin crumples like a collapsed tent. She admits it was "a monstrous and terrifying thing. I gaped bewildered, appalled."[66]

She knew that "evolution loves death more than it loves you or me."[67] A Christian, she did not "go and do likewise." From the Baal worshipers of the Old Testament to worshipers of blood and soil in the Third Reich, veteran missionary Lesslie Newbigin knew the idolatry of making nature our ultimate reference point. "There is no right and wrong in nature, the controlling realities are power and fertility. Nature sometimes has a charming smile but her teeth are terrible."[68]

Getting this wrong cost amateur naturalist, self-proclaimed eco-warrior, and friend of the bears Timothy Treadwell (1957-2003) his life. He's the subject of director Werner Herzog's disturbing documentary *Grizzly Man* (2005).

Treadwell, a controversial "protector" of bears, documented 13 summers living among the bears of Alaska. The last two years, his girlfriend reluctantly joined him. Treadwell scorned using an electric fence, pepper spray, or weaponry to protect himself or his girlfriend. He cultivated "a relationship" with the grizzlies. In 2003, the bears were fattening up for winter. A familiar bear, frustrated by failing to retrieve some fish from the nearby stream, ambled about the camp, finally turning on the couple, mauling, mutilating, and eating them amidst their hellish shrieks recorded on the videocam that was left running. Director Herzog is not reticent. "What haunts me is that in all the faces of all the bears that Treadwell ever filmed, I discover no kinship, no understanding, no mercy. I see only the overwhelming indifference of nature. . . . And this blank stare [of the bear that ate Treadwell] speaks only of a half-bored interest in food. . . . I believe the common character of the universe is not harmony, but chaos, hostility, and murder."

He should know. He processed the audio recording of Treadwell's and his partner's screams bearing harsh, shrieking witness to the ethics of nature. From the standpoint of the bears, human flesh, like pork chops, are just the other white meat.

Science, like nature, is amoral. While science can discover the praiseworthy, it can't command it. Further, science fails to locate any ethical scale that assures me that my killing of the bear is any more praiseworthy than his killing of me. This is why Einstein could say, "You are right in speaking of the moral foundations of science, but cannot turn round and speak of the scientific foundations of morality. . . . [E]very attempt to reduce ethics to scientific formulae must fail."[69] Science and nature provide the setting or stage for the drama, the "is." Human beings provide the storyline, the plot, the moral struggle, the "ought." Humans, not nature, make the ethical contribution to the drama. The higher shouldn't take its cues from the lower. The personal is superior to the impersonal. Humans are exceptional: only humans tell stories. Storytelling sets us apart.[70]

Scientism Can't Stand Up to Evil

We left Jacob Bronowski urging tentativeness, avoidance of dogma, a safe lukewarmness. This soft skepticism was applied to knowledge claims generally. But who was best equipped to save Bronowski's family — the philosophical skeptics or those with robust commitments to truth?

Just weeks before Hitler invaded Poland, German theologian Dietrich Bonhoeffer wrote his patron, the celebrated American theologian Reinhold Niebuhr of the celebrated Union Seminary. Bonhoeffer, already in America, had agreed to join the celebrated Union family as a celebrated theological boy wonder. But God hadn't called him to celebrity but to Germany. So he wrote Niebuhr: "I have made a mistake in coming to America. . . . I shall have no right to participate in the reconstruction of Christian life in Germany after the war if I do not share the trials of this time with my people."[71] He returned to Germany to participate in the resistance, ferry Jews to safety, and assist in a plot to assassinate Hitler.

Today, we admire those like Bonhoeffer — von Stauffenberg, Oster, von Galen, and even the deeply flawed Oskar Schindler — not because they were brilliant relativists or skeptics but because

they weren't. To the contrary, the vast majority of resisters and res-
cuers were theists who claimed knowledge of reality. The doctrine of
Creation taught them the dignity of the human person. The Abrahamic covenant and Israel's election taught them that the Jews were
God's memory in the heart of mankind. The Golden Rule was not
negotiable.

"Oh, we weren't really sure what the Nazis were up to" were
the words of the tentative and uncommitted during the most serious moral crisis of the 20th century.[72] They now get our scorn and
derision. But wasn't it Bronowski's agnosticism that reduced his
relatives to ash as certainly as Treadwell's romantic environmental
scientism reduced his girlfriend to protein?

Dietrich Bonhoeffer (1906-1945) was hanged in the Flossenbürg
concentration camp on April 8, 1945. Hitler, knowing the allies
were closing in, personally commanded that the execution continue.
That morning Bonhoeffer preached from Isaiah. The guards arrived
with their orders. The camp medical doctor saw Bonhoeffer kneel-
ing on the floor praying. "I was most deeply moved by the way this
lovable man prayed, so devout and so certain that God heard his
prayer." Bonhoeffer got up and became a dead man walking. "At the
place of execution, he again said a short prayer and then climbed the
steps to the gallows, brave and composed. His death ensued after
a few seconds." Those few seconds provided that doctor one of his
life's most burning lessons: "In the almost fifty years that I worked
as a doctor, I have hardly ever seen a man *die so entirely submissive
to the will of God.*"[73]

Bonhoeffer never flowered as an academic theologian. He was
only 39 when he was executed. He had, however, lived and died as
a "living epistle," teaching us more splendidly than his unfinished
magnum opus, *Ethics*, could possibly have done. He demonstrated
the *Cost of Discipleship*, the title of his most popular book. Had
Bonhoeffer been more tentative, adopting Bronowski's approach to
knowledge, we may have gotten his book, but we would have been
deprived of the example of his martyrdom, his living *Ethics*. That
would have been the tragedy. He provided us with knowledge that

the finest science can never discover, and only the finest of men can fully grasp and live, a knowledge more certain in death than in life.

"When Christ calls a man he bid him come and die," Bonhoeffer had written years before. The German theologian knew that was true, for he found that when he embraced Christ in his death or his death in Christ, he discovered his self — strengthened, coherent, firm, whole. Thus, he was empowered to leave us *sapientia*, not *scientia*. He discovered what so many cognitive scientists, neurobiologists, and writers like Stephen Pinker, E. O. Wilson, and Victor Stenger can't. They can tell us a lot, but they can't tell us what we need to know to become who we were created to be. Their scientism just doesn't have the tools.

Reductionism: Science Proves Life Is "Nothing But . . ."

"Science had persuaded the intelligent that the universe was but the mechanical interaction of purposeless bits of matter. Thoughtful people in the nineties [1890s] told themselves in all seriousness that they should no longer admire a sunset. It was nothing but the refraction of white light through dust particles in layers of air of variable density."

—JACQUES BARZUN (*The Use and Abuse of Art*, 1974)[1]

WHAT IS REDUCTIONISM?

Say "reduction" and most people hear weight loss. Chefs hear gourmet sauce. Philosophers and theologians hear trouble. Remember the tendency for scientific discoveries to get abused and turned into full-blown philosophies? Evolution becomes evolutionism. Relativity becomes relativism. So, too, with methods. The scientific method can be abused and turned into scientism. The method of reduction can be turned into reductionism. Just as methodological naturalism can become metaphysical naturalism, so too can methodological reductionism become metaphysical reductionism. So we need to make critical distinctions. Let's look at a few different "reductionisms."

1. One type of reductionism explains higher phenomena by its lowest components. For example:

- Worship (a theological or spiritual phenomenon) gets reduced to
  — a longing for an illusory cosmic father-figure (psychological) reduced to
  — a neural configuration in the brain (neurological) which is no more than

— electro-chemical firings between the ears (biochemical) reduced to

— subatomic particles operating according to quantum laws (physics).

Atheist Nobel laureate Francis Crick (1916-2004) announced 45 years ago: "The ultimate aim of the modern movement in biology is in fact to explain all biology in terms of physics and chemistry."[2]

POLITICAL RALLIES, IMMUNE SYSTEMS, GLOBAL FINANCIAL MARKETS, AND THE INTERNET HAVE WHAT IN COMMON?

2. Another type of reductionism claims that the whole can be reduced to the sum of its parts.

In 1981, Drs. Hubel and Wiesel shared the Nobel Prize in Physiology/Medicine for recording the electrical activity of *single neurons* in the visual cortex. Dr. Miguel Nicolelis was impressed. He was also impressed by the unrelated million protestors he had spent the afternoon with in São Paulo, Brazil, demanding "Elections now." When he returned to his lab, he asked his mentor, "Why not follow a strict reductionism like Hubel and Wiesel?"

Nicolelis gets dramatic:

My mentor's reply was as forceful as the roar . . . of the crowd in Sao Paulo: "We do not record from a single neuron, my son, for the same reason that the rally you attended . . . would be a disaster if, instead of one million people, only one person had showed up to protest. . . . Do you think that anyone would pay attention to the pleas of a single person screaming at a political rally? The brain does not pay attention to the electrical screaming of a single noisy neuron. It needs many more of its cells singing together to decide what to do next."[3]

He was saying a new reality emerged when neurons act together, just as a new reality emerged when a million people act together. The whole was definitely greater than the sum of its parts. The parts functioning together as a whole bring something new into existence.[4]

This Is Your Brain on God

3. Another type of reductionism dismisses the reality of an allegedly higher phenomenon by causing it through a lower, apparently unrelated cause.

Neuropsychologist Michael Persinger (b. 1945) had subjects don a fabricated "God-helmet" head covering so that he could apply mild electromagnetic bursts to the right temporal lobe of their brains. Lo and behold, people reported that they "sensed" God, Muhammad, UFOs, etc. *"Michael Persinger has found God in the brain,"*[5] says a gleeful Scott James in *An Introduction to Evolutionary Ethics* (2011), obviously pleased that religious experience has finally been discredited. Kudos are a tad premature.

First, ancient sorcerers generated the same result. In the Book of Revelation, "sorcerer" (Greek, *pharmakeus*) is the root of our "pharmacy" and "pharmaceuticals."[6] Ancient sorcerers or shamans induced quasi-mystical states through various substances and types of dance or chant. So too today through "entheogens" like LSD. For "acid guru" Timothy Leary (1920-1996), "drugs were the sacraments for the new religion."[7] Aldous Huxley (1894-1963), John Lilly (1915-2001), and many more share vibrant stories.[8] Only a flat-footed scientism would conclude that religious experiences are discredited because we can now do through electric shock what we have been doing for millennia through ingesting controlled substances. Who's the naïf here?

Second, artificially zapping the brain to simulate mystical experience does not explain whether or not authentic mystical experiences involve this portion of the brain. The ability to produce a counterfeit bill certainly is no argument against authentic bills.

Third, the only published attempt to replicate these effects failed. Critics correlated the unusual reports to personality characteristics and suggestibility.[9]

Fourth, the cause is too small for the effect. Reducing the history of worship, moral reasoning, theology, and mystical experience to a brain tickle just doesn't ring true. Persinger's experiments are too cramped a stage for the scope of the drama that he demands to be played there.

Reducing religious experience to a brain tickle is just one example of metaphysical reductionism.

ARE YOU A MAN OR A MOUSE?

Anthropomorphizing animals is fun. Paintings called *Dogs Playing Poker* or chimps dressed up riding tricycles always elicit laughter. On campus, however, "dressing" humans down is even more fun. By comparing DNA, homologous organs, or mating rituals, we draw humorous and sometimes not-so-humorous parallels between species.

The Great Ape Project, for instance, seeks legal recognition for human-like rights for the non-human great primates.[10] I don't know if biochemist Bruce Alberts (b. 1938) would lobby for the Great Worm Project but "in the last ten years we have come to realize humans are more like worms than we ever imagined."[11] The late geneticist Glen Evans (1954-2011), a pioneer in synthetic biology and formerly with the Salk Institute and the University of Texas Southwestern Medical Center, gladly agreed. Genetically speaking, he reports, "the worm represents a very simple human."[12] Other biologists think that humans favor oversized *Drosophila melanogaster* — fruit flies. "In essence, we are nothing but a big fly," insists Charles Zuker (b. 1957), genetic researcher at the University of California at San Diego.[13] Jane Roger of the Sanger Institute published the mouse genome in 2002. She has a tale for us. "We share 99% of our genes with mice, and we even have the genes that could make a tail." As reported: "The genetic blueprint of the mouse" demonstrates that "there isn't much difference between mice and men."[14] Are we really closer to mice than chimps (98 percent)? Only four nucleotides (A, C, G, T) write the entire genetic code, so a purely random assortment shows we share 25 percent of our DNA with any known life form, whether or not it even has a brain.[15] Since fish share 40 percent of our genes, can we boost their self-esteem and acknowledge them as 40 percent human?[16]

So who are humans?

- "The worm represents a very simple human."
- "What are you, a man or a mouse?"
- "In essence, we are nothing but a big fly."

Reducing the human to simply a more complex beast, different only in degree, not in kind, abuses the scientific method of reduction.

BEWARE THE "NOTHING BUTS"

Neuroscientist Donald M. MacKay (1922-1987) identified a verbal marker that functions like a radioisotope, alerting us to a disease of the tongue and/or mind. "Nothing but" is the phrase that leads to "nothing buttery." Humans are *nothing but* more complex apes. Love is *nothing but* oxytocin in good measure. Sex, like a sneeze, is *nothing but* an animal impulse. Whenever we hear "*nothing but*" we know that "metaphysical reductionism" is infecting our discussion. Level the playing field. Metaphysical reductionism sounds much less high-minded when called "nothing buttery."[17]

Nothing-buttery doesn't so much explain as *explains away*. "You can debunk love, or bravery, or sin . . . by finding the psychological or physiological mechanisms underlying the behaviour in question."[18] For example, bravery is "nothing but" overcompensation for one's short stature. Love is "nothing but" an increase in hormones.

English teacher and writer Jonathan Gottschall offers the first "unified theory of storytelling,"[19] based on scientific as well as traditional literary studies in *The Storytelling Animal: How Stories Make Us Human* (2012). He is always asked: "Don't you worry that science could explain away the magic of story?" His answer is a resounding "No! A thousand times, no!" And he is delightfully right. It's reductionism that explains away the magic of a story by saying it is "nothing but" a survival mechanism, which, by clear inference, is naturalistically wired into us by blind, irrational forces of nature. That isn't science. "Science adds to wonder; it doesn't dissolve it. Scientists almost always report that the more they discover about their subject, the more lovely and mysterious it becomes."[20] After decades as a particle physicist and now an Anglican priest, John

Polkinghorne testifies to scientific explanation's capacity to incite, rather than stifle, wonder. "The universe has not only proved to be astonishingly rationally transparent, making deep science possible," he writes, "but also rationally beautiful, affording scientists the reward of wonder for all the labours of their research. Why are we so lucky?"[21]

GRIEVING AT THE DEATH OF ORGANIC MOLECULES

"I am a collection of water, calcium and organic molecules called Carl Sagan. You are a collection of almost identical molecules with a different collective label. But is that all? Is there nothing in here but molecules? Some people find this idea somehow demeaning to human dignity. For myself, I find it elevating that our universe permits the evolution of molecular machines as intricate and subtle as we."[22]

Is Carl Sagan (1934-1996) best presented as his recipe or his résumé. Rather than painting pictures of dogs' molecules playing poker, he dresses up water and calcium as human beings. Sagan believes that matter is our ultimate origin and destiny. In between origin and destiny, he recommends we should frolic as though unaware that if he is correct, then Bertrand Russell's eloquent description best summarizes our plight and "that no fire, no heroism, no intensity of thought and feeling, can preserve an individual life beyond the grave; that all the labours of the ages, all the devotion, all the inspiration, all the noonday brightness of human genius, are destined to extinction in the vast death of the solar system, and that the whole temple of Man's achievement must inevitably be buried beneath the debris of a universe in ruins."[23] All that we frolic over is doomed. Sagan is whistling through the graveyard.

A recent survey still shows that the *collection of water, calcium, and organic molecules called Carl Sagan* remains deeply admired, though dead since 1996.[24] His wife, Ann Druyan (b. 1949), told the *Skeptical Enquirer* that "Carl faced his death with unflagging courage and never sought refuge in illusions. *The tragedy was that we knew we would never see each other again.* I don't ever expect to be reunited with Carl."[25]

We must tread gently here. Ann's grief is expected and appropriate. Yet she should not be patronized. Given their naturalistic philosophy, why was Carl's death a tragedy and not just in the natural order of things?[26] A tragedy occurs when a story that we expected to end happily, doesn't. The Sagans believed that humans "are the products of a long series of biological accidents."[27] The Sagan creed had never offered hope. Happy endings or beginnings were never in the cards. So, why tragic? Hadn't he simply finished his course? Hadn't he simply unfolded his genetic potentialities? Had anything happened that wasn't expected?

The Cosmos

"The cosmos is all that is, was and ever will be." Sagan's confession was easily memorized by all who attended his secular liturgy, celebrated at the shrine of our family altar, the television. He — high priest, oracle of science — presided over his PBS series *Cosmos*, repeating that there is nothing outside, above, under, or alongside the universe that gives it meaning, direction, or purpose. The universe is locked up, a closed system fortified against influence from outside the system. *"The cosmos is all that is, was and ever will be."*[28]

The *Cosmos* creed, of course, deliberately parodies the doxology "to the Father, and to the Son, and to the Holy Spirit. As it was in the beginning, is now, and ever shall be. . . ." Had he tried "From everlasting to everlasting thou art Cosmos" (cf. Ps 90:2) or "Come, let us bow down, let us kneel before the Cosmos, our maker" (cf. Ps 95:6), we might have laughed instead of nodding knowingly. The absurdity of bowing before an unintelligent brute force is not so apparent in his chosen motto as it is in those psalm equivalents.[29]

Is He a Wise Man or Only a Wise Guy?

Sagan mastered a certain set of facts, operations, and cultural practices in a society where celebrity scientists often pose as "oracles of science,"[30] sages for our time.

He wrote, many times, with moral seriousness. A man I wish I had known. Too often, however, he sounded like a scriptwriter for Biff Belson, village atheist: "I do not know of any compelling evidence for anthropomorphic patriarchs controlling human destiny from some hidden celestial vantage point. . . ."[31] Neither do I. But the God of Abraham, Isaac, and Jacob; the God and Father of Jesus Christ; and the First Mover of Aristotle hasn't left himself without witnesses or evidence.[32] At times, Sagan caricatures himself. "The idea that God is an oversized white male with a flowing beard, who sits in the sky and tallies the fall of every sparrow, is ludicrous."[33] Yes, of course. But why Sagan belittled God for the attention to detail, for which Google gets wealthy, is beyond me. He betrayed a silly mind over serious things.

George Buttrick, once chaplain at Harvard, disarmed students who declared, "I don't believe in God," by simply agreeing with them. "I probably don't believe in that god either." But what possesses an internationally renowned astrophysicist to construct a version of Christianity that my 11-year-old son would reject as silly, and then proceed to demolish it as though he was liberating the world from a dire misconception? Sagan didn't lack intelligence, style, humanity, or work ethic; he lacked wisdom, that virtue which interprets and values facts, draws lessons from experience, and exercises sound judgment in the face of imperfect knowledge. Wisdom resists reductionism because it won't lose the forest for the trees. Further, the biblical tradition insists that wisdom be rooted in a sense of awe before the Infinite Personal God of creation. "The fear of the Lord"[34] is the beginning of wisdom.[35]

So was Carl Sagan a wise man or only a wise guy? He could have instructed me any day on how the heavens go, but not on how to go to heaven. He could teach me the composition but not the meaning of "stardust." He could calculate the distance between Venus and me; I'd bet on it. Calculate the distance between me and my unreconciled college roommate? I'd cease to wager.

To the end of his life, Sagan remained a scorner,[36] too often dripping with the sarcasm that marked earlier generations of skeptics, like Voltaire and Diderot, who scoffed that the God of Genesis "loved his apples more than he did his children." Such clever but ultimately silly quips resemble adolescent sniping more than adult dialogue. Sagan, too often, drove his hot rod down that strip. He just couldn't resist the one-liner, tickling himself with zingers about oversized white males with flowing beards — a description that fit me for many years, and I know Sagan would never have mistaken me for Divinity. He knew the difference between God and man. A pity he couldn't discern the difference between God and the cosmos.

THE COSMOS: SPECTACLE OR MYSTERY?

"The Cosmos is all that is, was and ever will be. Our feeblest contemplations of the Cosmos stir us — there is a tingling in the spine, a catch in the voice, a faint sensation, as if a distant memory, of falling from a height. We know we are approaching the greatest of mysteries."

Sagan was, undoubtedly, inspired by creation's beauty. At times, his language is quasi-religious. His materialistic worldview, however, is in tension with his sense of reverence. Materialism, ultimately, forces people, at best, to prize the cosmos as spectacle rather than mystery. Mystery requires meaning, and meaning is a function of personhood — i.e., a consciousness with intention, identity, plan, desire, love. Meaning is not a feature of impersonal matter that is explained in mechanistic, deterministic, or legalistic terms. At best, Sagan's cosmos is a stimulating and splendid fireworks display. It may call for more research to uncover the mechanisms that govern. There is, however, no invitation to mystery, no call to commune with the Creator of the cosmos.[37]

WHO LIVES WITH ILLUSIONS?

Nevertheless, being created in the image and likeness of God, he cannot evade being *homo religiosus* — i.e., worshiping man. He feels a reverential relation toward the creation and wants to retain it. Yet he feels compelled to discard the idea of a Personal Creator. Carl Sagan, the man who wanted to live without illusion, now cheats. He theomorphizes the universe and kneels before its raw, brute exercise of impersonal power. He is living in denial of what he knows about the true character of matter; it is coldly, blindly, ruthlessly impersonal, unworthy of his reverence, just as Timothy Treadwell's bears were unworthy of his friendship. The universe smiles, but beneath the charming spectacle are very sharp teeth.

Ann also tries to preserve a sense of mystery for their love: "Every single moment that we were alive and we were together was miraculous — not miraculous in the sense of inexplicable or supernatural. *We knew we were beneficiaries of chance. . . .* [Amazed] *that pure chance could be so generous and so kind. . . ."*[38] But she, too, cheats. Chance is fortuitous; it is not "grace." Chance is not "kind" or "generous," nor does it dispense benefits. But Carl and Ann, made in the image and likeness of God, cannot avoid sensing that the world and their flourishing are somehow connected to a mystery properly called divine, and must be, in spite of their objection, deeply personal.

CRY OF THE HUMAN HEART: PATHOLOGICAL OR PRIME CLUE?

"The sockeye salmon exhaust themselves swimming up the mighty Columbia River to spawn, heroically hurdling cataracts, in a single-minded effort that works to propagate their DNA sequences into future generation. The moment their work is done, they fall to pieces. Scales flake off, fins drop, and soon — often within hours of spawning — they are dead and becoming distinctly aromatic.

"They've served their purpose.

"Nature is unsentimental.

"Death is built in."[39]

Unlike the salmon, Ann sees death as tragic. By seeing ourselves as "nothing but" calcium, hydrogen, and organic molecules, can we wash the tragedy out of death? Can we be more like the salmon? Ann Druyan, rightfully, refused to be so reduced.

Transcendence is the sense that humans and life are more than matter in motion, and that the whole is greater than the sum of its particular parts. Is the longing for transcendence a human pathology, or is it natural to us? Charles Taylor's magnum opus, *The Secular Age*, charges that the materialism or philosophical naturalism that dominates our public institutions does violence to us by closing "the window on transcendence, as though there were nothing beyond — more, as though it weren't a crying need of the human heart to open that window, gaze, and then go beyond, as though feeling this need were the result of a mistake, an erroneous worldview, bad conditioning, or worse, some pathology."[40]

But clearly, this is not how we experience it. Virtually all the great art of the Western world depends on balancing transcendence and immanence, and not letting "nature" eat up "grace," or the "machine" destroy "meaning," or "power" suppress "truth," or "determinism" extinguish "freedom," or the "impersonal" absorb the "personal." Students of the creative process and insight in science and philosophy know that creativity and insight flow from this human longing for transcendence.[41]

We should take a stand. Transcendence is natural, not pathological. Beware the doctor who tells us that our trait most cherished for its vitality is, after all, a cancer. Look for a new doctor. Refuse. Resist. Withhold your consent. The "authorities" of this age have no right to perform a spiritual lobotomy upon us.[42] We haven't signed some advanced directive that permits the euthanizing of our divine discontent. We intuit that life is more than matter in motion, and that makes far more sense within a theistic, rather than an atheistic, framework![43] So send that sorry physician out the door, tell him he's not welcome anymore, and sing "I will survive."

Look Upon the Beasts and Learn[44]

My oldest son Nick, then 17, sat with our deeply loved black Lab, Ben, as he passed from this world one early Saturday morning 10 years ago. Ben was the prime pet through the growing up years of four of our five children. His passing deeply saddened us, but it wasn't a tragedy, as those who have lost pets of long standing don't need me to explain. Death is natural for old dogs, as they slow down and then finally lie near the fire to pass from this life. Ben had fulfilled his "dogness" through our family in some wonderful way for which we could give thanks, which we did with an appropriate short burial service in our backyard, thanking God and honoring the great gift Ben had been to our family.

For human beings, death, St. Paul says, is our last enemy.[45] It isn't natural for us. Ann Druyan's worldview, however, holds death to be perfectly natural, yet she is aware of how violently it rips the fabric of all we hold dear. The death of a loved one is a quake, opening a crevice through which wafts an odd scent of meaning, a signal from beyond the stern unyielding, ironclad Cosmos that had become the idol Carl Sagan constructed to displace God. In the end, however, idolatry is a devil's bargain, and the Cosmos demanded all that Carl Sagan is, was, or ever would be. The calcium, water, and organic molecules that were called Carl Sagan degraded into the compost pile, which is his grave. Or did they?

SETI: CARL SAGAN'S PRACTICAL HOPE

"Hope deferred makes the heart sick."[46] Carl Sagan, not exempt from that proverb, sought hope to thrive. He found it where most of us don't look: the Cosmos. "There must be other starfolk. . . . There must be . . . many places in the galaxy where there are beings far more advanced than we in science and technology, in politics, ethics, poetry, and music."[47] Is it presumptuous to think that his search for extraterrestrial intelligence (SETI) flowed from his longing for something greater than himself?[48] This "oracle of science" was out on a limb[49] doing what he had so often condemned as irrational in others.[50] Unlike theism,[51] and the historic Resurrection of Christ,[52] there are no strong arguments to justify belief in purely naturalistic extraterrestrial life forms. The fruit of Christian hope sprouts from a rational root. The belief in extraterrestrials rests on personal incredulity — e.g., how can a universe this size not have other intelligent creatures?

Incredulity, however, is not an argument. Without evidence, Sagan also assumed his starfolk would be benevolent rather than imperialistic. "The receipt of a single message," he wrote, could save our civilization. With the arrival of the starfolk, "the animosities that divide the peoples of the earth . . . wither. . . ."[53] Carl had faith that these starfolk could teach the world to do what the United Nations, the papacy, the United States, the Red Cross, and Coca Cola[54] had failed to do: to teach the world to sing in perfect harmony.

Ironically, Carl said: "Reports [of the paranatural and supernatural] persist and proliferate because they sell. And they sell, I think, because there are so many of us who want so badly to be jolted out of our humdrum lives, to rekindle that sense of wonder we remember from childhood, and also, for a few of the stories, to be able, really and truly, to believe — in Someone older, smarter, and wiser who is looking out for us."

The irony is that this applies to Carl's SETI. By reducing himself to an impersonal recipe of water, calcium, etc., he abandoned cosmic hope in the human project and was forced to exercise an irrational, dare I say, blind faith in the most implausible of redemptive possibilities: extraterrestrials. "When people stop believing in God, they don't believe in nothing — they believe in anything."[55]

WHAT'S WRONG WITH EATING YOUR HEART OUT?

C. S. Lewis writes of our longing for heaven:

> All the things that have ever deeply possessed your soul have been but hints of [heaven] — tantalizing glimpses, promises never quite fulfilled, echoes that died away just as they caught your ear. But . . . if there ever came an echo that did not die away but swelled into the sound itself — you would know it. Beyond all possibility of doubt you would say "Here at last is the thing I was made for." . . . It is the secret signature of each soul, the incommunicable and unappeasable want, the thing we wanted before we met our wives or made our friends or chose our work, and which we shall still desire on our deathbeds, when the mind no longer knows wife or friend or work. While we are, this is. If we lose this, we lose all.[56]

Something is darkly wrong with a worldview that forces us to train our hearts to be hard and tamp down all our aspirations for love, significance, purpose, meaning, and goodness — all that makes life worth living. Something is wrong when alleged intellectual rigor demands that we dampen, even drown, every glowing ember of faith, hope, and love that lie nestled within us, pleading for nurture like a newborn's lips instinctively reaching for a mother's breast long before his poorly formed reason learns to question the existence of mothers.

Shouldn't we, rather, breathe on these tokens of meaning, the warm breath of faith, hope, and love? Shouldn't we live in joyful expectation, with minds keen for wisdom and direction, with wills strengthened and poised to execute a design for our flourishing and not our faltering? It is a fact that our souls do prosper when fueled with such hope. Why shouldn't that be eloquent testimony to our true origin and destiny? What dubious logic would force me to decide for hopelessness and death, while it is self-evident that hope confers life.[57] Faith, not suspicion, permits me to promise. Love, not gratification, enables me to sacrifice. This is what makes my life worth living. Those united to God, and seeking his will, do find that life is ultimately a comedy, not a tragedy; a wedding supper, not a funeral. For if God is for us, who or what can ultimately be against us?[58]

Relativism: Feet Firmly Planted in Mid-Air

"After all, what were the Ten Commandments? Were they municipal regulations to govern the immediate vicinity of Mt. Sinai? Or were they meant to be commands universal in their reach? The same God who authored a universal law of physics had not authored a separate moral law for Nigeria and Jersey City."

— HADLEY ARKES (*First Principles and Natural Law: The Foundations of Modern Political Philosophy*, 2012)[1]

WHAT IS RELATIVISM?

Sometimes it is helpful to do a simplistic comparison of a concept. What do various schools of thought consider "wonderful" or an unalloyed good?

- Christianity asks, "Isn't the Trinity wonderful?"
- New Ageism asks, "Isn't my divinity wonderful?"
- Secular humanism asks, "Isn't our humanity wonderful?"
- Hedonism asks, "Isn't pleasure wonderful?"
- Pragmatism asks, "If it works, it's wonderful?"
- Buddhism says, "Nothing is wonderful!"
- Hinduism says, "All is One-derful."
- Egotism says, "*I* am wonderful! No question."
- Relativism ends it: "If it's wonderful for you, now that's wonderful."[2]

The two most popular forms of relativism are egotistic relativism and cultural relativism. Crudely put, "If it's true for you, it's true. If it's right for you, it's right" and "If your culture says it's true, it's true. If your culture says it's right, it's right."

In fact, there are many relativisms that share core elements:

- No absolute conceptions of truth, morality, or beauty exist — i.e., no truth claim, moral principle or standard of beauty is absolutely true, good, or beautiful in all times, in all places, for all people.
- Truth, morality, and beauty are in the eye of the beholder.
- Contrary points of view can be equally valid.

HOW PREVALENT IS RELATIVISM?

In 1884, Pope Leo XIII (1810-1903) first used the word "relativism" in a papal document. John Paul II (1993) saw man "giving himself over to relativism and skepticism . . . in search of an illusory freedom apart from truth itself."[3] And in April 2005, Joseph Cardinal Ratzinger (soon to be Pope Benedict XVI) saw us "moving towards a dictatorship of relativism which does not recognize anything as certain and which has as its highest goal one's own ego and one's own desires."[4]

These shepherds see their flock, wandering around "like sheep . . . gone astray; . . . every one to his own way."[5] Allan Bloom famously confirmed: "There is one thing a professor can be absolutely sure of: almost every student entering the university believes, or says he believes, that truth is relative."[6] In *Finding God at Harvard*, Kelly Monroe claims that relativism masks insecurity, a form of intellectual cowardice: "Students feel safer as doubters, than as believers, and as perpetual seekers rather than eventual finders."[7] Hadley Arkes, professor of Constitutional Law at Amherst, spells it out:

> Students . . . seem to absorb deeply the doctrines of cultural relativism. . . . They come with the notion that the sophisticated view is to deny that we can know moral truths, genuine truths about the things that are right or wrong, just or unjust. . . . [Students claim these] judgments turn on matters of subjective feeling or irreducibly personal taste. . . . One person may not pass judgments on another. . . . These judgments are relative to the people who hold them and even more critically . . . they are relative to the teachings of that culture or that climate of

opinion in which people have been raised. . . . But the curious thing here is that students seem to have absorbed the tenets, the doctrines of cultural relativism as something that has a deeper hold on them than that monotheism in which they have been nominally raised.[8]

It's not just students. In 1994, the Barna Group discovered that three out of four Americans (72 percent) agreed with the following statement: There is "no such thing as absolute truth. Two people could define truth in totally conflicting ways, but both still be correct." In *One Nation After All*, Boston University's Alan Wolfe documents that even religious people are reluctant to make any moral judgments.[9] Libertarian social analyst Charles Murray finds that economically and socially successful whites shy away from publicly acknowledging the moral habits and dispositions that enabled their success for fear of sounding judgmental and preachy.[10]

Relativism as a Problem of International Culture

Catholic philosopher Frank Beckwith sat on a 1992 panel discussing sex, violence, and obscenity in media. Beckwith, then an evangelical Christian philosopher,[11] urged voluntary self-censorship from parents and broadcasters.

An agitated young woman raised her hand: "Who are you to judge?" She was not requesting Beckwith's résumé. These were fighting words.

Beckwith, ever the professor, saw a teachable moment: "I certainly do have a right to make moral judgments. I am a rational human person who is aware of certain fundamental principles of logical and moral reasoning. I think I'm qualified." Then came the *coup de grace*: "Your claim that I have no right to make judgments is itself a judgment about me. Your claim, therefore, is self-refuting." The audience voted with their laughter.

Beckwith knew that the young woman had displayed the cardinal failure of relativism: If all moral judgments are relative, then her own statement is refuted. Arkes notes the same phenomenon culture-wide:

The people who trumpet moral relativism . . . have grasped what might be called the logic of moralism. They are so persuaded there are no moral truths that they are adamant that it would be wrong, *wrong* for anyone to cast a reproach or a moral judgment on them. It's not merely that they dislike the notion; they [actually] think it is wrong. People ought not do it even if it gives them pleasure, even if it suits their own inclinations. . . . *Who are the ones who ought not do it?* Anyone. Everyone. In other words, *even the relativists have backed into the understanding of something that would be morally wrong for people to do.* No one, anywhere, ought to be imposing moral judgments on them! The "truth that dare not speak its name" is that the people who deny the existence of moral truths assert their denial of truth as the absolute, unvarying truth invulnerable against all attempts to refute it.[12]

Nevertheless, this remains the default for Americans as well as repressive political regimes. The Chinese, the North Koreans, and Muslim-dominated countries dismiss Western notions of human rights as culturally relative, just a Western thing. Knowing this, New York Mayor Rudy Giuliani roared on 9/11: "We're right and they're wrong. It's as simple as that. . . . The era of moral relativism between those who practice or condone terrorism and those nations who stand up against it must end. Moral relativism does not have a place in this discussion and debate."[13]

The Nuremberg Trials of 1945-1946 illustrate the problems universal human rights face in a global society. Nazi law marginalized and then massacred the Jews. These war crimes were legal under German law. The victorious Allies deemed the Holocaust a "crime against humanity." But after the war, the accused Nazis argued they were just removing the rodents, just cleaning house. Whose law had they broken? German law obligated them to "follow orders" in a time of national crisis and clean house, remove the rodents. The fatherland was in jeopardy.

Robert H. Jackson, chief counsel for the United States, and on a leave of absence as associate justice of the U.S. Supreme Court, embraced prosecution of Nazi war criminals as "infinitely more important than my work on the Supreme Court." Never had a conquered people been held responsible for their wartime actions *according to legal criteria from outside the vanquished's own society.* But Jackson knew the victor standing on the neck of the vanquished was an insufficient basis for international law. *He appealed to a higher moral law, universally accessible, known to all, capable of being obeyed*[14] *and morally binding across cultures,* something that "rises above the provincial and transient and seeks guidance not only from International Law but also from the basic principles of jurisprudence which are *the assumptions of civilization. . . .*"[15] Catholics call these "basic assumptions" *natural law,* meaning that some things are wrong regardless of what society or culture dictates.

A generation before, America's most widely cited jurist, U.S. Supreme Court Justice Oliver Wendell Holmes, Jr. (1841-1935) disagreed vehemently. In *The Common Law* (1881)[16] and in a 1926 letter to C. H. Wu, he argued: "[W]hen it comes to the development of a *corpus juris* [body of law] the ultimate question is what do the dominant forces of the community want and do they want it hard enough to disregard whatever inhibitions may stand in the way."[17]

Frederick Moore Vinson (1890-1953), former chief justice of the Supreme Court, spoke for many when he said: "Nothing is more certain in modern society than the principle that there are no absolutes."[18] Is the only allowable absolute the absolute insistence that there is no absolute?

HOW DID RELATIVISM BECOME THE CULTURAL DEFAULT?

Jackson triumphed! Natural law had been vindicated. Or had it? Western culture was discarding it elsewhere in law, ethics, and art. Art was the first to go. Aesthetic standards appear more subjective, so most people consent to skeptic David Hume's (1711-1776) famous line: "Beauty is no quality in things themselves: It exists merely in the mind which contemplates them; and each mind perceives a different beauty."[19]

But is there really a natural law regarding morality and ethics — i.e., a universal, objective morality? Or is it a useful social fiction?

Does it have a religious foundation? Where do we find it? Is it written up as divine revelation? Is it felt as an intuition? Do we learn it by observing the behavior of others? How did we get so relativistic in our popular culture?[20] Let's look at this last question first.

On May 29, 1919, Einstein's General Theory of Relativity was confirmed by photographs of a solar eclipse. Historian Paul Johnson narrates: "At the beginning of the twentieth century the belief began to circulate for the first time at a popular level, that there was no longer any absolutes; of time and space, of good and evil, of knowledge, above all of value. *Mistakenly, but perhaps inevitably, relativity became confused with relativism.*"[21] Einstein repeatedly but futilely tried to correct this fallacy.

But the relativistic horse was already out of the barn and galloping throughout the land. Yale's William Graham Sumner (1840-1910) had published *Folkways* in 1906. "An action is 'right,'" he wrote, because it conforms to the "folkways" of one's cultural group. The most influential American philosopher over the next generation would be John Dewey (1859-1952), for whom ethics were merely a social convention: "We institute standards of justice, truth, esthetic quality, etc., exactly as we set up a platinum bar as a standard measure of lengths. The standard is just as much subject to modification and revision in the one case as in the other. . . ."[22] Moral absolutes were dead among the educated elite. Cultural anthropologists Margaret Mead (1901-1978) and Ruth Benedict (1887-1948) popularized this view.[23]

Mead's *Coming of Age in Samoa* (1928) became cultural anthropology's best seller.[24] Critics maintain she was projecting her own desire for sexual emancipation upon the Samoans in imitation of Rousseau's "noble savage."[25] Nevertheless, she became America's most admired anthropologist, posthumously receiving the Presidential Medal of Freedom Award from President Carter in 1979, having answered questions about marriage, family, and childrearing in articles for popular magazines like *Redbook*.[26] Her mentor, the father of American anthropology, Franz Boas (1858-1942), developed a *research method* that rested on the commonsense observation that the elements of a culture are meaningful in that culture's terms, even if they may be meaningless (or take on a radically different meaning) in another culture. But like Einstein's "relativity" (relativism) and Darwin's "evolution" (evolutionism), Boas' limited method of "cultural relativism" was decoupled from its original scientific purpose and turned into an ethical conclusion. The tragic sexual chaos that followed has killed many and left even more with scars.[27]

An Awakening of Moral Realism

A more Christian mind began to reassert itself based on more extensive evidence.

First of all, human morality is universal. We have it. Aggressive chimps and pacific bonobos don't, fascinated as we are with empathy in primates or the poorly phrased "moral lives of animals." Human morality is qualitatively different from primate empathy. "The point is that we descend not from sharks, which fight over every scrap, but from highly social mammals that know trust, loyalty and solidarity."[28] Dutch primatologist Frans de Waal (b. 1948) studies primate empathy and cooperation at the Yerkes National Primate Research Center.[29] He wrote both the above and the following: "It is hard to believe that animals weigh their own interests against the rights of others, that they develop a vision of the greatest good of society, or that they feel lifelong guilt about something that they should not have done."[30] Non-humans can be "obligatorily gregarious" and show some cooperation and "sociability," but they are not aware of a moral code which they can "break."

"Human beings, unlike other animals, reflect on and make judgments about our own and others' actions. As a result, we are able to make considered moral choices . . . we are special and unique among the animal kingdom . . . and have the capacity consciously to change the way we behave and society as a whole,"[31] argues Dr. Helene Goldberg. Biological anthropologist Jonathan Marks (b. 1955) also makes the crucial distinction: "Apes should be conserved and treated with compassion, but to blur the line between them and us is an unscientific rhetorical device."[32] Let's learn about "Social Cognition and Cooperation in the Spotted Hyena" and how dolphins distinguish different whistles to maintain social cooperation.

But finally, we have the moral duty to protect the apes, spotted hyenas, and dolphins; they are under no similar moral obligation to protect us.

Second, relativists unwittingly deny moral improvement. If all is relative, what can improvement mean?

Third, moral relativism absolves us of the prophetic duty of denouncing evil. Imagine Jeremiah, Amos, and Malachi together wringing their hands and weeping, "Here we are called to be prophets but really, who are we to judge?"

THE MORAL *SENSE* OF HUMANITY

All human cultures distinguish between what is and what ought to be. In spite of Eastern and New Age thinkers who promise a state beyond good and evil, no human culture even tries. Everywhere a sense of right and wrong is foundational for human community. James Q. Wilson (1931-2012) discovered that *The Moral Sense* in humans is less a written code and more "an intuitively or directly felt belief about how one ought to act when one is free to act voluntarily." Examples include:

- *Sympathy* is our capacity to "feel" another's pain and the desire to relieve it.
- *Fairness* shows itself as a recognition of equity, impartiality, and reciprocity in social settings.
- *Self-control* means the foregoing of immediate pleasures for a perceived moral good.
- *Duty* is a sense of obligation strong enough that it extends to fulfilling vows or commitments under conditions of near isolation.[33]

As different as religions are, their moral codes share remarkable resemblances. The Golden Rule, for example, recurs frequently. Even attempts to update codes reveal more commonality than difference. For instance, in 1993, as president of the Foundation for a Global Ethic, theologian Hans Kung (b. 1928)[34] issued a declaration of common beliefs, including an extensive common ethic at the 1993 World Parliament of Religions.[35] Secular humanists are also engaged in demonstrating a global ethic.[36] These ancient and modern codes show remarkable overlap.

Why is this? Anthropologist Donald E. Brown of University of California, Santa Barbara, found over 300 unvarying patterns of behavior, including moral beliefs that "comprise those features of culture, society, language, behavior, and psyche for which there are no known exceptions."[37] The cultural relativism that had dominated anthropology was confronting reality. Literary scholar C. S. Lewis took on cultural relativism in Mead's heyday by simply compiling a list of underlying moral principles from Egypt, Babylon, Greece and Rome, the Vedas and Upanishads of Hinduism, Australian aboriginal customs, Old Norse law, and the Analects of Confucius. He called this awareness the "Tao."[38] In 1998, Martin E. P. Seligmann co-founded a new branch of psychology called "Positive Psychology." Six years later he identified and classified six broad virtues that consistently emerge across history and culture: wisdom, courage, humanity, justice, temperance, and transcendence.[39]

Moral practices vary, but a surprising unity of moral principle remains. For instance, some cultures permit a man more than one wife. He cannot, however, just grab any number of women he chooses. Betraying trusts, double-crossing, lying, and double-dealing are not celebrated. Specific situations might permit cheating or cowardice, but in no culture are they upheld as virtues.

WE DON'T ACT LIKE RELATIVISTS

Perhaps the most immediate evidence that relativism is false is that people simply don't live like relativists.

First, people behave and expect you to behave as though we shared a commonly understood and, therefore, binding moral code. Violate it and you aren't accused of being unpleasant — you are wrong. Let's take a small, even petty thing. Standing in line at the bank, someone rudely cuts in front of you. You don't think, "Oh, these lines are just social conventions. Who cares who goes first?" No, the real issue is the disrespect shown to me. We had an agreement and you just dismissed it, thereby treating me like a fool. We are obligated to do what we agreed to do. This is a small offense, and a mature person will rise above it. But he still maintains that a wrong, not an unpleasantry, has been committed. The wronged one might find excuses for the rude man. Maybe he didn't see me. Maybe he's having a bad day. Maybe nature called. If however, none of these apply, we will regard what he did as morally wrong. Even in small matters, we don't act like the relativists we claim to be when we are polled. And we certainly don't raise our children as though morality was just a matter of cultural or personal opinion. When even the self-identified relativist says to his son or daughter, "Be good," all share a fundamental understanding of what "good" means. Teenagers may engage in all types of casuistry to avoid the moral truths that bear down upon them. But their wriggling to get out from under them indicates just how firm is the case for those moral principles.

Second, created in the image of God, we are inescapably moral. It's in our nature, in our "DNA." Jonathan Haidt is a moral psychologist at the University of Virginia and author of one of the most talked-about books in 2012, *The Righteous Mind: Why Good People are Divided by Politics and Religion*. He begins:

> I chose the title *The Righteous Mind* to convey the sense that human nature is not just intrinsically moral, it's also intrinsically moralistic, critical, and judgmental. . . . I want to show you that an obsession with righteousness (leading inevitably to self-righteousness) is the normal human condition. It is a feature of our evolutionary design, not a bug or error that crept into minds that would otherwise be objective and rational. Our righteous minds made it possible for human beings — but no other animals — to produce large cooperative groups, tribes, and nations without the glue of kinship.[40]

Haidt is right. We are inescapably moral people, crusading against obesity, deadbeat dads, and bullying. We wear T-shirts urging us to do more to end breast cancer and paste bumper stickers on our cars that preach tolerance and co-existence. We believe people are morally obligated to support the right thing when it comes to secondhand smoke, child molesters, priests who break their vows, sexual harassment, presidents who can't keep their pants on, congressmen who won't keep their promises, people who squander charitable gifts, athletes who dope, swindlers like Bernie Madoff (and spongers like his brother), and companies that cause oil spills and rape the rain forests. Everybody reading that list shares a negative moral judgment about each entry. We disagree about the relative importance of these moral offenses, but I don't know a soul who treats them as a matter of moral indifference or mere opinion. *What people claim is moral relativism is really just an argument about what particular moral concerns should predominate.* Almost no one, in practice, lives the life of moral relativism.

The latest attempt to dispense with moral absolutes identifies them as merely evolutionary strategies for social cooperation necessary for survival. Cognitive scientist Steven Pinker recognizes that morality is "out there" as part of the evolutionary fitness landscape.[41] Atheist propagandist Sam Harris has recently argued that ethics could be objectively grounded in an understanding of neuroscience.[42]

This is helpful research. But their best efforts fail to explain distinctly human morality, such as why someone feels obligated to give blood, or remain chaste until marriage, or lay down his life for a stranger, or love one's enemies, or shout "Give me liberty or give me death." Instinct explains little. Telling us to obey instincts is like telling us to obey people. There are many of them, and they tell us different things. We must still choose. When these instincts conflict, something transcending those impulses arises within us, bidding us to choose a better way — and this "chooser" cannot be reduced to, or identified with, any of the instincts, for it must referee between them.

In *On Human Nature,* Edward O. Wilson reduces Mother Teresa's motivations to sociobiological compulsion or a calculated bargain to obtain heaven.[43] As Wilson computes, 80 years of service in exchange for unending millennia of bliss is not a bad bargain. But guess what? The world still admires Mother Teresa. *"Something beautiful for God"* doesn't easily morph into "self-aggrandizing behavior for the organism" or "selfish genes in action." She remains a rare flower in a human wasteland. We elevate her because we pretty much share her human evolutionary psychology and instincts.

What we don't have in common is her sacrificial nature, though that same "bargain" is available to us. She astonishes because we share her sociobiology but not her saintliness. Is the difference between us really to be explained along the lines of more fiber in the diet or a few extra endorphins?[44]

On what naturalistic evolutionary basis would it be sensible for a man to die for a stranger? Imprisoned for his anti-Nazi activities, Fr. Maximilian Kolbe watched the Nazis kill fellow prisoners within the concentration camp. One day a captive pleaded for his life. His wife and children needed him. As the Nazis dragged him to his death, Fr. Kolbe stepped up and offered to take his place. The Nazis, uncomprehending, refused. The priest insisted: "I don't have a family, I am old, and won't be missed." The Nazis finally relented. The priest entered the cult of martyrs. The man and his family survived the war. What plausible Darwinian explanation accounts for Fr. Kolbe's sacrifice?[45] Ernst Mayr (1904-2005) was a leading evolutionary biologist. He admitted that "altruism toward strangers is a behavior not supported by 'natural selection.'"[46]

CAN WE BE GOOD WITHOUT GOD?

It depends on who the "we" is. Atheistic states don't have a very good track record. Cops rather than conscience become the supreme authority in an atheistic state. Individual atheists, on the other hand, can, of course, be ethical without belief in God.[47] Made in God's image, they can recognize right and wrong, even as they deny the author of right and wrong. But aren't atheists reduced to saying, "If it's wonderful for you, that's wonderful," since they deny God as the foundation for a universal, objective morality? No, they aren't. There's an encouraging bit of intellectual history here.[48]

For most of the 20th century, the majority of philosophers and social scientists rejected the idea of "moral facts." The dominant philosophical school during the second third of the 20th century, logical positivism, regarded moral claims as unverifiable and therefore "meaningless." This suited atheists just fine since objective morality, like a finite universe, had always been more compatible with theism.

Recently, however, developments in philosophy of science, moral theory, and philosophy of language have undermined the argument against objective morality. "Moral realism" has displaced moral relativism.[49] One example is "new atheist" Sam Harris, who, relying on empirical arguments in neuroscience, argues in *Moral Landscape: How Science Can Determine Human Values* (2010) for objective morality.[50] Others still grant that objective morality favors, while not requiring, God's existence. Atheist philosopher J. L. Mackie, is one: "If there are objective values, they make the existence of a god more probable than it would have been without them. Thus we have a defensible argument from morality to existence of a god."[51]

Christopher Hitchens and Moral Absolutes

The late atheist Christopher Hitchens (1949-2011), author of *god is not Great: How Religion Poisons Everything*,[52] spoke with me shortly before he informed the world of the esophageal cancer he admitted earning from a lifetime of indulging whiskey and cigars. I asked how, as an atheist, could he objectively determine right from wrong? Wasn't he left with trying to guess the greatest good for the greatest number? And wouldn't that permit him to brutalize the few in the interests of the many as long as the hedonistic calculus[53] worked out?

He firmly denied it. So I asked him Dostoevsky's classic question: "If you had the opportunity to rid the world of war, hatred, inequality, and create heaven on earth, would you do it, if first, you must torture just one innocent child?" There was a markedly long pause. "Uh, yes, well, I've gone round and round on this. It is a devilish question, but a good one. No, I would not do it. It would be evil." It was my turn for a long pause.

Christopher Hitchens was no relativist. He believed in objective moral evil. Deep within his conscience he discovered a principle that I knew he had not laid upon himself and to which he realized he must assent.[54] This law, God's voice, was echoing in his depths. By recognizing a moral absolute, he encountered something transcendent to himself, something immaterial, immutable, and universal to which he was accountable. When we encounter law, we become conscious of sin. When we gaze into an excellent mirror, we detect unfamiliar blemishes. This is what C. S. Lewis in *Mere Christianity* titled "Right and Wrong as a Clue to the Meaning of the Universe." This moral sense is a datum about the nature of the human person and, consequently, the universe. St. Paul, in another context, describes its operation: "When Gentiles who have not the law do by nature what the law requires . . . they show that what the law requires is written on their hearts."[55]

People sometimes ask me if Hitchens was drawing nigh to the Kingdom. Those judgments remain God's, and for that reason we call Christopher's conscience his most secret sanctuary.[56] He did instruct those around him that he was going to his grave in a posture of defiance to God, even warning his comrades in the "secular revolution" that if they heard he had converted, then they would know that the cancer had reached his brain before it had finished him off.

But no longer a relativist, he began orbiting around a universal moral truth. In that orbit, our hearts can open to the interior conviction of sin, justice, and judgment wrought by the Holy Spirit.[57] We realize how we exaggerate our imaginary virtues even as we deny and then suppress our moral defects. And with others, we do just the opposite, thereby condemning ourselves by the very standards we erect to judge others. That's when the need for forgiveness becomes acute. If he reached out for forgiveness, it was available because God had already reached down for him. Calvary's sacrifice was necessary because relativism is false and God's law is absolute. The relativist *excuses sin*. God does something far more difficult: he *forgives it*.

PART THREE

Abusers of the
Past and Future

Christian Origins:
Redefining Orthodoxy

MEET SHEILA, YOUR NEW/OLD NEIGHBOR

"Hi, I'm Sheila Larson, a new RN. Robert Bellah, the sociologist, interviewed me for his book *Habits of the Heart?* Ya know, I told him I'm spiritual but not religious. I believe in God, but I am not a religious fanatic. I can't remember the last time I went to church. My faith has carried me a long way though. It's Sheilaism. Just my own little voice. My own little 'Sheilaism,' it's just a way to love yourself and be gentle with yourself. You know, I guess, take care of each other. I think God would want us to take care of each other. I just don't go in for organized religion."[1]

Setting aside the question of how any community can care for its members without being organized, we just think, "Where do I begin?" I've known many "Sheilas." They're gentle souls. Harried by the pace of modern life, they are good neighbors. I never worry about Sheila knocking on my door on a Sunday morning with a copy of *The Watchtower*, itching for a fight over the Trinity. But don't I know that if I just acquiesce in the reign of Sheilaism over Sheila, consistency would force me to acknowledge the reign of Mansonism over Manson, and he's not a lovely neighbor.[2] This radical individualism, this relativism of truth, doesn't lead anywhere I want to live.

"MY" RELIGION, "MY" SPIRITUALITY

For Sheila, "my" spirituality is a private leisure pursuit similar to "my" vacation, "my" golf game — a personal project for self-development. She's not unusual. In a 2012 Pew Forum poll, 1 in 5 Americans are religiously unaffiliated. They can do it their way. Another survey asked, "Why do you practice religion?" The most common answer (39 percent) was "To forge a personal relationship with God." In another poll, 80 percent of Americans agreed that "an individual should arrive at his or her own religious beliefs independent of any churches or synagogues."[3] Throughout Christian history, the faith was an inheritance received, not an invention created. Yet today, receiving a religious tradition is regarded, by many, as inauthentic.[4]

SCHOLARSHIP WITH AN AGENDA

A number of scholars are exploiting this individualism and "revisioning" Christian origins to more easily fit into a global religious unity.[5] Two representative figures are the late Joseph Campbell (1904-1987) and Karen Armstrong (b. 1944). Campbell, known for his *Power of Myth*,[6] called for "obstinate" Christianity to abandon the doctrine of the Fall as a "primeval event,"[7] along with the historic bodily Resurrection, and the unique Incarnation of the Son of God. Another popular writer, Karen Armstrong, ambassador for the U.N. Alliance of Civilizations, is a former nun[8] promoting her Charter for Compassion (2009) and activating the Golden Rule to unify the world's religions.[9] I wish she'd practice the Golden Rule toward St. Athanasius (296-373), whom she called a bully because he "managed to impose his theology" on the early Church.

REDEFINING HERESY AND ORTHODOXY

The revisionists also include Elaine Pagels (b. 1943), Bart Ehrman (b. 1955), Karen King (b. 1954), John Dominic Crossan (b. 1934), Robert Funk (1926-2005), Marcus Borg (b. 1942), and scores of others less well known. Some are members of the Jesus Seminar (1985- present). Some occasionally cooperate on projects.[10] Many hold compatible visions of Christian origins but disagree over the future of interreligious cooperation.[11]

Elaine Pagels, author of *The Gnostic Gospels* (1979), has exercised special influence.[12] She wrote the first popular introduction to the Nag Hammadi documents, chosen by Modern Library Association as one of the most significant nonfiction books of the 20th century. She and others have been promising for over 40 years that the Nag Hammadi library would radically refashion our understanding of

Christian origins.[13] "These discoveries are exploding the myth of a monolithic religion, and demonstrating how diverse — and fascinating — the early Christian movement really was."[14] This point was already well established. Any reading of the New Testament and the Church Fathers demonstrates anything but a monolithic institution. The apostolic Church was rich with discovery, debate, diverse opinion, discussion, and even doctrinal conflict.[15]

Their work is revisionist inasmuch as it actually denies that early Christianity had an authoritative, doctrinal core or set of authoritative teachers. *Heresy wasn't error, it was just different. Diversity of belief, they say, characterized the earliest Church.* The development of orthodoxy over a few centuries was purely a result of historical and political forces entirely apart from God's guidance or serious theological reflection.[16]

THE TRADITIONAL STORYLINE: TRUTH PRECEDES FALSEHOOD

The traditional storyline is represented by Eusebius' (263-339) *Ecclesiastical History* (c. 323). Jesus proclaimed and advocated the "truth" — i.e., "*orthodoxy*" (from Greek, meaning "*right belief*"). He commissioned the apostles and their successors to guard, defend, apply, and transmit this truth from generation to generation until he comes again. Fidelity, fidelity, fidelity was the score, but some preferred to create their own doctrinal playlist. These were called "heretics" (from Greek, *hairesis*, "a taking or choosing, a choice"). Heresies were deviations, corruptions of the truth. ***Orthodoxy preceded heresy.***[17]

THE REVISIONIST STORYLINE: DIVERSITY PRECEDES ORTHODOXY

German theologian Walter Bauer (1877-1960) recast the tradition: "[O]rthodoxy was only one of several competing systems of Christian belief, with no closer links to any original, so-called 'apostolic Christianity' than its rivals. . . . [I]t owed its victory . . . more to what we might call political influences than to its inherent merits."[18]

In Bauer's view, "orthodoxy" was imposed by ambitious, overbearing Church leaders through "polemical treatises, personal slurs, forgeries, falsifications, and formation of a closed 'canon' of authoritative texts."[19] In Bauer's view, personal choice, "heresy" represented the original condition of the Church. *Heresies were simply diverse Christianities.*

THE NAG HAMMADI LIBRARY

An ancient library likely related to Bauer's contention appeared in late 1945. Fifty-two documents — with exotic titles like the *Paraphrase of Shem*, the *Second Apocalypse of James*, the *Acts of Peter*, and the *Gospel of the Egyptians* — were discovered at Nag Hammadi, Egypt. This treasure trove was filled with literature authored by aberrant and heretical Jesus groups in the second, third, and fourth centuries, commonly placed under the umbrella term "Gnosticism."[20]

Bauer's *Heresy and Orthodoxy* claimed to deal with earliest Christianity — i.e., first century. But, unfortunately, the Nag Hammadi documents provide no reliable historical information to recover first-century "apostolic" Christianity.[21] None of these documents, with one possible exception, date back to the first century.[22] None were ever considered for inclusion in the New Testament.[23]

In spite of these deficits, impresarios continue to hype these Nag Hammadi documents and any other ancient find as "lost gospels," suppressed by a Church fearful of the truths they contain. When we object, saying that they are shamelessly exploiting the unsuspecting, they accuse the Church of hiding these documents. Nonsense.[24] Catholics love history. Just consider how we embraced the *Didache* after its discovery in 1873, in spite of material which at first glance would appear damaging to Catholic doctrine. We are, likewise, delighted to have the Nag Hammadi documents to help fill in the gaps of history. We just lament the often deliberate misrepresentation of our faith and the journalistic incompetence that permits constant misrepresentation of the truth, with no public accountability.

HOKUM HISTORY IS NOT HO-HUM HISTORY

Our opponents lob their missiles from the commanding heights of fairly serious, if speculative, scholarship and from the often silly underworld of popular culture, using vehicles like Dan Brown's (b. 1964) *Da Vinci Code* (2003) or hokum histories like Michael Baigent's (b. 1948) *Holy Blood, Holy Grail* (1982). Brown's misrepresentations have been amply dismissed, even by critics who themselves are hostile to Catholicism, such as Bart Ehrman.[25] I engage his ideas, not to beat a dead horse, but because the ideas he leans on are not his. They are presumed "common knowledge" in some circles where the Catholic Church is still called "the whore of Babylon"[26] and feared as a foreign power conspiring to destroy American freedom.[27] Dan Brown — like Oprah, Sagan, Graham, and so on — has become a representative type, a pop icon. In his case, he qualifies as the reckless Catholic-conspiracy hound. Brown's central ideas[28] can be found in *Holy Blood, Holy Grail*, a book deliberately constructed on a criminally fraudulent story *in which the original perpetrator was actually tried, convicted, and imprisoned.*[29] Such is Dan Brown's intellectual and ethical pedigree.

More than 80 million copies of the *Da Vinci Code* generate warped impressions and dark suspicions about Catholic history.[30] Brown poses as an instructor, no longer a mere novelist. He claims FACTS in a fictional framework. His publisher is shameless: "John Grisham teaches you about torts. Tom Clancy teaches you about military strategy. Dan Brown gives you a crash course in art history and the Catholic Church." Yeah, and Fred Flintstone gave me a crash course in paleoanthropology. For too many Americans, however, Dan Brown more plausibly narrates the history of the Church than Pope Francis. After all, they think, Brown is not a Catholic and can afford to be objective. What does he stand to gain by misrepresenting the truth? Sadly, many have never questioned how our public storytelling and investigations are distorted by the commercial considerations of big media and private entrepreneurs. Spectacle, sensationalism, song, sports, and sex sell much better than scholarship.[31]

COMMERCE, MEDIA, AND ACADEMIA

The relationship between commercial media and academia explains why so much suspicion is directed toward the history of the Church. *Time* magazine recently interviewed feminist scholar and Harvard Divinity School professor Karen King about a purported ancient document. Asked what Dan Brown got right, she, thankfully, said: "Well, there's so much that Dan Brown got wrong. Jesus and Mary Magdalene married — there's no evidence that they were. There's no evidence that they had a child. There's no evidence of a Catholic conspiracy. *What Dan Brown did for us as scholars was to provide a teaching moment, an opportunity when the public was actually interested in these questions.*"[32]

Commercial media and pop culture regularly distort the work of academics. But academics are just glad somebody's paying attention. People like Pagels, Armstrong, Ehrman, and Funk are not shy about using the attention to carry out larger personal-social agendas. A good example of mutual back scratching between commercial media and academics can be seen in the *National Geographic* (*NatGeo*) *Gospel of Judas* fiasco. *National Geographic* tried to mainstream the almost forgotten second-century *Gospel of Judas* with a new translation, glossy magazine cover story, critical editions, books, and a prime-time, made-for-TV spectacular on Sunday, April 9, 2006.

In haste, they mistranslated the work, turning black sheep Judas into a hero rather than a betrayer. The *New York Times* in a piece of journalistic malpractice tried to imply that the *Gospel of Judas* threw "new light on the historical relationship between Jesus and Judas."[33] Every academic knew such a statement was nonsense, along the lines of telling "Civil War historians [to] conduct a critical rereading of Ulysses S. Grant's memoirs in the light of Michael Shaara's 1974 novel of Gettysburg, *The Killer Angels.*"[34]

But the market, non-academic lay people, had just one major question. "Does it go back to Judas?" If it didn't, they weren't much interested in doctrinal disputes among second-century Gnostics in Egypt. So *NatGeo* had a problem.

James M. Robinson (b. 1924), America's leading expert on ancient Egyptian religious texts, told the *Boston Globe* that some participants in the *National Geographic* effort "are making the sly suggestion that the *Gospel of Judas* is more or less equally valid" with the gospels of the New Testament and that it "contains things that could pull the rug out from Christianity as we know it. This is just ridiculous." Repulsed, Robinson speculated that the release of *"The Gospel of Judas"* was aimed at capitalizing on interest in the film version of *The Da Vinci Code*, due to be released on May 19.[35] It was also near Holy Week that year.

The moral and professional shabbiness of the project came to light six months later. April DeConick, Rice University, an expert on non-canonical gospels retranslated *Judas*. The *NatGeo* team's translation "fell well outside the commonly accepted practices in the field."[36] The mistakes were so bad that she concluded that *NatGeo* was influenced by the money, not the scholarship. How misleading was the translation? Very. The difference was black and white. Two years later, Thomas Bartlett of the *Chronicle of Higher Education* confirmed DeConick's translation: "While *National Geographic's* translation supported the provocative interpretation of Judas as a hero, a more careful reading makes clear that Judas is not only no hero, he is a demon." Exactly opposite the intended *NatGeo* script. This is Elmer Gantryism in reverse, with dishonest secularists pretending miraculous discoveries to fleece the faithful. We should cooperate with the Catholic League for Religious and Civil Rights or other groups to publicly shame these exploitative opportunists.

In September 2012, Karen King of Harvard Divinity School announced discovery of a papyrus fragment that has a Jesus referring to "my wife."[37] Media outlets had a field day. The *Smithsonian* magazine was representative: "According to a top religion scholar, this 1,600-year-old text fragment suggests that some early Christians believed Jesus was married — possibly to Mary Magdalene."[38] This was totally false. Every scholar, including Karen King, denied that this was an authentic statement of the historical Jesus.[39] King was not even convinced that the fragment was genuine. Within days, experts at the International Congress of Coptic Studies in Rome suggested it was a forgery.[40] As I write, this remains the most likely story. I'm sorry to advise that you should not hold your breath waiting for the media outlets that titillated us with the original story to correct the misleading impressions they created.

WHAT ABOUT BAUER'S *ORTHODOXY AND HERESY*? NEW RESEARCH

Walter Bauer's (1877-1960) *Orthodoxy and Heresy in Earliest Christianity* (German 1934; English 1971) has been called "the most important book on the history of early Christianity to appear in the twentieth century."[41] Bauer's claim that "heresy" preceded "orthodoxy" now extends to virtually every related discipline. Many scholars no longer use the terms *orthodoxy* and *heresy* without the accompanying quotation marks.[42] Yet Bauer began his research, nearly 100 years ago, using a flawed method, and scholarship has since advanced.[43]

For instance, in 1989, Thomas Robinson reexamined Bauer's every location. According to Bauer, only Rome was decidedly "orthodox." Egypt and Edessa clearly were not. Asia Minor was mixed.[44] Robinson concluded that, indeed, "early Christianity was diverse."[45] But where the evidence was more abundant, in Ephesus and western Asia Minor, heresy was neither early nor strong. Full-fledged heretical Gnosticism appears only after the apostle John's (A.D. 6-100) and Ignatius of Antioch's time (c. 35/50-98/117). *In the only area where Bauer's thesis could be adequately tested, it failed.*[46] Orthodoxy preceded heresy and was numerically larger![47] A related study showed that the second-century Valentinians began as orthodox. Heresy came later.[48]

WAS EARLIEST CHRISTIANITY WITHOUT A DOCTRINAL AUTHORITY?[49]

No. For reasons of method, Bauer had surprisingly excluded the New Testament from his study of earliest Christianity. Later scholarship has remedied this neglect.[50] What follows is a list of evidences for first-century doctrinal authority in the New Testament:

a. Important questions — e.g., "Who do men say that I am?"[51] — were publicly asked and correct answers were expected. The New Covenant was not some individualized search for the god within. Nor was it a set of private philosophical positions. Rather, it was a *public* proclamation of good news.[52] Clarity and shared meanings helped build solid community.

b. Individuals were ordained to teach with authority.[53] Likewise, the Jerusalem Council definitively settled doctrinal questions related to the ministry of Paul and Barnabas. The council's pronouncements were circulated with the expectation of obedience.[54]

c. Jesus commissioned the twelve "apostles" (literally, "sent ones") as delegated authorities to present his "orthodoxy."[55]

d. Already in the first generation, Paul's teaching is esteemed as the Word of God and his letters as Scripture.[56]

e. Liturgical hymns, proto-creeds, and confessions represent authoritative norms and standards prior to the New Testament documents but which are evident within the New Testament.[57] *Christians sang those hymns and recited those creeds not because they were in the New Testament. Rather, they are in the New Testament because that is what the earliest Catholics sang and recited as the apostolic Tradition.*

f. The Pastoral Epistles command, "Follow the pattern of sound words which you have heard from me . . . guard the truth that has been entrusted to you by the Holy Spirit who dwells within us. . . .You must teach what is in accord with sound doctrine."[58]

g. Jesus' and Paul's warnings about "false Christs," "false teachers," "false apostles," and "false brethren" presuppose authoritative "true Christs" and "true teachers."[59]

h. The "rule of faith" was the Catholic worldview, the Catholic fix on the world order and the way to live. It functioned as a non-creedal authority.[60] Even Ehrman must agree that it was *permanently established by the opening of the second century.*[61]

THEN WHY THE CONTINUING APPEAL OF *AUTHORITY-FREE* CHRISTIANITY?

The Da Vinci Code, for instance, tells a story whose values, virtues, and vision appeal to late modern Americans in spite of its ludicrous historical claims:

- Consider our hierarchy of *virtues*: tolerance, diversity, and resistance to authority.
- Consider our hierarchy of *values*: personal peace, affluence, individual freedom, and autonomy.

- Consider the late modern *vision* of the blessed life: Our creed is "I believe in myself, the unencumbered, affluent and able, free to follow my own path and do as I please." This blessed life is anti-authoritarian in society, anti-traditional in morality and culture, and anti-institutional in religion.

THE GOSPEL OF DIVERSITY

A doctrinally flexible gospel, designed to eventually accommodate a united global religious movement, is now available as the "gospel of diversity." In *The Heresy of Orthodoxy: How Contemporary Culture's Fascination with Diversity Has Reshaped Our Understanding of Early Christianity*, two theologians, a Baptist, Andreas J. Kostenberger, and a professor at Reformed Theological Seminary, Michael J. Kruger, describe how this "gospel of diversity" functions:

> If it can be shown that early Christianity was not as unified as commonly supposed, and if it can be suggested that the eventual rise of Christian orthodoxy was in fact the result of a conspiracy or of a power grab by the ruling political, cultural, or ecclesiastical elite, this contributes to undermining the notion of religious truth itself and paves the way for the celebration of diversity as the only "truth" that is left. And thus the tables are turned — diversity becomes the last remaining orthodoxy and orthodoxy becomes heresy, because it violates the new orthodoxy: the gospel of diversity.[62]

The gospel of diversity leaves us free to follow our own path and fashion our own truth. We are excused from the demands of a universal Truth or conformity to a universal moral order. This spiritual hoboism threatens no one, and it holds no one accountable to anyone but one's own self.

In contrast, Jesus warned: To whom much was given much would be demanded. Great gifts meant great responsibilities; greater gifts, greater responsibilities.[63] His mother sang of God that he knocks tyrants off their high horses and pulls victims out of the mud. He sits the starving down to banquets, and the callous rich he sends out into the cold.[64] Her son would shake up our complacent "normalcies" by toppling those in authority and elevating those who had been ignored. *He wasn't about to let everyone pursue his own project.* The gospel of diversity bears no resemblance to Christ's gospel. It has no power to motivate people to imitate Christ in acts of sacrificial love. Just as Jesus wasn't executed for espousing his own little "Sheilaism," so, too, nobody lays down his life for the "gospel of diversity."

"Creedless Christianity" is as oxymoronic as "meatless barbecue" or "numberless mathematics." Its conceit is to imagine that by abolishing orthodoxy we liberate people to find their own way and thereby ensure tolerance. We might as well abolish the laws of logic and free people to their own private rationality. The champions of diversity imagine that this "emancipation" will allow every man to become a mystic. But does anyone really believe that what enslaves and prevents the modern person from achieving sanctity or mystic communion is the flatfooted rule of the Code of Canon Law or too rigorous an interpretation of *Humanae Vitae*? Isn't the problem more likely lazy conformity to the world's norm of the herd?

Dilettantism Is Not Diversity

More serious is our bondage to our electronic cocoon, in which we surround ourselves with self-selected music, political opinions, movies, Facebook friends, family videos, and news services tailored to deliver only stuff we want to see.

Yet we ironically pride ourselves on how eclectic and accepting we have become. We can adopt multiple identities and social roles. Who am I? How will I present myself today? A little country, a little glam, a little rocker? Or we boast "I'm a diversity voter because I can eat Mexican, Lebanese, or Szechuan, and I listen to Flo-Rida, Bach, and the early Miles Davis. Oh, and I don't make fun of headscarves or accents." This is dilettantism, not diversity. The tragic divisions of nation, ethnicity, creed, class, and race that threaten to destroy us, and which we are called to heal, don't dissolve by self-congratulating our expanded range of taste.

ORTHODOXY IS THE SUREST SAVIOR OF DIVERSITY AND COMMUNITY

Orthodoxy, is, in contrast, rude to style.[65] Hewing to right belief, right doctrine, and Truth binds us together regardless of my like or dislike of your playlist or politics, skin color or brain power. Paradoxically, by its indifference to engineering diversity, orthodoxy is its firmest guarantor.

In 1964's *Autobiography of Malcolm X* (1925-1965), he, the chief recruiter for the cultic Nation of Islam, is being bent towards a final transformation, from deviant to "orthodox" Islam. The "Honorable Elijah Muhammad" (1897-1975) taught that 6,600 years ago, the black scientist Yakub created whites, a "race of devils."[66] Malcolm's experience and then his theology taught him to hate the "blond-haired, blue-eyed, pale-skinned devils." He was the group's most effective proselytizer, preaching submission to the One God but enjoying this religious club where his talents were stroked and his hatred stoked.[67]

A phrase from an orthodox Muslim lodged in his soul: "No man has believed perfectly until he wishes for his brother what he wishes for himself." As he undertook the Haj, the pilgrimage that all Muslims must make, health permitting, at least once in their lifetime,[68] white Muslims showered him with hospitality, even as they were shocked by the myth of Yakub. He moved closer to Truth, which in this case is both Catholic and Islamic orthodoxy: "All nations form but one community. This is so because all stem from the one stock which God created to people the entire earth, and also because all share a common destiny, namely God."[69] Muslims of "all colors, from blue-eyed blonds to black-skinned Africans" were interacting as equals living the orthodox doctrine of the One Creator God. "I could see from this, that perhaps if white Americans could accept the Oneness of God, then perhaps, too, they could accept *in reality* the Oneness of Man — and cease to measure, and hinder, and harm others in terms of their 'differences' in color."[70]

A year later, Malcolm X was assassinated by his former co-religionists.[71] He never witnessed the Catholic Church celebrating *diversity rooted in orthodoxy.* He never saw the participants, the liturgies, the languages, or the riot of colors and sounds that constitute a World Youth Day. This is in our DNA — or, rather, in the bread and wine, the Eucharist, the sacrament of unity. This "oneness" is soaked up as every soul is immersed in the baptismal waters of Rio de Janeiro, Montreal, Johannesburg, Mumbai, Denver, Nairobi, San Diego, Sydney, or Moscow. Dynamic orthodoxy doesn't shrink our horizons. Rather, it throws open the gates of eternity, inviting all to build up the one mystical body of Christ: the Head in heaven and his body, the Church, extended through space and time on the earth.

What collective in history is more diverse than the communion of saints? Peter and John, Jerome and Thérèse of Lisieux, Kateri Tekakwitha and Thomas Aquinas, Hildegard of Bingen and Antony of the Desert, John Henry Newman and Solanus Casey — distinct personalities from every nation, kindred, and tongue: Armenian, Malankara Indian, Syrian, Coptic, Ethiopian, Gallic, Croatian, Greek, Celtic, Anglican, Spanish, Sino-Japanese, Slavic, and Saxon. For "it was not his will to sanctify a countless multitude of solitary souls but a corporate kingdom of saints. . . . For the grace of Christ never works in the individual in an isolated fashion, but always in the unity of his Body."[72]

This is lost on those who seek to rewrite Christian origins and dismiss the primacy of orthodoxy. They believe we can have union with God without the body of truth in which he shares his will for *us* and not just for *me*. They will fail. Orthodoxy doesn't impede spiritual vitality! Heresy can't spur community! Because "there can be no contradiction, or dissension or schism where God is. His truth cannot be otherwise than one truth, one life, one love. And therefore it can be realized in but one form, in a comprehensive fellowship that binds together all men in intimate unity."[73]

So How Does That Help Me Talk to Sheila?

Back to the basics of courteous invitation:

"Sheila, good to see you. People were talking about that interview you did. So you still have faith and still care for others. That's wonderful. Listening to your own little voice, your own little Sheilaism, as you put it, has carried you a long way. Jesus uses the same kind of language when he talks about faith and spirituality. He said 'I am the good shepherd. . . . My sheep hear my voice, and I know them, and they follow me.'[74] If you got this far just listening to your own little voice, your own little Sheilaism, what do you think will happen if you began listening for his voice?

"I started trying that a few years ago by reading the New Testament with friends. His voice is right there because Jesus said about his apostles, 'They who hear you, hear me.' So how to hear the apostles? That's what we talk about. We've got a small group that meets in my apartment once a week to talk about how to hear his voice and not just our own. You talk about faith and spirituality so freely that I think you would really contribute to the group. We are all learning together. Can you make it? Here's my number. Call me, maybe?"

Christian Origins: Rejecting the New Testament Text

A NEW BREED OF SCHOLAR?

Along with Jon Stewart's *Daily Show* and NPR's *Fresh Air*, *The Dallas Morning News* describes Dr. Bart D. Ehrman, author of *Misquoting Jesus: The Story Behind Who Changed the Bible and Why*, as a "new breed of biblical scholar."[1] Ehrman chairs the religious studies department at the University of North Carolina, Chapel Hill. A former fundamentalist Protestant, he's now agnostic at best, and a perfect combination for media producers who want a bona fide scholar, but one, who, like their audience, is disenchanted with organized religion.

He wants to dismantle the traditional understanding of Christian origins.[2] Is he a scholar? Yes. Is he a "new breed"? Not really. *The Dallas Morning News* employs "New" as a journalistic cliché just as Tide™ uses "New" as an advertising cliché. Commercial enterprises, like newspapers or soap manufacturers, thrive on novelty because what they offer us is so ephemeral and without distinction that they must always prop up their standing with "new" or "better" or "fresh," rather than actually create or discover something truly new. Ehrman is "new" only in that he has written a popular book on the driest, most tedious of topics: the manuscript basis for the New Testament, commonly called "textual criticism." He is a fine communicator, outlining what serious students of Scripture have long known but which rarely gets mentioned in sermons/homilies. When a book on the textual criticism of the New Testament hits the best-seller lists, we may not have new material, but we certainly have a new situation in our culture.

Ehrman's Abstract

Can we trust the New Testament? Historically? Theologically? Is it internally consistent? All are meaningless questions if we don't possess a *reliable text of the New Testament*. Do we have dependable manuscripts? Do we know what the biblical authors actually composed? Ehrman pronounces, "No."

Because we don't possess the original manuscript of any New Testament book, our opponents insinuate that we can't know what Paul wrote to the Corinthians, nor can we trust what Luke reported in the Acts of the Apostles. Thus Ehrman says:

> Not only do we not have the originals, we don't have the first copies of the originals. We don't even have copies of the copies of the originals, or copies of the copies of the copies of the originals. What we have are copies made later — much later. In most instances, they are copies made many centuries later. And these copies all differ from one another in many thousands of places. . . . There are more differences among our manuscripts than there are words in the New Testament.[3]

Neither Hypercriticism nor Fundamentalism

This sounds terrible, but immediately Ehrman is forced to make a reality check. He acknowledges what "new" and old scholars have long known: "Most of these differences [between manuscripts] are completely immaterial and insignificant." Ehrman's skepticism is more existential than evidential. It originates in his own autobiography more than the autographs. To be consistent, Ehrman would have to plead ignorance of Plato's *Republic* or Caesar's *Gallic Wars*. But that same method produces a thousandfold of doubt when applied to ancient Greco-Roman literature. Follow it and kiss off the Caesars, Alexander the Great, and the "glory that was Rome." Nor would we have Greek philosophy, the Roman influence on modern law, medical ethics, and worst of all, according to one Oscar-sensitive textual critic, "Russell Crowe could never have played the lead role in *Gladiator*."[4] Apply Ehrman's skepticism consistently and our knowledge of the ancient world evaporates like celluloid over a flame. "What we have here," one prominent expert wrote, "is a form of hypercriticism that is all too common in scholarly circles and sometimes seems to arise from confusing criticism with skepticism — that is, thinking that the more skeptical the position, the more critical it is. Radical skepticism is no more critical than is credulity."[5]

New Testament textual critic Daniel Wallace directs the Center for the Study of New Testament Manuscripts. He's digitally preserving all New Testament manuscripts so that scholars can examine them via enhancement software on the Internet.[6] By 2006, his center collected more than 35,000 high-resolution digital photographs of Greek New Testament manuscripts, including the most recently discovered texts. Wallace knows the complex and far-flung world of New Testament manuscripts as well as his friend Bart Ehrman, whose worries about the text he dismisses as unnecessary, unwarranted, and unfruitful: "The New Testament manuscripts stand closer to the original and are more plentiful than probably any other literature of that era. The New Testament is far and away the best attested work of Greek or Latin literature from the ancient world."[7] Lutheran theologian, lawyer, and historian John Warwick Montgomery confirms: "To be skeptical of the resultant text of the New Testament books is to allow all of classical antiquity to slip into obscurity, for no documents of the ancient period are as well attested bibliographically as the New Testament."[8]

Among scholars, this issue has been settled. Suspicion, however, reigns in pop culture among those who know least about textual criticism. Ehrman seems to lend plausibility to their conspiracy notions even though, on this point of textual reliability, he is eccentric and he himself rejects conspiracy. Has something happened recently to force a reevaluation? No. There are no troubling new discoveries. Ehrman presents virtually no new information. To the contrary, recent manuscript finds continue to strengthen our confidence in the textual reliability of the New Testament.[9] So why have so many people found him so plausible?

Why Now?

First, suspicion toward spiritual authority and revealed texts, like presidential favorability ratings, rely on many factors not necessarily related to the president's performance.

Second, Ehrman is a real insider, and to those unfamiliar with the field, he carries understandable authority.

Third, Ehrman writes to convert. He has an agenda. "In many ways . . . this is a very personal book for me, the end result of a long journey. Maybe, for others, it can be part of a journey of their own."[10] Having lost his faith, Ehrman wants to "dysevangelise" others.

Ehrman has an enviable popular touch. A respectful but disapproving colleague notes that Ehrman "has a strong ax to grind, and the fact that he grinds it well in fluid prose makes it all the more beguiling."[11]

But if Ehrman didn't present new evidence, what did he do? He drew back the curtain, and the general public peered for the first time into the rarefied world of biblical textual criticism. Like gazing upon an open skull and seeing gray brain matter for the first time, people were both appalled and fascinated. What they saw appeared as chaotic and disorganized as flea markets filled with old seed catalogs; half-burnt candles; fragments of papyri and unrolled scrolls; baskets of baubles and bangles; unwanted, uncataloged 78-rpm records; and forgotten *Mad* magazines, some with apparent signatures of Alfred E. Neuman. Whatever this stuff was, it doesn't bear any resemblance to the tidy, orderly volume tightly bound in leather upon which we place our hands and swear oaths before God in court.

The truth is, most of us have given little thought to how the New Testament came about. And just like the young person who finds the facts of life, the birds and the bees, a bit messier than he had imagined, many people are shaken by Ehrman's less-than-delicate handling of a specialized topic to an audience, virginal in their understanding of biblical criticism.

Ehrman's timing was also impeccable. In 2006, mistrust of Church authorities crested with *The Da Vinci Code*, the priest abuse scandals, the aggression of the "New Atheism," and a host of fruity Internet-pitched speculations like the movie *Zeitgeist*, seedy misrepresentations like the *Pagan Christ* or *Christ Conspiracy*, or the doubtful speculations of the Jesus Seminar. With skill, Ehrman delivered familiar old data with a prosecuting attorney's zeal and clarity. He charmed like an insider publicly whispering trade secrets.

THE LURE OF INSIDER KNOWLEDGE

Don't underestimate the rhetorical impact of insider information. Once upon a time, the barber doubled as a surgeon. His steady hand with a blade — and the anatomy learned from midwives, embalmers, and animal breeders — credentialed him in the blood-and-guts world of amputations, tracheotomies, and broken limbs. In time, however, the specialist surgeon emerged, along with a mushrooming new knowledge in biology, chemistry, physiology, anesthesiology, and the germ theory of disease. Eventually, a dozen years of education would certify a surgeon as an "expert" and separate him from the common lot of humanity. Specialization divides humanity up between lay and professional. Experts are privy to viewpoints, practices, experiences, and knowledge that are not understood or even welcomed by the uninitiated.

To the outsider, the nuanced observations of the art critic sound like poppycock. To the non-specialist, the abstractions of the analytic philosopher sound terribly unreal. To the grieving family, the procedures of the embalmer only intensify the trauma of loss. In spite of popular programs like *CSI*, *Bones*, and *NCIS*, the real world of the medical examiner still grosses us out, and forensic science demands serious study. So, too, in the fields of biblical scholarship, textual criticism, philosophical theology, and even, to a great degree, the world of church governance. Most laymen are as unfamiliar with the world of biblical scholarship as the cardiac patient is with the world of heart transplantation, or the average holder of a 401k with the world of investment banking or macroeconomics. Without a proper framework, the average believer is easily drowned in a flood of information and hypotheses. Professionals are trained to deal with all the ambiguities and uncertainties. Not so, the layman.

W<small>HAT</small> B<small>ART</small> E<small>HRMAN</small> F<small>AILS TO</small> D<small>ISCLOSE</small>

Luke, Paul, Jerome, Erasmus, and King James Knew the Bible Was a Human Book. Why Didn't Bart?

Given Ehrman's argument, why aren't we seeing a massive exodus of those with earned degrees in biblical studies leaving their Christianity for the Promised Land of agnosticism? As a colleague put it: "No student can earn a degree in Bible and not know this [the problem of copyists' errors and variant readings]. Yet Bible students are not defecting in droves."[12] Why not? Because, unlike the young fundamentalist Bart Ehrman, they assumed these errors didn't doom the project of reconstructing the original. New Testament critic Craig Evans laments the young Ehrman's "misplaced faith" in a common but false theory of biblical inspiration.[13] Here's the faulty line of reasoning that led to his disillusionment:

1. If God inspired the New Testament documents, then he would also prevent all manuscripts from being corrupted.
2. If God inspired the New Testament documents, then he would have preserved the original autographs with no blemishes — e.g., misspellings, clumsy constructions, and perfectly intact manuscripts.
3. New Testament manuscripts show numerous signs of corruption.
4. We do not possess the original autographs.
5. Therefore, God did not inspire the New Testament documents.

Setting aside for the moment the question of "corruption," the key premises are numbers 1 and 2. Has God anywhere promised to prevent the corruption of manuscripts or preserve original manuscripts? No, and it is clear from the evidence that he didn't. Are we then left with unreliable reconstructions of the original? Not at all.

We can reconstruct a largely uncorrupted facsimile of the original by using many corrupted copies. Consider music. A dozen singers can each seriously flub the same song, hitting notes off pitch or clashing with the rhythm. However, by comparing all their efforts, a musicologist can still recover the tonal center, melodic contours, and timing of the piece. Individual passages may be corrupted, but by playing them off against one another, we can still locate the original melody.

So, too, with reconstructing ancient texts. Ehrman's God was just too small, and his options too narrow. For Ehrman, apparently, one only possessed a reliable text had it been obtained in the manner of a court stenographer.[14] In the case of the New Testament, this kind of rigor was unnecessary. The comparatively widespread circulation and frequency of quotation in controlled settings like liturgies, as well as the replication of quotations through the Church Fathers and the sheer volume of manuscript copies, guaranteed a relatively intact original could be recomposed. The irony is that no other collection of documents in the ancient world is so frequently quoted or widely circulated and distributed. F. E. Peters (b. 1927) is professor emeritus of Middle Eastern and Islamic Studies and History at New York University and an expert in the manuscript traditions of the Greek and Latin classics, as well as the New Testament and Qur'an. "On the basis of manuscript tradition alone, the works that made up the Christians' New Testament were the most frequently copied and widely circulated books of antiquity."[15]

Ehrman taunts, "What if the book you take as giving you God's words instead contains human words?" This is a false dilemma. God created humans to work through them. We are created to image God. Human participation in divine tasks is what we were created for. Shouldn't we better ask, "Why must a book be either a divine or a human product? Why not a cooperative effort? Aren't our lives, never mind manuscript traditions, examples of God writing straight with crooked lines?" Why shouldn't we expect God to transmit the gospel tradition through manuscripts that also include a fair share of human style, limitation, and even copyists' mistakes? Mark's poor Greek, Luke's interest in eyewitness testimony, Paul's rabbinic training, Matthew's preoccupation with Palestinian Judaism, and the misspellings of some anonymous medieval scribe who needed more sleep and less communion wine are all personal, human concerns taken up as the Holy Spirit superintends the formation of inspired texts.

The sacred texts of Islam and Mormonism claim to have been *dictated* by God, errorless. This is fantasy. To the contrary, Catholics insist that the human agents are not mere stenographers, channellers, or mediums, but true authors working out of their own interests, worldviews, literary skills, longings, problems, and needs. God doesn't abolish or bypass the humanity of his human agents in forming, preserving, or restoring the biblical text.[16] We are content with the more mundane task of collecting, collating, critiquing, and combining thousands of manuscripts through tedious and rigorous attention to the minutest details of the writing tools and materials, the scribes' styles and syntax, and the manuscripts' age, location, and genealogy. Jerome and Augustine knew this. So did Erasmus and Luther. By his own admission, however, Ehrman's scholarship is a demolition job in the service of skepticism and unbelief — even if he is smiling all the time.[17]

How Does the New Testament Compare With Other Ancient Documents?

So well that New Testament textual critics are sheepish when talking to specialists in ancient Greek and Roman authors. There are roughly 5,500 known Greek manuscripts or portions of the New Testament. When we then add over 10,000 Latin Vulgate copies and at least 9,300 other early versions (Syriac, Ethiopic, Slavic, Armenian, Arabic, etc.), we have more than 24,000 manuscript copies or portions of the New Testament. No other work of ancient literature is so well-attested in terms of number of manuscripts. Some of them are also quite old, dating back to possibly the first and, certainly, second century, although our fullest and best manuscripts are later.[18]

So how does that compare with Plato, Homer, Caesar, Tacitus, etc.? Homer's *Iliad* ranks second to the New Testament with a "whopping" 643 manuscripts.[19] The first complete preserved *Iliad* is nearly 1,900 years after the *Iliad* was first recited. For Caesar's *Gallic Wars* (58-50 B.C.), we have only 9 or 10 good manuscripts, the oldest of which is 900 years after Caesar. So it is with all the Greco-Roman authors. Manuscripts are few and late. The historian Tacitus' *Annals* depends entirely on two manuscripts nearly a millennium after the original writing, and these are incomplete. Filling the gaps without manuscripts is absolutely necessary for most Greco-Roman literature; it is almost entirely unknown for the New Testament. There are three times more New Testament manuscripts within the first 200 years than the average Greco-Roman author has in 2,000 years.[20]

The New Testament textual critic is the envy of ancient historians. Imagine spreading the manuscripts in a line on a road. Greco-Roman literature would extend four feet; the New Testament over a mile. If the average Greco-Roman manuscript earned 20,000 dollars a year, the New Testament would earn over 20 million dollars. When Westcott and Hort prepared *The New Testament in the Original Greek* (1881), they inaugurated a new epoch in textual criticism. Since then, virtually all editions of the Greek New Testament rely on the Westcott-Hort text. So how did Hort compare the New Testament to other ancient literature? *"[I]n the variety and fullness of the evidence on which it rests the text of the New Testament stands absolutely and unapproachably alone among ancient prose writings"* (emphasis mine).[21]

Ehrman Contra Ehrman

In *Misquoting Jesus*, Ehrman poses as the ultimate skeptic. He changes his tune when writing for a scholarly audience, where he admits the vast superiority of the New Testament over other ancient sources. "Besides textual evidence derived from the New Testament Greek manuscripts and from early versions, the textual critic compares numerous scriptural quotations used in commentaries, sermons, and other treatises written by early church fathers. *Indeed so extensive are these citations that if all other sources for our knowledge of the text of the NT were destroyed, they would be sufficient alone for the reconstruction of practically the entire NT*."[22] Is that the same Bart Ehrman who troubled untold thousands of readers by writing *Misquoting Jesus*? Yes, it, is and the inconsistency is shameful.

Ehrman is his own worst enemy. In *Forged* (2011) he argues that Paul could not be the author of 1 and 2 Timothy and Titus. Why? Because their vocabulary doesn't match the vocabulary of the so-called authentic Pauline letters like Romans, 1 and 2 Corinthians, Galatians, Philippians, 1 Thessalonians, and Philemon. How can he make such a judgment unless he believes he knows what Paul actually wrote in Romans, etc. His radical skepticism forces him into self-defeating conclusions.

What About 400,000 Variant Readings?

"There are more variations among our manuscripts than there are words in the New Testament."[23] Ehrman says 400,000 variant readings. Others say 250,000, but to the layman both numbers, like differences in the federal government's budget figures, sound equally distressing. But what does Ehrman omit? Common sense. The fewer the manuscripts, the fewer the variants; the more the manuscripts, the greater the variants. We have so many variant readings because, thankfully, we have so many manuscripts, so many copies. Ehrman admits:

> It would be a mistake . . . to assume that the only changes being made were by copyists with a personal stake in the wording of the text. In fact, most of the changes found in our early Christian manuscripts have nothing to do with theology or ideology. Far and away, the most changes are the result of mistakes, pure and simple — slips of the pen, accidental omissions, inadvertent additions, misspelled words, blunders of one sort or another.[24]

So what are these mistakes? The vast majority are spelling differences. The next-largest category involves synonyms.[25] The third-largest category involves differences that are meaningful but not "viable." For instance, in 1 Thessalonians 2:9 one late medieval manuscript writes "the gospel of Christ" instead of "the gospel of God." The difference is meaningful, but there is no chance that a single medieval scribe retained the wording of the original text that had been missed by all other scribes over the previous centuries.

What About Intentional Changes to the Text?

Ehrman tries to emotionally trump by citing texts that scribes intentionally altered.[26] Even these, however, are usually harmless. For example, we have 2,000 manuscripts containing daily readings for Mass — i.e., lectionaries. In Mark, there is an 89-verse section in which the name of Jesus isn't mentioned once. It's always "*he* did" this or that. When this section is broken up over a week of Mass readings, you cannot begin the passage with: "When *he* was going to Jerusalem. . . ." You must specify, "When *Jesus* was going to Jerusalem. . . ." Such benign changes, however, get counted as a variant.[27] Intentional? Yes. Malignant? No.

There are, however, a few insertions long known that could not be part of the original manuscript. These insertions don't alter any dogma or doctrine. They might slightly shade our image of Jesus or particular doctrines. These include the "long ending" of Mark 16:9-20; the Trinitarian reference in 1 John 5:7-8; the woman caught in adultery in John 7. These are the most significant.

Why did they show up in manuscripts at all? We don't yet know. The Trinitarian passage seems to have originated as a comment in the margin of the text. Some medieval copyist may have thought an earlier scribe had failed to insert it. Omitting it doesn't alter our understanding of the Trinity since similar formulae are found in Matthew 28:19 and 2 Corinthians 13:14.[28] In the 16th century, Erasmus, whose Greek New Testament is still considered one of the great achievements of humanist scholarship, thought it was inauthentic.[29] Pope Pius XI on June 2, 1927, admitted that this passage was open to dispute. The *Nova Vulgata*, the revision of the Latin Vulgate approved for liturgical use by the Church, now excludes it.

Does Mark's gospel really end at 16:8 or was the original ending lost? We don't know but verses 9-20 differ in vocabulary, style, and theological content from the rest of Mark and are lacking in the most reliable manuscripts.

The story of the woman caught in adultery in John 7:53-8:11 is much loved. Most Bibles include a note like this: "The earliest and most reliable manuscripts and other ancient witnesses do not have John 7:53-8:11."[30] Perhaps the story was preached by the apostles but was not included in the originals of Matthew, Mark, Luke, or John. We find something similar in Acts 20:35, where Paul quotes Jesus: "It is more blessed to give than to receive." For some reason, Luke, the author of Acts, didn't include this saying in his gospel, yet it is an authentic Jesus saying. Like other historical figures, Jesus generated memories, stories, and sayings that exceeded biographers' abilities to collect them all in one volume. John laments that "there are also many other things which Jesus did; were every one of them to be written, I suppose that the world itself could not contain the books that would be written" (John 21:25). Perhaps a copyist, not wanting the story to be lost, inserted it in what he thought was an appropriate place.

Such alterations are few, well known, and don't threaten a single doctrine of the faith.[31] This has been known since the modern science of textual criticism began in 1707. Each new translation of the New Testament reaffirms that textual integrity. The *New Jerome Biblical Commentary* (1990) echoed this consensus: "[I]t is worth noting that the different readings, as numerous as they are, do not touch on any essential questions of Christian faith. In terms of the number of early copies preserved and of fidelity in copying, the NT is remarkable, esp. when compared with the masterpieces of Greco-Roman literature."[32] *Most surprising, however, is Ehrman's agreement: "Essential Christian beliefs are not affected by textual variants in the manuscript tradition of the New Testament."*[33]

CONCLUSION

So what do we know?

- The manuscripts contain lots of differences, but the overwhelming majority affect nothing substantial.
- Textual critical methods are good enough to have successfully located several inauthentic passages, and modern translations have been adjusted to reflect this. These have been known for centuries, and nobody expects any more such discoveries. Not one of the variations has altered "an article of faith or a precept of duty which is not abundantly sustained by other and undoubted passages, or by the whole tenor of Scripture."[34]

- The reconstruction of the New Testament by scholars can be assessed "excellent," even if not perfect. Textual critic Daniel Wallace shares the same academic pedigree as his friend and colleague Bart Ehrman. In his debates with Ehrman, he debunks his colleague's disproportionate skepticism: "Although we cannot be certain about every detail in the text, we can be certain about most. . . . [Only] a very small percentage of the New Testament text is in doubt."[35]
- Radical skepticism over the state of the text is as unwarranted as absolute certainty. *"Not only does the task [of reconstructing the New Testament] appear to be possible, but it would seem that it has already been accomplished. What is left to be done is mere fine-tuning"* (italics mine).[36]

How will this next generation respond to Christ's invitation to come unto him and find rest for their souls? We don't know. We can be certain, however, that we possess his invitation as it was composed in "The Gospel According to" Matthew, Mark, Luke, and John.

Christian Origins: Reinventing the New Testament Canon

Our opponents are trying to rewrite the history of Christian origins. To do this, they must redefine orthodoxy and heresy. This requires eliminating the traditional sources of authority, including our confidence in the collection of books we call the New Testament, which we receive as inspired by God. Most commonly, this is done by questioning the competence or the motives of those authorities who recognized particular texts as "inspired" and therefore authoritative.

WHAT IS CANON?[1]

Every field of human endeavor needs a standard. The greater the intended achievement, the greater the need for accurate measurements. Olympic athletes, nuclear physicists, cancer researchers, brain physiologists, and software technicians know that the more expert they get in their field, the more appreciative they are of the field's standards of measurement. In a perverse reversal of this commonsense wisdom, popular portrayals of religion, spirituality, and morality are left to individual judgment and private interpretation. Appeals to corporate or public standards are often shouted down as "legalism" or "dogmatism" or "traditionalism" or "authoritarianism."

The ancient Church, like the Hebrew tradition from which it emerged, was much more akin to the Olympians, scientific researchers, and innovators in technology. Truth-telling and the measuring of authentic spiritual experience were too important to be left to the vagaries of subjective individual experience. The Catholic Church encourages robust personal experience. It also encourages spiritual direction since experts in spirituality know the propensity of the human heart to self-deception.[2] The problem of our culture is that we no longer acknowledge that there can be "experts" in spirituality whose evaluation and opinion carry more weight than the average Joe's individual opinion or judgment.

The New Testament "canon" refers to the 27 books, from Matthew to Revelation, that comprise the New Testament — the "table of contents," so to speak. "Canon" (Greek, *kanon*) means "rule" or "measure" and is widely used to mean "standard of judgment," "the body of an author's authentic or representative work," a "criterion, rule, body of principles."[3] The Catholic Church maintains that these are the written crystallization of the apostolic Tradition. It doesn't exhaust the teaching, but it is perfectly accurate. When and how did the Church recognize and draw up a list of inspired, authoritative writings? Let's look at two different but equally misleading approaches.[4]

DA VINCI DECEPTIONS

The Da Vinci Code embodies many widespread misconceptions regarding early Christianity, such as: The Emperor Constantine bullied the bishops at the Council of Nicea in 325, forcing them to create a new Bible. This required destroying some 80 gospels that emphasized Jesus' humanity and "canonizing" books that would exaggerate his divinity.[5]

The undisputed truth is:

- It's all indisputably false. While Constantine did call for the council, neither he nor the bishops at the Council of Nicea even addressed this "canon" question.
- There were not 80 non-canonical *gospels*. We have direct evidence for 20 "gospels" found in collections of literature from the second and third centuries and beyond. Many of them were composed in the name of an apostle or other notable figure associated with Jesus or the apostles.[6] We hear of the *Acts of Paul and Thecla* or the *Apocalypse of Peter*. Only the *Coptic Gospel of Thomas* seems to have even a slender historical basis. As Darrell Bock observes in *Breaking the Da Vinci Code*, "The bulk of this material is a few generations removed from the foundations of the Christian faith, a vital point to remember when assessing the contents."[7] For that reason, the

early Church never considered any of these for inclusion in the canon of the New Testament.

- Contrary to the *Da Vinci Code*, Matthew, Mark, and Luke do not elevate Christ's divinity. Many scholars even claim that the deity of Christ can't be found in them.[8] Ironically, Constantine should have liked Matthew, Mark, and Luke for vividly portraying Jesus' weeping, getting angry, eating, sleeping, and so on. Undeniably human, he has a physical body according to first-century eyewitnesses.[9] By contrast, *all* the "Gnostic" gospels, beloved of Dan Brown, are second- or third-century productions, and they often deny Christ's human nature, split Jesus of Nazareth from the divine Christ, ignore the Passion narratives, and display Jesus performing bizarre, capricious "miracles."[10]

- Did Constantine create a new Bible? No! Where's the evidence of elaborate, systematic embellishment of manuscripts?[11] In 331, he requested 50 fancy bibles for the new churches in Constantinople. Eusebius of Caesarea got the call because Caesarea was the authoritative center for Old Testament textual studies and had skilled copyists, manufacturing capability, and authoritative texts. Further, Eusebius had just published his *Ecclesiastical History* and was the expert on the canon, largely settled since the second century.[12] The fourth-century Church Fathers had suffered torture protecting those gospels under Diocletian. They wouldn't have rolled over for Constantine, nor would they have shut up had he been messing with their contents.[13]

- Did Constantine invent the deity of Christ? No! Declarations of Jesus' deity show up early in John's gospel (1:1-3; 8:58; 10:30-33; 20:28), more than 200 years before Constantine's conversion.[14] All early Christians thought Jesus was divine in some way. The big argument was over the exact nature of his relation to "God" as understood by Jewish monotheism.

The Da Vinci Code's treatment of things Catholic is so awful that many people won't believe you when you tell them. So I always keep agnostic and skeptic Bart Ehrman's comments nearby. According to Ehrman, Dan Brown claimed that most

Christians understood Jesus to be human but not divine. That's absolutely false. Most people thought Jesus was divine centuries before Constantine. Second, it's not true that Constantine decided which books to include in the New Testament; he had nothing to do with it. And the Council of Nicaea didn't have anything to do with which books to include in the New Testament. . . . The books of the New Testament, in fact, don't go out of their way to call Jesus divine; and the books that were excluded from the New Testament do call Jesus divine. So it's wrong all around.[15]

ANOTHER MISLEADING AND FALSE REVISIONISM

First misleading claim: "The development of a New Testament canon was unexpected, an artificial imposition, something alien to the movement of the New Covenant spirit."

Three revisionist scholars forget the example of the Old Testament:

- "Nothing dictated that there should be a New Testament at all."[16] False. We already had the precedent of the Old Covenant with a written canon.[17]
- "No conscious or clear effort was made by these New Testament authors to produce Christian scriptures."[18] False. "[W]hen you received the word of God which you heard from us, you accepted it not as the word of men but as what it really is, the word of God" (1 Thess 2:13). Paul's preaching was considered the Word of God; the Word of God is automatically canonical.[19]
- "The idea of a Christian faith governed by Christian written Holy Scriptures was not an essential part of the foundation plan of Christianity."[20] Only if you disregard the precedent of the Old Testament.

The Old Testament pattern of salvation seems lost on these critics. God performs a redemptive act in history — e.g., *the Exodus*. To preserve the memory of that action for coming generations, he establishes a covenant with written stipulations — e.g., *the Law at Sinai*. Covenant and canon work together to spur remembrance through right belief, behavior, and belonging. This includes right worship, or liturgy — e.g., *Pentateuch, Ten Commandments, Tabernacle, priesthood, sacrificial system.*[21]

What was true of the Old Covenant is even more glorious and effective in the New Covenant. In the Old Testament, "[w]ritten texts were the central manner in which God testified to the terms of his covenantal relationships within ancient Israel, and thus would be the expected means of communication in the context of the new covenant."[22]

Some claim that "the [letter] kills, but the Spirit gives life" (2 Cor 3:6). Yes, the Pharisaic "letter" nearly strangled Israel's mission to the Gentiles. They were left merely a separated people protecting themselves behind barriers of ethnic sabbaths, circumcisions, and dietary laws. Jesus goes after those problems in the Sermon on the Mount: "You have heard it was said. . . . But I say to you. . . ."[23] Spirit and letter are no more metaphysically opposed to each other than faith and reason are opposed. As God speaks his Word, his breath — that is, his Spirit (*pneuma*) — goes out from him. Spirit and Word naturally flow together.[24]

The Spirit of Pentecost restores the international mission to the Israel of God with everyone hearing the gospel in his native tongue. God in the flesh is now available in the preaching of the apostles, the liturgy of the people of God, and the fellowship of the universal — i.e., Catholic — Church. The Spirit doesn't come to make written revelation obsolete. As Peter Jenson writes: "For Paul, what you did with the old covenant was read it,"[25] and now he is "competent as minister of the new covenant."[26] If a covenant is intimately connected to written texts, and Paul announces in a written text that he is the authoritative minister of a new covenant, it becomes difficult to avoid the implication that he also understands that new covenant as having written texts. As Francois Bovan writes: "A New Testament is the logical consequence and concrete expression of a revelation that articulates the event and its proclamation involving Jesus and his disciples."[27]

As a first-century Jew, Jesus accepted the binding authority of the Old Testament to the smallest detail. "Not a jot or tittle will pass away until all is fulfilled," "the Scripture cannot be broken."

The Church was NEVER without a written revelation, a canon of Scripture. It inherited and appealed to the Old Testament. Matthew's gospel contains over 200 quotations or allusions to the Hebrew Bible. Paul writes to Timothy, "All scripture is inspired by God and profitable for teaching, for reproof, for correction, and for training in righteousness, that the man of God may be complete, equipped for every good work."[28] He is referring to the Old Testament,[29] even as his writings are crystallizing into the New. Jesus' words quickly become canonical.[30] 1 Timothy 5:18 calls Luke 10:7 Scripture and is itself drawn from Deuteronomy 25:4. Both covenants are here linked.

Better than manuscripts, Jesus left a living community endowed with his ongoing teaching authority. To hear them would be to hear him. Immediately, apostolic writings achieve "canonical" status.[31] Peter writes that Paul's letters are "scripture" on par with the writings of the Old Testament.[32] His casual presentation indicates that no one should be rattled by the introduction of new Scripture. And why would they?[33] Like the Old Testament prophets, the New Testament apostles are foundational.[34] Listen to Peter, urge submission to "the predictions of the holy prophets and the commandment of the Lord and Savior through your apostles,"[35] clearly linking the authority of the covenants again. Augustine testifies to the authority of apostolic writings. If the apocrypha attributed to Andrew and John "were really theirs, they would have been accepted by the Church."[36] Clearly, Christians knew that written apostolic teaching was covenantal revelation.

Second misleading claim: "Nobody thought of a New Testament canon until Marcion published one in A. D. 144. Scrambling to outdo him, the silly bishops turn Marcion, a heretic, into the father of the New Testament canon."[37]

Elaine Pagels' mentor Helmut Koester wrote: "The New Testament canon of Holy Scripture . . . was thus essentially *created* by Irenaeus" in the late second century in response to the canon introduced by Marcion.[38] These revisionist scholars treat Marcion like an innovator, as though no written canon existed in the early

Church. This is simply false. The actual canon began in the earliest years of the New Covenant, with Christians continuing to hold the Old Testament as Scripture and apostolic writings fairly quickly achieving canonical status. In truth, Marcion was motivated by anti-Jewish convictions: "[Marcion's] design . . . appears to have been not so much an insight into the normative value of NT writings — that is, a biblical canon — as it was an anti-Jewish rejection of both the value of the OT scriptures and the Jewish influence on the Christian community."[39]

Marcion's rejection of the God of the Old Testament as evil led him to discard the Old Testament. The Catholic Church, however, taught that the Old Testament prophets had been moved by the Holy Spirit. The Catholic Church taught that God the Creator was good. His material creation was good. The Old Testament was our first canon.[40] Marcion also rejected Matthew, Mark, portions of Paul's letters, and other writings as too Jewish. What Marcion had launched, whether he intended to or not, was an attack on the canon that had begun emerging from the first preaching of the apostles. To Marcion, the bishops didn't say, "Wow, a canon of Scripture. What a cool innovation. Let's make up our own list and have a canon too." No, what they said was, "This fool's twisted theology is now messing with our canon." Marcion was attacking something that existed, and he was disfiguring it. He wasn't proposing some new idea that the Church now had to imitate. Orthodoxy preceded heresy once again.

The third misleading claim: "The revisionists, Bauer et al., claim that the canon wasn't 'closed' until well into the fourth century."

False. Athanasius lays out the first formal list of all 27 books in his Easter letter of 367. Does this mean that the Church had operated for three and a half centuries without a canon? Did the Church operate over that time with no particular concern to set its literary boundaries? Was the Church awaiting more revelation? Could there be more revelation after the death of the apostles?

1. The Church was never without a canon. It immediately inherited the "Hebrew Bible."[41] Jesus' words and Paul's let-

ters quickly became canonical. So the idea of a canon was already present.

2. The Church remained open to prophetic utterances and charismatic gifts, but these fell far short of the public revelation brought forth through the apostles and were not received as Scripture.[42] Great teachers and bishops, just like prophets and workers of miracles, also deferred to apostolic authority. Both Clement of Rome (fl. 95) and Ignatius wrote weighty, authoritative letters, but they disclaimed the authority of the apostles, which was of another magnitude. Dionysius of Corinth (fl. 171) wrote to the churches under his care that his letters were "inferior" to the Scriptures of the Lord, lest anyone think he was creating Scripture.[43] A certain Gaius from Rome reprimanded the Montanist prophets for their "recklessness and audacity . . . in composing new Scriptures."[44] If the canon was open, why wasn't Gaius welcoming the new material?

3. Public revelation had ended with the apostles. To be crude: This meant no more revelational contestants could enroll in the canon game. The deadline was over. The applications were closed. The contest was over. We didn't yet know all the winners, but we knew that if you were submitting the Acts of Bob Delaney, and Bob Delaney wasn't an apostle, nor was he born until A.D. 125, then his application was rejected.

4. The process was never wide open. For instance, the *Triple A Seal of Approval* set limits from the start: *Antiquity, Apostolicity, Acceptability:*[45]

   - All the New Testament books were accepted as written in the first century[46] [*Antiquity*].
   - They were believed to be connected with apostolic teaching [*Apostolicity*].
   - They were generally read in the liturgies [*Acceptability*].

These criteria begin "in the beginning." To acclaim that the canon begins with Athanasius creates misunderstanding to the point of misinformation and that is mischievous. A quick summary of canon formation might be of benefit.

Summarizing the History of the Canon

The early Church inherited the covenant/canon pattern of the Old Testament. In the first century, Jesus' words and Paul's writings, which he saw as the Word of God, were received with the same authority as the Old Testament. The earliest collections of books "to circulate among the churches in the first half of the second century" were our four gospels and the letters of Paul.[47] Justin Martyr (100-165) had a fourfold gospel called the *memoirs of the apostles* [*Apostolicity*]. He probably also had the Pauline letters.[48]

Around Justin's time (144), the heretic Marcion (85-160) was teaching that the God of the Old Testament was evil and that the Old Testament was incompatible with the gospel. Jesus came to liberate us from this world of evil matter created by this evil God. In keeping with this anti-Jewish theology, Marcion discarded the Old Testament and other early Christian literature like Matthew. Church leaders saw this as an attack on the emerging canon. Remember, *Marcion's problem starts with a false god, not a bad reading list.*

Irenaeus (fl. 180) metaphorically describes Matthew, Mark, Luke, and John as firm as the four corners of the earth. He also cites the prophet Ezekiel's visions of God: the four living creatures, each possessing four faces and four wings. Gaius affirms a 13-letter collection of Paul, the same as found in the Muratorian Canon (c. 170), the earliest known comprehensive but not exhaustive list of New Testament books recognized by the Church. The Muratorian Canon recognized every New Testament book except Hebrews, James, 1 and 2 Peter, and 3 John. No argument can be built upon the omissions since the Muratorian fragment is incomplete and full of transcriptional blunders.

In that second-century Muratorian canon, the popular *Shepherd of Hermas* was rejected and, therefore, unacceptable for liturgical use [*Acceptability*], but it was still recommended for private devotion. Because it was written "very recently, in our own times," it was disqualified for corporate use.[49]

By the end of the second century, the emerging canon seemed to include the four gospels, Acts, the thirteen Pauline epistles, "epistles by other 'apostolic men' and the Revelation of John."[50] Similar though not identical books were recognized by Irenaeus (fl. 180). At this point, the debate is largely settled. Many of the Gnostic gospels aren't even written, and those that exist can't meet the criteria. They aren't even considered.

Origen, in the early third century, lists all 27 books of the New Testament in a homily.[51] Elsewhere he writes that questions remain, but "he seems confident enough in the list to mention it in a sermon to those ordinary churchgoers in the pew. Moreover, he gives no indication in his homily that the contents of his list would have been regarded as controversial or unexpected to his hearers."[52] So while the earliest full formal listing of all the books in our New Testament comes from Athanasius in A.D. 367, there was already widespread agreement on most of these books by the end of the second century.

Marveling at this consensus, the dean of American New Testament textual criticism, Princeton's late Bruce Metzger (1914-2007) writes: "What is really remarkable . . . is that, though the fringes of the New Testament canon remained unsettled for centuries, a high degree of unanimity concerning the greater part of the New Testament was attained within the first two centuries among the very diverse and scattered congregations not only throughout the Mediterranean world but also over an area extending from Britain to Mesopotamia."[53]

A HOMAGE TO CANONS — CULTURAL AND SPIRITUAL

Over the last generation, our culture has been rebelling against the idea of "canon" in Western literature. "Hey, hey, ho, ho, Western culture has to go." That kind of thing. Cultures inevitably and inescapably form canons, just as they form traditions. These canons guide us, or challenge us, to take our measure by a previous generation's standard or rule. Thus, we broaden our sympathies. How much more so when encountering the Divine Revelation of the Incarnate Word? The apostolic Tradition radiating from that event is crystallized on the pages of the canonical New Testament.

If familiarity breeds contempt, it, first of all, breeds boredom and low expectation. What is more familiar than the spiritual and cultural standards of our own generation? That is why Jesus quotes to us the proverb, "A prophet is without honor in his own" — fill in the blank — "town" or "family" or "generation." This is true in identifying the divine in history just as much as identifying the prophet or saint in our midst. For if a prophet is without honor in his hometown, the Divine Presence is frequently without recognition in one's own generation.

Our times are so plain and so, so familiar. We are like fish understandably unenthusiastic about the presence of water. But remove that fish from its immersion in its familiar environment and he is shocked with a world in which his limitations are mortal, and he awakens to what is really at stake. He re-enters that water with a new appreciation of its life-giving presence. He's developed eyes to see or GILLS to breath, I suppose.

So it is with locating the Divine Presence in our day. I know where it is. I don't know where it is not. So I do my duty. In the sacraments of Christ and in service to others, I'm told, I can encounter the divine. Yes, but too often I encounter the merely familiar. When I read the New Testament, however, I am lifted out of my familiar environment and forced to gasp at new air. When I return to my generation, I see differently, more generously, more compassionately, for I now know what I've been missing.

Our culture grows increasingly fragmented, balkanized, and even tribal. We are missing a doctrinal center, a core of truths that would enable us to not just tolerate our differences but to actually work toward resolving them in the same way that physicists and art historians won't rest with contradiction and chaos.

The revisionists propose a gospel of diversity to replace the canon of the New Testament. This is a proposed cure that only inflames the disease by exponentially multiplying the number of revelators with which we have to deal. The Catholic tradition, with its dual emphasis on robust personal experience and the corporate canons of spirituality and faith, remains the best hope for personal, familial, and cultural blessedness.

OPPONENT #12

Evolutionism:
The New Cosmic Religion

"We need a new religion."

— RAY KURZWEIL (*The Singularity is Near:
When Humans Transcend Biology*)[1]

"The time is fulfilled, and the kingdom of God is at hand; repent, and believe in the gospel."

— JESUS (Mk 1:15; cf. Mt 4:17; Lk 4:43)

"Scientific materialism is itself a mythology defined in the noble sense. . . . The core of scientific materialism is the evolutionary epic . . . probably the best myth we will ever have."

— E. O. WILSON (*On Human Nature*, 1975)[2]

"THE SINGULARITY IS NEAR"

Ray Kurzweil (b. 1948) is a remarkable achiever. In 1965, Kurzweil, 17, was on the CBS television program *I've Got a Secret*, hosted by Steve Allen. Before the four-member celebrity panel, he performed a very short piano piece. Bess Myerson asked Kurzweil if he had composed that piece of music. No, he replied. Prickly comedian Henry Morgan was next, and he nailed it: "Was that thing written by a computer?" Yes. This 17-year-old had built his computer, created a pattern-recognition software program that analyzed the works of classical composers, and then synthesized his own songs in similar styles. Allen jokingly asked if his parents knew what he was doing behind their backs. With filial respect, Kurzweil also showed good humor: "My dad is a musician, and he doesn't like the competition." Steve Allen, a lover of ideas, knew genius when he saw it: "I predict a great future for you."

Kurzweil fulfilled those words beyond anything Allen could have imagined. Microsoft founder Bill Gates called Kurzweil the best in the world at predicting the future for having foreseen the collapse of the Soviet Union, the rise of the Internet, and the year a computer would beat a human chess champion. Kurzweil invented optical recognition software; the flatbed scanner; text-to-speech technology, including the first reading machine for the blind (Stevie Wonder was his first customer); the Kurzweil keyboard synthesizer (Billy Joel, Alicia Keys, Ray Charles, Vangelis, etc., etc.,); and most recently, Blio, the new e-reader software. He's a millionaire many times over, holding at least 24 patents.

I had the opportunity to interview him back in 1992. In over 25 years of interviews, I've muffed more than a few. But there are few failures I remember more painfully than my Kurzweil interview, after he had written *The Age of Intelligent Machines*. I have a raft of excuses to float on: too many guests that day, inadequate communication with the publisher, and artificial intelligence (AI) was not a field I was comfortable playing in. Back in 1992, artificial intelligence still seemed marginal, best known as a key plot element in science fiction (SF) like *2001: A Space Odyssey* (1968), with HAL, the renegade computer stalking Dave, the astronaut, and innumerable other examples. People may have been asking philosophical questions like: What is the "I" in AI? Can AI generate a sense of self? Can our brains fail to recognize where "reality" ends and "virtual" begins, as in *The Matrix*, *Avatar*, and *Tron*? It's just that I wasn't asking those questions.

Kurzweil was, thankfully, easy to talk to. He could have told me that soon a computer would beat the world chess champion (which I now know he was talking about at the time), and I would have just looked at him like a cow gazing at a fence. At the time, I had no idea whether that was plausible or not. A few years later IBM's Deep Blue did beat Gary Kasparov. I did try a question about spirituality since, after all, I was serving a Christian audience. I asked if these advances in artificial intelligence would threaten our understanding of human nature. Would we come to see man as only so much patterned information? Would it become folly to talk of spirituality? And then came the missed opportunity. He quickly shot back, "Only if you've got a mistaken idea of spirituality." Clearly, he was prepared to discuss spirituality. He may have even said what he is now saying today: "We need a new religion."[3] But to my embarrassment, I didn't pose any follow-up question. Another guest was waiting. The clock was imperious, and I was ignorant. Exit Ray Kurzweil, one of today's icons of the future.

SCIENCE FICTION AND SPIRITUALITY: THE POWER OF STORIES

As a boy, Kurzweil consumed the *Tom Swift* SF adventure books. "The moral of these tales was simple: the right idea had the power to overcome a seemingly overwhelming challenge. To this day, I remain convinced of this basic philosophy."[4] He's not alone. Einstein, Werner von Braun, Freeman Dyson, Carl Sagan, and Stephen Hawking are but a few illuminati of science who are also illustrious sci-fi buffs.[5]

Someone will say these are "nothing but" stories. Beware "nothing buttery" in the arts as well as the sciences. Scripture is, after all, rich with stories enhanced by lots of poetry functioning like a soundtrack in a movie. Stories are, in fact, essentially moving pictures. That's why they are so readily adaptable to the screen. Using films to build virtue and character strengths is the work of Niemiec and Wedding's *Positive Psychology at the Movies* (2008).

In 1958's *A Night to Remember*, it's "Women and children first" while the invincible Titanic is pitching and sinking. On deck, there's chaos. Edith Evans gives up her place on the last boat to Mrs. Brown, saying, "You go first; you have children waiting at home." Mrs. Isidor Strauss won't go; she won't abandon her husband. Arthur Ryersin strips off his life vest and donates it to his wife's maid. Below deck, men struggle to keep the pumps going in the face of certain death; the band keeps playing, moving from ragtime to hymns. We witness remarkable displays of love and selflessness. But there are others: the USS California's indolent crew only 10 miles away. They could have made all the difference, but they did nothing. We also see lifeboats half-full, with the occupants refusing to help. And then there's the man in the shawl, posing as a woman to get into the lifeboat first.

When that shawl is torn away from his head, we do not have to be told anything.[6] His face says it all.

The moral force of a story is the force of example.[7] It shows us men and women acting well or acting badly. The story points and says in effect, "Act like this; don't act like that." Stories communicate values, codes to live by, myths of origin and destiny, as well as straightforward history and biography.[8] "Story is not the icing; it's the cake." The Jewish feminist poet Muriel Rukeyser (1913-1980) got it right when she wrote, "The Universe is made of stories, not of atoms"[9]

Han Solo, jaded interstellar smuggler of *Star Wars*, cracks that "I've flown from one side of this galaxy to the other, I've seen a lot of strange stuff, but I've never seen anything to make me believe there's one all powerful force controlling everything. There's no mystical energy field that controls *my* destiny." And, of course, *Star Wars*, with all its sequels and prequels, is an elaborate and epic refutation of his unbelief.[10] The enormous popularity of *Star Wars* is also refutation of the claim that Americans are secularists at heart. We aren't. Americans respond to something greater than scientific materialism. We want science, and we want spirituality — and we want heroes who embody both.

George Lucas (b. 1944) understood this in college when he started reading Joseph Campbell's (1904-1987) *The Hero with a Thousand Faces* (1948). He molded the *Star Wars* movies into a new form of ancient hero mythology.[11] He told *Time* magazine, "I put 'The Force' into the movies to awaken a certain kind of spirituality in young people, not a belief in any particular religion, more a belief in God."[12] Lucas had no interest in theological orthodoxy, and it worked! Every tradition reads itself into the *Star Wars* mythology. Hinduism has *The Jedi in the Lotus: Star Wars and the Hindu Tradition*. Buddhism has *The Dharma of Star Wars*. Taoism has *The Tao of Star Wars*. Islam has "Allah is the Force."[13] Judaism has "Star Wars' Jewish Themes."[14] Christianity has *The Gospel according to Star Wars*.[15] We shouldn't be surprised. SF author Thomas Disch (1940-2008) notes that "SF has been trafficking in magic and mythology since first it came into existence."[16]

The intermingling of science fiction and theology — understood broadly to include religion, spirituality, and worldview — is not at all unusual. The first great SF story (at least in English),[17] Mary Shelley's *Frankenstein*, sports an epigraph drawn from what many consider the supreme epic poem about Creation and Fall, Milton's *Paradise Lost*:

Did I request thee, Maker, from my clay
To mould me Man, did I solicit thee
From darkness to promote me?[18]

Or, in short, "Did I ask to be born?" — in this case, the Monster to Victor Frankenstein, his creator.

University of Michigan's Eric Rabkin also notes how frequently religion shows up even in atheist SF writers. In H. G. Wells' *War of the Worlds*, "the parody vision of the three Martian machines with the dead Martians hanging out of them on a hilltop is a reminder of Calvary. It's not that [*Frankenstein* authoress, Mary] Shelley and Wells actually are religious. They are not, in fact. They are thoroughly secular, but they employ religion to strengthen their moral discussions, not to argue for any particular religion or even, in fact, for spirituality in general."[19] Arthur C. Clarke believed that he and Stanley Kubrick had made a "ten million dollar religious movie" when they completed *2001: A Space Odyssey* in 1968.[20]

Theists, pantheists, panentheists, and atheists have all given us work that is overtly spiritual. Remember The Wachowski's *The Matrix*; Clarke's *Childhood's End*, *The Star*, or *The Nine Billion Names of God*; Miller's *A Canticle for Leibowitz*; C. S. Lewis' *That Hideous Strength*; Carl Sagan's *Contact*; Richard Sawyer's *Calculating God*; James Blish's *A Case of Conscience*; Orson Scott Card's *Ender's Game* and *Speak for the Dead*; and Mary Doria Russell's *The Sparrow*. Philip K. Dick (1928-1982) — noted for his disturbed, even psychotic, spirituality — was the first SF writer to be included in the *Library of America* series. His stories even influenced Hollywood by being turned into popular and innovative movies like *Blade Runner*, *Total Recall*, *Minority Report*, and *The Adjustment Bureau*, and by influencing the theme of alternate realities in movies like *The Truman Show* and *The Matrix*.

There is a free trafficking between science fiction and speculative science. "In his book *The Age of Spiritual Machines*, Ray Kurzweil has exposed a possible future that is both shocking as well as exhilarating, and bears an uneasy resemblance to the world of Dick's novels."[21] Speculative science and science fiction often resemble each other. Both presuppose, broadly speaking, theological questions and often rest on religious assumptions. Robert Sawyer, author of *Calculating God*, sees SF as "the most effective tool for exploring the deepest of all questions."[22]

While spirituality, morality, and religion play important roles in SF, it has never been a bastion of orthodoxy. Arthur C. Clarke (1917-2008), Isaac Asimov (1920-1992), and Robert Heinlein (1907-1988), the great triumvirate of the SF universe, were all inveterate and vocal atheists or, at least, "agnoskeptics." All came of age when the myth of the warfare between science and religion was largely unquestioned.[23] This is no longer the case. Many SF writers, no doubt, retain the residue of their atheism and skepticism. Many others, however, are awakening to the fact that the "warfare between science and religion" creates a false dilemma which is unhistorical and potentially damaging to one's writing since it demeans a way of seeing the world that is common to the vast majority of one's reading audience.[24]

Christian Writers Baptize the Imagination

Catholics and other Christians are often ignorant of how many members of Christ's body are at work in speculative fiction. This ignorance can lead to unnecessary discouragement. Western literature, even modern literature, owes a debt to the Catholic faith. Literary biographer Joseph Pearce (b. 1961) introduces us to some of these in *Literary Converts: Spiritual Inspiration in an Age of Unbelief* (2006) and many profiles.[25]

I wonder how many Catholics and other Christians are aware that today's most popular writer of suspense thrillers, Dean Koontz (b. 1945), is a serious Catholic thinker. He has just recast the *Frankenstein* story in six best-selling volumes. In another series, he has developed a character, *Odd Thomas*, a twentysomething fry cook, who lives in a universe which is simultaneously natural, preternatural, and supernatural. Koontz' novels are often preternatural thrillers in which the moral premise relates to human exceptionalism.[26]

Best known for creating the Scotland Yard investigator/poet Adam Dalgliesh, is P. D. James (b. 1920), an Anglican laywoman who believes our cultural malaise has theological causes. Her *A Taste for Death* has a church setting in which a nihilistic-sadist "kills in order to prove that the cosmos is empty of divinity."[27] Her *Children of Men*, adapted to film, is set in a dystopia created by a birth dearth. The drama hinges on the preciousness of offspring.

Marylynne Robinson (b. 1943) is another critically acclaimed novelist (*Gilead*, *Housekeeping*, and *Home*) and essayist (*Death of Adam*, *Absence of Mind*) working from a Reformational point of view, as well as Larry Woiwode (b. 1941), author of *Beyond the Bedroom Wall*. The great SF writer and editor Anthony Boucher (1911-1968) was a lifelong Catholic whose most noted SF story, "The Quest for Saint Aquin," features a superhumanly intelligent robot that embraces the Catholic faith through sheer logical reasoning. His novel *The Case of the Seven of Calvary* is "excellent fun."[28] William Fitzgerald Jenkins, known as Murray Leinster (1896-1975), a Catholic, "The Dean of Science Fiction," as he was sometimes known, was an award-winning SF writer who wrote and published over 1,500 short stories and articles, 14 movie scripts, and hundreds of radio scripts and television plays.[29] Tim Powers (b. 1952),[30] "the reigning king of adult historical fantasy," was a close friend of Philip K. Dick but describes himself as a "conservative Catholic." His short story "The Way Down the Hill" turns on the assumption that unborn human life is . . . human. His novels *Last Call* and *Declare* work within a clear Catholic moral framework to tell a story.

Walker Percy (1916-1990) is one of the most respected American novelists of the last century. While not a SF writer, he had a scientific education and took on the scientism that underlies much SF. Percy, a Catholic, is often mentioned along with John Updike (1932-2009), William Faulkner (1897-1962), and Saul Bellow (1915-2005),[31] as the greatest American novelists of the 20th century. We must also mention one of America's greatest short-story writers, Flannery O'Connor, a deeply committed Catholic who found grace in the grotesque. These writers didn't go into their "craft" to be propagandists. They wanted to be excellent writers. While none of them were known for their personal piety or "inspirational" or "devotional" writing, all are noted for the seriousness and respect with which they take spirituality, faith, or religion.[32] Many believe this accounts for the continuing appeal of their work.

Brit C. S. Lewis' science fiction doesn't rank as highly in its class as does his expository prose in apologetics and theology. But he personally enjoyed and saw the cultural importance of SF, even debating by correspondence with Arthur C. Clarke regarding pros and cons of space colonization and offering an opinion on Olaf Stapledon's *Star Maker*.[33] In 1939, in answer to a question about his *Out of the Silent Planet*, Lewis wrote that "any amount of theology can now be smuggled into the reader's mind under cover of a good romance, without their knowing it."[34] Lewis' own concern about the theological implications of H. G. Wells' "evolutionism" and Olaf Stapledon's *Star Maker*, which Lewis thought concluded with "sheer devil worship," prompted him to write his own Space Trilogy.[35] Lewis' friend, J. R. R. Tolkien, who played a major role in Lewis' conversion to Christ, blessed us with *The Hobbit*[36] and *The Lord of the Rings*, arguably the most significant fantasy of the 20th century.

Christians shouldn't be intimidated; they should be striving to create masterpieces of imaginative fiction. The public is still hungry for believable, edifying, and entertaining stories that have a distinctly moral premise and take seriously a cosmos in which ultimate reality includes divinity, spirit, intelligence, and so on. I've mentioned but a few of the dozens of Catholics, other Christians, and spiritually minded non-Christians who are among the most respected writers of the last 50 years.

SF AS PROPAGANDA FOR ATHEISM?

Robert Sawyer laments the 50 percent decline in non-*Star War*, non-*Star Trek* SF sales. Sawyer wonders if there is a future for serious science fiction.[37] Yes, he concludes, if SF writers become propagandists for scientism. "Inculcate the belief that rational thought, that discarding superstition, that subjecting all beliefs to the test of the scientific method, is the most reasonable approach to any question, then . . . will science fiction have a key role to play in the intellectual development of the new century . . . and at last, help humanity shuck off the last vestiges of the supernatural, the irrational, the spurious, the fake."

Robert Sawyer's atheism betrays a lack of imagination, a premature closing of possibilities, an admission that he is hostage to the sense of a blocked future. His advice will only continue the decline in non-*Star Wars*, non-*Star Trek* SF. First, he imagines we all know that the race is progressing beyond religion and spirituality. We certainly do not! The popularity of *Star Wars* has been counter-evidence to that. Think what you will of it as SF, but from its appearance in 1977, parents and children enjoyed *Star Wars* together because it reintroduced into the grim world of 1970s filmmaking (e.g., *Last Tango in Paris*, *The Swarm*, *Zardoz*) a shamelessly heroic tale, with a universe inhabited by wildly and wonderfully diverse creatures who still had to deal with the old traditional moral categories of good and evil and the struggle against temptation. Morality was not relative. Heroism was not trashed. The "Force" provided a feeling of transcendence.

Second, Sawyer also seems unaware that many sociologists disagree with him about religion's future. Last century, many sociologists theorized that modern societies were undergoing secularization — i.e., the social process by which religious ideas, influences, and institutions are pushed from the center of public life to its margins. But under the nose of the mainstream press, the public and cultural significance of religion and faith was reasserting itself in North America, India, China, and the Middle East. Sociologist Peter Berger, one of the developers of secularization theory, "recanted" in *The Desecularization of the World: Resurgent Religion and World Politics* (1999), where he wrote: "The assumption we live in a secularized world is false. . . . The world today is as furiously religious as it ever was."[38]

Many like Sawyer want, at least temporarily, the fruit of theism, without accepting the root of theism, a Transcendent, Infinite,

Personal God. They want to retain a religious glow to the universe, a faith that life is meaningful, so that religiously minded people won't be downcast and without motivation. They want to enlist and control the religious impulse without the inconvenient burden of God revealing himself in ways that contradict their unfolding vision of the new humanity, new society, new liberation movement, and so on.

Evolutionary Optimistic Humanism

Melding evolution and religion has been one of the great intellectual projects of the 20th and now 21st centuries. Let's begin with UNESCO's first director, Julian Huxley, the grandson of Darwin's great ally, Thomas Huxley. Julian sought a *"Religion Without Revelation"*[39] when he realized that UNESCO "needed a philosophy that was a global, scientific, evolutionary humanism."[40] This appears in his 1955 "Introduction" to Fr. Teilhard de Chardin's magnum opus on "evolutionism," *The Phenomenon of Man*, which, as we'll see later, was one of the most important books of the 20th century in giving evolutionism its religious glow.

Immediately after the spiritual catastrophe of World War II, America's most influential philosopher, John Dewey, proposed a *"Common Faith"* (1947), which would free "faith," or the human religious impulse, from the authority of divine revelation, dogmatic theology, and denominationalism. Having decoupled the religious sense from any supernatural authority, he proposed a "faith in ideals apprehended by the imagination as being intrinsically valuable possibilities. . ."[41] Again, the aim is to eliminate "God" in any theistic sense.

To be crude, the primary question is: Does religion have survival value? Does it help the human organism adapt to difficult cultural environments? *Darwin's Cathedral: Evolution, Religion and the Nature of Society* is the work of David Sloan Wilson, a gifted teacher and a man of evident respect for religion.[42] He is the "nice atheist." In tone, he is about as far removed from Dawkins, Harris, and Hitchens as Gorbachev was from Stalin. Wilson argues that the religious impulse evolved early in hominid history because it bound communities together and enhanced fraternal feelings, which enabled a better defense against adversaries. As much as any atheist, Wilson, as a communitarian, appreciates religion's capacity to form community. But evolution goes beyond community formation and is the central organizing principle of his entire intellectual vision. His many books are about using evolution to "improve my city," "change the way we think about our lives," "rethink storytelling," "promote altruism."[43]

This is "religious naturalism," the attempt to form a religious philosophy of life rooted in nature. In religious naturalism, "God" can be identified with the totality of the cosmos. Or "God" becomes the creative genius or force within the universe. Many religious naturalists simply discard "God" as confusing and prefer to talk of "Nature" or "Cosmos" or "the All."[44]

James A. Herrick analyzes the rhetorical strategy of these surrogate religions or spiritualities that are finding voice through SF and popular culture. In his *Scientific Mythologies: How Science and Science Fiction Forge New Religious Beliefs*, he warns: "Scientific mythologies are powerful cultural engines for inventing . . . a worldview that stands in marked contrast to, and seeks to move its audience away from . . . the Judaeo-Christian tradition."[45] He locates many, but two of the recurring themes that characterize these "scientific mythologies" are:

- Evolution as Religion or Spiritual Journey
- Myth of the New Humanity[46]

EVOLUTIONISM AS RELIGION

A strange blend of SF writers, speculative scientists, and philosopher/theologians has proposed "evolutionism" as the overarching storyline to make sense out of life. British philosopher Mary Midgley (b. 1919) recognized that "Evolution is the creation myth of our age. By telling us our origins it shapes our views of what we are. It influences not just our thoughts but also our feelings and actions in a way which goes far beyond its official function as a biological theory."[47] Evolutionism functions as a religion, philosophy, or myth because it answers those questions of ultimate concern normally associated with religion and philosophy, as well as those normally beyond scientific verification or falsification.

Is talk of "the myth of evolution" a sly way of discrediting the biological theory of evolution? No. C. S. Lewis wrote long ago: "I do not mean that the doctrine of evolution as held by practicing biologists is a myth. . . . It is a genuine scientific hypothesis. But we must sharply distinguish between Evolution as a biological theorem and popular Evolutionism or Developmentalism which is certainly a Myth."[48] He also presents earlier examples of "evolutionism" in literature and the arts. Sometimes writers avoid "myth" and use "Metanarrative," "Grand Story," "Universe Story,"[49] "Great Story,"[50] or "Everybody's Story."[51]

Secular humanists, like the late Julian Huxley (1887-1975), promoted evolutionism as the unfolding of the potential of matter, a "religion without revelation." Philosopher Michael Ruse (b. 1940), a vocal defender of biological evolution as science, blew the whistle on those, like Huxley, who would turn the scientific theory into a surrogate religion: "Evolution is promulgated as an ideology, a secular religion — a full-fledged alternative to Christianity, with meaning and morality. . . . This was true of evolution in the beginning, and it is true of evolution still today."[52]

Cosmic humanists or New Age thinkers promote evolutionism as the unfolding of mind. In late 1977, Marilyn Ferguson, author of the *Aquarian Conspiracy*, sent a questionnaire to 210 "persons engaged in social transformation." One hundred eighty five of these "Aquarian conspirators" responded to a question asking whose ideas had most influenced them. Pierre Teilhard de Chardin — the Jesuit paleontologist best known for his controversial effort to sacralize, even Christianize, evolution — was the clear favorite, outranking 20th-century luminaries like C. G. Jung, Abraham Maslow, Carl Rogers, Aldous Huxley, Robert Asagioli, and J. Krishnamurti.[53]

THE NEXT STEP

Both secular and cosmic evolutionary humanism place the human person in the vanguard guiding the process in the future. For example, in 1979, molecular biologist William Day explored the chemical origins of life in *Genesis on Planet Earth: the Search for Life's Beginning*. He concludes: "[A] new species, Omega man, will emerge. . . . It is reasonable to assume that man's intellect . . . merely represents a stage intermediate between the primates and Omega man."[54] We are not yet what we will be. Day, frustrated by nature's slowness, doesn't want to wait 10,000 years or more for biology to do its work, so he asks, "How then can Omega man arise in so short a time? The answer is unavoidable. Man will make him."[55]

But what is the next step? If evolution has been directional, progressive, and always improving, what is the next phase of evolution? Here's the dirty little secret. Nobody knows. This is where we watch Kurzweil in action and encounter the myth of Humanity 3.0.

Myth of Humanity 3.0: Human Enhancement Through Technology

"I want to create a world without weakness . . . this is no longer about curing ills; it is about finding perfection."

— DR. CURTIS CONNOR (as he develops cross-species genetics in *The Amazing Spiderman*, 2012).

"Mr. Parker, do you know what it means to feel like god?"

— DR. MOREAU (played by Charles Laughton, in *The Island of Lost Souls*, 1932)[1]

"You're playing God." "Somebody has to!"

— DR. MICHAEL HFUHRUHURR (played by Steve Martin, in *The Man with Two Brains*, 1983)

THE MYTH OF HUMANITY 3.0

Evolutionism, climaxing with the myth of the New Humanity, now holds the default position for those in the West who have rejected or never considered the Christian story of Creation, Fall, Redemption, and Consummation. In both stories, the human race aims at a new birth, a new race, a new kind, a transformation of the self. The Catholic's goal is to be purged of disordered self-love, find union with Christ, and serve, in love, his Creator and all of his creation. Generally, the Christian seeks an enhancement of his capacity to love and worship. Evolutionism's goal is technological enhancement of our basic biology, the old self is accessorized up to a higher life. This may involve genetic engineering, although most media attention is being given to the use of artificial intelligence in neural implants and brain-computer or brain-machine interfaces. The Transhumanist, primarily, focuses on enlarging his intelligence.[2] Is the new self actually the same self renewed or a different species altogether?

Humanity's future was the subject of the September/October 2004 issue of the influential journal *Foreign Policy*. It posed the question: *"What ideas, if embraced, would pose the greatest threat to the welfare of humanity?"*

THE THREAT OF TRANSHUMANISM

Foreign Policy asked this question of eight respected public intellectuals. Francis Fukuyama of the Johns Hopkins School of Advanced International Studies answered unambiguously: "Transhumanism . . . an essentially idolatrous religion proffering a counterfeit salvation . . . a strange liberation movement" that wants "nothing less than to liberate the human race from its biological constraints."[3] The goal: *"Humans must wrest their biological destiny from evolution's blind process of random variation and adaptation and move to the next stage as a species."*[4]

WHAT IS TRANSHUMANISM?[5]

For *Reason* magazine's Ronald Bailey (b. 1953), Transhumanism "epitomizes the most daring, courageous, imaginative, and idealistic aspirations of humanity."[6]

Philosopher Nick Bostrom (b. 1973), co-founder of the World Transhumanist Association (WTA, a.k.a. H+) agrees that it is bold but not unnatural.[7] What is wrong with eradicating disease, eliminating suffering, reversing aging, extending the life span, and expanding all human intellectual, physical, and emotional capacities?[8] Other Transhumanist themes include creating superintelligent machines, space colonization, and restructuring our social, economic, cultural, and political designs.[9] Three emphases show us the vision.

Improving Human Nature

This is to be done "through the ethical application of science."[10] Catholics will appreciate some of the aspirations but will certainly disagree with some of the ethics. James Hughes, a former executive director of the WTA, sees "pro-life" concerns as "throwbacks to the authoritarianism of the church and totalitarian states . . . to dogma and fear." In particular, the human embryo is not a person. "It is a biological product, so we must think we can use it for good ends."[11] Doesn't Hughes understand that in his vision of the world, he is also only "a biological product?" Shall we use product Hughes "for good ends?"

Sometimes Transhumanists pose as descendants of the Enlightenment, with its ideal of the perfectibility of man. But Enlightenment thinkers (1650-1800), unlike Transhumanists, weren't skeptical about human nature's fundamental stability. It could be perfected, but it needn't be reinvented. They identified virtue and vice, right and wrong, with a confidence that would scandalize most Transhumanists. For instance, in his *Enquiry Concerning the Principles of Morals* (1751), Hume confidently declared:

> The end of all moral speculation is to teach us our duty; and, by proper representations of the deformity of vice and beauty of virtue, beget corresponding habits, and engage us to avoid the one, and embrace the other.[12]

Transhumanists need to be asked how, without an essential human nature, they know what they are perfecting or improving? You can hardly specify an existing *telos*, or aim of human nature, if you are in the process of inventing human nature. Something is shifty here.

Increasing the Human Health Span

This is a euphemism for "Chasing Methuselah" — i.e., eliminating aging entirely.[13] Former Cambridge geneticist Aubrey de Grey (b. 1963) has co-authored *Endless Aging* (2007) and co-founded the Methuselah Foundation, which aims at eliminating cellular aging.[14] De Grey expects life spans of several millennia as early as 2025.

Transhumanists present orthodox Christians as opponents of "life extension."[15] This is preposterous. If we can engineer cellular anti-aging processes, beat back disease, and advance human life spans, we should. Nothing is off-limits except sin. After all, Jesus Christ's promise of eternal life placed an authentic version of "life extension" at the center of the human quest. What is the relationship between our aspiration for eternal life and extended biological life? What are the technological means available to extend human life from 75 years to 125 years? What about "several millennia," as de Grey claims? We may think this is an impossible task. We may not want to fund it. We certainly would want to ensure that human life is protected. But there is no *necessary* reason to treat the life extension project with contempt, horror, or moral disdain. If we can ease one consequence of original sin, pain in childbirth, why shouldn't we push back against another: death and aging?

Catholics will insist on protecting human dignity during the experimental phase, while Transhumanists seem to adopt a "by any means necessary" approach.

Extending Our Intellectual and Physical Capacities[16]

Transhumanism's agenda makes Lance Armstrong's and Barry Bonds' trainers look like pikers. Doping is just so primitive compared to enhancements potentially available through brain-computer interfaces and advances in neuropsychopharmacology or genetic engineering. The National Nanotechnology Initiative[17] is developing new delivery systems and therapies. Nanomedicine will monitor, control, construct, repair, defend, and improve all human biological systems, working from the molecular level. The expectation is that we, within a few decades, will be able to repair or replace most organs, including the skin, with materials superior to those supplied by nature. These biotechnologies are not just for healing anymore. Fantasies of Captain America and the Bionic Man are on the verge of realization[18] according to many observers.

THERAPY OR ENHANCEMENT?

Traditionally, therapy corrects some deficiency, deficit, disease, or disorder. Enhancements improve already healthy performance to a more optimal level. "By definition enhancements are not aimed at preventing, treating or mitigating the effects of a disease or disorder."[19] For the most part, Transhumanists reject this common-sense distinction between therapy and enhancement as a distinction without a difference. Pro-enhancement advocates stress the continuities between the new methods of enhancement and the old. "How is taking Modafinil[20] fundamentally different from imbibing a good cup of tea? How is either morally different from getting a full night's sleep? Are not shoes a kind of foot enhancement, clothes an enhancement of our skin?"[21]

Morally responsible parents can be led into many transgressions if convinced it will benefit their children. Michael Sandel, (b. 1953), political philosophy professor at Harvard, in *The Case Against Perfection: Ethics in an Age of Genetic Engineering* (2007), introduces us to a deaf lesbian couple who were proud members in the deaf-pride community. Deafness, they said, was their cultural identity, their way of life, not a personal disability. They found a sperm donor with five generations of deafness, and their son was born deaf. Is it wrong to make a deaf child by design? If so, what makes it wrong — the deafness or the design?[22]

Sandel dishes up another. "An infertile couple was seeking an egg donor. . . . She had to be five feet, ten inches tall, athletic, without major family medical problems, and . . . a combined SAT score of 1400 or above. In exchange for an egg from [the right] donor, [the infertile couple] offered payment of $50,000."[23] Even if there is no harm or deficit inflicted on the child, aren't we uncomfortable with ordering up a child on specification?

Transhumanists retort that elite families always arrange marriages to "move up" the fitness ladder. Is choosing a spouse or arranging a daughter's marriage the same as ordering up a designed child? Is it permissible because the results are less predictable? But why should unpredictability make a moral difference? How is leaving it to chance a superior approach? Some Transhumanists argue that parents are morally obligated to provide all enhancements they can afford for their children's sake, including prenatal surgeries and genetic engineering and, in time, the technological creation of our descendants.

Catholics, of course, have the wisdom of the Church on in vitro fertilization.[24] Sadly, however, the culture has moved so far down the pike that most people haven't a clue what we are talking about. In truth, most Catholics aren't even listening. Are we waiting for them to come to their senses and realize how wise the Church is? Or are we ready to be ambassadors of Christ and ministers of reconciliation.[25] Q: "Isn't it dangerous to play God?" A. *Somebody has to.* My flippancy makes the point that Transhumanism flatly rejects some of our most cherished assumptions about providence, progress, and parental responsibility. If we don't represent the Catholic way of life, others will assume there is none.

TRANSHUMANISM AND CHRISTIANITY

The overall Transhumanist ethos is hostile to Christianity.[26] An exception is Tihamer Toth-Fejel, a research engineer with General Dynamics, a friendly acquaintance working in the field of nanotechnology. He's a Catholic[27] and refuses to be marginalized and written out of the humane promise that these technologies offer. He's reported for the National Catholic Bioethics Center.[28] At the 2004 Toronto TransVision conference, words like "Christian" and "religious" were often used scornfully. Christian opposition to the destruction of human embryos in research was described as "a Luddite dragging in of Trojan horses."[29] Simon Young's *Designer Evolution: A Transhumanist Manifesto* (2006) shows that most Transhumanists are thoroughly secular.[30]

TRANSCENDING *STAR TREK*, LAB RATS, AND BIOLOGY

Until the recent media attention given to Transhumanism, serious artificial intelligence (AI) was rarely on public display. IBM's computer "Watson" beat champion *Jeopardy* contestants in a 2011 match, and IBM's Deep Blue bested world chess master Gary Kasparov in a 1997 match.[31] Most of our encounters with the secularist New Man, robotics, machine minds, and uploading intelligence, however, have come through innumerable SF books, films, and TV programs like *I, Robot* (1950, 2004), *Blade Runner* (1982), *Neuromancer* (1984), and *Star Trek: The Next Generation*, episode 35, "The Measure of a Man" (1989).

Recently some pro-Transhumanist light fare has been offered. Catholic blogger and molecular biologist Rebecca Taylor notes that Disney's *Lab Rats*[32] and *Captain America* present their superpowers as the result of rational planning and perfecting a humanity that

nature or God didn't get quite right on the first draft. Most super-
heros acquire their distinctive powers by some quirk of history or
fate, an accident that makes their power more a result of "grace,"
or at least gratuitousness rather than rational planning. Not so the
superheroes of Transhumanism.

Steve Rogers, Captain America, is the ideal Transhumanist
superhero, according to *Discover* magazine. First, he is deliberately enhanced by someone. Second, Rogers deliberately chooses
to become enhanced. He seeks strength and speed to defend and
protect others. Third, and most important, "Captain America is
literally super-moral,"[33]not just physically superior.

Soon we will attain superhuman status through the development of artificial intelligence, if Ray Kurzweil and Larry Page of
Google get what they are banking on.[34] Shortly, we will supersede
modern Homo sapiens more definitively than we surpassed *archaic
Homo sapiens.*

In 2005, Ray Kurzweil seized the public's attention with *The
Singularity Is Near: When Humans Transcend Biology,*[35] updating his
1998 *The Age of Spiritual Machines: When Computers Exceed Human
Intelligence.*[36] He was already working this theme in 1990 when he
and I discussed his *The Age of Intelligent Machines,* though, at the
time, I lacked ears to hear. "With neurological architecture, sufficient complexity, and the right combination of analog and digital
processes, *computers will become 'spiritual'[conscious] like we are.*"[37]

Bill Gates maintains that "Ray Kurzweil is the best in the world
at predicting the future of artificial intelligence," and he predicts
"2045: The Year Man Becomes Immortal"[38] will be an utterly
unique, unrepeatable moment after which nothing is the same:[39]
The Singularity. *Artificial intelligence will have enhanced human intelligence to such a degree that only by actually blending or merging the
two can we ride the rate of change. To fail to do so will risk our creation
outpacing us and eventually arraying itself against us.* To retain control,
human intelligence will have to reinvent or raise itself in a superior
form. A new species will have emerged with "no distinction . . .
between human and machine or between physical and virtual reality."[40] This is the New Man. We have become our own creation.[41]

WHERE ARE WE NOW? HOW PLAUSIBLE IS THIS SCENARIO?

Duke University neuroscientist Miguel Nicolelis looks at medical breakthroughs in *Beyond Boundaries: The New Neuroscience of Connecting Brains with Machines and How it will Change Our Lives* (2011).[42] "Melding brains and machines had, for decades, appeared to be a far-fetched dream or, at best, the stuff of science fiction. [Now] . . . brain machine interfaces had crossed the threshold into the rarefied halls of real science."[43]

Scientific American, *Nature*, *MIT Technology Review*, and other respected professional and popular journals have tracked the progress. In a special issue of *Nature* in 2001, over 10 years ago, the question was not if, nor even when, but how.[44] Already, one brain implant uses voluntary brain activity to control a robotic arm. "Locked in"[45] patients can already communicate with the external world through an EEG-based Brain Computer Interface (BCI). With similar BCIs, severely paralyzed patients can steer a wheelchair. Technical problems remain. But expectations remain high.

Beginning in the 2020s, Kurzweil expects to reprogram the information processes underlying biology, including reverse engineering of the brain. Afterward, he sees neural implants in the brain that will download information and multiply intelligence a billion fold. By the 2030s,

> We've eliminated the heart, lungs, red and white blood cells, platelets, pancreas, thyroid and all the hormone-producing organs, kidneys, bladder, liver, lower esophagus, stomach, small intestines, large intestines and bowel. What we have left at this point is the skeleton, skin, sex organs, sensory organs, mouth and upper esophagus and brain. . . . We will ultimately be able to improve on the skin with new nanoengineered supple materials that will provide greater protection from physical and thermal environmental effects while enhancing our capacity for intimate communication.[46]

All this is precursor to 2045, the Singularity. Transhumanists agree that Fukuyama was right in his vetting but wrong in his fretting. The Singularity is just the "inevitable next step" in the evolutionary process. Nature's biological evolution has been extended through humanity's technological evolution.[47] The evolutionism epic climaxes with matter turning into mind or the physical turning into spirit, as though matter was some burden from which mind or spirit had to be liberated.

Not all who subscribe to and marvel at the epic of evolutionism buy the Singularity as a moment of radical discontinuity with the past. William Gibson (*Neuromancer*, 1985) — who regularly gets credit for popularizing the concepts of "the matrix," "cyberspace," and "reality" TV, as well as with blurring the line (which he claims doesn't exist) between virtual and real — is called the *noir* prophet of Cyberpunk Science Fiction. He lampoons Kurzweil's Singularity scenario as the "Geek rapture," which, I suppose, means that we Catholics are, again, going to be "*Left Behind.*" Gibson notes with irony Kurzweil's "belief that [the Singularity] will be a sudden, quasi-religious transformation . . . positively 4th century in its thinking."[48]

Suppressing the Truth, Given Over to Fantasy

In Scripture, God's judgments come upon those who suppress his truth. They are given over to the lie that they have told themselves. They now live in bondage to their own fantasies.[49] They live in fear of the unreal, they lose the capacity to test reality, and they allow their sensuous imaginations to buffer them from their experience of the "real" world.

Christians, on the other hand, still believe that adherence to truth requires distinguishing "virtual" and "real." The distinction between image and reality deserves honor because God created space/time and history as the setting in which a providential drama would be played out. We balance the inner and the outer worlds because the human person is a union of body and soul. Neither the soul alone nor the body alone is the person. We aren't just an "inner" world — i.e., mind, spirit. We aren't just an "outer" world — i.e., matter, body. Souls are given to us, as the form of our bodies. Bodies give us boundaries and distinguish us from other immaterial identities while at the same time uniting us with our kind. This reminds us that the physical is good, not meaningless or unworthy of the "spiritual" person.

Kurzweil's discontinuity of life before and after the Singularity fails to respect the intrinsic continuity between body and soul. Gibson stresses continuity, but one that leads to the same phony emancipation from distinctions between the real and the virtual, the physical and the spiritual, the material and the mental. For Kurzweil and Gibson both, the end game is a new emergent species of consciousness with no distinction between human and machine or between physical and virtual reality. For both, the human has become his own creation. Is this a fulfillment of Bernard Levin's (1928-2004) quip, "Whom the mad would destroy, first they make gods"?

CHOOSING A FUTURE, REMEMBERING A PAST

Is this our future? *From Chance to Choice*, a bioethics of enhancement text, makes our continued evolution dependent on our decision to choose to walk our evolutionary path. We must choose to have a choice. Francis Fukuyama doesn't disagree:[50] "It may be that we are . . . destined to take up this new kind of freedom . . . that the next stage of evolution is one in which we will deliberately take charge of our own biological makeup rather than leaving it to the blind forces of natural selection. But if we do, we should do it with eyes open."[51]

From 1910 to 1940, the world's leading nations were swept up in a movement that ignored the Catholic vision of the human person. Eugenics claimed that the gene pool was deteriorating because the best human beings were not breeding as rapidly as the inferior ones. Who was inferior? Foreigners, immigrants, Jews, promiscuous women, homosexuals, the poor, degenerates, the unfit, and the "feeble minded."[52] Crude but popular. At least four U.S. presidents called for "eugenics." Leading entertainers, writers, economists, and even clergy[53] and most of the population thought the common good would be served by passing laws protecting the gene pool by forcibly sterilizing those deemed unfit. Over two dozen states passed compulsory sterilization laws, which were upheld by the U.S. Supreme Court in a decision[54] written by one of our most celebrated jurists.[55]

But after World War II, nobody was a eugenicist, and nobody had ever been a eugenicist. Nobody admitted to even knowing a eugenicist. Biographers of the celebrated avoided addressing their subjects' attitudes on this policy. Eugenics ceased to be a subject for college classrooms, even history classrooms.[56]

What happened? We learned that even as we fought the Nazis on the European front, we had been their allies in a war against the weak on the cultural front. They modeled their immigration policy after our 1924 law. We helped them in the forming of their sterilization laws. They forcibly sterilized 300,000. We managed 63,000.

WHO RESISTED?

Didn't anybody resist? Fundamentalist and evangelical Protestants, with their high view of biblical inspiration, refused to accommodate to the myths of "evolutionism" and "the new humanity." They stuck to the biblical story of Creation and thought America needed to get "saved," not sterilized. The more effective resistance came from the Catholic Church. The scientific expertise of our laity and our grasp of natural law put us at the center of the debate.[57] Catholic laity and clergy worked effectively together.

Will Transhumanism seize the imagination of the public as eugenics did? If so, we had better be ready for round two. It shares similar goals of improving the human race by applying largely untested technologies derived from the biological sciences. Eugenics, like Transhumanism, was an "avant-garde notion that attracted the most liberal and progressive minds of a generation."[58]

IS HUMAN NATURE BROKEN OR UNFINISHED?

The doctrine of Creation is the bright line dividing us and our evolutionism opponents. We do not have to accept a fundamentalist approach to reading Genesis to understand that life will be conceived differently by those who believe life was created by a benevolent God and by those for whom life is the product of natural forces that had no prevision of the end they were achieving.

Transhumanists rejoice that "the human species in its current form does not represent the end of our development but rather a comparatively early phase."[59] Bostrom says:

Transhumanists view human nature as a work-in-progress, a half-baked beginning that we can learn to remold in desirable ways. Current humanity need not be the endpoint of evolution. Transhumanists hope that by responsible use of science, technology, and other rational means we shall eventually manage to become posthuman, beings with vastly greater capacities than present human beings have.[60]

This is the myth of evolutionism and the new humanity 3.0.

In contrast, our side is composed of "the prudentialists." These are theists and humanistic naturalists that include Pope Benedict XVI (b. 1927), Pope John Paul II (1920-2005), Leon Kass (b. 1939), Michael Sandel (b. 1953), Francis Fukuyama (b. 1952), Robert George (b. 1955), Jurgen Habermas (b. 1929) — or reaching further back, Hannah Arendt (1906-1975), C. S. Lewis (1898-1973), and Hans Jonas (1903-1993).[61]

Despite the substantial philosophical and theological differences among the prudentialists, they accept the "givenness" of the human race as it is. Even if not a theist, the prudentialist can have a sense of being "gifted," inasmuch as he knows the world and humanity are not a result of his doing.[62] The prudentialist isn't waiting for humanity to be unveiled. Human nature is largely fixed, objectively "good," and presently demands our respect. "Humanity is not something still to be 'realized' by technological reshaping but finds its worth or dignity in its finite, vulnerable, embodied nature — that is, in precisely those features that Transhumanists hope to alter or transcend.[63]

Catholics receive Genesis not only as divine revelation but also as the most radical statement of "humanism" in the history of human literature. We are created by God, immortal beings possessing an intrinsic dignity derived not from the elements out of which our bodies were produced but by the divine Word that invests those elements with transcendental significance. "To believe that our talents and powers are wholly our own doing is to misunderstand our place in creation, to confuse our role with God's."[64] We believe God created us in his image and likeness, and though marred by sin, we are basically intact, commanded to carry out a co-regency with God, stewarding and cultivating his creation in a Kingdom direction. Has anyone ever envisioned a higher calling?

Christians see our physical, material side as fundamentally good, even when deformed in some way. The Transhumanists see our biology as limiting, and they look to human technology as the pathway to a new form of humanity without these limitations. Is this actually a death wish? Don't Transhumanists want the end of their own embodied kind, the humanity that we know and are?

E. Christian Brugger holds the J. Francis Cardinal Stafford Chair of Moral Theology at St. John Vianney Theological Seminary in Denver. He's thought about the challenge of Transhumanism and our culture's inability to grasp and/or embrace the Catholic vision of the human person. Into that vacuum we find new visions — spawned by SF, speculative science, and vigorous intellectual movements — presenting themselves as the inevitable, irresistible next phase of our life together.[65]

Right now, Brugger explains, many of the elite citizens of our nation are denying five key aspects of Catholic anthropology. First, they deny the doctrine of divine creation in favor of the myth of evolutionism. Second, they deny the reality of original sin and believe that human nature is perfectible without divine grace.[66] Third, they deny an immortal human soul, which cannot be reduced to the body or reduced to our waking consciousness and is not subject to decay.[67] Fourth, they often deny what commonly is called "free will." This leads to a denial of moral responsibility. Fifth, they deny that our bodies are an essential part of our personhood. They see the body as an accessory, or mere tool of the mind.[68]

In *Childhood's End*, Arthur C. Clarke wrote, "But they knew in their hearts that once science had declared a thing possible, there was no escape from its eventual realization." I'm not convinced. That we can do something doesn't require that we will eventually do it. The possibility of doing evil doesn't necessitate that we commit evil.

The greatest safeguard against the notion that we will do whatever our science and technology will permit us to do, irrespective of the moral law, is to remember God. In so doing, we realize that we are creatures under command. The future is always subject to an Other than ourselves.

The new scientistic mythology that we've been sketching generally rejects God, creaturely limits, and the inevitability of sin distorting even the best of our intentions. In Philip K. Dick's troubling story *Valis*, we get a picture of our culture on the cusp of a new era:

> As the three of us walked back to the house, Kevin said, "Was all that just quotations from the Bible?"
>
> "No," I said.
>
> "No," David agreed. "There was something new; that part about us being our own gods, now. That the time had come where we no longer had to believe in any deity other than ourselves."

PART FOUR

Abusers of Power
and Wealth

Caesar Redivivus: Better Living Through Secularized Government

"Religion . . . is one of the greatest instruments of morality and civilization which God ever decided to employ."

— ALEXIS DE TOCQUEVILLE (*The European Revolution and Correspondence with Gobineau*)

"A kind of perverse theocracy . . . seemed to be encouraged even by the implacable Church-haters."

— LESZEK KOLAKOWSKI (citing Machiavelli, Hobbes, Spinoza, and Montesquieu in *Modernity on Endless Trial*, 1990)[1]

THE CHAFEE WHO STOLE CHRISTMAS

Maverick Rhode Island governor Lincoln Chafee (b. 1953) angered many, but surprised no one, when he renamed the state Christmas tree a "holiday" tree. While a Republican senator, he refused to defend traditional marriage, ban partial-birth abortion, or even vote for fellow Republican George W. Bush. Once governor, he decriminalized marijuana on his inauguration day. Chafee even refused to attend Episcopalian services in order to keep church and state separate. The Anglican vestryman, known as the "Father of the Country," George Washington was not as careful as the governor and recklessly proclaimed days of prayer and fasting, invoked "divine providence," and left the new republic some scandalous wisdom in his Farewell Address (1789): "Of all the dispositions and habits, which lead to political prosperity, Religion and Morality are *indispensable* supports."[2] More progressive than thou, Chafee and his political kin have evolved beyond these quaint pieties.

"Do you understand how some people feel as though you have somehow negated their traditions?" asked a reporter. Chafee grinned: "Yes, you are absolutely right. People against gay rights or [against accepting] immigrants." And then, "digging" some Bob Dylan, he pronounced: "*They don't want to believe the times are changing*."[3]

There you have it. The old Christmas tree was demoted for a vision of social progress that belittles those who cling to Christmas and oppose redefining marriage. This "progressive" Chafeevision is shared by many entertainers, business leaders, academicians, and officeholders, including President Barak Obama, who deputized Chafee as a campaign surrogate in 2012. Behind it is John Fitzgerald Kennedy's (JFK's) secularist hope: "All men's problems were created by man, and can be solved by man."[4] In short, man is the measure of all things; this world is the end of all things. Make the most of it. Beneath these politics, the cultural tectonic plates are shifting: Christianity is again colliding with "optimistic evolutionary humanism," or "evolutionism."[5]

CULTURE CLASH

No intellectual figure dominated American "progressive" education and democratic humanism[6] in the first half of the 20th century more than John Dewey (1859-1952). At the time of his death, historian Hilda Neatby (1904-1975) wrote, "Dewey has been to our age what Aristotle was to the later Middle Ages, not a philosopher, but *the* philosopher."[7] Dewey celebrated the new social sciences with their promise of social planning rather than frontier-style individualism.[8] He tried to unite "individual self-realization and freedom, democratic social reconstruction, and the scientific search for practical truth including moral values."[9] No American better typifies the cultural, intellectual, and social transition from the 19th to the 20th century.

Born the year that Darwin's *On the Origin of Species* was published (1859), Dewey expected evolution to "transform . . . knowledge, and hence the treatment of morals, politics, and religion."[10] He discarded the "familiar furniture of the mind [that] rested on the [2,000-year] assumption of the superiority of the fixed and final."[11] Nothing was fixed and final. Everything was in flux. Change was the only constant.

Once an active Congregationalist, Dewey's mature philosophy, after 1894, explicitly rejected Christianity:[12]

- There is no divine, purposeful creation.
- There is no revelation. God, if he exists at all, hasn't communicated any reliable norms concerning the ordering of our lives together.
- There is no law of God or nature that establishes any moral boundaries. Morality is a function of evolutionary adaptation or a cultural invention.
- There is no fixed or stable human nature. The human being is an unfinished, incomplete process whose future is plastic.[13]

Dewey claimed to be a "scientific" thinker whose view of politics and social theory was "religiously-neutral." But neutrality is impossible since "political judgments are inevitably permeated with moral and religious assumptions."[14] Dewey holds particular views of ultimate reality, the good, the true, and the beautiful just as certainly as Thomas Aquinas does. To govern requires answering fundamentally religio-philosophical questions like: What is liberty? What is right and good? What are human beings for? Is the state interested in good men or only good citizens? These cannot be settled with appeals to "science."

While church and state must be institutionally separated, the ideas of religion and politics cannot be isolated from one another. History demonstrates that they are distinct, but not separable. For instance, Carl Becker's *The Heavenly City of the Eighteenth Century Philosophers* (1932/2005) shows that the vision of the future society held by the secular Enlightenment was not religiously neutral. The Enlightenment "demolished the Heavenly City of St. Augustine only to rebuild it with more up-to-date materials."[15] Progress replaces providence, the revolution replaces the apocalypse, and Christ's saving blood is replaced by the sacrificial victims of the revolutionary violence that brings in the "kingdom."[16] Nineteenth-century philosophers also had their "heavenly city." Liberal Protestant millennialists falsely taught that Christianity would perfect the world *before* Christ's return.[17] So-called secularists followed suit, only without Christ. "[Dewey's] vision of a progressively and transcendently realized liberal society invested early twentieth-century liberalism with the powerful cultural legacy of Protestant millennialism."[18]

When we construct a government, we must answer fundamentally religious questions, since that is the way existence is ordered. Human beings are religiously wired and will be guided by some "ultimate concern."[19] They will make moral judgments. They will create. They will seek and find meaning.[20] They will seek the good, even eternal, life. As theologian and missionary Lesslie Newbigin (1909-1998) wrote after a long lifetime of cross-cultural communication on "religious" matters: "No state can be completely secular in the sense that those who exercise power have no beliefs about what is true and no commitments to what they believe to be right." The Christian demands more. "It is the duty of the church to ask what those beliefs and commitments are and to expose them to the light of the gospel."[21] Let's try.

DIFFERENT ASSUMPTIONS GIVE POLITICS A DIFFERENT MEANING

Western political thought always assumed human beings possessed a fixed nature. Evolutionism changes that. We are in process, in flux; a verb, not a noun; a process, not a product. What does it mean to govern a self which is unfinished and in flux? If there are no "designed natures and no intrinsic purposes, where do we find any natural duties that we are obligated to obey?"[22] Dewey held that "an individual is nothing fixed, given, ready-made. [He is] something achieved, . . . with the aid and support of . . . economic, legal and political institutions as well as science and art. . . ."[23] *In the absence of God or a purposeful Nature, the unfinished human has only himself or the state to fashion his formation and fulfillment. Only the state has the "power" to accomplish that task for society at large.*

TRANSFORMING THE HUMAN: HUMANIST AND CATHOLIC

Dewey saw each human person in formation. In contrast, today's evolutionary humanists see the entire human species in formation. They continue garnering respect. Princeton philosopher Peter

Singer, known for his animal-rights advocacy, now supports Transhumanist geneticist Aubrey de Grey's radical anti-aging agenda.[24] Ray Kurzweil's Singularity Institute partners with the CEO of Google.[25] Dewey's generation posed democratic education as the instrument of personal transformation. Today's Transhumanists are far more ambitious. Biotechnology is their mechanism for transformation of the entire species.[26]

Catholics and humanists agree that the present state of human beings is less than ideal. Dewey championed democracy as an ethical ideal to replace Christianity and the Church.[27] He expected to "scientifically" engineer moral as well as political progress.[28] Christians also favor democracy.[29] But where Dewey and the later Transhumanists practice *democratic idealism*, Christians who believe in the Fall and the perversity of the human heart, practice *democratic realism*.[30] Rather than using democracy to perfect humanity and bring in secular utopia, Christians praise democracy as a way of protecting humanity from concentrations of power in too few hands.

Christians also see humanity as fallen, a marred masterpiece needing restoration to its original purpose. For centuries, the redemption of the person has been the work of the Catholic Church. Eucharist, penance, fasting, prayer, and the spiritual and sacramental disciplines are the Church's "technology" to cultivate the virtues. We strive for purity of heart and develop "eyes to see" in hope of seeing God once again.[31] The evolutionary humanist, on the other hand, doesn't believe there was any original masterpiece. We are nature's botched draft that must be scrapped in order to create a new species.

Christians and humanists also disagree about the reality and extent of "sin."

Christians believe that "sin — humanity's inescapable tendency to pervert and destroy even its best achievements"[32] — not lack of education, is the primary problem. Only grace — not artificial intelligence, nanotechnology, free elections, or well-crafted constitutions — can shake sin loose. Catholics object to the humanist agendas because they propose a political or technological solution to what is, first of all, a moral, spiritual problem. In Christianity, death is the rotten fruit of moral disobedience and self-centeredness, not the inevitable limitation of biology.

Transhumanists seem unaware that our technological power will continue to be great, but it is never pure — i.e., "never characterized by singularity of purpose in pursuit of the good." Their ambition eases into Nietzsche's vision of an enhanced "master race, masters of the earth . . . a new, tremendous aristocracy" who will "employ democratic Europe as their most pliant and supple instrument . . . so as to work as artists upon 'man' himself."[33]

THE PROGRESSIVE AGENDA

- A rigidly secular state[34] is included because "religion's failure to help people in this process of development is an obvious fact" and "a society of the faithful will be a society of sheep."[35]
- Individual rights are to be expanded as long as other individuals are not directly harmed.[36]
- Beyond the Bill of Rights' "freedom rights" is a "second bill of rights,"[37] including "benefit rights" like education, housing, and even a guaranteed minimum income.[38]

Consequently, we will see

- a growing regulatory state in order to promote a healthful environment, safe products, universal access to health care, and to increasingly eliminate systemic risk in the markets.[39]

Better living through secularized government extends the progressive tradition of Teddy Roosevelt's *Square Deal* through Lyndon Johnson's *Great Society*. Like Woodrow Wilson's *New Freedom*[40] and JFK's *New Frontier*, it seeks to use "every means . . . by which **society may be perfected through the instrumentality of government.**"[41]

THE STATE REPLACES THE CHURCH AS MORAL AUTHORITY

Often, the king, the emperor, the party — i.e., the state — has been the primary source of social morality. Through American history, however, families and churches formed the "nurseries of virtue" that served as the nation's moral compass. Today, however, even private philanthropists like Ted Turner and Bill and Melinda Gates make super contributions[42] that enhance the moral status of public, governmental organizations. Social morality is increasingly placed upon a secular foundation and auspices.

This is unprecedented for, in America, religious faith normally plays the central role in social crises like slavery, prohibition, anti-communism, civil rights, and abortion. As Fr. Richard John Neuhaus pointed out: "There are no a-religious moral traditions of public force in American life. . . . Among the American people, religion and morality are conjoined. Religion in our popular life is the morality-bearing part of culture, and in that sense the heart of culture."[43] Is that changing? Churches and synagogues no longer command respect as the "soul of the nation." Note these examples where the state judges the church's morality inferior, interfering with its social aims:

- The Justice Department admitted that "the [Catholic] bishops have been 'resoundingly successful in increasing assistance to victims of [human] trafficking.'"[44] Yet because the Catholic Church, for moral reasons, did not provide contraceptives, abortion, or sterilization, the federal government refused to work with the bishops protecting victims of human trafficking.[45]
- Illinois discontinued its partnership with the highly respected Catholic Charities/Social Services in various dioceses because they would not release adoptive children to unmarried couples, same-sex or heterosexual.
- In April 2008, Crystal Dixon, an African-American associate vice president for human resources at the University of Toledo, was fired for a column in the *Toledo Free Press*. She objected to calling homosexuals "civil-rights victims." She signed it as a private citizen. Nevertheless, she was fired for "the public position you have taken in the *Toledo Free Press*." Apparently, Christians, like Dixon, can't hold managerial positions at public universities[46] where diversity devolves to gender and skin pigmentation but not point of view.

• Nor is preaching sacrosanct. In 2005, Bishop Fred Henry was hauled before the Alberta Human Rights Tribunal. His offense? A simple pastoral letter on marriage.[47] In Ontario, a parishioner brought her parish before the Human Rights Tribunal for erecting a monument opposing a woman's right to abortion. St. Paul warned Christians against choosing the judgment of Caesar over Christ.[48]

Caesar and Christ

The earliest Christian confession "*Jesus is Lord*" or "*Christ is King*" sounds strange to our ears. Americans don't do kings or lords. But for Paul, these were fighting words.[49] The cult of the emperor was the social glue holding the diverse, tolerant Roman Empire together. Every conquered people's gods were welcome in Rome's pantheon. One emperor even placed a Jesus figurine in his household shrine. The empire could tolerate all religions just because it was inflexible about something above religion: the veneration of the emperor, which was the cohesive force keeping the empire from disintegrating.[50] "Caesar is Lord" was the password to imperial unity. "Jesus is Lord" directly contradicted it. Caesar wasn't the supreme organizing principle for Christian lives. He was not Lord; Jesus was.[51] The earliest Christians weren't persecuted for "religious reasons" but instead for challenging who held the world together.[52]

Modern regimes still threaten citizens with higher allegiances. "In China today, Christianity is experiencing an ongoing campaign by the Communist regime to bring religious belief in general, and Christian belief in particular, under control. Numerous Chinese Christians have been martyred."[53] We expect that from communist regimes, but France? In December 2012, French President François Hollande announced the "National Observatory of Secularism" to promote state secularism and "formulate propositions for the transmission of 'public morality'" in the schools. The state will monitor a Catholic-oriented group working for the "establishment of the social Kingship of Christ."[54] Apparently "Jesus is Lord" or "Christ is King" still threatens the social organization of France.[55] Secularism is not neutral; it is a jealous creed.

WILL CAESAR BE ORWELL'S BIG BROTHER OR HUXLEY'S WORLD CONTROLLER?

In 1984, Orwell's *1984* was nowhere in America or Western Europe. But the other great anti-utopia of the 20th century, Aldous Huxley's *Brave New World* (1932), was alive and well.

"What Orwell feared," Neil Postman wrote, "were those who would ban books. What Huxley feared was that there would be no reason to ban a book, for there would be no one who wanted to read one. Orwell feared those who would deprive us of information. Huxley feared those who would give us so much that we would be reduced to passivity and egoism. Orwell feared that the truth would be concealed from us. Huxley feared the truth would be drowned in a sea of irrelevance. Orwell feared we would become a captive culture. Huxley feared we would become a trivial culture. . . ."[56] Orwell's society controlled by inflicting pain; Huxley's by inflicting pleasure. Orwell gave us "Big Brother," an external oppressor. Huxley showed us how we would come to love our oppressor.

When America's Caesar emerges, I suspect, he will take his cues from Huxley, not Orwell. *A culture that has become a burlesque can seduce us into forgetting Christ before a prison culture can coerce us into renouncing him.* "When a population becomes distracted by trivia, when cultural life is redefined as a perpetual round of entertainments, when serious public conversation becomes a form of baby-talk, when, in short, a people become an audience and their public business a vaudeville act, then a nation finds itself at risk; culture-death is a clear possibility."[57]

Big Brother controls most effectively, not by watching us, but by ensuring that we enjoy watching him. Lives of perpetual entertainment, easy access to mood enhancers, three squares a day (plus munchies), undemanding employment, and erotic encounters on demand create a sedate political constituency that remains uncurious, conformist-demanding "bread and circuses."[58] How close are we? Americans aged 12 and older with Internet access now spend 6.1 hours daily with video-based entertainment, up from 4.6 in 1996.[59] NFL players' and teachers' salaries illustrate how we value amusement above learning, entertainment above exposition.

Prescription opioid pain relievers (Huxley's "soma"?) increased 402 percent between 1997 to 2007.[60] Our extravagant expectations feed fantasies that can't be realized any more than salt water can quench thirst.[61] We expect more and enjoy less.

Secularists accuse religious people of shackling their minds and being easily led. No, these children of indulgence are the shrunken selves of our society, forming a voting bloc of sheep easily sheared. The civil authorities can "manufacture consent,"[62] exploiting the passivity of these citizens whose "god is the belly."[63]

Where We Are Today: The God Gap

Election 2012's most serious demographic gap was the God gap. Of those who attend religious services more than once a week, 63 percent voted for Romney, 36 percent for Obama. Of those who never attend religious services, 62 percent voted for Obama, 34 percent for Romney.[64] Why?

America is becoming increasingly divided over God and the human person. On one side are those who accept human life as a finished product, divinely created, possessing inalienable rights and dignity.[65] We aren't awaiting a major renovation before we respect human nature as pretty much fixed and stable.

On the other side are those who regard the human project as a purely naturalistic product of undirected, blind evolution. *Homo sapiens* stands midway between *homo erectus* and *homo* _____ (i.e., whatever he is going to be). These two worldviews stand in complete antithesis to one another not only in philosophical content but in their natural results — i.e., the sociological and governmental results that flow from them, including law, governance, and statecraft.

How Ought We to Order Our Lives Together?

Long before the rise of the modern nation-state, Aristotle posed his first political question: "How ought we to order our lives together?" My first question upon hearing this was, "Who is the *we*?" The tribe, the family, the empire, the polis, the nation-state? What assemblage of persons makes up our primary "we."

For Catholics, it is "the baptized." We constitute a body, a people, "a holy nation."[66] When Christ bids us to come and follow him, we may leave father, mother, sister, brother, nation, race, wealth, fame, etc. His call supersedes all our earthly obligations, including party loyalty. We are not ultimately liberals or conservatives, Democrats or Republicans; we are supposedly "Catholics."

In the 2012 election, 40 percent of Mass-attending Catholics voted for President Obama, a self-identified *champion* of two intrinsic evils: abortion, including partial-birth abortion, and the redefinition of marriage.[67] Most elections don't permit of such black-and-white assessments.[68] The U.S. bishops teach, "A Catholic cannot vote for a candidate who takes a position in favor of an intrinsic evil, such as abortion or racism, if the voter's intent is to support that position."[69]

In this case, however, Bishop Thomas Paprocki of Springfield, Illinois, concluded without qualification: "A vote for a candidate who promotes actions or behaviors that are intrinsically evil and gravely sinful makes you morally complicit and places the eternal salvation of your own soul in serious jeopardy."[70] Clearly, our own house is not in order. When the Church is so compromised that it fails to serve as a counter community forming a counter culture based on counter values and telling a counter story, we jeopardize our own salvation and our nation's well-being. Our problem isn't in Washington; it's in our parishes. Only if we first build the Church, can we, will we, bless the nation. It's happened before.

In 1927, premier jurist Oliver Wendell Holmes wrote in *Buck v. Bell* (1927) that Virginia could forcibly sterilize 21-year-old Carrie Buck because "three generations of imbeciles is enough."[71] Afterward, new state laws led to 65,000 mandatory sterilizations.[72] Catholics and Biblicist Protestants resisted.[73] When the Church is instructed and united, the innocent are protected against Caesar. As Fr. Neuhaus put it: "Of all the institutions in society, only religion can invoke against the state a transcendent authority and have its invocation seconded by '*the people*' to whom a democratic state is presumably accountable."[74] This is why the vote of "the peculiar people" remains important.

VOTING FOR CHRIST THE KING

Many Catholics thoughtlessly boast that their faith doesn't influence their vote. What a pitiful evasion of adult spirituality. In a representative democracy, Christ speaks through us. He is not indifferent to the plight of the poor, religious liberty, war and peace, the unborn, marriage, and so on. What he teaches about the world, humanity, and freedom helps both church and state to order our lives together.

For Catholics, *the world* is not a chaos of undirected, purpose-less forces in desperate need of state power, a *Leviathan*,[75] to impose order.

For Catholics, *humanity* bears God's image. For this reason, Catholics have a special identification with the weak, the poor, the powerless, the alien, and the oppressed for whom Christ died. They are not the unfinished product of blind forces of nature. Don't these differences make for different policies?

For Catholics, true *freedom* does what it ought, not merely what it wants. Ordered liberty cultivates excellence and virtue, and this produces a very different social agenda than what emerges when people believe freedom is license to do whatever one wants as long as others aren't directly hurt.

History shows the power of the gospel to transform men and nations. Eighteenth- and 19th-century England avoided violent revolution by renewing the nation's moral landscape through the influential revivals of John Wesley (1703-1791), which began in the 1740s. A late-life Wesleyan convert, William Wilberforce (1759-1833), member of Parliament, portrayed in the feature film *Amazing Grace* (2006), gathered together mostly lay prayer warriors, activists, and philanthropists to form a small group in his parish church of Clapham. Wilberforce and his team went on to abolish the slave trade and "reform the manners" of England.[76] So successful were they that historian of European morals W. H. Lecky ranked the British anti-slavery movement "among the three or four perfectly virtuous pages . . . in the history of nations."[77] As one evangelical apologist and thinker wrote: "Revival is measured by the transformation of human lives and the transformation of culture as a result of those transformed lives."[78] But Wesley did not preach to change politics or culture. He preached to change human hearts and urged the seeking of Christ's Kingdom above Caesar's rule. That was the one thing necessary.

When we seek first his Kingdom, we discover just how accessible and present it is. Christ's promise that the gates of hell won't prevail against his Church has seen a marvelous fulfillment in the last generation. The unpredicted collapse of the Soviet empire and the unpredictable role played by the Bishop of Rome has fascinated Cold War historians. How "coincidental" that the only Polish pope in history arrived at just the right time to support the Polish trade union, Solidarity. As a result, Catholic Poland is the first to start ripping apart the Iron Curtain.[79] The gates of hell did not prevail against the battering ram of the Polish Church. Romania, Czechoslovakia, East Germany, and others followed. In all cases, Christians and Christian institutions played decisive roles.

"Corpses piled high like cords of wood" mark 20th-century Soviet Russia, Nazi Germany, Maoist China, secular Mexico, and Pol Pot's Cambodia. In each case, the state displaced and exiled the church as the "generator and bearer of values." Fr. Neuhaus puts it differently: "In the eyes of the state the dangerous child today is not the child who points out that the emperor has no clothes but the child who sees that the emperor's garments of moral authority have been stolen from the religion he has sent into exile from the public square."[80] Being called "dangerous" by the authorities, young mothers, grandfathers, small-business owners, Catholic sisters, high school valedictorians, and insurance salesmen have a hard time believing that they are a threat. But the authorities are right: we are dangerous, because we know that the nation's Supreme Court is not literally Supreme. Someone reigns over Caesar.

Conflict is inevitable when we obey the rightful King and seek first his Kingdom. Try to avoid the necessary conflicts, and you will end up betraying Christ. On that first Good Friday, at the very moment Jesus was informing Pilate of a kingdom utterly unlike any Pilate had known, Jesus' enemies were gathering for a vote. Pilate, frustrated and wanting out, turned to the mob and proposed an immediate referendum, a show of hands, a renegade vote. Where were Jesus' people? They were gone — afraid, intimidated, tired, confused, wary. Their absence enabled Barabbas to be democratically elected and released as the people's choice.

Ironically, by fleeing conflict, Jesus' friends found the blood of an innocent man on their hands, while Barabbas, the revolutionary, stepped out into the first sunlight he had felt in months. "Curse the Romans, those filthy occupiers," he muttered. "Forget Yahweh, he promises a Messiah, and all we get is an armed Roman occupation." The thought that it was time to leave the old faith and take control of Israel's future bucked him up. Was he playing God? Ha, someone had to. Thoughts of again gathering the Zealots pleased him, and he began humming in Aramaic, "The times they are a-changin'." At that very moment, Caesar unwittingly unveiled the original Catholic crucifix — a brutal, shocking, living display of God's fierce love. God is love, and his times aren't a-changin', for hanging cruciform, with arms outstretched in invitation, is the lover who remains the same yesterday, today, and forever.

OPPONENT #15

Consumerism: Branding the Heart

"Marx may have had it exactly backward. He argued that classes are defined by their means of production. But it could be true that, in the information age at least, classes define themselves by their means of consumption."

— DAVID BROOKS (*Bobos in Paradise*, 2000)[1]

"One of the most striking ways we are trained and reinforced in the consumptive way of life is exactly through a flood of ever-proliferating choices. In 1976, the average American supermarket carried nine thousand products; today it stocks thirty thousand. The typical produce section in 1975 had 65 items; today it stocks 285."

— RODNEY CLAPP (from his article in *Christianity Today*)[2]

"All of us experience the sad effects of blind submission to consumerism. In the first place it represents crass materialism. At the same time it represents a radical dissatisfaction because one quickly — unless one is shielded from the flood of publicity and the ceaseless and tempting offers of products — learns that the more one possesses, the more one wants, while deeper aspirations remain unsatisfied and perhaps even stifled."

— JOHN PAUL II (encyclical letter *Sollicitudo Rei Socialis*, December 30, 1987)[3]

Khao Lak, Thailand, December 26, 2004, 10:30 a.m.: One of the most beautiful women ever photographed is unconscious, bobbing up and down in filthy black water — her bare, bleeding arms wrapped around a palm tree. The searing pain shooting through her carefully sculpted and Midas-insured legs, wrenches her back to consciousness. Waves of oil-slicked, muddied water choked with debris, lap at her body. Almost in mockery, the sky's still-blue brilliance matched her fiancé's eyes. And then, she gagged, startled by the remembrance. She and Simon Atlee, her lover-photographer, were lounging in their vacation bungalow when "a rush of water rose up so suddenly there was not even a second to think, a rush of water that came from all directions, hurtling us out into the furious current. . . . 'Petra!' he screamed. 'Petra! What's happening?' I couldn't answer. . . Then I lost sight of him. Seconds later I saw him again, whirling in the rumbling waters. He was a few yards ahead of me. Behind him a rooftop was sticking out of the water. 'Catch the roof! Catch the roof!' I shouted. Then he was gone. . . . I prayed that he would catch hold. I was sure he would. He was a strong swimmer."[4]

But who is a strong swimmer against a tsunami releasing the energy of 23,000 Hiroshima-type atom bombs? A massive underwater earthquake had unleashed a series of killer waves that sped across the Indian Ocean at the speed of a jet airliner.[5] That morning, the gentleness of her lover's kiss and their nostalgic viewing of *White Christmas* vanished as nature's ferocity cast them and 150,000 other souls into a wide, watery grave. Simon's body was discovered on a Sumatran shore months later. Even the photographer in him wouldn't have released the picture.

After eight more hours, Petra, now cradled by a palm tree, was discovered naked, caked with mud, bleeding internally, and broken. Petra Němcová, 25 years old, first gained supermodel status by gracing the cover of *Sports Illustrated*'s 2003 swimsuit issue.[6] Growing up in a coal-mining district of communist Czechoslovakia, she wasn't groomed to jet set with Donald Trump or Prince Albert of Monaco, wear $20,000 dresses, or be chauffeured in cars once carrying JFK and Marilyn Monroe.

But in a split second, her celebrity now confronted her obituary. Two competing visions of the "good life" wrestled for preeminence. One "good" her fans enjoyed in press releases and would look so shockingly trivial on a gravestone: *"Here lies Petra Němcová, beloved for her long legs, high cheekbones, and gleaming white teeth, she prized exquisite taste in restaurants and punctuality at shoots. 1979-2004. R.I.P."* A second "good" can be heard in the words of Jesus:[7] "No one can serve two masters. . . . You cannot serve God and mammon. Therefore I tell you, do not be anxious about your life, what you shall eat or what you shall drink, nor about your body, what you shall put on. Is not life more than food, and the body more than clothing? . . . For what will it profit a man, if he gains the whole world and forfeits his life? Or what shall a man give in return for his life?"[8]

After Petra's hospitalization and recovery, she told reporters that "she no longer cared about her old life of fashion, fame, and fortune. 'Believe me, it isn't really important,' she said. 'There are so many more important things in the world, like health and love and peace in your soul.'"[9] Petra's reassessment of her responsibilities to the broken world that her industry worked so hard, through the art and science of image and illusion, to ignore is as rare as her beauty. Though she continues modeling to make a living, she thinks very differently about living a life.[10] Petra rearranged her priorities, created and continues to chair the Happy Hearts Fund, a non-profit foundation that has restored hope and opportunity to 41,000 children and 340,000 community members afflicted by natural disasters and who need support after the emergency workers and cameras leave. She is now 34 years old. The fashionistas will no doubt discover and anoint a younger specimen of nubile magnificence. Such is the demand of the "leisure class," who need to be perpetually stimulated to maintain the pursuit of "conspicuous consumption."[11] No need to worry when they do, for the "wretched of the earth" will then rise up and call Petra Němcová blessed.

Our world is in dire need of those who will break format and broadcast a different message: a message of authentic human interaction and care and service for others that helps the world see the truth that human beings image God. The satanic strategy is to so trash and trivialize God's image as to render the existence of God implausible. The aim of that devilish strategy is to kill God in effigy. Those of us practicing the Samaritan strategy strive for the opposite. We continue to expand the circle of love and concern around those for whom we will take responsibility. By signaling the preciousness of the person who images God, we bear witness to God's existence and character. In this chapter, we look at the lure and spell of our consumer culture, how it erodes human dignity, and then look at some tools to break the enchantment.

What Is Consumerism?

"Consumerism" was first defined in the 1960 Oxford English Dictionary as the "emphasis on or preoccupation with the acquisition of consumer goods."[12] Yes, but it is so much more than maxed-out credit cards and spats over family budgets. John Paul II saw that "a given culture reveals its overall understanding of life through the choices it makes in production and consumption. It is here that *the phenomenon of consumerism* arises."[13] Consumerism has a seemingly endless ability to generate wants, produce innumerable competing brands of breakfast cereals and toothpastes, enable 24-hour electronic shopping, extend nearly limitless credit, encourage planned obsolescence, and conveniently dispose of and replace purchases, leading to perpetual repurchasing. Benedict XVI noted that consumerism implies that we can change our condition by convenient commercial transactions. This "wrongly [convinces the person] that he is the sole author of himself, his life and society."[14] Psychologists also note that irrational purchases often accompany manic disorders, and that compulsive shopping/spending mimics addictive behavior.[15]

For British Green Party radical Jonathan Porrit (b. 1950),[16] consumerism is

> the idea that we should all, actively, be consuming more and more every year and that this is the best measure of economic progress. Consumerism puts consumption at the very heart of the modern economy and everything is done to persuade us to go and consume more — advertising hoardings, billboards, newspapers, magazines and TV. We are bombarded day in and day out by these advertising messages. You may think they're all selling you something different, different products, different brands, but at the same time they're selling you one big idea; that the more we consume, the better our lives will be.[17]

CONSUMERISM AND ITS PATHOLOGIES

Consumerism is the life orientation that human fulfillment is to be found in our purchases. That is the fundamental lie. Lies lead to breaks with reality. Breaks with reality lead to pathologies. Consumerism abounds with them:

- Consumerism arrests our development and keeps us children by continually weakening impulse control. Chief Rabbi of the United Hebrew Congregations of the Commonwealth, Jonathan Sacks, summarized the psychological research for the Pontifical Gregorian University: "We know . . . children with strong impulse control grow to be better adjusted, more dependable, achieve higher grades in school and college and have more success in their careers than others. Success depends on the ability to delay gratification, which is precisely what a consumerist culture undermines. At every stage, the emphasis is on the instant gratification of instinct. In the words of the pop group Queen, 'I want it all and I want it now.' A whole culture is being infantilised."[18]

- Consumerism bypasses rationality, manipulates emotions, and conflates wants and needs, making responsible stewardship more difficult. John Paul II warned: "If direct appeal is made to [man's] instincts — while ignoring the reality of the person as intelligent and free — then *consumer attitudes* and *life-styles* can be created which are objectively improper and often damaging to his physical and spiritual health."[19] Isn't this, however, the work of modern "neuromarketing"?[20] Former vice president of marketing for Starbucks, Scott Bedbury, admits that "consumers don't truly believe there's a huge difference between products, so to sell a $4 cup of coffee the real goal is to establish emotional ties."[21]

- Consumerism promises more than it can deliver, thereby increasing pessimism about life's outcomes. Psychologists David Myers and Ed Diene, discovered that "people have not become happier over time as their cultures have become more affluent. Indeed, in most nations, the correlation between income and happiness is negligible — only in the poorest countries, such as Bangladesh and India, is income a good measure of emotional well-being."[22]

• Consumerism creates the illusion that community and spirituality can be had by commercial means. Howard Schulz, the founder of Starbucks, says what his company actually sells is "the romance of the coffee experience, the feeling of warmth and community people get in Starbucks stores."[23]

• Consumerism reduces persons to products. It manufactures them as celebrities, a cheap substitute for heroes. "Shakespeare, in the familiar lines, divided great men into three classes: those born great, those who achieved greatness, and those who had greatness thrust upon them. It never occurred to him to mention those who hired public relations experts and press secretaries to make themselves look great. . . . Our power to fill our minds with more and more 'big names' has increased our demand for Big Names and our willingness to confuse the Big Name with the Big Man. Again mistaking our powers for our necessities, we have filled our world with artificial fame."[24]

• Consumerism obscures that we have "a billion desperately poor neighbors . . . another two billion struggle in near poverty with very little hope for a decent life. . . . Hundreds of biblical texts tell us that God still measures our societies by what we do to the poorest. Jesus' words still remind those with abundance that if they do not feed the hungry and clothe the naked, they go to hell."[25] Consumerism does its best to ignore these social realities and these truths of divine revelation by tempting us to spend disproportionately on ourselves. Writer Chuck Palahniuk (b. 1962), *Fight Club*, describes it: "We're consumers. We are by-products of a lifestyle obsession. Murder, crime, poverty, these things don't concern me. What concerns me are celebrity magazines, television with 500 channels, some guy's name on my underwear. Rogaine, Viagra, Olestra. . . ."[26] This attitude deprives the poor and hungry of justice and makes a mockery of Catholic teaching on the "universal destination of goods,"[27] the corporal works of mercy, the problem of structural evil and injustice, the basic responsibility Catholics have to love, serve, confront, admonish, encourage, pray for, and bear one another's burdens, including those of the hungry, the poor, and the diseased.

• Consumerism encourages the illusion of limitlessness. This undermines responsible stewardship of God's creation for which we all bear responsibility. John Paul II warned: "Using [our natural resources] as if they are inexhaustible endangers their availability not only for the present generation but for generations to come. . . . [The] earth and its atmosphere are telling us that there is an order in the universe which must be respected. The human person has a grave responsibility to preserve the order for the well-being of future generations."[28]

How Big a Problem Is It?

In short, consumerism affects the language, visual culture, urban architecture, and educational objectives of our entire culture. Ad expert James B. Twitchell[29] observes that "commercial speech — advertising — *makes up most of what we share as a culture.* No one is happy about this, not even the people who make it. They call it clutter, which is rather like a doctor complaining about a frantic patient after he has shot him full of adrenaline."[30] The marketers are relentless. David Lubars, a senior ad executive in the Omnicom Group, "jokes" that consumers "are like roaches — you spray them and spray them and they get immune after a while."[31] The answer? Spray more! Bob Garfield at *Advertising Age* magazine doesn't even like it:

> You cannot walk down the street without being bombarded. You stand in an elevator looking at advertising in the corner of the elevator car. And you go to play golf and you go to pick the ball up out of the cup, and there's an ad in the bottom of it. And you look up at the sky, and there's skywriting. And you look at a bus passing, and there's advertising. And you walk in Times Square and you go, "Is this Las Vegas on the Hudson? Am I entrapped inside a pinball machine?"[32]

In 1915, my Austrian grandfather — in either Vienna, which he left, or New Haven, Connecticut, his new hometown — would see only one or two advertisements in a week. Today, the American Association of Advertising Agencies estimates that the typical American is subjected to three thousand commercial ad impressions each day.[33] We all swim in this cultural sea, no more conscious of our all-encompassing environment than a fish is of water.

How acclimated to consumerism are we? Did you know that marketing to children from ancient times until recently has been considered a form of molestation? The Code of Hammurabi (c. 1772 B.C.) prohibited entering into contracts with children under penalty of death. At the end of the first century A.D., do you think the author of the *Didache* would have built a mutual fund portfolio? "Never turn away the needy; share all your possessions with your brother, and do not claim that anything is your own."[34] Did you know that the great St. Augustine, arguably one of the five most influential thinkers in the history of Western civilization, flatly declared, "Business is in itself an evil," and that St. Jerome suspected that "a man who is a merchant can seldom, if ever, please God"?[35] Did you know that the charging of interest was once considered sinful and forbidden by the Church?[36] Or that the Scholastic theologians struggled to determine a "just" price.[37] And "just" didn't mean "just" what the market would bear.

Rather than engaging their conversation and questioning our own culture's assumptions, we tend to ignore them because they didn't swim in the same waters we inhabit. That's true. They did, however, understand their cultural pool, and we, by some effort, can understand both. In a world of runaway consumer debt, shopping addictions, 24-hour shopping channels, and a nation that spends more on pet food than on foreign missionary enterprises — in which every second teenager is considering how to parlay his YouTube account into an audition, and when brands like Nike and Starbucks compete for spiritual allegiances with the Catholic Church — maybe they saw something we haven't.

Not only has consumerism dominated our language and pop-cultural environment, but our skylines also reflect massive social changes. The late art historian Kenneth Clark (1903-1983), after a lifetime of art criticism, opened his documentary series, *Civilization* (1969), by pointing out that "one could tell more about a civilization from its architecture than from anything else it leaves behind. Painting and literature depend largely on unpredictable individuals. But architecture is to some extent a communal art — at least it depends upon a relationship between the user and the maker much closer than in the other arts."[38] If so, what do we learn about changes in our skylines over the last few centuries? Since at least the 14th century, churches and cathedrals were the focal points of towns, villages, and cities.[39] Into the late 19th and early 20th centuries, the cathedral could often be seen for miles from outside the city. Within the city, the cathedral often occupied the center of the town square and served as the pulse of the community.

What type of buildings dominates our skylines today? Which serve as hubs of our urban centers? London's tallest buildings are the Willis Building and the National Westminster Tower 42, an insurance company and bank, respectively. In New York, One World Trade Center will be the tallest building in the Western Hemisphere when completed in 2013.[40] With the renaming of Chicago's Sears Tower as the Willis Building, Fr. Robert Barron points out, it now appears that three of the four tallest buildings in Chicago are all named for, and owned by, insurance companies and one by a bank.[41] Is this ironic? Increased anxiety accompanies increased affluence, and so we are compelled to spend more on insurance to feel less vulnerable and more secure.[42]

Even our image of liberal learning and the aims of education have been changed radically. In the 1990s, incoming college students began answering an old question in a new way. For years, they were asked what they expected to get out of their college education. The answers varied. Most of the time it had to do with mastery of a subject, hope of making a new discovery, broadening their perspective, or being equipped to serve other people. The new dominant answer became "To make more money." John Paul II acknowledged that "it is not wrong to want to live better; what is wrong is a style of life which is presumed to be better when it is directed towards 'having' rather than 'being.' "[43] These incoming students are vulnerable to Emile Gauvreau's biting words: "I was part of that strange race of people aptly described as spending their lives doing things they detest, to make money they don't want, to buy things they don't need, to impress people they don't like."[44]

How Does This "Branding of the Heart" Work?[45]

In the late 19th and early 20th centuries, advertising changed. Earlier ad campaigns were built around new technologies or inventions, and they largely delivered product-information bulletins. Conveying information soon took a back seat to building an appealing image around a particular logo and brand-name version of a product. Why the change? Mass production of soaps, beers, cigarettes, cereals, flour, washers, and widgets meant that manufacturers could not distinguish their products from one another in the marketplace. The local shopkeeper who once could be trusted to stand behind the flour and rice he would scoop out of his barrels was being replaced by Aunt Jemima and Uncle Ben. Image advertising would flourish from the demand to produce *apparent* distinctions between products that had no real performance differential.

These invented "corporate personalities" could speak directly to consumers. In the early 1920s, legendary adman Bruce Barton turned General Motors into a metaphor for the American family, "something personal, warm and human," while GE was not so much the name of faceless General Electric Company as, in Barton's words, "the initials of a friend."[46] The emotional appeal of products grew. How else to explain the legendary Marlboro Man, the longest-running ad campaign in history (1954-1999)? He was such an embodiment of the brand that, in time, he needn't even hold a cigarette. What was he doing after all? Was he stalking game? Exercising? Thinking of a lost love? Fasting in the wilderness? The ambiguity of the image was part of the magic. One could project, as with certain types of political candidates, one's own impressions and hopes upon the image. If handled correctly, the image could even embody the contradictory and the impossible. For instance, Marlboro Man was enjoying robust health among the mountains and the plains, inhaling all that fresh air apparently to offset the cancerous vapors he was selling through his mighty man persona.[47] As a boy, I remember watching Miss Rheingold sing, "My beer is Rheingold, the dry beer." That it was impossible for a woman with that kind of figure to be much of a beer drinker didn't seem to bother anyone.

In the 1980s, "the product" began to recede into the background, and people were no longer buying sneakers, beer, or moisturizing cream but instead lifestyles, personal signature statements, meaning systems. The degree of emotional investment people began to feel in the brands with which they identified bordered on the spiritual and, in some instances, pathological. The stories grew tragically bizarre.

Michael Thomas' grandmother warned him: "Don't wear those shoes to school. You know somebody might like them and just take them." Was she kidding? These were no ordinary shoes or sneakers. These were Nike's Air Jordans. You don't just like them. They were to die for. Michael knew that strutting into class with his blue jeans tightly rolled up around the ankle so the $110 high-tops were fully exposed would bring his classmates to their knees. These weren't mere shoes; they were a revelation awakening his peers to his real identity. They told people how they should think of him. By wearing those shoes, he was participating in the legend of Jordan. The wearer expected homage. How could she, how could anyone, expect 15-year-old Michael to not wear his Air Jordans to school? So Michael assured his grandmother, "Granny, before I let anyone take those shoes, they'll have to kill me." Two weeks later, his 17-year-old basketball partner strangled Michael to death and ran off with those coveted athletic shoes bearing a Nike logo. He must have thought his flight could match the magic depicted by the silhouetted Michael Jordan soaring, his basketball palmed and hoisted, his legs spread in magical stride. One fan described the logo as "an almost angelic symbol: Sport mixed with divinity."[48] That seemed fitting for gym shoes said to evoke "something larger than athletics, and perhaps life itself."[49]

Police Lt. Thomas Malacek investigates these apparently senseless crimes. In 1990, he said: "It's becoming a growing problem, because apparently these items have a lot more identity value than in the past."[50] Nike has worked hard to link power, success, and status to its brand. Sociologist Elijah Anderson argues that many urban youth lack the means to acquire robust, healthy identities. Instead, "they value these 'emblems,' these symbols of supposed success. The gold, the shoes, the drug dealer's outfit."[51] Nike certainly never intended this when "nurturing relevant emotional ties between the Nike brand and the consumer." But maybe these murders aren't so senseless after all. The murderers seem to have a sense of values. Journalist Skye Jethani grimly notes, "After all, no one has been murdered for a pair of Keds."[52]

Naomi Klein's *No Logo* argues that by the early 1990s, the super brands — like Nike, Starbucks, and the Body Shop — were engaging in a kind of pseudo-spiritual marketing, providing belief, shaping behavior, and creating a sense of belonging to a community open to new initiates for the simple purchase of a product. "Nike said that they were about the meaning of sports, but more than that, that they were about transcendence through sports. Starbucks said that they were about the idea of community, of place — that is, a third place that is not home, not work. Benetton was, of course, selling multiculturalism, racial diversity."[53] Disney became the essence of family. The Body Shop was marketing environmentalism. "So brands started filling a gap that citizens, not just consumers, used to get elsewhere, whether from religion, whether from a sense of belonging in their community."[54] But there was something illusory about this. Klein points out, "Nobody was actually selling what they were selling."

Douglas Rushkoff's documentary *The Persuaders* takes us to school: "This lesson — that a brand could forge an emotional, even spiritual bond with today's cynical consumer — wasn't lost on corporate America."[55] Douglas Atkin, an expert on the relationship between consumers and brands, used to be brand manager at Proctor and Gamble. In the old days, he had to "make sure the product was good, develop new advertising copy, design the pack." Today, "the brand manager has an entirely different kind of responsibility . . . to create and maintain a whole meaning system for people, through which they get identity and understanding of the world."[56]

Atkin remembers his moment of epiphany:

> I was in a research facility watching eight people rhapsodize about a sneaker. And I thought, "Where is this coming from? This is, at the end of the day, a piece of footwear." But the terms they were using were evangelical. So I thought, if these people are expressing cult-like devotion, then why not study cults? Why not study the original? Find out why people join cults and apply that knowledge to brands. And the conclusion was this, is that people, whether they're joining a cult or joining a brand, do so for exactly the same reasons. They need to belong, and they want to make meaning. We need to figure out what the world is all about, and we need the company of others. It's simply that.[57]

All we wanted to do was distinguish soaps from one another. How did we end up with a multibillion-dollar industry churning out illusions, generating wants, promising us the world remade in the interest of our appetites, increasing our consumer choices beyond anything the world has ever seen. (In 1976, American grocery stores carried 9,000 items; now they carry 30,000.) But worse, commercially driven meaning systems that function as counterfeit spiritualities require belief, codes of behavior, and a rite for belonging. Believing a lie leads to bondage, even if it comes from golden handcuffs.

FAITHFUL WITNESS IN THE AGE OF THE CONSUMER

So in the face of this unusual, largely non-ideological opponent, do Catholics offer a different way of life? Yes. Here are a just a few tools we have to bear witness to the Kingdom of Christ in a world more interested in Disney's Magic Kingdom.

1. The Sabbath Principle

The Sabbath offers an antidote to consumerism. "Sabbath, in the first instance, is not about worship. It is about work stoppage. It is about withdrawal from the anxiety system of Pharaoh, the refusal to let one's life be defined by production and consumption and the endless pursuit of private well-being."[58] Work, of course, is stopped *in pursuit of worship*, even in the Exodus story. "He who wants to enter the holiness of the day must first lay down the profanity of chattering commerce . . . and fury of acquisitiveness."[59] In contrast to this "fury of acquisitiveness," Benedict XVI urges us to recover "the astonishing experience of gift. . . . Man is wrongly convinced that he is the sole author of himself, his life and society."[60]

Observing the Sabbath, the Lord's Day, testifies that we did not create ourselves. Time is not our own. Matter is not our own. Even energy is not our own. We are dependent creatures, not Atlas shouldering the world. Sabbath rest trains us to stop, receive life's gift as grace, recover wonder and awe, rediscover the sacred, and refuse the profane. To that end:

- We cease from buying and selling — i.e., laboring to acquire as though we could secure our well-being apart from the grace of God.
- We cease ranking and comparing our "consumption" status with our fellow worshippers.
- We remember that we were created as friends of the God who made heaven and earth and not as slaves in Egypt. We were created to be something long before we were to have anything.
- We take the time to savor more so we might consume less. Nutritionists tell us to chew more, if we want to eat less. So, too, when it comes to using the things of this earth. So much of our consumption is done in a rush. If we enjoy more, we will guzzle less.
- We steward our resources better in order to share what we have received. "If we truly enjoyed eating more, we would want to share more."[61]

2. Know Pain, Know Gain. Learning Contentment Through Suffering

St. James begins his letter with a paradox: "Count it all *joy*, my brethren, when you meet various *trials*."[62] Rejoice — don't lament, don't wallow in self-pity — because the painful trial will refine your faith so that "you may be perfect and complete, lacking in nothing." We find true contentment — lacking nothing — in the midst of those everyday trials we don't choose: what James calls the "trial of suffering." When we recognize and embrace a trial of suffering and pursue it according to God's will, we mature to the "discipline of suffering." This is the mind of Jesus in Gethsemane. He turns what he didn't immediately choose into that which he embraced as God's will. Do our immediate desires conflict with God's will? Yes. Confess it, acknowledge it as Jesus did. "My Father, if it be possible, let this cup pass from me." When we say, "nevertheless, not as I will, but as you will,"[63] the Spirit of Christ is in us, surrendering our immediate desires in hope of a greater good. Like Jesus, we embrace the cross for the joy set before us because we have given little to gain eternity.[64]

The Kingdom of heaven is like a treasure hidden in a field.[65] When a man comes upon it, he joyfully sells everything he has and buys the field. This is not irrational or against our nature. Any rational person would release something of little value to gain something of greater value. As C. S. Lewis put it: "We are half-hearted creatures, fooling about with drink and sex and ambition when infinite joy is offered us, like an ignorant child who wants to go on making mud pies in a slum because he cannot imagine what is meant by the offer of a holiday at the sea. We are far too easily pleased."[66] We desire what won't endure because our desire for the eternal is weak. Our desires are not too strong; they are too feeble.

We need to recover this hunger and thirsting for God, the only desire we can work to make insatiable, if we are to bear witness to a higher life than that provided by consumerism:

- "As a deer longs for flowing streams, so longs my soul for you, O God. My soul thirsts for God, for the living God. When shall I come and behold the face of God?"[67]
- "God, you are my God, I seek you, my soul thirsts for you; my flesh faints for you, as in a dry and weary land where no water is."[68]

- "Take delight in the LORD, and he will give you the desires of your heart."[69]
- "[Men] feast on the abundance of your house, and you give them drink from the river of your delights."[70]

Contentment is best discovered through the thanksgiving that becomes the Thanksgiving in the Eucharist.

3. The Eucharist

For Christians, Sunday is the Easter banquet. We consume the Eucharist, Christ's body and blood. We get the extraordinary opportunity to participate in the divine life that created and pulsates through the universe. Rabbi Tsvi Blanchard speaks from the Jewish tradition of "consecrated consumption."[71] How do we consecrate our consumption? The Greek word for "thanksgiving" is *eucharistia*.[72] "For everything created by God is good, and nothing is to be rejected if it is received with thanksgiving; for then it is consecrated by the word of God and prayer."[73] The practice of thanksgiving reorders priorities. The right practice of the Eucharist "demonstrates so beautifully that when consumption is done right, it *is* transformative."[74]

We are to model lives that make the consumerist model look immature, weak, trifling, and shallow. We don't do this by simply reading *Brideshead Revisited* rather than *Fifty Shades of Grey*. Rather, we live lives that are characterized by the Eucharist, Thanksgiving.

St. Paul weaves this theme throughout his letters: ". . . always and for everything giving thanks in the name of our Lord Jesus Christ to God the Father."[75] He repeats this point over and over, so we have no excuse to miss the centrality of thanksgiving in Catholic spirituality. The Eucharist is the "source and summit of our faith." We must never drive a wedge between the daily and hourly and momentary acts of thanksgiving we perform in the face of the consumerist culture that claws for our attention and the sacramental expression of thanksgiving we call the Eucharist. They "feed" each other, if you will. We need to strengthen the link between the Eucharist and daily life, between sacramental belief and daily behavior.

Consumer culture breeds worry and status seeking. Not so Christ: "Have no anxiety about anything, but in everything by prayer and supplication with thanksgiving let your requests be made known to God. And the peace of God, which passes all understanding, will keep your hearts and your minds in Christ Jesus."[76] This directly challenges the consumerism that tells us to look immediately to go shopping to put things right and get what we want. Scripture tells us to first pray before we act to fulfill these desires. If we do so, we will be able to separate legitimate from illegitimate desires.

Notice the repetition. Time and again, thanksgiving is prescribed as central to our relationship with God and the world:

- "As therefore you received Christ Jesus the Lord, so live in him, rooted and built up in him and established in the faith, just as you were taught, abounding in thanksgiving."[77]
- "And let the peace of Christ rule in your hearts, to which indeed you were called in the one body. And be thankful. . . . And whatever you do, in word or deed, do everything in the name of the Lord Jesus, giving thanks to God the Father through him."[78]
- "Continue steadfastly in prayer, being watchful in it with thanksgiving."[79]

These are hard words but beautiful. They give us no room to move. The "everything" includes *all things*. In other words, our lives should be characterized by Thanksgiving. Yes, people should look upon God's people and say, "My, how they love one another." But equally, they should observe, "This is a thankful people."[80]

Finally, "give thanks in all circumstances; for this is the will of God in Christ Jesus for you. Do not quench the Spirit."[81] We are back to where we began. The refusal to give thanks thwarts the work of the Holy Spirit in our lives. The Holy Spirit is given, John tells us, to reveal and bear witness to Christ.[82] If our lives are absent thanksgiving, then our lives are absent Christ, and we might just as well follow the consumerist path and follow the popular Epicureanism that marked St. Paul's generation: "If Christ has not been

raised . . . [then] we are of all men most to be pitied. . . . 'Let us eat
and drink, for tomorrow we die.'"[83]

The final apologetic for the Catholic is not an argument as much
as a way of life. Catholicism is true to the way things are. Caryll
Houselander phrased it differently but tried in her writing to demonstrate the concreteness, vividness, corporeality, the "is-ness" of
Catholic spirituality: "The acceptance of life as it is must teach us
trust and humility. This is because every real experience of life is an
experience of God."[84] Because the Catholic faith deals with reality
and human nature as God designed it, then we should expect it
to sharpen reason, enrich experience, strengthen families, deepen
spirituality, and lead to right worship, enhance relationships, and
establish *shalom* among all creatures, and enliven the artistic imagination as well as empower the moral imagination. We must never
deny the importance of reason or experience. Nor are we to weaken
on the truths of divine revelation. By the same token, we must
understand the limits of argument and authority.

Often a life well lived can do more to illustrate the truth, "adorn
the doctrine" — as St. Paul tells Titus[85] — than the most brilliant words. I started discussing consumerism with the example of
a woman of extraordinary beauty who, when she saw the limitations
of physical attractiveness, added charitable service to her portfolio.
I'm sure her friends saw her as more, not less, beautiful as a result.
Beauty, the attraction of a godly life, the beauty of holiness as exhibited in the lives of the saints, beckons us to make their example
ours. Again, the lives of the saints, but especially your becoming a
saint, may be the most neglected tool in the missionary/apologist's
work bucket.[86]

Notes

Epigraph

1. George Orwell, "The Freedom of the Press (*Animal Farm*)" in *Essays*, ed., By John Carey, New York: Alfred A. Knopf, 2002, pp. 888-897.
2. Moira Allen, *On Religion in SF and Fantasy: An Interview with Orson Scott Card* www.writing-world.com/sf/card.shtml, 2000.

INTRODUCTION
We Have Enemies to Love and Challenge

1. Letter from Vincent van Gogh to Theo van Gogh, Laeken, November 15, 1878; http://www.webexhibits.org/vangogh/letter/7/126.htm.
2. Catherine Claire Larson, "Vincent Van Gogh and Seeing" in Kelly Monroe Kullberg and Lael Arrington, *Faith and Culture*, Grand Rapids: Zondervan, 2008, pp. 125-126. My thanks to Larson for linking Van Gogh's artistic vision with his missionary aspirations.
3. Letter from Vincent van Gogh to Theo van Gogh, Antwerp, c. December 19, 1885; http://www.webexhibits.org/vangogh/letter/16/441.htm.
4. C.S. Lewis, *The Weight of Glory*, New York: HarperCollins, orig. 1949, rep. 1980, p. 46.
5. The story is well told in Cliff Edwards, *Van Gogh and God: A Creative Spiritual Quest*, Chicago: Loyola Press, 2002.
6. Letter from Vincent van Gogh to Emile Bernard, Arles, June 24, 1888; http://www.webexhibits.org/vangogh/letter/18/B09.htm?qp=health.fatigue.
7. As he persecuted Christians, the Pharisee Saul was struck by a revelation of Jesus Christ. Disoriented, he asked, "Who are you Lord?" The answer: "I am Jesus whom you are persecuting." Christ, the bridegroom is mystically united with his bride, the Church. He is fully identified with his body on earth. To attack the Church is to attack Christ. See Acts 8:1-3 & 9:1-5; Cf. 1 Cor 15:9; Gal 1:13; Phil 3:6; 1 Tim 1:12-13; 1 Cor 10:32.
8. Rom 12:18.
9. Ratzinger (b. 1927-) credits American Baptist theologian Harvey Cox's (b. 1929-) *Secular City* (1965) with this version. Both acknowledge that the original version probably originates with the Lutheran philosopher Soren Kierkegaard (1813-1855). See Joseph Ratzinger, *Introduction to Christianity*, San Francisco: Ignatius Press, orig. 1968, rep. 1990, pp. 15-16. The call to proclaim the faith is being felt at all levels of the Church. Certainly see John Paul II's and Benedict XVI's encyclicals which are built on the assumption of the Church not merely having a mission but being a mission. See Avery Cardinal Dulles, "John Paul II and the New Evangelization" in *Church and Society: The Laurence J. McGinley Lectures, 1988-2007*, New York: Fordham University Press, 2008; also, Dulles, *Evangelization for the Third Millennium*, New York: Paulist Press, 2009. Cardinal Paul Poupard & The Pontifical Council of Culture, *Where is Your God? Responding to the Challenge of Unbelief and Religious Indifference Today*, Chicago: Liturgy Training Publications, 2004.

Part One / Abusers of Spirituality and Revelation

OPPONENT #1
From New Age to the New Self-Styled Spirituality of Oprah

1. Robert Fuller, *Mesmerism and the American Cure of Souls*, Philadelphia: University of Pennsylvania Press, 1982, p. 129.

2. Wouter J. Hanegraaff, *New Age Religion and Western Culture: Esotericism in the Mirror of Secular Thought*, Albany: State University of New York Press, 1998, p. 314.

3. Rev 19:7-10; See also Is 54:5-7; Hos 2:19; 4; Eph 5:32; Mt 22:2-1; Jn 15-17.

4. "Keeping the Faith" February 9, 2010 http://www.oprah.com/oprahshow/Lisa-Ling-Goes-Inside-a-Convent; "Marrying Christ" November 10, 2010 http://www.oprah.com/oprahshow/Marrying-Christ-Video.

5. Martha Sherrill, "Welcome to the Banquet," *O, The Oprah Magazine*, vol. 9, number 5, May 2008, p. 281.

6. Elizabeth Gilbert, *Eat, Pray, Love: One Woman's Search for Everything Across Italy, India and Indonesia*, New York: Penguin Books, 2006, p. 208.

7. Quoted at http://shatteredparadigm.blogspot.com/2010/12/is-oprah-christian.html.

8. This only refers to soft drink sales of Coca Cola and Pepsi. It doesn't refer to diet drinks or market cap, net profit, gross revenues, number of employees, or total holdings. http://www.usatoday.com/money/industries/food/2011-03-17-diet-coke-2.htm. Judaism, Islam, and Religious Studies covered 40, 20, 35 feet respectively. I did not attribute them to any larger category.

9. Elizabeth Gilbert, *Eat, Pray, Love*, New York: Penguin Books, 2006, p. 26.

10. Elizabeth Gilbert, *Eat, Pray, Love*, New York: Penguin Books, 2006, pp. 199-200.

11. See Ross Douthat's keen insight on Gilbert's journey in *Bad Religion: How We Became a Nation of Heretics*, New York: Free Press, 2012, p. 213ff.

12. During the movie version of *Eat, Pray. Love*, Gilbert is surrounded in Italy by Catholic nuns and churches. Not once, however, is Catholicism even considered as a worthy path to self-understanding.

13. Shirley MacLaine, *Out on a Limb*, New York: Bantam Books, 1986, pp. 234-235.

14. A music executive confessed: "The term 'New Age' has developed a negative connotation in society and is now generally associated with crystals, reincarnation, and the harmonic convergence. It has become the 'in' gredient in the social recipe for humor and the 'out' cast in social trends. It is now the trite way to describe the eccentric boundaries of a period of social change. And, unfortunately, it is not the section of the record store in which mainstream consumers think they are going to find great music" See Gary L. Chappell, "'New Age' Term Is Detriment," *Billboard*, February 8, 1992.

15. Nathan O. Hatch, *The Democratization of American Christianity*. New Haven: Yale University Press, 1989. From the time Anne Hutchinson (1591-1642) and Roger Williams (1603-1683) brought schism to the New England Puritans, Americans resist being told what to believe. See John Barry, *Roger Williams and the Creation of the American Soul*, New York: Viking Press, 2012; Eve LaPlante, *American Jezebel, the Uncommon Life of Anne Hutchinson, the Woman who Defied the Puritans*. San Francisco: Harper Collins, 2004.

16. Many Transcendentalists despised Spiritualism which principally sought to communicate with the spirits of departed loved ones who had gone on to higher realms of existence or planes of consciousness. Spiritualism grew exponentially after the bloodbath of the Civil War with its 500,000 deaths.

17. Christian Science (1879-), New Thought (1850s-) and its offshoots like the Unity School (1889-), Divine Science (1880s), and Religious Science (1927-) all descend from Quimby and Transcendentalism.

18. Ross Gregory Douthat, *Bad Religion: How We Became a Nation of Heretics* New York: Free Press, 2012.

19. "What works for them" is a pragmatic criterion. Syncretism is the attempt to merge various, even contradictory, religious elements into a satisfying worldview. This pragmatic test for truth is given a high-minded interpretation by William James in his *Varieties of Religious Experience: A Study in Human Nature*, Norcross, GA: Trinity Press Intl, orig. 1902, rep. 2013. For the less high-minded, it is simply mixing and matching one's spiritual beliefs like going to a grocery store and shopping around. See Douthat, *Bad Religion* 2012; James B. Twitchell, *Shopping for God: How Christianity Went from In Your Heart to In Your Face*, New York: Simon & Schuster, 2007.

20. See Avery Cardinal Dulles, "John Paul II and the New Evangelization" in *Church and Society: The Laurence J. McGinley Lectures, 1988-2007*, New York: Fordham University Press, 2008.

21. Kathryn Lofton, *Oprah: The Gospel of an Icon*, Berkeley: University of California Press, 2011, p. 4.

22. Mt 16:15-16.

23. 2 Cor 11:1-6; Mt 7:15-23; 1 Thess 5:21.

24. Historic Christian orthodoxy describing the person of Christ is summarized in the First Council of Nicaea (325), First Council of Ephesus (431), and Council of Chalcedon (451).

25. John M. Allegro, *The Sacred Mushroom and The Cross: A study of the nature and origins of Christianity within the fertility cults*, Gnostic Media and Researching, orig. 1970, rep. 2009.

26. See Stephen Prothero, *American Jesus: How the Son of God Became a National Icon*, New York: Farrar, Straus, & Giroux, 2004. Cf. Stephen J. Nichols, *Jesus Made in America: A Cultural History from the Puritans to "The Passion of the Christ,"* Downers Grove, IL: InterVarsity Press, 2008.

27. *A New Earth* Online Class, chapter 1 Transcript www.oprah.com. Contrast with Jn 3:16-18; 14:6; Acts 4:12.

28. "This book [Butterworth's *Discover the Power Within You*] changed my [Oprah's] perspective on life and religion. Eric Butterworth teaches that God isn't 'up there.' He exists inside each one of us, and it's up to us to seek the divine within." See "Oprah Winfrey: The Oprahfication of America," Russ Wise, http://www.christian information. org/article.asp?artID=103. After Butterworth's death, Oprah discovered Eckhart Tolle (1948-). Butterworth's *Discover the Power of God Within You* and Tolle's *A New Earth* are 1 & 2 on her favorite book list.

29. John 5:17-18; 8:42; 10:30; 12:45; 14:7, 10-11; 17:21-23; 19:7; Acts 4:12. See C.S. Lewis, *Mere Christianity*, New York: Macmillan, 1952, pp. 40-41.

30. "Not that He as a man was any better [than any of us] but He was the embodiment of a higher Wisdom, more so than any man who has ever lived." See Phineas P. Quimby, *The Quimby Manuscripts*, ed. Horatio W. Dresserk New Hyde Park, NY: University Books, 1961, p. 283. He cites some curious displays of supernatural power and miracles working through the Catholic Church. Google books, *The Complete Collected Works of Phineas Parkhurst Quimby*, p. 440.

31. Eric Butterworth, *Discover the Power Within You*, New York: HarperCollins, orig. 1968, rep. 1989, p. 9. Similarly, Elaine Pagels, "Gnosis: Self-Knowledge as Knowledge of God" in *The Gnostic Gospels*, New York: Vintage, 1979, pp. 143-169.

32. Charles Fillmore, *Talks on Truth*, Lee's Summit, MO: Unity School of Christianity, 1926, p. 169.

33. Elaine Pagels, "Gnosis: Self-Knowledge as Knowledge of God" in *The Gnostic Gospels*, 1979, pp. 143-169; Experts debate whether Gnostics would so identify themselves. See Miguel Connor, ed., interview with Karen King, *Voices of Gnosticism*, Dublin: Bardic Press, 2011, p. 158. Carl A. Raschke, *The Interruption of Eternity: Modern Gnosticism and the Origins of the New Religious Consciousness*, Chicago: Burnham Inc Publishing, 1980.

34. Gnosticism seeks liberation from physical reality but also invites us to escape history and particularity. For example, as Gilbert resolves her divorce, she imagines her ex-husband hovering above their ashram and comments: "I started to cry ... but quickly realized I didn't need to. Tears are part of this bodily life...we had nothing to do with the body...[we were] not even people anymore... [we] weren't even ex-spouses; none of this was relevant....[we were] just two cool blue souls who already understood everything." They were ultimately unbound by their bodies, unbound by the complex history of their past relationships. See Gilbert, *Eat, Pray, Love*, p. 186ff.

35. H. Emilie Cady, *Lessons in Truth*, http://trueacu.com/Lessons_In_Truth, Lesson 3:7.

36. Cady unwittingly rejected God's assessment of the material creation, 'This is very good' " Gen 1:31.

37. *CCC*, 571-573; 601; "The Scriptures had foretold this divine plan of salvation through the putting to death of 'the righteous one, my Servant' as a mystery of universal redemption, that is, as the ransom that would free men from the slavery of sin." Cf. 1 Cor 15:3; Acts 3:14-18; 7:52; 13:29; 26:22-23; Isaiah 53:7-12; Acts 8:32-35; Mt 20:28; Lk 24:25-44; Jn 8:34-36.

38. This statement rejects centuries of Catholic, Protestant and Orthodox Christian teaching as well as the plain meaning of Jesus' own words: "The Son of Man came as a ransom for many" (Mt 20:28). The author of Hebrews is also clear:"Without the shedding of blood there is no forgiveness" (Heb 9:22; Cf. Lev16:29-30; 17:11; 23:27-28; Isaiah 53:7-12; Likewise 1 Cor 15:3 & Rom 5:11).

39. "Oprah Winfrey: Jesus Did Not Come to Die On the Cross," http://www.youtube .com/watch?v=xM5ILOsHLnw.

40. New Testament studies recently reaffirmed and clarified the worship of Jesus in the early Church. See Larry Hurtado, *Lord Jesus Christ: Devotion to Jesus in Earliest Christianity*, Grand Rapids: Eerdmans, 2005; Larry Hurtado, *How on Earth Did Jesus Become a God?* Grand Rapids: Eerdmans, 2005 and James D. G. Dunn, *Did the First Christians Worship Jesus?* Louisville, KY: Westminster/John Knox, 2010. See also Luke Timothy Johnson, *Religious Experience in Earliest Christianity*, Minneapolis: Augsburg/ Fortress, 1998.

41. *CCC*, 2096- 2097. In Catholic doctrine, to "Worship" is to declare the worth of another. It can be applied to God and creatures. "Adoration, which is known as *latria* in classical theology, is the worship and homage that is rightly offered to God alone. It is the acknowledgement of excellence and perfection of an uncreated, divine person. It is the worship of the Creator that God alone deserves. Veneration, known as *dulia* in classical theology, is the honor due to the excellence of a created person. This refers to the excellence exhibited by the created being who likewise deserves recognition and honor." The Blessed Virgin Mary receives *hyperdulia* which is just a whole lot more *dulia*. Cf. *CCC*, 971; 2132. See Mark Miravalle, *What is Devotion to Mary?*

42. John 20:28.

43. Ross Gregory Douthat, *Bad Religion: How We Became a Nation of Heretics*, New York: Free Press, 2012, pp. 213-214, quoting Gilbert, pp. 158, 176, 199-200.

44. Paul Coelho, *The Alchemist*, New York: HarperCollins, 1993, p. 152. This is adjusted to make pronouns and tenses agree.

45. Martin Buber, trans. Ronald Smith, *I and Thou*, New York: Scribner's, orig. 1923, rep. 2000. "The close association of the relation to God with the relation to one's fellow-men is my most essential concern."

46. Thomas Merton, *The Climate of Monastic Prayer*, Spencer, MA: Cistercian Publications, 1973, pp. 113-114. See also Ps. 139:2-24.

47. The same Hebrew word, *qana*, can be translated either jealous or zealous depending on the context. In Gen 37:11 and Num 5:14, 20 we see the negative, "jealous." In Num 25:11, 13 and 1 Kgs 19:10, 14, we see the positive, "zealous." John teaches that "God is love" (1 Jn 4:8, 16b) and Paul teaches that love is not jealous (1 Cor 13:4). Words count. Because God's relation to Israel is that of love,. disloyalty to God is spiritual promiscuity or adultery See Hosea 2:19; 4:1; 6:6; 10:12; 12:6. Adultery and apostasy are frequently paralleled in Scripture. See Francis A. Schaeffer, *The Church at the End of the Twentieth Century*, Downers Grove, IL: InterVarsity Press, 1970, appendix- "Adultery & Apostasy."

OPPONENT #2
The Dark Side of the Bright New Age Movement

1. Catholic teaching documents on New Age thought:
   * *Jesus Christ the Bearer of the Water of Life: A Christian Reflection on the New Age,"* Pontifical Council on Culture/ Interreligious Dialogue, 2003.
   * John Paul II, *Address to the Bishops of Iowa, Kansas, Missouri and Nebraska*, 1993.
   * Congregation for the Doctrine of the Faith (CDF), *On Certain Aspects of Christian Meditation,*1989.

- International Theological Commission, *Questions Concerning Eschatology,* 1992, 9-10.
- International Theological Commission, *Questions on the Theology of Redemption,* 1995, I/29 and II/35-36.
- Irish Theological Commission, *A New Age of the Spirit,* 1994.
- Godfried Danneels, *Christ or Aquarius?* Pastoral Letter, Christmas 1990, Veritas, Dublin.
- Edward Anthony McCarthy, *The New Age Movement,* Pastoral Instruction, 1992.
- Working group on New Age, ed., *Sects and New Religious Movements,* Washington (USCC), 1995.
- Sharon Lee Gigante, former New Ager, maintains an helpful website at http://newagedeception.com/new/.
- Constance Cumbey first sounded the trumpet alerting Christians to dangerous New Age influence among evangelical Protestants in the early 1980s. She continues monitoring related socio-politico trends at http://cumbey.blogspot.com/.

2. Shirley MacLaine, *It's All in the Playing,* New York: Bantam Books, 1987, p. 91.

3. Eric Jantsch, *The Self-Organizing Universe: Scientific and Human Implications of the Emerging Paradigm of Evolution,* Oxford: Pergamum Press, 1980, p. 84.

4. Larry Brilliant, in a remarkable career, helped eradicate small-pox, allegedly under command of his guru.

5. Jobs read *Be Here Now* by former Harvard LSD researcher, Richard Alpert, aka, Ram Dass. "It was profound. It transformed me and many of my friends." Acid guru Timothy Leary declared that personal computers had become the new LSD. His famous motto, "Turn on, tune in, drop out" was changed to "Turn on, boot up, jack in." See Walter Isaacson, *Steve Jobs,* New York: Simon and Schuster, 2011, p. 58.

6. Walter Isaacson, *Steve Jobs,* p. 16.

7. Ibid., p. 15.

8. Ibid., p. 455.

9. Isaacson describes "the roller-coaster life and searingly intense personality of a creative entrepreneur whose passion for perfection and ferocious drive revolutionized six industries: personal computers, animated movies, music, phones, tablet computing, and digital publishing. You might even add a seventh, retail stores, which Jobs did not quite revolutionize but did reimagine (*Steve Jobs,* p. xx, xxi). Cf. http://www.smh.com.au/digital-life/digital-life-news/steve-jobs-the-man-who-changed-the-way-we-live-20110825-1jbjm.html#ixzz28m2MBHJN.

10. See Graham Smith, "Steve Jobs doomed himself," *Daily Mail,* October, 14, 2011. Andrew Weil, who directs integrative medicine at the University of Arizona College of Medicine, says Amir is uninformed. "No one knows how long he would have survived or what his quality of life would have been had he opted for immediate surgery and used only conventional treatment." See http://www.cnn.com/2011/10/27/opinion/weil-steve-jobs/index.html.

11. "25 most powerful people in business – #1: Steve Jobs." *Fortune.* http://money.cnn.com/galleries/2007/fortune/0711/gallery.power_25.fortune Retrieved April 19, 2010.

12. Jobs initial spiritual formation drew from *Cutting Through Spiritual Materialism* by Chögyam Trungpa Rinpoche, a Tibetan lama spreading Buddhism to those who went beyond "psychedelic insight." He also read *Zen Mind, Beginner's Mind* by Shunryu Suzuki-roshi, founder of San Francisco Zen Center. In "What Kind of Buddhist Was Steve Jobs Really?" Steve Silberman, investigative reporter for *Wired* claims Zen had much deeper impact on Jobs than Isaacson allows. See http://blogs.plos.org/neurotribes/2011/10/28/what-kind-of-buddhist-was-steve-jobs-really/.

13. "Vedic" is that branch of Indian philosophy focused on the self and its union with Ultimate Being. "Yoga" is the branch focused on the disciplines and techniques to reach union.

14. See "The Science of Kriya Yoga" in Paramahansa Yogananda, *Autobiography of a Yogi*, Los Angeles: Self Realization Fellowship (SRF), 1946 orig., 13ᵗʰ ed., 1990, pp. 149-154.

15. *Autobiography of a Yogi*, p. 276. Cf. Isaacson, *Steve Jobs*, p. 453.

16. The book is an elaborate apologetic for Yogananda's master Sri Yukteswar. The entire report indicates that the mortuary director detected a faint brown dot on the nose, a sign of deterioration on day 20. Yet, he claimed it was "unparalleled" in mortuary history.

17. Buddhist John Lambert blogs: "If we look at the time that Steve Jobs grew up in, we can see that his Buddhism was probably more of a New Age type of religion or practice rather than a real practice of classical Buddhism. He used mind altering drugs, visited ashrams, and probably took what he thought was useful from the Zen tradition and incorporated into his life." See http://spreadtheflame.com/2011/10/steve-jobs-was-a-buddhist-what-does-that-mean.

18. See Joseph Campbell (1904-1987), *Hero with a Thousand Faces*, New York: New Library, orig. 1949, rep. 3ʳᵈ ed., 1988.

19. Fr. Benedict Groeschel (b. 1933-) told me the tragic story of his friend and colleague Helen Shucman (1909- 1981), the scribe or medium for Jesus in *Course in Miracles*. By the end of her life, she was cursing the *Course* in the vilest terms. See http://www.beliefnet.com/Faiths/2004/07/The-Making-Of-A-Course-In-Miracles. aspx. Cf. Sharon Lee Gigante's preliminary critique of *Course in Miracles* at http://www.newagedeception.com/new/free-resources/22-does-qa-course-in-miraclesq-really-mean-what-it-says.

20. See Thomas Keating, *Intimacy with God: An Introduction to Centering Prayer*, New York: Crossroads Publishing, 2009. See the Congregation for the Doctrine of the Faith (CDF), *On Some Aspects of Christian Meditation*, 1989. Also Jesuit Fr. Mitch Pacwa recounts New Age influence encountered in seminary, retreat centers, chanceries, and parish churches in *Catholics and the New Age*, 1992.

21. See http://www.auramag.com/.

22. See Donald Meyer, *The Positive Thinkers: Popular Religious Psychology from Mary Baker Eddy to Norman Vincent Peale and Ronald Reagan*, rev., Wesleyan, 1988. More recently, Barbara Ehrenreich, *Bright-Sided: How Positive Thinking is Undermining America*, New York: Picador, 2009.

23. Deepak Chopra, *The Seven Spiritual Laws of Success: A Practical Guide to the Fulfillment of Your Dreams*, New York: New World Library, 1994.

24. Carl T. Jackson, "The New Thought Movement and the Nineteenth Century Discovery of Oriental Philosophy" in *The Journal of Popular Culture*, 1975, ix:3, pp. 523–548.

25. Jerry Adler, "Decoding 'The Secret,' " *Newsweek*, March 3, 2007 available on http://www.newsweek.com/2007/03/04/decoding-the-secret.html.

26. Maja D'Aoust, Adam Parfray, *The Secret Source: The Law of Attraction and its Hermetic Influence Throughout the Ages*, Fort Townsend, WA: Process Media, 2012. D'Aoust and Parfray's unusual history of the Law of Attraction contends that it is only one of the Seven Ancient Hermetic Laws.

27. Mary Baker Eddy founded the Church of Christ, Scientist or, more commonly, Christian Science (1879) on her text, *Science and Health with Key to the Scriptures*, Boston: Christian Science Board of Directors, orig. 1875, rep. 1994.

28. Paramahansa Yogananda, *Scientific Healing Affirmations: Theory and Practice of Concentration*, Los Angeles: Self-Realization Fellowship, 1958.

29. Benjamin Kidd (1858-1916), *The Science of Power* (1919) is one of only two books recommended by Napoleon Hill (1883-1970), famed author of *Think and Grow Rich* (1937).

30. In the documentary, *The Enemies of Reason*, Chopra, questioned by Richard Dawkins admits that he uses the term "quantum theory" metaphorically. See Richard Dawkins, *The Enemies of Reason*, Part 2, 2007, aired August 20, 2007, BBC channel 4. Cf. Deepak Chopra, Leonard Mlodinow, *War of the Worldviews: Science vs. Spirituality*, New York: Harmony, 2011, p. 207.

31. Ingrid Hansen Smythe located these references and made these observations at http://www.skeptic.com/eskeptic/07-03-07/#note03.

32. Michael Beckwith, *The Secret* DVD.

33. John F. Demartini, *The Secret* DVD.

34. James Arthur Ray, *The Secret* DVD.

35. Ed Gungar, *There Is More to the Secret*. Nashville: Nelson, 2007, p. 2.

36. Biblical wisdom cultivates a positive mental attitude. To expect such attitudes to be rewarded by some immutable cosmic law as impersonal and invariable as the law of gravity is folly E.g., "A joyful heart is good medicine, but a crushed spirit dries up the bones" (Prov. 17:22). Cf. Mt 6:25-31; Jn 14:27; Rom 5:1; Heb 13:6; Phil 4:6; 1 Pet 5:7.

37. See Gary Zukav, *The Seat of the Soul*, New York: Free Press, 1990, p. 209.

38. Lisa Nichols interviewed in Rhonda Byrne, *The Secret*, DVD.

39. As cited in Jerry Adler, "Decoding 'The Secret,' " *Newsweek* March 3, 2007 available at http://www.newsweek.com/2007/03/04/decoding-the-secret.html.

40. H.P. Blavatsky, *Key to Theosophy*, orig. 1889, rep. 2007, section nine, at Theosophical University Press Online Edition, http://www.theosociety.org/pasadena/key/key-9.htm. Cf., Christmas Humphreys, *Karma and Rebirth*. London: Curzon Press, orig. 1948, rep. 1983, p. 55.

41. *CCC*, 303; Cf. Ps 115:3; Rev 3:7; Prov 19:21.

42. Byrne's presentation is heavily dependent on other people's material. She "borrowed" the image of the genie from Robert Collier's *How to Get Anything You Want with the Law of Attraction*, Melrose, FL: Laurenzana Press, 2011. The original edition was published under the mercenary title *The Secret of Gold: How to Get What You Want*, 1927.

43. The Pontifical Councils for Culture and Interreligious Dialogue elaborate: "The *New Age* concept of God is rather diffuse, whereas the Christian concept is a very clear one. The *New Age* god is an impersonal energy, really a particular extension or component of the cosmos; god in this sense is the life-force or soul of the world. Divinity is to be found in every being, in a gradation 'from the lowest crystal of the mineral world up to and beyond the Galactic God himself, about Whom we can say nothing at all. This is not a man but a Great Consciousness,' " quoting Benjamin Creme, *The Reappearance of Christ and the Masters of Wisdom*, London: Tara Press, 1979, p. 116 in *Jesus Christ, The Bearer of the Water of Life: A Christian Reflection on the New Age*, 2003, chapter four.

44. Rhonda Byrne, *The Secret*, New York: Atria, 2006, p.131.

45. Lisa Nichols as quoted in Rhonda Byrne, *The Secret* DVD.

46. See Jonathan Walton, a professor of African-American religions at the University of California at Riverside who asks: "Has the so-called Prosperity gospel turned its followers into some of the most willing participants—and hence, victims—of the current financial crisis?"(David Van Biema, "Maybe We Should Blame God for the Subprime Mortgage Mess," *Time*, Oct 3, 2008). See an earlier Van Biema TIME cover piece "Does God Want You Rich?" at http://www.time.com/time/magazine/article/0,9171,1533448,00.html.

47. Esther Hicks, *The Secret* DVD. Cf. http://www.abraham-hicks.com/lawofattractionsource/about_abraham.php.

48. Ingrid Hansen Smythe, "The Secret Behind *The Secret:* What is Attracting Millions to the *Law of Attraction*?" http://www.skeptic.com/eskeptic/07-03-07/#note03.

49. "Those who desire to be rich fall into temptation, into a snare, into many senseless and hurtful desires that plunge men into ruin and destruction. For the love of money is the root of all evils; it is through this craving that some have wandered away from the faith and pierced their hearts with many pangs" (1 Tim 6:9).

50. Cf. Mt 6:24; 13:22; Lk 12:12-21; 1 Tim 6:1; Heb 13:5. See *CCC* 2113.

51. Cf. Mt 16:26; Mk. 8:36.

52. Deepak Chopra, *The Seven Spiritual Laws of Success: A Practical Guide to the Fulfillment of Your Dreams*, New York: New World Library, 1994, pp. 3-4.

53. "Positive Psychology" builds "thriving individuals, families, and communities." Like the mid-20th century humanistic psychology of Rogers, Fromm, and Maslow, founder Martin Seligman wants a psychology *not* defined by what's wrong with people

but what's right. Positive Psychology focuses on formation of character rather than treating disease, abnormalities, neuroses and psychoses. The phrase, "Positive Psychology" is from Maslow's *Motivation and Personality*,1954.

54. Jules Evans, *Prospect Magazine: Albert Ellis*. Issue 137, August 1, 2007: D. Smith, "Trends in counseling and psychotherapy," *American Psychologist*, Vol. 37:7, July, 1982.

55. Albert Ellis, *Overcoming Resistance:Rational Emotive Therapy With Difficult Clients*, New York: Springer Publishing, 1985, p. 147.

56. G. K. Chesterton, *Orthodoxy*, New York: John Lane and Co., orig. 1919, rep. 2013, p. 136.

57. Walter Isaacson, *Steve Jobs*, p. 453. This assumes, of course, that his postponement of surgery was an attempt to *will* the problem away.

58. In fairness, Steve Jobs would never have embraced the crass thinking behind *The Secret*.

59. Paraphrased from the International Theological Commission, *Certain Questions on Eschatology*, 10.2, 1992.

60. What we call the New Age gospel finds many parallels with the so-called Gnostic Christians of the second and third centuries. Elaine Pagels' groundbreaking but dated *The Gnostic Gospels* (New York: Vantage, 1979, pp. 143ff.) contains an entire chapter entitled "Gnosis: Self Knowledge as Knowledge of God."

61. Lilly describes the peak experience of the serious New Age mystic although Lilly's experience was induced through psychedelics.

62. James Sire, *The Universe Next Door*, 5th edition, Downers Grove, IL: InterVarsity Press, 2009, p. 192; cf. John Lilly's *Center of the Cyclone*, New York: Julian, 1972, pp. 148-149.

63. Shirley MacLaine, *Dancing in the Light*, New York: Bantam Books, 1985, p. 350.

64. Aldous Huxley, *Doors of Perception* and *Heaven and Hell*, New York: Harper & Row, 1963, p. 23.

65. Carlos Casteneda, *A Separate Reality*, orig. 1971, rep. 1992.

66. Deepak Chopra, *The Third Jesus: The Christ We Cannot Ignore*, 2009, p. 23.

67. Jon Klimo, *Channeling: Investigations on Receiving Information from Paranormal Sources*, 1998, pp. 174-76.

68. *CCC*, 163. Eastern Orthodox spirituality uses the term "theosis" to describe our participation in the divine life. "Deification" is another term.

69. *CCC* 163, 2548-2550; 1 Cor 13:12; 1 Jn 3:2.

70. John 15:15.

71. Cf. Gal 2:30.

72. Fr. David Vincent Meconi, SJ, *Union with God: Living the Christ Life*, London: Catholic Truth Society, 2006, p. 3.

73. Phil 4:13; Col 1:27.

74. John Paul II, *Crossing the Threshold of Hope*, New York: Alfred A. Knopf, 1994, pp. 85, 87.

75. Yogananda, *Autobiography of a Yogi*, p. 98.

76. Mother's Nobel lecture is available at http://www.nobelprize.org/nobel_prizes/peace/laureates/1979/teresa-lecture.html.

77. Occasionally, the dead bodies of saints avoid decomposition without embalming. Through this phenomenon, God supernaturally testifies to and honors their sanctity. "Also, that the holy bodies of holy martyrs, and of others now living with Christ, — which bodies were the living members of Christ, and the temple of the Holy Ghost, and which are by Him to be raised unto eternal life, and to be glorified, — are to be venerated by the faithful; through which (bodies) many benefits are bestowed by God on men" (Council of Trent, 25th Session, On the Invocation, Veneration, and Relics, of Saints, and on Sacred Images). Like other relics and sacramentals, incorruptibles "prepare us to receive grace and dispose us to cooperate with it" (*CCC* 1670; Cf. 1667-1679). When fellow Christians dismiss relics as mere superstition, ask them to explain 2 Kgs 13:20-21; Mt 9:20-22; Acts 5:15-16; 19:11-12. The *CCC* 2110-2141explains faith, superstition, magic, idolatry, etc. Relics, like incorruptibles, can enhance our communion with the saints and awaken us to the reality of

the invisible world. See Joan Carroll Cruz, *The Incorruptibles: A Study of the Incorruption of the Bodies of Various Catholic Saints and Beati*, Charlotte. NC: TAN Books, 1977.

78. 1 Cor 15:1-6.

79. Ps 16:10; cf. Acts 13:36; Ps 49:9-15; 86:13.

Opponent #3
The East in the West: The Case of Reincarnation

1. As of this writing he has returned to number one.

2. Gary Smith, "The Chosen One," *Sports Illustrated*, Dec 23, 1996 at http://sports illustrated.cnn.com/vault/article/magazine/MAG1009257/index.htm.

3. For an intelligent range of opinions on the appropriateness of Hume's remarks go to http://religionblog.dallasnews.com/2010/01/texas-faith-brit-hume-and-tige.html/.

4. These prestige journalists let their antipathy or ignorance of spiritual matters blind them to the most moving aspect of the story. Hume was simply one beggar telling another beggar where to find food. In 1998, Hume's 28 year old son, Sandy, a talented, Washington journalist, suddenly committed suicide after a DUI arrest. Hume, the grieving father, received hundreds of Mass cards and offers of prayer. Moved by this outpouring, he determined to pursue the Christian faith. Hume was willing to step out of his comfort zone and into the breach for Tiger. Rather than write this as a heartwarming offer from a father who overcame professional aloofness to offer spiritual consolation, they skewered him for exploiting Woods' vulnerability.

5. Sarah Pulliam Bailey at *Christianity Today* gives Hume a chance to explain more fully. See http://www.christianitytoday.com/ct/2010/januaryweb-only/11-42.0.html.

6. John Paul II, *Crossing the Threshold of Hope*, New York: Alfred A. Knopf, 1994, p. 87.

7. Anglican theologian Keith Ward, *Religion and Human Nature* (Oxford: Clarendon Press, 1998, p. 59ff), notes that certain groups following the Hindu god Vishnu do not see karma as a mechanical process, but as a saving path leading to the grace of Krishna. Doesn't grace deprive reincarnation of its rationale as a working out of the impersonal laws of cosmic justice? Nevertheless, rebirth is central to even these followers of Vishnu. "Even in these more theistic versions of Hinduism, karmic retribution combines with the idea of multiple human incarnations, so that all suffering in this life can be explained by each individual's prior wrongdoing, whether in this or in a prior life, and all wrongdoing in the present life will be punished in either this or a future life. In this way, Indian thought is able to endorse a complete and consistent retributive explanation of evil: *all suffering can be explained by the wrongdoing of the sufferer himself*" (italics mine).

8. Stephen Prothero, "What Would Buddha Do?" *USA Today*, Jan 10, 2010 at http://www.usatoday.com/NEWS/usaedition/2010-01-11-column11_ST_U.htm?csp=34.

9. Cf. Mark Muesse, *Religions of the Axial Ages*, Vol. 1 "Death and Rebirth," Chantilly, VA: Teaching Company, 2007, p. 92. "Samsara," the cycle of life, death, and rebirth "has found acceptance in all orthodox Hindu traditions- monistic, pluralistic, theistic and pantheistic- and also in religions that emerged from them, such as Buddhism, Jainism and Sikhism." See William A. Dyrness and Veli-Matti Karkkainen, ed., *Global Dictionary of Theology* Downers Grove, IL: InterVarsity Press, 2008, p. 738.

10. A.R. Wadia, "Philosophical Implications of the Doctrine of Karma," *Philosophy East and West*, University of Hawaii Press, Vol. 5, No. 2, April 1965, p. 145. Since "grace" dominates Western theological discussion, "karma" also splits Eastern Hindu/Buddhist from Western Christian spirituality, as well as philosophy.

11. "Orthodox" Indian philosophy is based on the testimony of the Vedas ("knowledge"), the earliest strata of Sanskrit literature dating back to c. 1500 B.C. There are other Hindu sacred texts. The Vedas, however, have a special status as texts that are "revealed"; the non-Vedic sacred texts are described as texts that are "remembered." Schools are considered orthodox if they esteem the Vedas as infallible revelation and not of human origin. Between 1000 B.C. and the first few centuries A.D., orthodox Hindu philosophy crystallized into six different schools. The six schools with an identifying word or phrase are: *Vedanta* (Ultimate realization of self as Brahman), *Yoga* (Union, contemplative method), *Samkhya* (Enumeration, dualist, atheistic) *Vaisesika* (Atomist, reductionistic

method to physical world), *Nyaya* (Logic, resembles analytic philosophy), and *Mimasa* (Investigation, Textual interpretation) The unorthodox schools are *Jain*, *Buddhist*, and *Carvaka*. They respect but do not rely on the Vedas authority.

12. The major Western philosopher who would be most at home with Indian philosophy would be Baruch Spinoza (1632-1677). He also has the odd distinction of being the only person who managed to get excommunicated by both Jews and Christians (Calvinists). Indian teachers who succeeded in the West include Soyen Shaku (1860-1912), Swami Vivekananda (1863-1902), Sri Aurobindo (1872-1950), D.T. Suzuki (1870-1966), Paramahansa Yogananda (1893-1952), A. C. Bhaktivedanta Swami Prabhupada (1896-1977), Swami Muktananda (1908-1982), Maharishi Mahesh Yogi (1918-2008), Śri Sathya Sai Baba (1926-2011), Dalai Lama (Tenzin Gyatso, b. 1935-).

13. *Maitrayaniya Upanishad* (c. 300 BC) is the first mention of the six-fold form of yoga. Patanjali (fl. 150 BC) is widely regarded as the compiler of the formal yoga philosophy. The *Yoga Sutras of Patanjali* are foundational.

14. This is tricky. Some Indian schools stress the impersonal character of Brahman. Others insist that personhood is somehow preserved. Combining the opposites in this way can be misleading since they may only represent the emphasis of competing schools of Indian philosophy and not "Hinduism" as a whole. Nevertheless, this both/and approach appeals to Westerners.

15. *CCC*, 2705-2724 discusses meditation's difference from contemplative prayer. See the CDF's "Letter to the Bishops of the Catholic Church on Some Aspects of Christian Meditation" at http://www.vatican.va/roman_curia/congregations/cfaith/documents/rc_con_cfaith_doc_19891015_meditazione-cristiana_en.html.

16. This summary is excerpted with my changes from Philip Goldberg, *American Veda: From Emerson and the Beatles to Yoga and Meditation: How Indian Spirituality Changed the West*, New York: Harmony, 2010, pp. 10-12.

17. *CCC*, 1013, citing *Lumen Gentium* 48:3. Cf. Hebrews 9:27.

18. At some point, God acts so that the animal form receives the creative word of God and a human person is created who will live for eternity. This is a qualitative, not merely a quantitative difference between the human and the non-human. Creating human beings from pre-existing animal forms constitutes no greater moral, theological or biblical problem than with the formation of the human from pre-existing inanimate matter, i.e., the "clay of the earth" (Gen 2:7). The Hebrew verb, *yatsar*, is used to describe a potter molding clay into a pot. See Is 45:9; Jer 18:6; Job 33:6.

19. "In Buddhism, we do not actually use the word 'reincarnation.' We say 'rebirth.' " (Thich Nhat Hanh, *Living Buddha, Living Christ* NY: Penguin, 1995, p. 134). Related phrases are "transmigration of souls" and "metempsychosis."

20. Quoted in Lisa Miller, "Remembrances of Lives Past," *New York Times*, August 27, 2010 at http://www.nytimes.com/2010/08/29/fashion/29PastLives.html?pagewanted=all.

21. Geddes MacGregor, *Reincarnation in Christianity: A New Vision of the Role of Rebirth in Christian Thought*, Wheaton, IL: Theosophical Publishing House, 1978, p. 5. Arthur Herman, in his classic *The Problem of Evil and Indian Thought*, similarly asserts the superiority of karma to all Western theodicies: "Unlike the Western theories, ... the doctrine of rebirth is capable of meeting the major objections against which those Western attempts all failed" (Herman, 1976, p. 287). His confidence is unjustified as we will see below.

22. Quincey Howe, *Reincarnation for the Christian*, Wheaton, IL: Theosophical Publishing House, 1974, p. 51.

23. The only way to rid ourselves of the doctrine of hell is to eliminate the human person's eternally significant ability to make moral choices. Quoted in Lisa Miller, "Remembrances of Lives Past," *New York Times*, August 27, 2010. See http://www.nytimes.com/2010/08/29/fashion/29PastLives.html?pagewanted=all.

24. Stevenson published *Twenty Cases Suggestive of Reincarnation* (1974), *Children Who Remember Previous Lives* (1987), *Where Reincarnation and Biology Intersect* (1997), *Reincarnation and Biology*, (1997), and *European Cases of the Reincarnation Type* (2003).

The Division of Perceptual Studies at the University of Virginia School of Medicine continues his work and can be accessed at http://www.medicine.virginia.edu/clinical/departments/psychiatry/sections/cspp/dops/home-page. Carol Bowman also works with stories of reincarnation from children. See http://www.childpastlives.org/.

25. See "Hypnotic Regression to Previous Lives: A Short Statement by Ian Stevenson, M.D." at http://www.medicine.virginia.edu/clinical/departments/psychiatry/sections/cspp/dops/regression-page.

26. See Raymond Moody, *Coming Back: A Psychiatrist Explores Past Life Journeys*, New York: Bantam, 1992.

27. While one isn't surprised that these unconventional mental health professionals have failed to persuade their colleagues, one is surprised to find it even tried given the weakness of the empirical argument for reincarnation. Weiss, for instance on pp. 43-44 refers to a Catherine who persuaded her skeptical father of her paranormal powers by going to the horse races and picking "the winner of every race." Weiss claims this as "tangible proof" but he doesn't provide any documentation nor does he tell us where we can find these two living in the lap of luxury from Catherine's ability to pick race winners. He then claims thousands of similar cases but again leaves us without any compelling documentation or even well credited eyewitness testimony. One may have subjective reasons for believing in reincarnation but they shouldn't pose as objective. Cf. Lisa Miller, "Remembrances of Lives Past" *New York Times*, August 27, 2010.

28. Jurgen Moltmann, *Is There Life After Death?* Milwaukee: Marquette University Press, orig. 1998, rep. 2007, p. 39.

29. Suffering is at the heart of Buddhism. "When he [Gotama Buddha] looked at human life, Gotama could see only a grim cycle of suffering, which began with the trauma of birth and proceeded inexorably to 'aging, illness, death, sorrow, and corruption'(*Majjhima Nikaya*, 26)..." He concluded that these suffering states must have their positive counterparts; there must be another mode of existence, therefore, and it was up to him to find it. Cf. Karen Armstrong, *Buddha*, NY: Penguin, 2001, pp. 3, 99.

30. Thich Nhat Hanh, *Living Buddha, Living Christ*, New York: Penguin, 1995, p. 61.

31. Rajiv Mehrotra, *All You Ever Wanted to Know From His Holiness the Dalai Lama on Happiness, Life, Living, and Much More*, Carlsbad, CA: Hay House, 2009, p. 83.

32. Rajiv Mehrotra, op cit., pg. 82.

33. Geddes MacGregor, *Reincarnation and Christianity: A New Vision of the Role of Rebirth in Christian Thought*. Wheaton, IL: Theosophical Publishing House, 1978, p. 16.

34. Ibid, p. 17.

35. Hebrews 9:27. Many other passages from both Old and New Testaments dealing with death read most naturally as denials of reincarnation. See 2 Sam 12:23; 14:4; Job 7:9-10; Ps 78:39; Matt 25:31-46; Luke 23: 39-43; Acts 17:21; 2 Cor 5:1; 4:8; Rev 20: 11-15.

36. Phil 3:20-21.

37. Mal 3:1; 4:5.

38. Luke 1:17 (emphasis added).

39. 2 Kings 2:11.

40. See Ex 3:2; 13:21; 19:18. Volkmar Fritz, *A Continental Commentary: 1 & 2 Kings* Minneapolis, MN: Fortress Press, 2003, p. 235. "It is assumed that Elijah climbs onto the chariot sent from heaven and is translated there. Elijah is the only figure in the Hebrew Bible who enjoys this particular privilege. Even Moses, the greatest of the prophets so far, had to die in the land of Moab... Otherwise, only Enoch was translated by God (Gen 5:24)...That the fate of death is suspended nowhere else in the Hebrew Bible (apart from Enoch) is what makes Elijah's translation exceptional."

41. Matt 17; Mark 9.

42. John 9:2-3.

43. Ananda Coomaraswamy, *Buddha and the Gospel of Buddhism*, New York: Harper and Row, 1964 p. 108.

44. See also Ps. 109:14; Isa. 65:6-7. Norman L. Geisler and Ron Rhodes, *When Cultists Ask: A Popular Handbook on Cultic Misinterpretations*, Grand Rapids, MI: Baker Books, 1997, pp. 174-75.

45. Ex 20:5. See also Nu 16:31-34; Josh 7:24.

46. Joseph Head, S.L. Cranston, *Reincarnation: The Phoenix Fire Mystery*. NY: Warner Books, 1979, p. 134. Similarly see Shirley MacLaine, *Out on a Limb (New York: Bantam, 1986)*, pp. 234-235.

47. They often misdate and confuse the councils of Nicea with Constantinople. The two ecumenical councils of Nicea were in A.D. 325 and 787, not 553. Neither dealt with reincarnation. Second Constantinople convened in A.D. 553 but didn't address the question of reincarnation.

48. Geisler and Nix identify 36,289 New Testament citations from the Fathers of the second to the fourth century. This is enough to reconstruct the entire NT sans eleven verses. See Geisler and Nix, *General Introduction to the Bible*, 1968, revised 1986.

49. G.R.S. Meade, *Pistis Sophia: A Gnostic Gospel*, Garber Communications, 1921 reprinted 1984, pp. 8-10, 262-3 at http://www.gnosis.org/library/psophint.htm.

50. Justin Martyr, *Dialogue with Trypho*, 4–5 (c. 135).

51. See Ireneaus, *Against Heresies* , Books I, chapter 25 and II, chapter 33. Hippolytus, *The Refutation of all Heresies*, Book VII, chapter 20.

52. Clement of Alexandria, *Stromata* IV, 12; VI 4. One can hold a doctrine of pre-existing souls without adopting reincarnation, as do the Mormons (Church of Jesus Christ of Latter Day Saints).

53. Second Constantinople condemned Origen's belief that souls exist in heaven before coming to earth. Origen writes against reincarnation in his *Commentary on John* 6:7 and his *Commentary on Matthew* 10:20; 11:17; 13:1.

54. Tertullian, *On the Soul*, chapter 23-4, 29-35.

55. John Hick's *Death and Eternal Life*, Philadelphia: Westminster/John Knox Press, 1994 has an extensive discussion of the church fathers and reincarnation.

56. *Certain Questions on Eschatology*, International Theological Commission, 1993, #9.3 at http://www.vatican.va/roman_curia/congregations/cfaith/cti_documents/rc_cti_1990_problemi-attuali-escatologia_en.html.

57. Eph 1:6-8.

58. *Certain Questions on Eschatology*, International Theological Commission, 1993, #9.3.

59. "As a man casts off his worn-out clothes and takes on other new ones, so does the embodied [self] cast off its worn-out bodies and enter other new ones," proclaims the *Bhagavad Gita*, 2:22; Cf. *Svetashvatara* Upanishad, V, 10.

60. Currently, N.T. Wright's *The Resurrection of the Son of God*, Minneapolis: Fortress Press, 2003 is the most scholarly, yet accessible, presentation of the Resurrection. Less academic but very sound are Gary R. Habermas, Michael Licona, *The Case for the Resurrection of Jesus*, Grand Rapids: Kregel, 2004; Michael Licona, *The Resurrection of Jesus: A New Historiographical Approach*. For a debate, "Is There Historical Evidence for the Resurrection of Jesus? A Debate between William Lane Craig and Bart D. Ehrman" March 28, 2006, College of the Holy Cross, Worcester, Massachusetts, http://academics.holycross.edu/files/crec/resurrection-debate-transcript.pdf.

OPPONENT #4
Islam: A Competing Kingdom on Earth

1. John Paul II, *Crossing the Threshold of Hope*, New York: Alfred A. Knopf, 1994, p. 93.

2. William Lane Craig, "The Jesus of the Bible vs. the Jesus of the Qur'an," lecture, La Mirada, CA: Biola University, disc one. n.d. www.reasonablefaith.org.

3. William Lane Craig, "The Jesus of the Bible vs. the Jesus of the Qur'an," lecture, La Mirada, CA: Biola University, disc one. n.d. www.reasonablefaith.org.

4. See Vatican II *Nostra Aetate* [Declaration on the Relation of the Church to Non-Christian Religions], #3; Michael L. Fitzgerald and John Borelli, *Interfaith Dialogue: A Catholic View*, "Christian-Muslim Relations," Maryknoll, NY: Orbis, 2006, pp.85-162; Maurice Borrmans, *Guidelines for Dialogue Between Christians and Muslims* by the Pontifical Council for Interreligious Dialogue, Mahwah, NJ: Paulist Press, 1981. Unfortunately, this suffers from preceding the rise of the new Jihadist groups.

5. Sura 4:171; These passages are taken from taken from the most popular English translation of the Qu'ran by Abdullah Yusuf Ali, *The Holy Qur'an: Text, Translation, and Commentary*, new revised Edition, Brentwood, MD: Amana Corporation, 1989. The original work was published in 1938. English translations of the Qur'an are discussed at http://www.meforum.org/717/assessing-english-translations-of-the-quran.

6. Sura 18:5.

7. Sura 4:116.

8. Sura 5: 79, 82.

9. Whether the sin is literally unforgiveable or not is debated. See Sura 4:116.

10. Allah is the general Arabic word for "the God." Pagans used it in pre-Islamic Arabia.

11. Ruqaiyyah Maqsood, *Islam*, Chicago: NTC Publishing Group, 1994, p. 45. In *A Common Word Between Us and You* by The Royal Aal al-Bayt Institute for Islamic Thought, Jordan, October 13, 2007 (www.acommonword.org or www.acommonword.com), God's oneness and denial that he has a son or "associate" leads the document. "The Prophet Muhammad, said: '*The best that I have said—myself, and the prophets that came before me—is: 'There is no god but God, He Alone, He hath no associate, His is the sovereignty and His is the praise and He hath power over all things.'*" The document does not start by seeking common ground. Rather, it leads with the profound differences between Christianity and Islam and issues a call to conversion. Catholics prefer to begin by stating what we share. Even urbane Muslim scholars prefer to begin with the difference. After all, this is Islam's reason for existence: to assert God's oneness and deny Christ's divine sonship.

12. Ibn Taymiyyah, "The Status of the Arabic Language in Islam," www.sunnah online.com/ilm/quran/0021.htm.

13. In some countries, women may gather together with the men for public prayer as long as the women stay together at the back of the mosque.

14. Jihad, translated "struggle," is the sixth pillar of Islam. While it can refer to the inner struggle against temptation, jihad, historically, refers *primarily* to armed struggle for the faith. Since the 1924 abolition of the caliphate, Muslims have necessarily favored the non-armed definition. Historically, jihad was offensive as well as defensive. See Johns Hopkins University international affairs scholar, Mary Habek's *Knowing the Enemy: Jihadist Ideology and the War on Terror*, New Haven: Yale University Press, 2007. Cf. Paul Fregosi, *Jihad in the West: Muslim Conquests from the 7th to the 21st* Centuries, Amherst, NY: Prometheus Books, 1998: "The jihad has been the most unrecorded and disregarded major event of history."

15. See Seyyed Hossein Nasr, *The Garden of Truth: The Vision and Promise of Sufism*, 2007; Carl W. Ernst, *Sufism: An Introduction to the Mystical Tradition of Islam*, 2011; William C. Chittick, *Sufism: A Beginner's Guide*, 2007. Paulist Press' *Classics of Western Spirituality* series contains Sufi contributions. Neo-Sufism as an organized social force is defined as a "competitor to radical Islam in terms of shaping the Islamic reaction to modernity. The crucial difference is that radicals want to seize political power, while neo-Sufis generally want to change people's souls" See John L. Allen, *Future Church*, New York: Doubleday, 2009, p. 111. The "Gulen" movement is "a sort of Islamic analogue to Opus Dei" that originates with and is led by two Turks, Said Nursia (1878-1960) and his disciple, Fethullah Gulen (b. 1947-). This "Gulen" movement emphasizes building schools rather than wielding political power. Gulen, who met with John Paul II in 1998, is also a pioneer in inter-faith dialogue.

16. Revivals of *Sharia*, commonly lead to persecution of Muslim "sects at variance with the dominant practice of the country, such as Sufis, Ibadis,... Ahmadis, or Shi'ite minorities in Sunni countries and vice-versa." Sufism, however, does not necessarily immunize against forceful implementation of *Sharia*. Grand Ayatollah, Ruhollah Khomeini (1902-1989), past leader of Iran, the Chechan jihadists, and founder of the Muslim Brotherhood, Hasan al-Banna (1906 – 1949), all loved Sufism. Robert Spencer, "Libya: Sufis face continuing persecution after revolution" at *JihadWatch.org*, Feb 2, 2012.

17. Marshall Hodgson, *The Venture of Islam; Conscience and History in a World Civi-*

lization argues that Sufism does not appear in the Islamic world until large numbers of Christian monks and hermits, especially in Syria and Egypt, come under Muslim rule. Sufism's differences with Sunni or Shia a result of Christian mystical or contemplative influence? For an exchange between Muslim and Eastern Orthodox thinkers see James S. Cutsinger, ed., *Paths to the Heart: Sufism and the Christian East*, Bloomington, IN: World Wisdom, Inc., 2002.

18. Kenneth Cragg, *The Call of the Minaret*, New York: Oxford University Press, 1964, p. 39.

19. Sura 112 al-Ikhlas, "the purity of faith."

20. Sura 2:116.

21. Comment on Sura 2:116, Abdullah Yusuf Ali, *The Holy Qur'an: Text, Translation, and Commentary*, new revised edition, Beltsville, MD: Amana Publications, 1989, p. 49. He repeats the same thought in his comment on Sura 112.

22. Quoted in Anis A. Shorrosh, *Islam Revealed*, Nashville: Thomas Nelson, 1988.

23. *CCC* 239, "We ought...to recall that God transcends the human distinction between the sexes. He is neither man nor woman; he is God. He also transcends human motherhood and fatherhood, although he is their origin and standard: no one is father as God is Father." Cf. Ps 27:10; Eph 3:14; Is 49:15.

24. *CCC*, 239, 240, 246; Council of Florence (1438). Origen (185-254) seems to have introduced the term, "eternal generation of the Son." Catholic, Orthodox, and Lutheran creeds teach it, as do the Reformed Belgic Confession (c. 1562) and Westminster Confession of Faith (1646). The key NT passages are Jn 1:14-18; 3:16-18; 1 Jn 4:9; Heb 11:17. Calvin did hold Christ's eternal sonship but found "eternal generation" too speculative (*Institutes* I, xiii. 29). Most "Calvinists," however, did not follow him and retained the earlier Catholic understanding.

25. It happened but rarely. See Deut 1:31; 8:5; 14:1; 32:6; 2 Sam 7:14; Pss. 2:7; 89:26; 106:13; Jer 3:4-19; 31:9; Is 1:2; 63:16; 64:8; Hos 11:1; Mal 1:6; 2:10; 3:17.

26. See Sirach 23:1-4; 51:10 where we have the prayer of an individual calling God "father." Cf. Wisdom 2:13-16; 14:3; Tob 13:4; Jub 1:24, 28; 19:29; 3 Mac 5:7; 6:4-8; T. Levi 18:6; T. Judah 24:2; Ps. Sol 13:8 and also the Joseph Prayer in the Qumran scrolls 1QH 9:35f; 4Q372 1:16f. where Joseph calls God my Father.

27. It appears on his lips some 65 times in the Synoptic Gospels and 111 times in John. God as Father and Christ as Son often occur together, as in the phrase "the God and Father of our Lord Jesus," See Rom 15:6; 1 Cor 1:3; 2 Cor 1:3; 11:31; Eph 1:3, 17; Col 1:3; 1 Thess 1:1; 1 Pet 1:3.

28. Louis Bouyer, "Father" in *Dictionary of Theology*, Tournai, Belgium: Desclee Co., 1965, p. 162.

29. Catholics accept Muslims as fellow monotheists. Arabic Catholics use "Allah" as their word for God. *Nostra Aetate's* statement on Muslims is fairly positive although it doesn't address Islam as a system or Mohammad as a prophet. It refers to the Muslims' *belief* and *their claim* to be Abrahamic.

30. Alhaj A.D. Ajijola, *The Essence of Faith in Islam*, Lahore, Pakistan: Islamic Publications Ltd. , 1978, p. 55.

31. Alhaj A.D. Ajijola, *The Myth of the Cross*, Lahore, Pakistan: Islamic Publication Ltd., 1975, p. 170.

32. Jaroslav Pelikan, *Imago Dei: The Byzantine Apologia for Icons*, orig 1987, rep 2011. "Iconoclasm was defeated — by Byzantine politics, by popular revolts, by monastic piety, and, most fundamentally of all, by theology, just as it had been theology that the opponents of images had used to justify their actions." Cf. John of Damascus, *On the Divine Images*; Léonide Ouspensky, *Theology of the Icon*, 1992. FAQ on icons and images from an Eastern Orthodox blogger http://orthodoxinfo.com/general/icon_faq.aspx.

33. Phil Parshall, *The Crescent and the Cross*, Kindle edition, location 188 of 3177.

34. Vatican II, *Nostra Aetate*, 3.

35. One common argument to illustrate the Triunity of God and deny tritheism requires us to note that the New Testament describes Father, Son, and Holy Spirit as God. Yet there is only one God. The Church reconciles those two facts by showing that

in the nature of the one God there subsists three persons, Father, Son and Holy Spirit. We don't think in terms of arithmetic, 1+1+1=3 for that would be tritheism. Rather, we think multiplication, 1x1x1=1 which is Trinitarian monotheism.

36. Miroslav Volf, *Allah: A Christian Response*, New York: HarperOne, 2011, p. 165.

37. Strangely, Ibn Taymiyya (1263-1328), the spiritual ancestor of the modern Salafi movement, e.g., the Wahhabis, argues that God actively loves before creation. Therefore, Allah's love is essential. Who or what does Allah love? God loves his own self. Remarkably, this sounds like the beginning of divine plurality, some kind of binitarianism. Compare Miroslav Volf, *Allah: A Christian Response*, p. 166ff. and Seyyed Hossein Nasr, *The Garden of Truth: The Vision and Promise of Sufism, Islam's Mystical Tradition*, San Francisco: HarperOne, 2007, p. 61.

38. *CCC* 374 uses the language of friendship. Cf. 277, 396, 1468.

39. See Paul's letter to the Romans, chapters 5-8 esp. 8:18ff.

40. Covenants aim at extending sacred kinship or family bonds and comprise major turning points in salvation history. See Scott W. Hahn, *Kinship by Covenant: A Canonical Approach to the Fulfillment of God's Saving Promises*, New Haven: Yale University Press, 2009. His more popular works rely on the centrality of a covenant-making God. See *A Father Who Keeps His Promises: God's Covenant Love in Scripture*, 1998 as well as *Swear to God: The Promise and Power of the Sacraments*, 2004. In Islam, the word "covenant" bears little resemblance to the biblical tradition. "God's covenant with people *has been the same* since He created Adam." See Suras 2:83,125; 3:71,187; 5:7-12. See http://www .islamicanswer.org/wordpress/?p=1804 and http://www.islaam.net/main/display_article _printview.php?id=1382. In Scripture, through Abraham, Moses, David and to Jesus and the New Covenant, the scope and immediacy of the covenants grow. We see God acting in history to expand the covenant and insure increased closeness and intimacy with his people. This climaxes with the Incarnation and the New Covenant in which God shares his very life with us through Eucharist.

41. If he is so "Other" can I say I know him? Baptist theologian and apologist Norman L. Geisler describes this problem in *Answering Islam*. Grand Rapids: Baker, 1993, pp. 134-145.

42. Also, it seems clear that "Allah does not love the unbelievers" Sura 3:32.

43. Some Muslims claim that Allah is not literally close. He certainly is not intimate as in the biblical portrayal which includes family, even nuptial, language. He is close in the sense of knowing what's going on. He is close because he knows all things. His omnipresence is just another word for his omniscience. Allah is so far transcendent to creation that to claim his presence here is blasphemous. The jugular verse may refer to Allah's messengers, guardian angels not Allah himself.

44. See Hans Kung, *Islam: Past, Present, Future*, Oxford: OneWorld, 2004.

45. Ismael al-Faruqi, *Christian Mission and Islamic Da'wah: Proceedings of the Chambèsy Dialogue Consultation* [held 1976 in Chambèsy, Switzerland], Leicester: The Islamic Foundation, 1982, pp. 47-48.

46. Scott Hahn, lecture *Abba or Allah*, n.d. Lighthouse Catholic Media, http://lighthouse catholicmediablog.blogspot.com/2012/05/abba-or-allah-by-dr-scott-hahn.html. While Paul identifies himself as a servant of Christ Jesus, the language of family and friendship have a priority given Jesus' words: "I no longer call you servants...but friends" (Jn15:15). He also shares his intimacy with the Father with us (Jn 14:1-7, 15-18; 15:1-17; 17:1-10; 22-26). We are adopted in God's family and made his children, receiving his Spirit and sharing Christ's inheritance. See Romans 5-8.

47. http://www.ncregister.com/daily-news/a-muslim-finds-the-catholic-faith-through -geography-and-theology/#ixzz248EppXmx.

48. "Muslims Tell ... "Why I chose Jesus" http://www.30-days.net/testimony/why -jesus/. The cry of the human heart for loving union with God, our heavenly Father, to "find a friend in Jesus" are well illustrated in Bilquis Sheikh and Richard H. Schneider, *I Dared to Call Him Father : The Miraculous Story of a Muslim Woman's Encounter with God*, Grand Rapids: Chosen Books, orig. 1978, rep. 2003.

49. Congregation for the Doctrine of the Faith, *Dominus Iesus*, 2000. "The Church's

tradition… reserves the designation of *inspired texts* to the canonical books of the Old and New Testaments, since these are inspired by the Holy Spirit."

50. The Qur'an cannot be received by Catholics as binding revelation. "God has revealed himself fully by sending his own Son…The Son is his Father's definitive Word; so there will be no further Revelation after him" (*CCC*, 50, 67, 73).

51. Annemarie Schimmel and Abdoldjavad Falaturi, *We Believe in One God*, New York: Seabury Press, 1979, p. 5.

52. This is always qualified by the testimony of the Sufis.

53. *Lumen Gentium*, 11.

54. Anne Lamott, *Help, Thanks, Wow: The Three Essential Prayers*. New York: Riverhead, 2012.

55. Again, historically Sufism is not considered "normative" Islam. I like to think that human beings are often better than their theologies and worldviews. Being made in the image and likeness of God, worship is central to being human and this can't forever be suppressed. It will be like the odd flower that pushes its way through the cement sidewalk. I see the Sufi phenomenon developing in spite of mainstream Islam, not because of it.

56. See Hilaire Belloc, *The Great Heresies*, Freeport, NY: Libraries Press, 1937, especially chapter four.

57. John 2:5.

58. Fulton J. Sheen, *The World's First Love: Mary, Mother of God*, San Francisco: Ignatius Press, orig. 1952 rep. 2011, p. 207.

59. See Carl G. Schulte, C.M., *The Life of Sister Marie de Mandat-Grancey* and *Mary's House in Ephesus* are published in a joint edition, Charlotte, NC: TAN, 2011.

60. See http://www.zeitun-eg.org/pz0001.htm.

61. Vatican II, *Nostra Aetate*, 3.

62. John Paul II, *Crossing the Threshold of Hope*, New York: Alfred A. Knopf, 1994, p. 91. John Paul II also recognized Islam's importance to Thomas Aquinas, by noting "the dialogue that Thomas carried on with the writings of the Arab [Ibn Rushd, Averroes] and Jewish [Rabbi Moses Maimonides] thinkers of his time." Suzanne McCarthy, "Out of Cordoba," Nov 20, 2011, http://bltnotjustasandwich.com/2011/11/20/out-of-cordoba/. Interstingly, Thomas Aquinas dubbed Aristotle, "the philosopher"; Ibn Rushd or Averroes, "the Commentator" and Moses Maimonides as "the Rabbi." There was clear difference but no lack of respect.

63. Though it would have taken us far afield, Islam denies one of the most certain and best attested facts of ancient history irrespective of one's theology or philosophy or worldview: the crucifixion of Jesus of Nazareth and his empty tomb.

64. John Paul II, *Crossing the Threshold of Hope*, New York: Alfred A. Knopf, 1994, p. 92-93. Similarly, Benedict XVI/Cdl. Ratzinger affirms all that can be affirmed but never failing to clearly and charitably set forth the differences. On November 30, 2006, Benedict XVI visited Istanbul's Blue Mosque. Standing alongside Grand Mufti Mustafa Cagrici, he engaged in a moment of shared silent prayer. The Catholic Church, however, does not regard all religions as equally true or helpful. In fact, years earlier, as prefect of the CDF, Cardinal Ratzinger warned that inter-religious prayer was not "a concession to that relativism which negates the very meaning of truth." See John L. Allen, *The Future Church: How Ten Trends are Revolutionizing the Catholic Church*, New York: Doubleday, 2009, p. 95.

65. *Nostra Aetate*, 3; Paul Moses, "Pope: Francis's `dialogue' with Muslims should inspire us," *Commonweal*, January 28, 2010; http://www.commonwealmagazine.org/blog/?p=6509. While political historian Samuel Huntington warned of a possible "clash of civilizations," Catholics remain ministers of reconciliation and ambassadors of Christ (2 Cor 5:18-20). How apt is the prayer attributed to St. Francis. "Lord, make me an instrument of your peace… Where there is hatred, let me sow love. Where there is injury, pardon." We were born for such a time as this and called to such a task as this. See Samuel P. Huntington, *The Clash of Civilizations and the Remaking of World Order*, New York: Simon & Schuster, orig. 1996, rep. 2011.

66. This incident between the Saint and the Sultan remains an object of inquiry. See *When the Saint Met the Sultan: A Medieval 'Summit' with 21st-Century Lessons?* from

the Fordham Center on Religion and Culture website: http://www.fordham.edu/images/
undergraduate/centeronreligionculture/Feb%2017%20Saint%20Sultan__Transcript.pdf.

Part Two / Abusers of Science and Reason

OPPONENT #5
Science and Warfare With Religion

1. Anthony T. Kronman, *Education's End: Why Our Colleges and Universities Have
Given Up on the Meaning of Life*, New Haven: Yale University Press, 2007, pp. 207-08.
2. Quoted in James L. Heft, *Believing Scholars: Ten Catholic Intellectuals*, New York:
Fordham University Press, 2005, p. 82. The often unequal discussion between "science"
and "theology" is due to a basic category mistake. In popular discussion, science is treated
as though it were a synonym for "nature" or "the way the world is." In contrast, theology
is treated as a product of fallible human culture, i.e., what people opine about God or
the bible as though there is no hard object to be investigated. In truth, both science and
theology have hard objects to investigate and both human disciplines create a culture
around the discipline. Science has a culture to it as much as theology and is as fallible an
enterprise. See James K.A. Smith, "Science and Religion Take Practice: Engaging Science as a Culture," *Perspectives on Science and Christian Faith: The Journal of the American
Scientific Affiliation*, Vol. 65, Number 1, March 2013, pp. 3-9.
3. Albert Einstein, "Science, Philosophy, and Religion," 1940 as quoted in Alice
Calaprice, ed., *The Quotable Einstein*, Princeton: Princeton University Press, 1996.
4. *Does science make belief in God obsolete?* A Templeton Conversation, Templeton
Foundation, 2010; http://www.templeton.org/belief/.
5. *Beyond Belief: Science, Religion, Reason and Survival* hosted by the Science Network. La Jolla, CA, 2010; http://thesciencenetwork.org/programs/beyond-belief-science
-religion-reason-and-survival.
6. Virtually all the *"Great Books"* authors (c. 150) "discourse on the divine. The rare
exceptions are a few mathematicians and physicists." See Mortimer Adler, *Great Books
of the Western World*, Robert Maynard Hutchins, ed., Chicago: *Encyclopedia Britannica*,
1994, vol 2, p. 561.
7. I list here some contemporary professional philosophers who deal with theistic
argumentation as both professionals and as Christians of various sorts: Richard Swinburne, Alvin Plantinga, William Alston, George Mavrodes, William Lane Craig, Dallas Willard. Bernard Lonergan, Keith Ward, Brian Davies, David Burrell, Elisabeth
Anscombe, Peter Geach, Jacques Maritain, Gabriel Marcel, Josef Pieper, Fergus Kerr,
Henry Veatch, Norris Clarke, Robert Sokolowski, Charles Taylor, John Rist. See Thomas
V. Morris, *God and the Philosophers*, New York: Oxford, 1996; Phillip Blond, ed., *Post-
Secular Philosophy*, New York: Routledge, 1998; Chris L. Firestone and Nathan A. Jacobs,
editors, *The Persistence of the Sacred in Modern Thought*, Notre Dame, IN: University of
Notre Dame Press, 2012. Boldly enlisting the atheistic critique to purify Christian
thought and life is Merold Westphal, *Suspicion & Faith: The Religious Uses of Modern
Atheism*, New York: Fordham University Press, 1998: "When our holiness has halitosis
we need someone to let us know and on such occasions those who wish us no good can
be helpful" (p. 284). More popular presentations are Kreeft's & Tacelli's *Handbook of
Catholic Apologetics*; Lewis' *Mere Christianity*. Feser's *Last Superstition: A Refutation of the
New Atheism*. Williams' *Existential Reasons for Belief in God*. William Lane Craig's debate
with Christopher Hitchens is available on the internet and DVD.
8. Wiker & Witt's *A Meaningful World*; Spitzer, *New Proofs for the Existence of God*;
God and Modern Physics, DVD; Gonzalez & Richards, *The Privileged Planet*; Varghese
& Flew *There is a God*.
9. Paul Davies, *The Mind of God*, London: Simon and Schuster, 1992, p. 232. Since
then Davies has clarified that by God he means something quite different from historic Catholicism. See his article "What Happened Before the Big Bang?" http://www
.beliefnet.com/News/Science-Religion/2001/01/What-Happened-Before-The-Big
-Bang.aspx#ixzz1jrh2DNSA.

10. Richard Swinburne, *The Existence of God,* 2d ed., Oxford University Press, 2004, pp. 293-327; Also "Arguing God from Religious Experience," http://www .closertotruth.com/video-profile/Arguing-God-from-Religious-Experience-Richard -Swinburne-/953; D. Elton Trueblood, *The Knowledge of God,* pp. 144-152. For a popular effort to mix an apologetic for religious experience with actual testimonies see Al Kresta and Nick Thomm, *Moments of Grace,* 2010.

11. "New atheists" Richard Dawkins, Sam Harris, and the late Christopher Hitchens all credit the religiously motivated violence of September 11th as key. See Dawkins: *A Devil's Chaplain,* 2004, p. 156; Harris: *The End of Faith* p. 67; Hitchens: *Hitch 22: A Memoir* 2010, p. 241 and *God is Not Great.* 2006, p. 283.

12. See John Lennox, *God and Stephen Hawking: Whose Design is it Anyway?* Physicist Stephen Barr responds in *First Things,* Sep 10, 2010. Fr. Robert Spitzer's 7 minute video at http://www.investingforcatholics.com/articles/Hawkings_Attack_on_God_Draws _Logical_Response.aspx. Also the "The Curious Metaphysics of Dr. Stephen Hawking" available at magisreasonfaith.org. A collection of responses to Hawking from serious thinkers http://vibrantdance.org/_blog/Articles/tag/Hugh_Ross/.

13. In spite of Hawking's wishes and overpromising, the problem of why there is something rather than nothing is still not resolved by astrophysics and cosmology. See William E. Carroll, "Thomas Aquinas, Creation, and Big Bang Cosmology" in Chris Impey and Catherine Petry, *Science And Theology: Ruminations on the Cosmos,* Vatican City: Vatican Observatory, 2004. Philosopher William Lane Craig also critiques Hawking's boundary conditions at http://www.reasonablefaith.org/stephen-hawking-and-god.

14. John Updike, *Roger's Version,* New York: Random House, 1996.

15. *Religion and Ethics NewsWeekly:* "John Updike," November 19, 2004, PBS, Episode 812. http://www.pbs.org/wnet/religionandethics/week812/exclusive.html; Katelyn Beaty, "John Updike, 'Theological Novelist,' Dies at 76," *Christianity Today,* January, 30, 2009. http://blog.christianitytoday.com/ctliveblog/archives/2009/01/john_updike_nor.html.

16. The "God of the gaps" was a self-defeating strategy that helped spur the rise of modern atheism. Michael J. Buckley S.J, *At the Origins of Modern Atheism,* 1990; Brad S. Gregory, *The Unintended Reformation: How a Religious Revolution Secularized Society,* 2012; James C. Turner, *Without God, Without Creed: The Origins of Unbelief in America,* 1986.

17. Dan Graves, *Scientists of Faith: 48 Biographies* Grand Rapids: Kregel, 1996; Paul M. Anderson, *Professors Who Believe,* Downers Grove, IL: InterVarsity Press, 1996; *Jesuits and the Sciences,1540-1999* at http://www.lib.luc.edu/specialcollections/exhibits/show/ jesuitsandthesciences.

18. Richard Dawkins, *The Blind Watchmaker: Why Evidence of Evolution Reveals a Universe Without Design,* New York: Norton, 1996, pp. xvi, 1, 22, 36. Stephen Hawking, *A Brief History of Time,* New York: Bantam, 1988, p. 191. In 1988, Hawking claimed that when physicists find the theory he and his colleagues are looking for - a so-called "theory of everything" - then they will have seen into "the mind of God." God, however, is not a person but an abstract mathematical principle. Seeing into his mind is ultimately a triumph of human reason not a revelation of divine love.

19. Stephen Jay Gould, *Rocks of Ages: Science and Religion in the Fullness of Life,* New York: Ballantine Books, 2002. These magisteria overlap when Scripture makes historical claims subject to the science of archaeology. Gregory W. Dawes, "Could There Be Another Galileo Case? Galileo, Augustine and Vatican II," *Journal of Religion & Society* Volume 4, 2002, http://moses.creighton.edu/jrs/2002/2002-2.pdf.

20. There are many ways of framing the relationship between science and faith. Astrophysicist George Coyne, S.J., former head of the Vatican Observatory recommends five discourses of John Paul II on science and faith:
- To the Pontifical Academy of Sciences on 10 November 1979;
- On October 28, 1986, fiftieth anniversary of the Pontifical Academy of Sciences;
- To the Director of the Vatican Observatory, on tricentennial of Newton's *Philosophiae Naturalis Principia Mathematica* (1687);
- To the Pontifical Academy of Sciences on October 22, 1996;

- Encyclical *Fides et Ratio* [Faith and Reason], September 14, 1998 at http://www.disf.org/en/OtherTexts/Coyne.asp.

21. See Justin Barrett's *Born Believers: The Science of Children's Religious Belief,* New York: Free Press, 2012. Cf. http://www.gnxp.com/blog/2006/04/10-questions-for-justin-l-barrett.php.

22. Rom 1:18-32. From the earliest cave paintings and burial sites through today's country gospel music, we find human beings bearing witness to an ambiguous but real "consciousness of God." Religion's relationship to human brain architecture, ritual, art, morality, language or primitive communities is much disputed. Human religious sensibilities seem present from the beginning of *Homo sapiens.* Religion, like language, seems to be a human universal. No human civilization has been without religion and none have been able to suppress or eliminate it. The earliest cave art and ritualized burials (c. 100-125,000 years ago) include grave goods indicating belief in an afterlife. Wherever we find modern humans, we find religious expression. See Philip Lieberman, *Uniquely Human: The Evolution of Speech, Thought, and Selfless Behavior.* Cambridge: Harvard University Press, 1991. A generation ago, Austrian Jesuit priest, linguist, and anthropologist Wilhelm Schmidt (1868-1954) published his 12-volume *Der Ursprung der Gottesidee (The Origin of the Idea of God,* 1912-1954) and argued that religion has *devolved* from an original monotheism. His works translated into English include, *The Origin and Growth of Religion* (1931) as well as *Primitive Religion* (1939). His research, if not his thesis, was greatly respected even though he rejected the dominant "myth of evolutionism." For a look at the origin of religion, see Rodney Stark, *Discovering God: The Origins of the Great Religions and the Evolution of Belief,* New York: HarperOne, 2007.

23. David Berlinski, *The Devil's Delusion: Atheism and Its Scientific Pretensions,* New York: Basic Books, 2009. See also Karl Giberson and Mariano Artigas, *Oracles of Science: Celebrity Scientists Versus God and Religion,* New York: Oxford University Press, 2009.

24. "The heavens declare the glory of God." Other relevant texts on creation include Rom 1:18-32; Gen 1-3; Prov 8:22-36; Gen 9:8-17; Job 38-42; Ps 8, 19, 148; Is 40:9-31; John 1:1-18; Col 1:15ff. See Swinburne's *Is There a God?* (2010); Wiker & Witt's *A Meaningful World* (2006); Spitzer, *New Proofs for the Existence of God* (2010) as well as the documentary DVD, *God and Modern Physics* (2011) Gonzalez & Richards, *The Privileged Planet* (2004); Meyer's *Signature in the Cell* (2010); Varghese & Flew *There is a God* (2008); Robert Jastrow, *God and the Astronomers* (1978/2000); Owen Gingerich, *God's Universe* (2006); Keith Ward, *Why There Almost Certainly is a God* (2009).

25. White *falsely* claims Copernicus feared for his life, that many early "scientists," including Friar Roger Bacon, were repeatedly persecuted, that the Inquisition had "Galileo tortured and humiliated as the worst of unbelievers." This is false and wrongheaded. See Ronald Numbers, *Galileo Goes to Jail,* (2009); Benjamin Wiker, *The Catholic Church & Science,* (2011); Jeffrey Burton Russell. *Inventing the Flat Earth: Columbus and Modern Historian* (1991); Thomas Dixon, *Science and Religion: A Very Short Introduction* (2008), pp. 18-36.

26. Steven Shapin, *The Scientific Revolution.* Chicago: University of Chicago Press, 1998, p. 196.

27. Alfred North Whitehead, *Science and the Modern World,* orig. 1926, rep. 1997, pp. 13, 61, 141.

28. See Cameron Wybrow, *Creation, Nature, and Political Order in the Philosophy of Michael Foster (1903–1959),* Lewiston, New York: Edwin Mellen Press, 1992; Edward B. Davis, "Christianity and Early Modern Science: The Foster Thesis Reconsidered" in *Evangelicals and Science in Historical Perspective,* Oxford University Press, 1999, pp.75–95.

29. For instance, Herbert Butterfield, *The Origins of Modern Science,* New York: Free Press, orig. 1949 rev. 1997 as well as primary documents like Harvey's "On the Motion of the Heart and Blood" which assumes a divinely ordered Nature or various portions of the 19th century *Bridgewater Treatises On the Power, Wisdom and Goodness of God As Manifested in the Creation* and, of course, William Paley's *Natural Theology.*

30. "New Age" cosmologies reject materialism, naturalism and physicalism. They are commonly pantheistic or pandeistic. They frequently try to commandeer quantum

physics and consciousness studies to illustrate their conception of the cosmos. See Chopra & Mlodinow, *War of the Worldviews* (2011), Capra, *The Tao of Physics* (1975); Zukav, *The Dancing Wu Li Masters* (1979); Haisch's, *The God Theory* (2009) and *The Purpose-Guided Universe* (2010).

31. Ken Wilber, *The Marriage of Sense and Soul: Integrating Science and Religion*, New York: Three Rivers Press, 1998, p. ix, x.

32. J.L. Heilbron, *The Sun in the Church: Cathedrals as Solar Observatories*, Cambridge: Harvard, 1999, p. 3.

33. Galileo, his family and friends did not react to the Church with the same intense indignation we witness today from ideologues hundreds of years removed. See Dave Sobel, *Galileo's Daughter: A Historical Memoir of Science, Faith and Love*, New York: Penguin Books, 1999. Also Ronald Numbers, *Galileo Goes to Jail* Harvard, 2009; Wade Rowland, *Galileo's Mistake*, Melbourne: Arcade, rev., 2012; Gregory W. Dawes, "Could There Be Another Galileo Case? Galileo, Augustine and Vatican II," *Journal of Religion & Society* Volume 4, 2002, at http://moses.creighton.edu/jrs/2002/2002-2.pdf. In 1992, Pope John Paul II apologized for the mistakes made by Catholics on the tribunal that presided over the Galileo trial. He called Galileo "a brilliant physicist...who practically invented the experimental method." The popular press made it appear as though the Pope was finally getting around to accepting Galileo's view of the cosmos. This is ludicrous.

34. Arthur Koestler, *The Sleepwalkers: A History of Man's Changing Vision of the Universe*, New York: Penguin Books, orig. 1959, rep.1990.

35. Gary Ferngren, ed., *Science and Religion*, Baltimore: Johns Hopkins University Press, 2003, p. xi.

36. Lawrence Principe, *Science and Religion*, "Warfare Thesis" lecture two, Teaching Company: Chantilly, VA: 2006, transcript p. 23. Cf. Russell (Ferngren, ed., *Science & Religion: A Historical Introduction*, Baltimore: Johns Hopkins University Press, 2002, p. 7). Also Brooke in *Science and Religion: Some Historical Perspectives;* Lindberg & Numbers, eds. *God and Nature: Historical Essays on the Encounter between Christianity and Science.*

37. For an excellent survey of the complexities, conflicts, co-operations and complementarities see David B. Wilson, "The Historiography of Science and Religion" in Gary B. Ferngren, Edward J. Larson, & Darrel W. Amundsen, eds., *The History of Science and Religion in the Western Tradition: An Encyclopedia*, London: Routledge, 2000, pp. 2ff.

38. David C. Lindberg, "Medieval Science and Religion" in Gary B. Ferngren, Edward J. Larson, & Darrel W. Amundsen, eds., *The History of Science and Religion in the Western Tradition: An Encyclopedia* p. 296.

39. Does Wilber really think that the bodily resurrection strains the credulity of 21st century people more than the laborers, slaves, farmers, fishermen, tax collectors, prostitutes and corrupt procurators in the 1st century. Ask any first or 21st century person: "Have you ever had a relative raised from the dead?" The numbers of those who answer yes will run about the same. That dead men stay dead is fairly self-evident whatever century one lives in.

40. Elaine Ecklund, *Science vs. Religion: What Scientists Really Think*, New York: Oxford University Press, 2010. See also http://blog.beliefnet.com/roddreher/2010/04/science-vs-religion-what-do-scientists-say.html. Also the National Academy of Sciences' document *Science and Creationism* reads, "Scientists, like many others, are touched with awe at the order and complexity of nature. Indeed, many scientists are deeply religious."

41. See Michael Heller, *Philosophy in Science: An Historical Introduction*, New York: Springer, 2011; *Creative Tension: Essays on Science and Religion*, Philadelphia: Templeton, 2003.

42. Charles Taylor, *A Secular Age*, Cambridge: Belknap of Harvard University Press, 2007.

43. George V. Coyne and Michael Heller, *A Comprehensible Universe: The Interplay of Science and Theology*, New York: Springer, 2008; *Wayfarers in the Cosmos: The Human Quest for Meaning*, New York: Crossroads, 2002.

44. http://www.usatoday.com/news/religion/2009-10-14-PopeNIH_N.htm. See Collins, *The Language of God: A Scientist Presents Evidence for Belief* (2006).

45. Justin Barrett, *Born Believers: The Science of Children's Religious Belief*, New York: Free Press, 2012.

46. John Lennox, *The Theory of Infinite Soluble Groups*, London: Clarendon Press, 2004; *Seven Days That Divide the World: The Beginning according to Genesis and Science*, Grand Rapids: Zondervan, 2011; *God's Undertaker: Has Science Buried God?*, revised, London: Lion UK, 2009; *Gunning for God: Why the New Atheists are Missing the Target*, London: Lion UK, 2011; *God and Stephen Hawking: Whose Design Is It Anyway?*, London: Lion UK, 2011.

47. John Polkinghorne, *Quantum Physics and Theology: An Unexpected Kinship*, New Haven: Yale University Press, 2008; *Quantum Theory: A Very Short Introduction*, Oxford: Oxford University Press, 2002; *Quarks, Chaos & Christianity: Questions to Science And Religion*, New York: Crossroads, 2002 revised.

48. Ian Hutchinson, *Monopolizing Knowledge*, Boston: Fias Press, 2011.

49. As quoted by Gabriel Meyer, "Pontifical Science Academy Bans on Stellar Cast," *National Catholic Register*, December 1-7, 1996, as cited on http://atheismexposed.tripd.com/nobelistsgod.htm.

50. Phillip Clayton, et al, *Science and the Spiritual Quest: New Essays by Leading Scientists* (New York, NY: Routledge, 2002).

51. Martin Nowak and Roger Highfield, *Supercooperators: The Mathematics of Evolution, Altruism and Human Behaviour (Or, Why We Need Each Other to Succeed*, New York: Free Press, 2012. Martin Nowak, *Evolutionary Dynamics: Exploring the Equations of Life*, Cambridge: Belknap Press of Harvard University Press, 2006. Many others are reassessing the adequacy of natural selection and mutation as causes for the changes we call "evolution" even apart from the creationist or intelligent design or theistic evolution criticisms. Persistent mathematical challenges, the incredulity of many cognitive scientists and the fragmentary nature of the fossil record keep people re-searching. This does not mean, however, that anyone has presented a more plausible picture of the genealogy of species than the current historical account. As often happens in the history of science (it happened with Galileo) one can have the right conclusion but the wrong chain of reasoning. The genealogy of species is independent of but not entirely unconnected to the mechanism of natural selection. See Jerry Fodor and Massimo Piattelli-Palmarini, *What Darwin Got Wrong*, New York: Picador, 2010, pp. 1-16; Cf. Massimo Piattelli-Palmarini, Juan Uriagereka, Pello Salaburu, eds., *Of Minds and Language: A Dialogue with Noam Chomsky in the Basque Country*, New York: Oxford University Press, 2011, pp. 408-409.

52. John Paul II, *Fides et Ratio* [Faith and Reason], 1998 should dispel any notion of Catholic hostility towards reason. Also Vatican I, *Dei Filius* 4: DS 3017 "Though faith is above reason, there can never be any real discrepancy between faith and reason." Cf. CCC, 159, *Gaudium Spes* 36:1. "Consequently, methodical research in all branches of knowledge, provided it is carried out in a truly scientific manner and does not override moral laws, can never conflict with the faith." Benedict XVI, *The Regensburg Lecture* edited and commentary by James V. Schall, San Francisco: Ignatius Press, 2007.

53. Richard Dawkins, Lecture "The "know-nothings," the "know-alls," and the "no-contests," *The Nullifidian*, December,1994, http://www.simonyi.ox.ac.uk/. He uses the same sentence elsewhere in his *The God Delusion*, 2006.

54. See Thomas Dixon, *Science and Religion: A Very Short Introduction*, "What are Science-Religion Debates All About," Oxford: Oxford University Press, 2008, pp. 1-17.

55. Jonathan Wright, *The Jesuits: Missions, Myths, and Histories*, London: HarperCollins, 2004, p. 182.

56. A.C. Crombie, *Robert Grosseteste and the Origins of Experimental Science 1100–1700*. Oxford: Clarendon Press, 1953, pp. 98, 107, 111. Cf. Leslie Stephen and Sidney Lee, ed., "Grosseteste, Robert" in *Dictionary of National Biography*. London: Oxford University Press, 1921 – 1996; C.C. Gillispie, ed., "Grosseteste, Robert." *Dictionary of Scientific Biography*, New York: Scribner's, 1970.

57. "Roger Bacon," *Stanford Encyclopedia of Philosophy*, http://plato.stanford.edu/entries/roger-bacon/#OpuMaiFouFivSixMatNatDeMulSpePerSciExp. See also David Lindberg on Andrew Dickson White's hagiography of Bacon as the scientist persecuted

by the medieval Church. See his "Science as Handmaiden: Roger Bacon and the Patristic Tradition," in Michael H. Shank, ed., *The Scientific Enterprise in Antiquity and the Middle Ages*, Chicago: University of Chicago Press, 2000.

58. Also Karl Alois Kneller, *Christianity and the Leaders of Modern Science: A Contribution to the History of Culture during the Nineteenth Century*, New Hope, KY: Real-view Books, 1995.

59. Two serious but concise debates are Harold W. Attridge, ed., *The Religion and Science Debate: Why Does It Continue?* New Haven: Yale University Press, 2009; Daniel C. Dennett & Alvin Plantinga, *Science and Religion: Are They Compatible?*, Oxford: Oxford University Press, 2010. See also Karl Giberson, *Worlds Apart: The Unholy War Between Religion and Science*, Kansas City: Beacon Hill Press, 1993.

60. E.g., the National Academy of Sciences booklet *Science and Creationism*: "Scientists, like many others, are touched with awe at the order and complexity of nature. Indeed, many scientists are deeply religious. But science and religion occupy two separate realms of human experience. Demanding that they be combined detracts from the glory of each."

61. This is like telling Christian athletes that Christ's command to love our enemies inhibits their competitiveness. How priceless to see the faces of Christians like Reggie White, Johnny Unitas, George Foreman, Tony Dungy, Lou Holtz, Danny Abramowicz, Mike Ditka, Roger Staubach, Pat Shurmur, Kurt Warner, A.C. Green, Mike Singletary, Mike Sweeney, Tom Landry, Mike Piazza, Pat McCaskey, Rich Donnelly, Sal Bando, Pat Veerbeck, David Robinson, and thousands of others when told their faith crippled their game. Research is competition against the problem. Such competition is good not sinful.

62. Daniel Callahan's 1974 article "Bioethics as a Discipline" is a watershed. Catholics, however, were doing bioethics since the first century *Didache* condemned abortion. See the *National Catholic Bioethics Quarterly* and the *Linacre Quarterly*. Pope Paul VI's *Humane Vitae* or *Evangelium Splendor* and *Veritatis Splendor* by John Paul II.

63. See Artigas et al, *Negotiating Darwin: The Vatican Confronts Evolution, 1877-1902*, 2006. Schonburn, *Chance or Purpose?* 2007. Ratzinger, *In the Beginning* 1995; Horn, ed., *Creation and Evolution*, 2009; Cf. Berlinski, *The Devil's Delusion: Atheism and its Scientific Pretensions*, New York: Basic Books, 2008.

64. Malcolm Ritter and Karl Ritter, "2 scientists win Nobel Prize for discoveries that offer alternative to embryonic stem cells" in *Detroit Free Press*, Oct 9, 2012.

65. Richard Dawkins, "Ratzinger Is an Enemy of Humanity," September 22, 2010, http://www.guadian.co.uk/commentisfree/belief/2010/sep/22/ratzinger-enemy-humanity. See Kaczor, *Seven Myths*, p. 31.

66. Steven Myers, "Catholic Church Declares Support For Adult Stem Cell Research," *Forbes*, Jan 23, 2012; http://www.forbes.com/sites/rickungar/2012/01/23/catholic-church-declares-support-for-adult-stem-cell-research/.

67. *CCC*, 2294.

68. *CCC*, 2258.

69. Robert George, *Embryo: A Defense of Human Life*, 2011; Francis Beckwith *Defending Life: A Moral and Legal Case Against Abortion Choice*, 2007; Christopher Kaczor, *The Ethics of Abortion: Women's Rights, Human Life, and the Question of Justice*, London, 2010.

70. Nicanor Pier Giorgio Austriaco, O.P., *Biomedicine and Beatitude: An Introduction to Catholic Bioethics*, Washington D.C., Catholic University Press of America, 2011, p. 11.

71. William E. May, *Catholic Bioethics and Gift of Human Life*, Huntington, IN: 2008; Janet E. Smith and Christopher Kaczor, *Life Issues, Medical Choices: Questions and Answers for Catholics*, Cincinnati: Servant Books, 2007.

72. See Thomas Aquinas in conversation with contemporary schools of thought in Jean Porter, *The Recovery of Virtue*, 1990; Hibbs, *Virtue's Splendor: Wisdom, Prudence, and the Human Good*, 2001.

73. Nicanor Pier Giorgio Austriaco, O.P., *Biomedicine and Beatitude: An Introduction to Catholic Bioethics*, Washington D.C., Catholic University Press of America, 2011, p. 11.

74. *CCC*, 1756, 1759; Cf. Rom 3:5-8.

75. Nicanor Pier Giorgio Austriaco, O.P., *Biomedicine and Beatitude: An Introduction to Catholic Bioethics*, Washington D.C., Catholic University Press of America, 2011, pp. 211-212.

76. The Catholic Church has anticipated our culture's bioethical confusion about human cloning, embryonic stem cell research, artificial intelligence, human enhancement, etc. Our teaching documents include:

- *Humanae Vitae* [Of Human Life] Pope Paul VI on the regulation of birth, 1968;
- *Donum Vitae* [Gift of Life] Instruction on Respect for Human Life in Its Origin and on the Dignity of Procreation, 1987;
- *Evangelium Vitae* [Gospel of Life] on the value and inviolability of human life, 1995;
- *Charter for Health Care Workers*, Pontifical Council for Pastoral Assistance to Health Care Workers, 1995;
- *Instruction Dignitas Personae* [Instruction on the Dignity of the Person] *on Certain Bioethical Questions*, Congregation for the Doctrine of the Faith, 2008.

The National Catholic Bioethics Center (NCBC, 1972) conducts research and consultation promoting human dignity in health care and the life sciences. Dr. John Haas has assembled a team of ethicists like Fr. Tadeusz Pacholczyk who earned degrees in philosophy, biochemistry, molecular cell biology, and chemistry. He went on to laboratory research on hormonal regulation of the immune response. He also earned a Ph.D. in Neuroscience from Yale University, where he focused on cloning genes for neurotransmitter transporters which are expressed in the brain. He also worked for several years as a molecular biologist at Massachusetts General Hospital/Harvard Medical School. Fr. Tad studied for 5 years in Rome where he did advanced work in dogmatic theology and in bioethics. The NCBC is providing Catholic insight at a time our culture is demonstrating technological brilliance but ethical bankruptcy. Also read Rebecca Taylor, who knows these issues from working as a molecular biologist. She blogs at http://www.marymeetsdolly.com. For years, Wesley Smith has been monitoring threats to human exceptionalism at http://www.nationalreview.com/human-exceptionalism.

77. See John Haught in *Science and Christianity: From Conflict to Conversation*, Paulist Press, 1995.

78. John Paul II repeated the phrase in 1992 when he clarified the Galileo incident. In 1615, Galileo, when asked by the Grand Duchess Christina to explain his philosophy attributes the phrase to Cardinal Baronius in 1598.

79. Bacon (1561-1626) served as Chancellor, Solicitor General and Attorney General at various times under Elizabeth I and James I. Though he persecuted Catholics, his greatest influence was in what we now call "philosophy of science." He emphasized that the new science must reject Aristotle's formal and final causes. Only the efficient and material causes were the proper sphere for scientific investigation. For better or worse, this attitude prevails today. His use of the Genesis "dominion mandate" tied the scientific enterprise to Scripture without falling into what we today call "fundamentalism." See http://www.newadvent.org/cathen/02192a.htm.

80. Francis Bacon, "Of Atheism" in *Essays*, London: Oxford University Press, orig. 1625, rep. 1943. Joseph de Maistre (1753-1821) regarded Bacon's "orthodoxy" as a disguise for his atheism. Others have described Bacon's Christianity as "sincere but unenthusiastic." The late Classics scholar and historian of Western science, Benjamin Farrington (1891-1974), regarded him as a man with a significant religious mission. Bacon tried to set up scientific institutes throughout England and composed a prayer to be used in them. See *The Christianity of Francis Bacon* at http://www.sirbacon.org/farrington.htm.

81. A brief but helpful approach to Genesis can be found in Christopher Kaczor, *The Seven Big Myths About the Catholic Church*, San Francisco: Ignatius Press, 2012, pp. 24-29.

82. Cf. *CCC*, 2293

83. Francis Bacon, *Novum Organum* II, end. Quoted in Benjamin Farrington "The Christianity of Francis Bacon," http://www.sirbacon.org/farrington.htm.

84. Benedict XVI, Wednesday audience, March 24, 2010 on St. Albert the Great.

85. For a Catholic approach to Scripture study and interpretation you can't do better in a single volume than Steven C. Smith, *The Word of the Lord: 7 Essential Principles for Catholic Scripture Study*, Huntington, IN: Our Sunday Visitor, 2012; Mark Shea, *Making Senses Out of Scripture: Reading the Bible as the First Christians Did*, Basilica Press, 1999; For real beginners in Scripture study see "How a Catholic Starts to Read the Bible" at http://www.salvationhistory.com/studies/lesson/genesis_how_a_catholic_starts_to_read_the_bible/. For the more mature student see Peter S Williamson, *Catholic Principles for Interpreting Scripture: A Study of the Pontifical Commission's. The Interpetation of the Bible in the Church*, Vatican City: Biblical Institute Press, 2001. See also the journal *Letter and Spirit*, edited by Scott Hahn which discusses issues surrounding interpretation of Scripture.

86. Vatican I, *Dei Filius* 4; "Though faith is above reason, there can never be any real discrepancy between faith and reason." Cf. *CCC*, 159, *Gaudium spes* 36:1. "Consequently, methodical research in all branches of knowledge, provided it is carried out in a truly scientific manner and does not override moral laws, can never conflict with the faith."

OPPONENT #6
Scientism: Science Can Explain Everything

1. Rudolf Carnap, *The Logical Structure of the World*, trans. R. George, Berkeley: University of California Press, 1967, p. 290.

2. Owen J. Gingerich, *Christian Herald*, Dec. 1978, p. 34 quoted in Michael D. Aeschliman, *The Restitution of Man: C.S. Lewis and the Case Against Scientism*, Grand Rapids: Eerdmans, 1983, p. 49.

3. Keith Ward, *Why There Almost Certainly Is a God: Doubting Dawkins*, Lion, London, 2008, p. 30.

4. E.g., *Encyclopedie ou Dictionnaire Raisonne des Sciences, des Arts et des Metiers* [Encyclopedia or Reasoned Dictionary of Sciences, Arts (Technologies), and Trades] edited by Denis Diderot and published in 23 volumes during the years 1751 to 1777.

5. Ian Hutchinson, *Monopolizing Knowledge: A Scientists Refutes Religion-denying, Reason-destroying Scientism*, Belmont, MA: Fias Publishing, 2011.

6. Edwards v. Aguillard: U.S. Supreme Court Decision Amicus Curiae Brief of 72 Nobel Laureates, et al. in support of Appellees.
http://www.talkorigins.org/faqs/edwards-v-aguillard/amicus1.htm.

7. Stephen Jay Gould in "Impeaching a Self-Appointed Judge," *Scientific American*, July 1992, p. 119 cited in Gerald L. Schroeder, *The Science of God: The Convergence of Scientific and Biblical Wisdom*, 2009, pp. 18 & 220.

8. See Rene van Woudenberg, "Limits of Science and the Christian Faith," *Perspectives on Science and the Christian Faith: Journal of the American Scientific Affiliation*, Vol. 65, Number 1, March 2013, pp. 24-36. See the hard to find Ronda Chervin, Eugene Kevan, *Love of Wisdom: An Introduction to Christian Philosophy*, San Francisco: Ignatius Press, 1988. Also a good popularly written book is Esther Lightcap Meek, *Longing to Know: The Philosophy of Knowledge for Ordinary People*, Grand Rapids: Brazos Press, 2003.

9. The "historical" method builds a case based on reliable and trustworthy sources and witnesses, inferences to the best explanation including the use of statistical comparisons and arguments from analogy. The aim is to persuade a "judge" or "jury" to a high degree of probability or "beyond a reasonable doubt."

10. Norman Cousins (1912-1990) in *The Most Brilliant Thoughts of All Time (in two lines or less)*, ed., John M. Shannon, New York: HarperCollins, 1999, p. 202.

11. A fine example of wisdom based on human observation and not divine revelation. Delightfully brief and transparent, his message is poignant and memorable. Jobs had the cancer that would kill him. He had undergone surgery and seemed to be under the impression that he had put it behind him. See http://www.forbes.com/sites/davidewalt/2011/10/05/steve-jobs-2005-stanford-commencement-address/.

12. T.S. Eliot, "The Rock," 1934 quoted by Peter Y. Chou, ed., *Stories of the Human Spirit*, Mountain View, CA: WisdomPortal.com, 2003. See http://www.wisdomportal.com/Technology/TSEliot-TheRock.html.

13. There are also truths of mathematics and things which are true by definition.

For instance, bachelors are unmarried. The information in the predicate (unmarried) is already contained in the subject (bachelors). This is considered non-informative or a tautology. In addition, what kind of knowledge are the "laws of logic?" Immaterial, immutable, and universal yet they do not convey information as much as govern the way we think and assess the value of other knowledge statements.

14. Michael D. Aeschliman, *The Restitution of Man: C.S. Lewis and the Case Against Scientism*, Grand Rapids: Eerdmans, 1983, p. 50; See Catholic thinker and novelist Walker Percy, trained as a man of science, he challenged both reductionism and scientism. See Micah Mattix, "Walker Percy's Alternative to Reductive Scientism in *The Thanatos Syndrome*," in *Perspectives on Political Science* Volume 40, Issue 3, 2011, pp. 147-152. Also, Theodore Roszak, "The Monster and the Titan: Science, Knowledge, and Gnosis," *Daedalus*, 103, Summer, 1974, p. 26.

15. How sensations become perceptions and then conceptions goes far beyond what I'm trying to do here.

16. "Scientism is… the view that empirical science constitutes the most authoritative worldview or most valuable part of human learning to the exclusion of other viewpoints … and the reduction of all knowledge to only that which is measurable." Tom Sorrel, *Scientism: Philosophy and the Infatuation with Science*, New York: Routledge Press, 1994.

17. "Scientism" - PBS.org. *Faith and Reason;* http://www.pbs.org/faithandreason/.

18. Scientism" definition 2, *Oxford English Dictionary* web edition, accessed October 16, 2009.

19. Alexander Rosenberg, *The Atheist's Guide to Reality: Enjoying Life without Illusions*, New York: Norton, 2011, pp. 5, 6.

20. For example, Herbert Spencer's *The Principles of Ethics* (1879-1893); Ernst Haeckel's *The Riddle of the Universe* (1899); Pierre Teilhard de Chardin's *The Phenomenon of Man* (c. 1930s, pub. 1955) or Carl Sagan's *Cosmos* (1980).

21. Marilynne Robinson, *The Absence of Mind: The Dispelling of Inwardness from the Modern Myth of the Self*, New Haven: Yale University Press, 2011, p. 124.

22. Denyse O'Leary, "Teaching evolution as religion harms science," *Science*, March 20, 2003.

23. See Keith Ward, *Is Religion Dangerous?* and the discussion by William P. Alston, "Religious language and Verificationism" in Paul K. Moser, Paul Copan, *The Rationality of Theism*, New York: Routledge. pp. 26–34.

24. Christians believe in a uniformity of natural causes in an open system, i.e., open to human free will and divine intervention. Atheists, generally, believe in the uniformity of natural causes in a closed system, i.e., closed to anything that can't be detected through the methods of science.

25. Anthony Rizzi, *The Science Before Science: A Guide to Thinking in the 21st Century*, Baton Rouge, LA: Institute for Advanced Physics Press, 2004.

26. See Michael Polanyi, *Personal Knowledge: Towards a Post- Critical Philosophy.* Chicago, University of Chicago Press, orig. 1958, rep. 1974.

27. The same relative indifference that followed the telescope recurred with the microscope, electrical energy and pneumatics. See Toby E. Huff, *Intellectual Curiosity and the Scientific Revolution: A Global Perspective*, New York: Cambridge, 2010, p. 5. See also his *The Rise of Early Modern Science: Islam, China and the West*, New York: Cambridge University Press, 2003. He sees the cultural revolution of the high Middle Ages as critical in explaining why modern science made its breakthrough in the Christian west. In a few works, e.g., *Islam Through Western Eyes*, *The House of Wisdom: How the Arabs Transformed Western Civilization*, Jonathan Lyons blames Western historians for devaluing Muslim contributions to the founding of modern science. He misses the point. Muslim contributions in algebra, chemistry, medical teachings, geography, engineering, etc., are well-acknowledged. Islamic thinkers, however, failed to generate the necessary enthusiasm and commitment to launch the scientific revolution. On this point see David Lindberg, Edward Grant, Lawrence Principe, Bernard Lewis, A.C. Crombie, and Toby Huff.

28. Edward Grant, *The Foundations of Modern Science in the Middle Ages*, New York: Cambridge University Press, 1998 [1996], p. 168.

29. Nancy Pearcey, "The War That Wasn't: Why Christianity is a Science-Starter" in *Areopagus Journal*, Volume 5, No. 1, Jan-Feb 2005.

30. Rodney Stark, *For the Glory of God: How Monotheism Led to Reformations, Science, Witch Hunts, and the End of Slavery*, Princeton: Princeton University Press, 2003, pp. 160-163; 198-199.

31. See also Robert Cohen, "Alternative Interpretations of the History of Science," in *The Validation of Scientific Theories*, ed. Philipp G. Frank, Boston: Beacon Press, 1956, p. 227. M.B. Foster's 3 articles in *Mind* 1934-36; Cf. Stanley Jaki, O.S.B., *Science and Creation*, Edinburgh: Scottish Academic Press, 1974; *Origin of Science and the Science of Its Origins*, South Bend: Regnery/Gateway, 1978 and Reijer Hooykaas, *Religion and the Rise of Modern Science*, Vancouver: Regent College Publishing, 2000, orig. 1972. See Nancy Pearcey & Charles Thaxton, *The Soul of Science*, Wheaton, IL: Crossway Books, 1994, p. 29.

32. See Cameron Wybrow, et al, *Creation, Nature, and Political Order in the Philosophy of Michael Foster (1903–1959)*, Lewiston, NY: Edwin Mellen Press, 1992. Also Edward B. Davis, "Christianity and Early Modern Science: The Foster Thesis Reconsidered" in *Evangelicals and Science in Historical Perspective*, Oxford, 1999, pp.75–95.

33. Alfred North Whitehead, *Science and the Modern World*, orig., 1926, rep. 1997, pp. 13, 61,141.

34. Nancy Pearcey, "The War That Wasn't: Why Christianity is a Science-Starter" in *Areopagus Journal*, Volume 5, No. 1, Jan-Feb 2005, p. 5.

35. Joseph Needham, *The Grand Titration: Science and Society in East and West*, Toronto: University of Toronto Press, 1969, p. 327. Cf. Nancy Pearcey, *The Soul of Science*, Wheaton, IL: Crossway, 1994, p. 22, 29.

36. P. E. Hodgson, review of *Science and Creation* by S. L. Jaki in *Nature*, Vol. 251, Oct. 24, 1974, p. 747.

37. Quoted in John Lennox, *God and Stephen Hawking (Whose Design Is It Anyway?)*, Oxford: Lion Hudson Plc, 2011, p. 32.

38. Albert Einstein, "Physics and Reality," *Journal of the Franklin Institute*, March 1936. The actual quote is: "The eternal mystery of the world is its comprehensibility... The fact that it is comprehensible is a miracle."

39. "It seems to me immensely unlikely that mind is a mere by-product of matter. For if my mental processes are determined wholly by the motions of atoms in my brain I have no reason to suppose that my beliefs are true. They may be sound chemically, but that does not make them sound logically. And hence I have no reason for supposing my brain to be composed of atoms" (J.B.S. Haldane, "When I am Dead" in *Possible Worlds*, 1927). Later in life, he changed his position. C.S. Lewis, who was quite familiar with Haldane, discusses this very problem at length in "The Cardinal Difficulty of Naturalism" in *Miracles: A Preliminary View*, New York: Simon & Schuster, 1996, pp. 20-35.

40. Douglas R. Hofstadter, *Gödel, Escher, Bach: An Eternal Golden Braid*, New York: Basic Books, 1979, p. 20.

41. Nancy Pearcey & Charles Thaxton, *The Soul of Science: Christian Faith and Natural Philosophy*; Wheaton, IL: Crossway Books, 1994, p. 29; David Lindberg, *The Beginnings of Western Science: The European Scientific Tradition in Philosophical, Religious, and Institutional Context, Prehistory to AD 1450*, Chicago: University of Chicago Press, 2008.

42. Quoted in Brand Blanshard, "Reply to Lewis Edwin Hahn," *The Philosophy of Brand Blanshard*, 1980, p. 901.

43. Richard Dawkins, *The Blind Watchmaker: Why Evidence of Evolution Reveals a Universe Without Design*, New York: Norton, 1996, p. 1.

44. Antony Flew and Roy Abraham Varghese, *There is a God: How the World's Most Notorious Atheist Changed His Mind*, New York: HarperOne, 2007. Gary Habermas, "My Pilgrimage from Atheism to Theism: An Exclusive Interview with Former British Atheist Professor Antony Flew" in *Philosophia Christi*, Vol. 6, No. 2, Winter 2004.

45. William Graham, *The Creed of Science: Religious, Moral and Social*, London: C. Kegan Paul & Co, 1881.

46. Letter of Charles Darwin to William Graham, July 3, 1881 in the Darwin Correspondence Database at http://www.darwinproject.ac.uk/entry-13230.

47. Plantinga recently revised an argument in *Where the Conflict Really Lies: Science, Religion, and Naturalism*, New York: Oxford University Press, 2011. Plantinga replies to his critics in James Beilby, *Naturalism Defeated? Essays on Plantinga's Evolutionary Argument against Naturalism*, Ithaca: Cornell University Press, 2002. C.S. Lewis argued against naturalism in *Miracles: A Preliminary Study*, org. 1947, rep. 1996, pp. 20-35. Cf. Victor Reppert, *C. S. Lewis' Dangerous Idea: In Defense of the Argument from Reason*, Downers Grove, IL: InterVarsity Press, 2003. See also, John G. West, *The Magician's Twin: C.S. Lewis on Science, Scientism, and Society*, Seattle: Discovery Institute Press, 2012; Michael D. Aeschliman, *The Restitution of Man: C.S. Lewis and the Case Against Scientism*, Grand Rapids: Eerdmans, 1983.

48. Jacob Bronowski, *The Ascent of Man*, New York: Little, Brown, 1973, p. 374, Episode 5, "Knowledge or Certainty?"

49. Richard Weikart, *From Darwin to Hitler: Evolutionary Ethics, Eugenics, and Racism in Germany*, New York: Palgrave MacMillan, 2004, p. 227.

50. Found in Fritz Lenz' very popular 1931 book, *Menschliche Auslese und Rassenhygiene (Eugenick)*, [Human Selection and Race Hygiene (Eugenics)] Munich: Lehmann, 1931, p. 417. Cf. Robert Proctor, "Nazi Biomedical Technologies" in *Lifeworld and Technology*, ed., Timothy Casey and Lester Embree, Washington D.C.: University Press of America, 1989, p. 23. The slogan was picked up by Rudolf Hess, Deputy Fuhrer of the Nazi party, at a rally in 1934. See Stefan Kuhl, *The Nazi Connection: Eugenics, American Racism, and German National Socialism*, New York: Oxford University Press, 1994, pp. 34-38. Hess' comments are also recounted in Robert Lifton, *The Nazi Doctors: Medical Killing and the Psychology of Genocide*, New York: Basic Book, 1986, p. 31. Lifton laments the uncritical reliance on Haeckel's scientism which had infected all areas of life including the humane disciplines like ethics, history, the arts, and theology, i.e., the *human*ities: "Haeckel was a constantly cited authority for the *Archiv fur Rassen- und Gesellschaftsbiolgie (Archive of Racial and Social Biology)*, which was published from 1904 until 1944, and became a chief organ for the dissemination of eugenics ideas and Nazi pseudo science" (Lifton, *The Nazi Doctors* p, 441).

51. Richard Weikart, *From Darwin to Hitler: Evolutionary Ethics, Eugenics, and Racism in Germany*, New York: Palgrave MacMillan, 2004, p. 225.

52. John Cornwell, *Hitler's Scientists*, p. 80. Andre Pichot, *Pure Society: From Darwin to Hitler* (2009). Likewise, Richard Weikart, *From Darwin to Hitler: Evolutionary Ethics, Eugenics, and Racism in Germany* (2005); Richard Weikart, *Hitler's Ethic: The Nazi Pursuit of Evolutionary Progress*, 2009.

53. See John Cornwell, *Hitler's Scientists: Science, War, and the Devil's Pact*, New York: Penguin, 2003, p. 111. Cf. Jean Bethke Elshtain, *Books and Culture* May/June 2004 reviewing Geoffrey Cocks, *Psychotherapy in the Third Reich: The Goring Institute*; James E. Goggin and Eileen Brockman Goggin, *Death of a 'Jewish Science': Psychoanalysis in the Third Reich*; Robert N. Proctor, *The Nazi War on Cancer*.

54. The standard histories by Richard Evans and Michael Burleigh investigate the role of science in Nazi success. See also Mark Walker, *Nazi Science: Myth, Truth, and the German Atomic Bomb*, New York: Basic Books, 2001; Eric Katz, *Death By Design: Science, Technology, and Engineering in Nazi Germany*, London: Longmans, 2006; Jean Medawar, David Pyke, *Hitler's Gift: The True Story of the Scientists Expelled by the Nazi Regime*, New York: Arcade, 2001. Robert N. Proctor, *Value-Free Science?: Purity and Power in Modern Knowledge*, Cambridge: Harvard University Press, 1991.

55. Quoted in Richard Weikart, *From Darwin to Hitler: Evolutionary Ethics, Eugenics, and Racism in Germany*, New York: Palgrave MacMillan, 2004, p. 43. Weikart provides the German language citations.

56. In the 1890s and 1900s this attitude is expressed on a postcard sent by Willibald Hentschel, a former student of Haeckel's to Christian von Ehrenfels, a philosopher and eugenics enthusiast. Quoted in Richard Weikart, *From Darwin to Hitler*, p. 43. By 1935, the worldview of Nazism and the science of biology had merged creating an agenda for public education. From a secondary school teacher we read: "Concerns emanating from National Socialism will undoubtedly impact the direction of [biological] research such

that the biological worldview of Nazism and the science of biology are united into one. We are merely standing at the beginning of such a symbiotic penetration and development. Only the future will shed light on the results of this symbiosis" (Dr Werner Siedentop, German Higher Secondary School Biology Teacher 1935) in Sheila Faith Weiss, *The Nazi Symbiosis: Human Genetics and Politics in the Third Reich*, Chicago: University of Chicago Press, 2010, p. 1. Cf. Sheila Faith Weiss, *Race Hygiene and National Efficiency: The Eugenics of Wilhelm Schallmayer*, Berkeley: University of California Press, 1987.

57. Quoted in Richard Weikart, *From Darwin to Hitler* p. 45.

58. Ibid.

59. Ibid. See Alexander Tille, *Von Darwin bis Nietzsche*, [From Darwin to Nietzsche] Leipzig: 1895, p. 232-4.

60. See Jerry Walls, *Hell: The Logic of Damnation*, South Bend, IN: University of Notre Dame Press, 1992, p. 121.

61. Rebecca West, *The Meaning of Treason*, in Aeschlimann p. 50.

62. Michael Burleigh, "The Legacy of Nazi Medicine in Context," in *Medicine and Medical Ethics in Nazi Germany*, ed. Francis Nicosia and Jonathan Huener, Oxford, NY: Berghahn Books, 2002, p. 119. Gustav Ratzenhofer (1840-1904) wrote extensively on the social implications of Darwinism in his book, *Positive Ethiks* [The Positive Ethic] (1901). See Richard Weikart, *From Darwin to Hitler* p. 44.

63. Paul Lawrence Farber *The Temptations of Evolutionary Ethics* University of California Press, 1994; Paul Lawrence Farber, *Mixing Races*, Baltimore: Johns Hopkins University Press, 2011; Duane McCampbell, "The Development and Failure of the Nineteenth-Century Evolutionary Theory of Ethics," in *Restoration Quarterly*, Vol. 26, Number 3, 1983.

64. "Progress is no invariable rule" counseled Darwin. We must "prevent the reckless, the vicious, the ... inferior members of society from increasing at a quicker rate than the better class." If we fail, "the nation will retrograde." My thanks to Ben Wiker's eye for these quotes in *The Darwin Myth: The Life and Lies of Charles Darwin*, Washington, D.C.: Regnery, 2009 taken from Charles Darwin, *The Descent of Man*, Part II, ch. XXI, pp. 405, 403.

65. Quoted in Richard Weikart, *Hitler's Ethic: The Nazi Pursuit of Evolutionary Progress*, New York: Palgrave Macmillan, 2009, p. 189.

66. Annie Dillard, *Pilgrim at Tinker Creek*, New York: Harper Perennial 1974 p. 6.

67. Annie Dillard, *Pilgrim at Tinker Creek*, p. 178. This unblinkered look at nature resembles Lao Tzu's "Heaven and earth are ruthless, and treat the myriad creatures as straw dogs."

68. Lesslie Newbigen, *Truth to Tell: The Gospel as Public Trust*, Grand Rapids, MI: Eerdmans, 1991, p. 62.

69. See Max Jammer, *Einstein and Religion*, Princeton: Princeton University Press, 1999 p. 69.

70. See Jonathan Gottschall, *The Storytelling Animal: How Stories Make Us Human*, New York: Houghton Mifflin, 2012.

71. Dietrich Bonhoeffer, Letter to Reinhold Niebuhr, July, 1939.

72. Eric A. Johnson and Karl-Heinz Reuband, *What We Knew: Terror, Mass Murder, and Everyday Life in Nazi Germany*, New York: Basic Books, 2006; Andy Andrews, *How Do You Kill 11 Million People?: Why the Truth Matters More Than You Think*, Nashville: Thomas Nelson, 2012.

73. Eric Metaxas, *Bonhoeffer: Pastor, Martyr, Prophet, Spy*, Nashville: Thomas Nelson, 2011, p. 532.

OPPONENT #7
Reductionism: Science Proves Life Is "Nothing But ..."

1. Jacques Barzun, *The Use and Abuse of Art*, Princeton: Princeton University Press, 1974, p. 53. See also M.H. Abrams, *The Mirror and the Lamp: Romantic Theory and the Critical Tradition*, New York: Oxford University Press, 1953.

2. Frances Crick, *Of Molecules and Men*, 1966, quoted in A.R. Peacocke, *Creation and the World of Science*, New York: Oxford University Press, 1979, p. 118.

3. Miguel Nicolelis, *Beyond Boundaries*, New York: Times Books, 2011, Kindle location 288/6908.

4. Philosophers debate the ontological status of emergent properties. For our illustrative purposes, however, it is unnecessary to resolve these very significant questions.

5. Scott James describing Persinger's experiments in "neuro-theology" which began in the 1990s. See Scott James, *An Introduction to Evolutionary Ethics*, Malden, MA: Wiley Blackwell, 2011 pp. 165-166.

6. Rev 9:21; 18:23; 21:8; 22:15.

7. Quoted in Francis A. Schaeffer, *How Should We Then Live*, orig. 1976, rep. 2005, pp. 206-209. See Charles Slack, *Timothy Leary, the Madness of the Sixties and Me*, New York: Wyden, 1974.

8. Carlos Castaneda, *The Teachings of Don Juan*, 1968. In 1976, Richard de Mille published *Castaneda's Journey* and insisted that contradictions, twisted chronologies and other lapses require Castaneda's many books to be received as fiction. See Robert Marshall, "The Dark Legacy of Carlos Castaneda," *Salon*, April 12, 2007 http://www.salon.com/2007/04/12/castaneda/. Psychedelic use is described by Aldous Huxley, *The Doors of Perception*, 1954; John Cunningham Lilly, *The Center of the Cyclone* 1972. John Allegro, *The Sacred Mushroom and the Cross*, 1971. Ömer C. Stewart, *Peyote Religion* 1993; Michael H.N. Shermer, "Brave New World versus Island – Utopian and Dystopian Views on Psychopharmacology" in *Medicine, Health Care and Philosophy*, Netherlands: Springer 10:119-128, 2007 at http://www.huxley.net/utopian-dystopian.pdf.

9. The most respected engagement of Persinger's experiments can be found at P. Granqvist; M. Fredrikson, et al, "Sensed presence and mystical experiences are predicted by suggestibility, but not by the application of transcranial weak complex magnetic fields" in *Neuroscience Letters*. Amsterdam: Elsevier, 379 (1): 1–6, 2005: "The magnetic fields are far too weak to penetrate the cranium and influence neurons within." Persinger replies and a counterreply from his critics follow in the next issue. For a summary, see the December 2004 issue of *Nature*. He still insists that he has generated "mystical experiences and altered states." See Persinger, et al. "The Electromagnetic Induction of Mystical and Altered States Within the Laboratory," *Journal of Consciousness Exploration & Research* 1 (7) 2010, pp. 808-830.

10. See *The Great Ape Project: Equality Beyond Humanity* by Peter Singer & Paola Cavalieri; For a spirited counterpoint, see Peter Geach, *Providence and Evil*, Cambridge: Cambridge University Press, 1977, pp. 79–80; Also, Peter Geach, *The Virtues*, Cambridge: Cambridge University Press, 1977, p. 19. Christian animal welfare perspectives include Matthew Scully's *Dominion: The Power of Man, the Suffering of Animals, and the Call to Mercy*, 2003 and Andrew Linzey's, *Animal Gospel*, 1999. British philosopher John Gray's *Straw Dogs: Thoughts on Humans and Other Animals* accuses liberal humanism's high view of the person and faith in progress of little more than Christian heresy. "The irony of evangelical Darwinism is that it uses science to support a view of humanity that comes from religion…. A truly naturalistic view of the world leaves no room for secular hope…The idea of progress is a secular version of the Christian belief in providence. That is why among the ancient pagans it is unknown" (p. xii, xiii). For an antidote to Singer and Gray both, enjoy the fiction of Dean Koontz and activist Wesley J. Smith's, *A Rat is a Pig is a Dog is a Boy*, New York: Encounter Books, 2010. Smith blogs at http://www.nationalreview.com/human-exceptionalism#.

11. John G. West, *Darwin Day in America: How Our Politics and Culture Have Been Dehumanized in the Name of Science*, Wilmington, DE: ISI Books, 2007. Quoted in Nicholas Wade, "Animal's Genetic Program Decoded, in a Science First," *New York Times*, December 11, 1998.

12. Quoted in Ibid.

13. Quoted in Maggie Fox, "Fly Gene Map May Have Many Uses, Scientists Say," *Reuters*, March 23, 2000.

14. Patricia Reaney, "'Are You Man or Mouse?' Check Your Genes…," *Reuters*, Dec 4, 2002.

15. For an extended analysis of the relation between brain, mind, and soul see Mario Beauregard and Denyse O'Leary, *The Spiritual Brain: A Neuroscientist's Case for the Existence of the Soul*, New York: HarperOne, 2007, p. 16.

16. Jonathan Marks, *What It Means to Be 98% Chimpanzee: Ape, People, and Their Genes*, Berkeley: University of California, 2001, p. 197.

17. John D. Barrow in *The World within the World*, New York: Oxford, 1990, pp. 304-05 distinguishes 3 different types of reductionism. *Ontological reductionism* reduces everything to elementary particles and forces. *Methodological reductionism* claims all explanations must be deterministic, and mathematical. *Epistemological reductionism* reduces all psychology to biology, all biology to chemistry, and all chemistry to physics. .

18. Donald M. MacKay, *The Clockwork Image*, Downers Grove, IL: InterVarsity Press, 1974, p. 43. For a richer Catholic philosophical perspective, see David Aitken, "Bernard Lonergan's Critique of Reductionism: A Call to Intellectual Conversion" in *Christian Scholars Review*, XLI:3, Spring 2012, pp. 233-251.

19. Jonathan Gottschall, *The Storytelling Animal: How Stories Make Us Human*, New York: Houghton Mifflin, 2012, p. xi.

20. Jonathan Gottschall, author of *The Storytelling Animal*, during Amazon.com interview at http://www.amazon.com/Storytelling-Animal-Stories-Make-Human/dp/0547391404 accessed March 3, 2013, 4:36 pm. Wordsworth once said that we must murder in order to dissect. I disagree. Right analysis doesn't kill. Science can help explain the power stories have over us; it cannot eliminate the magical experience of entering into a story or the inevitability of seeing our lives in narrative terms.

21. John Polkinghorne, *Science and Religion in Quest of Truth*. quoted in "How Science and Faith Can Work Together," Yale University Press Blog, October 24, 2012; http://yalepress.wordpress.com/2012/10/24/how-science-and-faith-can-work-together/.

22. *Cosmos*, p. 127; carlsagan.com provides ongoing access to his projects.

23. Bertrand Russell, "A Free Man's Worship" available in many editions and locations. http://www.philosophicalsociety.com/archives/a%20free%20man's%20worship.htm.

24. Karl Giberson and Mariano Artigas, *Oracles of Science: Celebrity Scientists versus God and Religion* , New York: Oxford, 2007, p. 123.

25. Ann Druyan, "Ann Druyan talks about science, religion, wonder, awe … and Carl Sagan," *Skeptical Inquirer* (Committee for Skeptical Inquiry) November/December 2003; 27, 6.

26. Carl Sagan and Ann Druyan, "What Thin Partitions…" in *Shadows of Forgotten Ancestors*, New York: Ballantine Books, 1992, p. 159.

27. *Cosmos*, p. 282.

28. Sagan claimed he could not disprove God until he could prove an eternal cosmos. He is a practical atheist, however. He stands in perpetual opposition to organized religion. He finds himself unable to present any religious position in a way that an adherent would recognize as fair and accurate. He assumes that a materialistic universe is all there is, was or ever will be. The 1997 film *Contact* adapted from his novel may provide counter-evidence by hinting at religion-science co-operation. The film treatment of H.G. Wells, *War of the Worlds*, however, departs from Wells anti-religious position in order to draw audience. Why not Sagan?

29. "Sagan's Grand Slogan isn't scientific by any standard. His statement about the Cosmos certainly isn't empirically testable…It's atheistic pseudo-science just like intelligent design is Christian pseudo-science. Or, perhaps more accurately, it's *scientism*." See Planet Atheism, August 2011, Eric Steinart Archive; http://planetatheism.com/author/eric-steinhart/page/4/.

30. Karl Giberson, Mariano Artigas, *Oracles of Science: Celebrity Scientists versus God and Religion*, New York: Oxford University Press, 2007.

31. Carl Sagan, *Broca's Brain: Reflections on the Romance of Science*, New York: Ballantine Books, 1986, p. 282.

32. Many believe that God's existence can be inferred from the design or fine-tuning

of the natural world. These are not strict proofs but attempts to demonstrate the plausibility of theistic belief and implausibility of atheism. See Owen Gingerich, *God's Universe*, 2006; Robert Jastrow, *God and The Astronomers*, rev. ed., 2000; Antony Flew, *There is a God*, 2007; *Cosmic Origins* DVD produced by Magis Institute for Faith and Reason, 2011. Also *New Proofs for the Existence of God*, Robert J. Spitzer, 2010; Ben Wiker, *A Meaningful World*; Stephen C. Meyer, *Signature in the Cell: DNA and the Evidence for Intelligent Design*, 2010. Richard Swinburne's *Is There a God?*, 2010, maintains that theism does — and materialism does not — provide a very simple ultimate explanation of the world.

33. Carl Sagan, *Broca's Brain: Reflections on the Romance of Science*, New York: Ballantine Books, 1986, p. 330.

34. Prov 1:7; "Fear of the Lord" is the trembling awe the finite feels in the presence of the infinite, the sinful feels in the presence of the holy. A good example of "fear of the Lord" or "in awe of the Lord" would be Isaiah 6:1-8. More philosophically minded observers might say, it is "the appropriate sense of radical contingency one experiences in the presence of the numinous."

35. See Proverbs 8. In Prov 15:21ff wisdom confers abundant life upon us. "My son, do not forget my teaching... [It] will mean health for your flesh and vigor for your bones... life to your soul."

36. See Ps 1.

37. Sagan sometimes used the word "spiritual" to refer to the depth of his interior response rather than any objective feature of the cosmos.

38. Ann Druyan, "Ann Druyan talks about science, religion, wonder, awe ... and Carl Sagan," *Skeptical Inquirer*, November/December 2003.

39. Carl Sagan and Ann Druyan, *Shadows Of Forgotten Ancestors: A Search For Who We Are*, New York: Ballantine, 1993, p. 153.

40. Charles Taylor, *A Catholic Modernity?* New York: Oxford University Press, 1999, pp. 26, 27.

41. See Fergus Kerr, *Immortal Longings: Versions of Transcending Humanity*, South Bend, IN: University of Notre Dame Press, 1997; Hans Urs von Balthasar, *Love Alone is Credible*, San Francisco: Ignatius Press, 2005. Balthasar has insight into how God incites man with his divine love and encourages him to ponder his encounters with beauty. Fr. Thomas Dubay, *Evidential Power of Beauty: Science and Theology Meet*, San Francisco: Ignatius Press, 1999. Madeleine L'Engle, *Walking on Water: Reflections on Faith and Art*, Portland, OR: Waterbrooks Press/Multnomah, 2001. *Creativity enables an artist of integrity to* "see matter rendered spiritual...even when the artist does not personally believe in God." Such a principled artist would become "a genuine servant of the glory which he does not recognize."

42. Randle McMurphy is an unsavory Christ figure in Ken Kesey's novel and film *One Flew Over the Cuckoo's Nest*. McMurphy's longing for transcendence is shown in his adolescent longing for freedom and, often, innocent mischievousness. Those aspirations are finally ripped from him by hospital authorities through a frontal lobotomy. His death becomes the source of his friend, the Chief's freedom.

43. Charles Taylor, *A Catholic Moderrnity?* p. 19; Charles Taylor, *A Secular Age*, Cambridge: Belknap Press of Harvard, 2007.

44. Prov 6:6.

45. 1 Cor 15:26.

46. Prov 13:12.

47. Carl Sagan, *The Cosmic Connection: An Extraterrestrial Perspective*, Garden City: Anchor, 1980, pp. 257-258.

48. See Norman L. Geisler, *Cosmos: Carl Sagan's Religion for the Scientific Mind*, Dallas, TX: Quest Publications, 1983, pp. 49-53.

49. See Benjamin D. Wiker, "Alien Ideas Christianity and the Search for Extraterrestrial Life" found at the Catholic Resource Education Center http://catholiceducation .org/articles/religion/re0591.html. "Given the antiquity of the question, we might be even more surprised to find that the Catholic Church has never issued any formal pronouncement, one way or the other, about the existence of extraterrestrial life." Patristics

scholar Fr. Joseph Lienhard, however, has said, "In no case I know of did a Father of the Church postulate corporeal beings living on some other planet."

50. Sagan admitted that "at the present time, there is no unambiguous evidence for even simple varieties of extraterrestrial life ..." See *Intelligent Life in the Universe*, p. 22.

51. For arguments from observing the empirical world see endnote 32, Opponent #7. For a short list of apologetic works, see endnotes 7-10, Opponent #5.

52. Currently, N.T. Wright's *The Resurrection of the Son of God*, 2003 is the most scholarly, yet accessible presentation of the Resurrection; Less academic but very sound are Gary R. Habermas, Michael Licona, *The Case for the Resurrection of Jesus*, 2004; Michael Licona, *The Resurrection of Jesus: A New Historiographical Approach*. For a debate, "Is There Historical Evidence for the Resurrection of Jesus? A Debate between William Lane Craig and Bart D. Ehrman" March 28, 2006, College of the Holy Cross, Worcester, Massachusetts http://academics.holycross.edu/files/crec/resurrection-debate-transcript.pdf.

53. Carl Sagan, *Broca's Brain: Reflections on the Romance of Science*, New York: Ballantine Books, 1986, pp. 272-275.

54. Famous 1971 Coca Cola ad campaign.

55. This is commonly misattributed to G.K. Chesterton when it actually comes from page 211 of Émile Cammaerts' book *The Laughing Prophet: The Seven Virtues and G. K. Chesterton* (1937). Nigel Rees in a 1997 *First Things* is credited with finding the source. For a fuller look go to http://en.wikiquote.org/wiki/G._K._Chesterton and look under Misattributed.

56. C.S. Lewis, *The Problem of Pain*, New York: HarperCollins, orig. 1940, rep. 1996, pp. 150-151.

57. "Take away a man's lie and take away his hope" quoted in Francis A. Schaeffer, *The God Who is There*, Downers Grove, IL: InterVarsity Press, orig. 1968, rep. 1998, p. 115 where he summarizes Norwegian dramatist Henrik Ibsen's "Take the life-lie away from the average man and straight away you take away his happiness." See Reilling, in Ibsen's *The Wild Duck*, act 5, 1884.

58. Paraphrasing St. Paul's *Letter to the Romans* 8:28-39.

OPPONENT #8
Relativism: Feet Firmly Planted in Mid-Air

1. Hadley Arkes, Lecture #1, *Modern Scholar: First Principles, Natural Law: Foundations of Modern Political Philosophy*, Prince Frederick, MD: Recorded Books, 2012.

2. I developed this list out of a rump list I stumbled across on the Internet years ago and am clueless as to its origin.

3. Pope John Paul II, *Veritatis Splendor*, [The Splendor of Truth], #1, 1993.

4. Joseph Ratzinger, Homily, *Pro Eligendo Romano Pontifice* in *The Essential Pope Benedict: His Central Writings and Speeches*, John F. Thornton and Susan B. Varenne, eds., New York: HarperCollins Publishers, 2007, 21-24. See also Gediminas T. Jankunas, STD, *The Dictatorship of Relativism: Pope Benedict XVI's Response*, Staten Island, NY: Alba House, 2011. Also Joseph Ratzinger, Marcello Pera , *Without Roots: The West, Relativism, Christianity, Islam*, New York: Basic Books, 2006.

5. Is 53:6.

6. Allan Bloom, *The Closing of the American Mind*, New York: Simon & Schuster, 1987, p. 25, 38.

7. Kelly Monroe, ed., *Finding God at Harvard*, Grand Rapids: Zondervan, 1996, p. 15. Though she isn't striving to be philosophically precise, British soul singer Joss Stone sings movingly that she has a "*Right to be Wrong*." The song moves back and forth between a valuable right to one's own opinion (how else can one learn without testing reality and forming judgments?) and the worthless notion that one has a right to one's own facts and a right not to be corrected or challenged.

8. Hadley Arkes, Lecture #1, *Modern Scholar: First Principles, Natural Law: Foundations of Modern Political Philosophy*, Prince Frederick, MD: Recorded Books, 2012.

9. Alan Wolfe, *One Nation, After All: What Americans Really Think About God, Country, Family, Racism, Welfare, Immigration*, New York: Penguin, 1999.

10. Charles Murray, *Coming Apart: The State of White America, 1960-2010*, New York: Crown Forum, 2012.

11. Frank Beckwith's return to the Catholic Faith after serving as President of the Evangelical Theological Society is told in *Return to Rome: Confessions of an Evangelical Catholic*, Grand Rapids: Brazos, 2008. His work is presented at http://www.patheos.com/blogs/returntorome/.

12. Hadley Arkes, Lecture #1, *Modern Scholar: First Principles, Natural Law: Foundations of Modern Political Philosophy*, Prince Frederick, MD: Recorded Books, 2012.

13. Rudolph Giuliani, *Address to the United Nations General Assembly*, October 1, 2001 at http://www.washingtonpost.com/wp-srv/nation/specials/attacked/transcripts/giulianitext_100101.html. Repressive regimes dismiss human rights as a culturally relative product of the West. E.g., Pollis and Schwab in "Human Rights: A Western Construct with Limited Applicability" in *Human Rights: New Perspectives, New Realities*, 2000. In contrast, Jack Donnelly, relies on the UN Declaration of Human Rights and Western liberalism's social contract theory in his *Universal Human Rights in Theory and Practice*, 2002. For a sounder approach, see Michael J. Perry, *The Idea of Human Rights: Four Inquiries*, New York: Oxford University Press, 2000. Secular rights theories are incoherent. Only by regarding every human being as "sacred" or "inviolable" can we guarantee even the possibility of sustained protections against powers that can overwhelm persons. For an explicitly Christian approach to legal foundations see John Warwick Montgomery (b. 1931-), *Human Rights and, Human* Dignity, 1986. For a brief overview, see Richard Amesbury and George M. Newlands, *Faith and Human Rights: Christianity and the Global Struggle for Human Dignity*, 2008, p. 70ff.

14. Moral judgments differ from other kinds of opinions we have on how people ought to behave. Steven Pinker writes: "Moralization is a psychological state that can be turned on and off like a switch, and when it is on, a distinctive mind-set commandeers our thinking. This is the mind-set that makes us deem actions immoral ('killing is wrong'), rather than merely disagreeable ('I hate brussels sprouts'), unfashionable ('bell-bottoms are out') or imprudent ('don't scratch mosquito bites')" at http://www.nytimes.com/2008/01/13/magazine/13Psychology-t.html?pagewanted=all&_r=0. I would argue that when people are in this state of "moralization," they are engaging and discerning the natural law. They may get a particular prescription wrong but they can't escape the natural law's universality and its demand that those who violate must pay the price. See outstanding Catholic presentations in Russell Hittinger, *The First Grace: Rediscovering the Natural Law in a Post-Christian World*, 2003; J. Budziszewski, *What We Can't Not Know*, 2011and *The Line Through the Heart: Natural Law as Fact, Theory, and Sign of Contradiction*, 2009; Fr. Joseph Koterski, *Natural Law and Human Nature*, 24 lectures Teaching Company.

15. Robert H. Jackson, "Closing Address in the Nuremberg Trial," in *Proceedings in the Trial of the Major War Criminals before the International Military Tribunal*, 1948, quoted in John Warwick Montgomery, *The Law Above the Law*, Minneapolis: Bethany House, 1975, p. 24.

16. Holmes argued that legal rules are not deduced from natural law but rather emerge from experience. His 1881 book *The Common Law*, tried to reformulate or reinvent "common law." He rejected natural law.

17. Holmes' cultural relativism led eventually to an egoist or individual relativism in American jurisprudence. In *Planned Parenthood of Southeastern Pennsylvania v. Casey* (1992), the Court boldly declared, "At the heart of liberty is the right to define one's own concept of existence, of meaning, of the universe, and of the mystery of human life." This is a stunning admission of how little we share as a common culture. We should be dismayed when we think that "my own concept of existence, of meaning, of the universe, and of the mystery of human life" is the foundation of American jurisprudence. One is certainly entitled to his own opinion but not his own facts. *Casey* was rendered even more significant by its use in the 2003 Lawrence v. Texas decision. What does the future hold if the individual's project of defining his own reality becomes the basis or goal of law?

18. Quoted in Erik von Kuehnelt-Leddihn, *Leftism Revisited: From de Sade and Marx*

to Hitler and Pol Pot,Washington, D.C: Regnery Gateway, 1990, p. 188. Cf. Felix Morley, in *Barron's Magazine*, June 18, 1951.

19. David Hume, *Of the Standard of Taste and Other Essays*, New York: Prentice Hall, orig. 1777, rep. 1965.

20. Russell Hittinger, *The First Grace: Rediscovering the Natural Law in a Post-Christian World*, Wilmington, DE: ISI Books, 2003.

21. Paul Johnson, *Modern Times: The World from the Twenties to the Eighties*, New York: Harper & Row, 1983, p. 4.

22. John Dewey, *Logic: The Theory of Inquiry*, New York, Henry Holt and Co., 1938, p. 216.

23. The primary academic critique is that of Derek Freeman and Martin Orans. For more popular presentations see Joyce Milton, *The Road to Malpsychia*, 2002, chapter 1; E. Michael Jones, *Degenerate Moderns*, 1993, pp. 19-41; Benjamin Wiker, *Architects of the Culture of Death*, pp. 249-265.

24. Some claim Napoleon Chagnon's *Yanomamö: The Fierce People* (1968) is cultural anthropology's number one.

25. Benjamin Wiker, *Architects of the Culture of Death*, San Francisco: Ignatius Press, pp. 249-265.

26. An Episcopalian all her life she helped revise the Episcopal Book of Common Prayer which was finally published in 1979. How she reconciled her cultural relativism with historic Christian morality is a question I have not seen treated anywhere.

27. John N. Vertefeuille, *Sexual Chaos: The Personal and Social Consequences of the Sexual Revolution*, Wheaton, IL: Crossway Books, 1988.

28. Frans de Waal, "The empathic ape," *New Scientist*, October 8, 2005.

29. Ibid at http://www.annular.org/~sdbrown/the-empathic-ape.html.

30. Frans de Waal, *Good Natured: The Origins of Right and Wrong in Humans and Other Animals*, Cambridge: Harvard University Press, 1996, p. 209.

31. Responding to books like the *Moral Lives of Animals* and *Wild Justice: The Moral Lives of Animals*, Goldberg denies true morality to animals: "Only humans have morality, not animals." See *Psychology Today*, June 18, 2011; http://www.psychologytoday.com/blog/reclaiming-childhood/201106/only-humans-have-morality-not-animals. Philosopher Peter Geach takes a look at animal/human morality in *Providence and Evil*, Cambridge: Cambridge University Press, 1977, pp. 79-80; Also, Peter Geach, *The Virtues*, Cambridge: Cambridge University Press, 1977, p. 19.

32. Jonathan Marks, *What It Means to Be 98% Chimpanzee: Ape, People, and Their Genes*, Berkeley: University of California, 2001, p. 192; We need activists to preserve "human exceptionalism." See Wesley J. Smith's blog , www.nationalreview.com/human-exceptionalism.

33. James Q. Wilson, *The Moral Sense*, New York: Free Press, 1993.

34. On December 18, 1979, Fr. Kung was stripped of his licence to teach as a Roman Catholic theologian. He denied papal infallibility. His priestly faculties have never been revoked.

35. Hans Kung and Karl-Josef Kuschel, eds., *A Global Ethic*, New York: Continuum Press, 1993. See also Kimberly Hutchings *Global Ethics: An Introduction*, New York: Polity, 2010; Thomas Pogge, *Global Ethics: Seminal Essays*, New York: Paragon House, 2008.

36. Rodrigue Tremblay, *The Code for Global Ethics: Toward a Humanist Civilization*, New York: Trafford Publishing, 2009 and his *The Code for Global Ethics: Ten Humanist Principles*, Buffalo, NY: Prometheus Books, 2010.

37. Donald E. Brown, *Human Universals*, New York: McGraw Hill, 1991. Harvard cognitive scientist Steven Pinker tries to reduce the moral sense to nothing more than a function of evolutionary psychology in *The Blank Slate*. New York: Viking, 2002. "The human moral sense turns out to be an organ of considerable complexity, with quirks that reflect its evolutionary history and its neurobiological foundations." He also has a utilitarian test for "sainthood" see http://www.nytimes.com/2008/01/13/magazine/13Psychology-t.html?pagewanted=all&_r=0. For a list of Brown's universals see http://condor.depaul.edu/mfiddler/hyphen/humunivers.htm.

38. C.S. Lewis, *The Abolition of Man*, New York: Simon & Schuster, 1944, new edition 1996. Lewis includes as illustrations of the Tao, the Laws of General and Special Beneficence, Duties to Parents, Elders and Ancestors as well as Duties to Children and Posterity, Laws of Justice, Good Faith, Veracity, Mercy, Magnanimity.

39. Christopher Peterson & Martin E.P. Seligman, *Character Strengths and Virtues: A Handbook and Classification*, Oxford: Oxford University Press, 2004.

40. Jonathan Haidt, *The Righteous Mind: Why Good People Are Divided by Politics and Religion*, New York: Pantheon Books, 2012, p. xiii.

41. Steven Pinker, *The Better Angels of Our Nature: Why Violence Has Declined*, New York: Viking, 2011.

42. Sam Harris, *The Moral Landscape: How Science Can Determine Human Values*, New York: Free Press, 2010. In a related book, Harris takes on *Free Will*. Philosopher Alvin Plantinga reviews his work, http://www.booksandculture.com/articles/2013/janfeb/bait-and-switch.html.

43. Edward O. Wilson, *On Human Nature*, Cambridge: Harvard University Press, 2004, pp. 164-165.

44. What we are learning about her experience of darkness sounds like she may have been lacking those endorphins which makes her fidelity and service all the more remarkable. See Carol Zaleski, "The Dark Night of Mother Teresa," *First Things*, May, 2003; Cf. Fr. Brian Kolodiejchuk, Mother Teresa, *Come Be My Light: The Private Writings of the Saint of Calcutta*, New York: Doubleday Image, 2007.

45. See Dinesh D'Souza, *What's so Great about Christianity?*, Washington, D.C.: Regnery, 2007, p. 235 uses the story of the Kolbe martyrdom.

46. Ernst Mayr, *What Evolution Is*, New York: Basic Books, 2001, p. 259. Some prominent researchers now add *cooperation*, i.e., one individual paying a cost for another to receive a benefit to natural selection and mutation to explain biological change in species. Martin Nowak, a Catholic who directs the Program for Evolutionary Dynamics at Harvard, co-authored *Supercooperators: The Mathematics of Evolution, Altruism and Human Behaviour (Or, Why We Need Each Other to Succeed*, 2012. He also wrote *Evolutionary Dynamics*, 2006 and has lectures on Christianity and evolution. See http://president.cua.edu/res/docs/NowakPresentation.pdf. " The 'Evolution and Theology of Cooperation' research project at Harvard University was a three-year interdisciplinary undertaking formed to discuss the implications of the evolutionary phenomenon of 'cooperation' for the understanding of the relation of the evolutionary processes and classic theism(s)" http://www.fas.harvard.edu/~etc/index.html.

47. It is not so easy to judge whether a society can be good without God. See Glen Tinder, "Can We Be Good Without God: On the Political Meaning of Christianity" in *Atlantic Monthly*, December 1989.

48. William Lane Craig vs. Sam Harris *Is the Foundation of Morality Natural or Supernatural?* at http://www.reasonablefaith.org/is-the-foundation-of-morality-natural-or-supernatural-the-craig-harris#ixzz29FDNXoUi. William Lane Craig *Can We Be Good Without God?* at School of Oriental and African Studies, Christian Union, London at http://www.reasonablefaith.org/media/can-we-be-good-without-god-london#ixzz29FESsSAZ.

49. See Russ Shafer-Landau, *Whatever Happened to Good and Evil?* and *Moral Realism: A Defence*; Also Geoffrey Sayre-McCord , ed., *Essays on Moral Realism*. Catholic moral theology does deal with the status of moral facts. See Germain Grisez, *The Way of the Lord Jesus*, esp. chapter 4 available online at http://www.twotlj.org/. Other rebuttals of relativism include Christopher Norris, *Reclaiming Truth: Contribution to a Critique of Cultural Relativism*,1995; Ruth Macklin, *Against Relativism: Cultural Diversity and the Search for Ethical Universals in Medicine*, 1999; Joseph Ratzinger, Marcello Pera , *Without Roots: The West, Relativism, Christianity, Islam*, 2006. See the extensive work of Catholic legal scholar and philosopher Michael J. Perry. For a blog devoted to Catholic legal theory, see http://www.mirrorofjustice.blogs.com/.

50. Sam Harris, *The Moral Landscape: How Science Can Determine Human Values*, New York: Free Press, 2010.

51. J.L. Mackie, *The Miracle of Theism*, Oxford: Clarendon, 1982, pp. 115-116. Regarding moral realism or relativism, see his *Ethics: Inventing Right and Wrong*, 1991.

52. Christopher Hitchens, *god is not Great: How Religion Poisons Everything*, New York: Hachette Book Group, 2009. Peter Hitchens, Christopher's journalist brother, is a practicing Anglican who tells "how atheism led me to faith" in *The Rage Against God*, Grand Rapids: Zondervan, 2010. "Two brothers, two beliefs, two revolted, one returned."

53. "Hedonistic calculus" is a phrase from the father of utilitarianism Jeremy Bentham. He believed ethics was to determine the greatest good for the greatest number. How to figure that out is a problem. So hedonistic calculus is "a method of working out the sum total of pleasure and pain produced by an act, and thus the total value of its consequences."

54. Christopher became an atheist at nine by realizing in one clear impression that the universe wasn't designed. His brother comments: "It is astonishing, in one so set against the idea of design or authority in the universe, how often he appeals to mysterious intuitions and 'innate' knowledge of this kind, and uses religious language such as 'awesome' – in awe of whom or what? Or 'mysterious.' What is the mystery, if all is explained by science, the telescope and the microscope? *He even refers to 'conscience' and makes frequent thunderous denunciations of various evil actions. Where is his certain knowledge of what is right and wrong supposed to have come from? How can the idea of a conscience have any meaning in a world of random chance, where in the end we are all just collections of molecules swirling in a purposeless confusion?*" Peter Hitchens, "Hitchens vs Hitchens." *Mail Online.* <http://www.dailymail.co.uk/pages/live/articles/news/newscomment.html?in_article_id=459427&in_page_id=1787&in_a_source> August 7, 2008.

55. Romans 2:14-15. For an lucid overview of Catholic moral theology see Servais O.P. Pinckaers, Michael Sherwin and Alasdair MacIntyre, *Morality: The Catholic View*, South Bend, IN: St. Augustine's Press, 2003; William May, *An Introduction to Moral Theology*, Huntington, IN: Our Sunday Visitor, 2003; John Paul II, *Veritatis Splendor*, [Splendor of Truth], 1993; Servais O.P. Pinckaers, *The Sources of Christian Ethics*, Washington, D.C.: Catholic University Press of America, 1995.

56. These words on conscience are drawn from the *Catechism of the Catholic Church*, 1776.

57. Rom 5:13; Gal 3:24; John 16: 8.

Part Three / Abusers of the Past and Future

Opponent #9
Christian Origins: Redefining Orthodoxy

1. This conversation is adapted from Robert Bellah, "Habits of the Heart: Implications for Religion," lecture at St. Mark's Catholic Church, Isla Vista, California, February 21, 1986 at http://www.robertbellah.com/lectures_5.htm.

2. After interviewing Manson, Oxford's R.C. Zaehner (1913-74) wrote: "Charles Manson…claimed to have had an 'enlightenment' experience which transported him into an eternal Now in which time was transcended and in which, therefore, all the opposites which confront us on earth were seen to be either non-existent or identical. 'All is One, and One is All, and there is no difference anywhere', seems to have been his basic philosophy." See R.C. Zaehner, *Our Savage God: The Perverse Use of Eastern Thought*, NY: Sheed and Ward, 1974, p. 12.

3. Elaine Ecklund, *Science vs. Religion: What Scientists Really Think*, New York: Oxford University Press, 2010; Robert Bellah, "Habits of the Heart: Implications for Religion" at http://www.robertbellah.com/lectures_5.htm.

4. *CCC*, 74-100; 830-833; 860-862.

5. This does not require a dark, backroom conspiracy. Scholars, who disagree on many particulars, easily cooperate if they share a certain life orientation or set of control beliefs, presuppositions or prejudices in their scholarship. Sometimes their unity is forged through a common enemy. In this case, classical Christian orthodoxy, especially Catholicism, represents the common obstacle to their vision of things to come.

6. For Campbell, the "mortal sin" of modern Christianity was to accept the literal truth of doctrines like the Incarnation, Resurrection, Virgin Birth, etc. Insistence on historic fact destroyed the power of the myth. See Joseph Campbell with Bill Moyers, *The Power of Myth*, June 1988 PBS and the accompanying book.

7. *CCC*, 390.

8. Armstrong's works include *The History of God: the 4,000 Year Quest of Judaism, Christianity, and Islam*, New York: Ballantine, 1994; *The Case for God*, New York: Anchor, 2010; *Jerusalem: One City, Three Faiths*, New York: Ballantine, 1997; *Muhammad: A Prophet for Our Time*, New York: HarperOne, 2007; *Twelve Steps to a Compassionate Life*, New York: Anchor, 2011.

9. Charter of Compassion, http://charterforcompassion.org/the-charter; Karen Armstrong, *Twelve Steps to a Compassionate Life*, New York: Anchor, 2011.

10. King and Pagels, for instance, co-authored the revisionist *Reading Judas: The Gospel of Judas and the Shaping of Christianity* (2007).

11. E.g., the former evangelical Protestant Bart Ehrman is now agnostic or atheist. He has no investment in inter-religious unity. He is a leader, however, in recasting the story of Christian origins.

12. Her first two books, *The Johannine Gospel in Gnostic Exegesis* (1973) and *The Gnostic Paul* (1975) were academic tomes but credentialed her in the field of Christian origins. In 1979, *The Gnostic Gospels* catapulted her to popular prominence. *Beyond Belief: The Secret Gospel of Thomas* (2003), lets us know her scholarly quest is more than academic; it is inescapably shaped by her own spiritual need. Her other books are *Adam, Eve, and the Serpent: Sex and Politics in Early Christianity* (1988), The *Origin of Satan: How Christians Demonized Jews, Pagans, and Heretics* (1995), *Reading Judas: The Gospel of Judas and the Shaping of Christianity* (2007), and, most recently, *Revelations: Visions, Prophecy, and Politics in the Book of Revelation* (2012).

13. http://www.nytimes.com/2006/04/06/science/06cnd-judas.html?_r=0.

14. http://www.nytimes.com/2006/04/06/science/06cnd-judas.html?_r=0. In their own writings, at least Pagels, Ehrman, and Robert Funk of the Jesus Seminar have openly admitted their personal agendas and its influence on their scholarship. See also *Fabricating Jesus: How Modern Scholars Distort the Gospels*, Downers Grove, IL: InterVarsity Press, 2008, pp. 19-33.

15. How can anybody who has read Paul's letters possibly think that earliest Christianity was "monolithic?" Cf. Arland Hultgren and Steven Haggmark, *The Earliest Christian Heretics: Readings from Their Opponents*, Minneapolis: Fortress Press, 1996. Even Pagels knows the limits of "diversity." In *Reading Judas: The Gospel of Judas and the Shaping of Christianity*, she states the obvious. "Leaders like Irenaeus devoted decades of their lives to establishing the structures of creed, canon, clergy believing that the movement's survival depended on them – and in some ways they may have been right, for there are limits to how many different views any groups can accommodate, perhaps especially in times of trouble" (p. 101-102).

16. Philip Jenkins, *Jesus Wars: How Four Patriarchs, Three Queens, and Two Emperors Decided What Christians Would Believe for the Next 1,500 years*, New York: HarperOne, 2009 sees the formation of dogmatic definitions as simply political squabble. For a critical review see Roger E. Olson, *Christianity Today*, June 23, 2010.

17. "Heresy is the obstinate post-baptismal denial of some truth which must be believed with divine and catholic faith, or it is likewise an obstinate doubt concerning the same." "Apostasy" is "the total repudiation of the Christian faith" and "schism" is "the refusal of submission to the Roman Pontiff or of communion with the members of the Church subject to him."

18. This is taken from Bauer's own summary quoted and translated by NT scholar, I. Howard Marshall (b. 1934-): "Orthodoxy and Heresy in Earlier Christianity" (*Themelios*, 2.1 September 1976, p. 6). Bauer's work wasn't translated into English until 1971, From the beginning, however, it was challenged, in Europe. Immediately, in 1935 by Walter Volker, in "Walter Bauer's 'Rechtglaubigkeit und Ketzerei im Altesten Christentum'," translated by Thomas P. Scheck in *Journal of Early Christian Studies* 14,4, 2006, pp.

399-405. Most recently see Andreas J. Kostenberger and Michael J. Kruger, *The Heresy of Orthodoxy: How Contemporary Culture's Fascination with Diversity Has Reshaped Our Understanding of Early Christianity*, Wheaton, IL: Crossway, 2010 for a stinging critique.

19. Listed in "Table of Contents" in Bart Ehrman, *Lost Christianities: The Battles for Scripture and the Faiths We Never Knew*, New York: Oxford University Press, 2003.

20. There was also non-gnostic literature like Plato's *Republic*. In *Voices of Gnosticism*, pp. 157-58, Karen King says: "It's clear that the term Gnosticism, as such, with the –ism on the end was not invented until the 18th century... [I]n all of the Nag Hammadi literature ... they don't call themselves that...That kind of language only comes from opponents who were writing against them, and Irenaeus who is a church father, writing in the second century, is the one who talks about the *gnostikoi* in his work *Against Heresies*, and he mentioned them a couple of times."

21. Marvin W. Meyer and James M. Robinson, *The Nag Hammadi Scriptures*: The Revised and Updated Translation of Sacred Gnostic Texts Complete in One Volume, New York: HarperOne, 1988, rep. 2009. See Paterson Brown, "Are the Coptic Gospels Gnostic?" at http://www.metalog.org/files/gnostic.html.

22. The Jesus Seminar holds the minority position that the *Gospel of Thomas* is mid-first century. Even Pagels, its greatest champion, dates it at the end of the first century. Robert E. Van Voorst voices the consensus: "Most interpreters place its writing in the second century, understanding that many of its oral traditions are much older" See *Jesus Outside the New Testament: An Introduction to the Ancient Evidence*, Grand Rapids: Eerdmans, 2000, p. 189.

23. Many are *"pseudepigrapha"* i.e., texts "whose real author attributed to a figure of the past"(Richard Bauckham, "Pseudo-Apostolic Letters," *Journal of Biblical Literature*, Vol. 107, No. 3, September 1988, pp.469–494).

24. The Church loves recovering ancient documents dealing with apostolic Christianity. Occasionally, one shows up as 1873 when the *Didache* was discovered. The church embraced it as soon as its historicity was settled even though it contained what some thought were doctrinal irregularities. Questions about dating and intended audience remain.

25. See Ehrman interviewed in *BeliefNet* n.d. http://www.beliefnet.com/Faiths/Christianity/2005/06/Unpacking-The-Code.aspx#ixzz20Ytpk3A7. See also Bart D. Ehrman, *Truth and Fiction in The Da Vinci Code: A Historian Reveals What We Really Know about Jesus, Mary Magdalene, and Constantine*, New York: Oxford University Press, 2006. Though Ehrman's book has its own problems, his portrayal of Dan Brown's errors is indisputable.

26. See Rev 17, 18 and EWTN Colin Donovan's "Whore of Babylon" http://www.ewtn.com/expert/answers/whore_of_babylon.htm; Catholic Answers' "Hunting the Whore of Babylon"; http://www.catholic.com/tracts/hunting-the-whore-of-babylon.

27. See John T. McGreevy, *Catholicism and American Freedom*, New York: W.W. Norton, 2003 esp. pp. 166-189; Leaders throughout American history who have kept this particular fear alive have been Lyman Beecher, Samuel Morse, Ellen White, Joseph Smith, Charles Taze Russell, Avro Manhattan, Lorraine Boettner, Carl McIntire, Bob Jones, the Blanshard brothers, Norman Vincent Peale, Jack Chick. They include mainline as well as fundamentalist Protestants as well as secular humanists and those identified as "cult leaders."

28. Jesus married to Magdalene with child, a secret society the Priory of Zion, the Vatican's unnumbered deceptions, etc. For CBS' 60 Minutes look at the Priory of Sion http://www.cbsnews.com/stories/2006/04/27/60minutes/main1552009.shtml

29. This wasn't done in a corner. French media produced exposes and a full-length book laid out the truth for all to see. Cf., Bill Putnam and John Edwin Wood, *The Treasure of Rennes-le-Chateau: A Mystery Solved*, London: History Press, 2003. Brown was aware of the legal proceedings.

30. Remember Brown alleges that the Emperor Constantine and the bishops maliciously conspired to destroy sacred texts and invent others as well as suppress authentic history about Jesus. All for crass political purposes. *U.S. News and World*

Report quickly analyzes the historical claims http://www.usnews.com/usnews/news/articles/060522/22davinci.htm.

31. On the positive side, animals and children are winners in commercial media as well.

32. See http://world.time.com/2012/09/25/an-interview-with-the-discoverer-of-jesus-wife/#ixzz29KdnGUXV.

33. John Noble Wilford and Laurie Goodstein, "In Ancient Document, Judas, Minus the Betrayal," *New York Times*, April 7, 2006.

34. Ross Douthat, *Bad Religion: How We Became a Nation of Heretics*, New York: Free Press, 2012, p.151

35. In his, *The Secrets of Judas: The Story of the Misunderstood Disciple and His Lost Gospel*, San Francisco: HarperSanFrancisco, 2007, Robinson describes the secret maneuvering between various parties seeking to financially exploit this find. Cf. Father Steven Tsichlis, St. Paul's Greek Orthodox Church, Irvine, CA http://www.goarch.org/ourfaith/ourfaith9560.

36. April DeConick, "Gospel Truth," *New York Times*, December 1, 2007.

37. http://world.time.com/2012/09/25/an-interview-with-the-discoverer-of-jesus-wife/

38. September 18, 2012 http://www.smithsonianmag.com/history-archaeology/The-Inside-Story-of-the-Controversial-New-Text-About-Jesus-170177076.html#ixzz29Kf87qhc.

39. The fragment has no clear context, seems to be 3rd century, the author and intended audience aren't known. Even the chain of manuscript transmission is unclear. Karen King told TIME: "Assuming, of course, that it's authentic, it gives us a portrait of discussions that were happening at the end of the 2nd century, about 150 years after the death of Jesus, concerning marriage, sexuality, reproduction, family and discipleship. Those issues are still obviously of considerable contemporary concern." http://world.time.com/2012/09/25/an-interview-with-the-discoverer-of-jesus-wife/#ixzz29KWbMp20

40. http://world.time.com/2012/09/25/an-interview-with-the-discoverer-of-jesus-wife/#ixzz29KcLcHIE.

41. Ehrman, *Lost Christianities*, p. 173.

42. Robert A. Wild, review of Thomas A. Robinson, "The Bauer Thesis Examined" in *Catholic Biblical Quarterly* 52, 1990, pp. 568-69. Quoted in Andreas J. Kostenberger and Michael J. Kruger, *The Heresy of Orthodoxy: How Contemporary Culture's Fascination with Diversity Has Reshaped Our Understanding of Early Christianity*, Wheaton, IL: Crossway, 2010, p. 38.

43. In 1935, Volker and others seriously challenged Bauer to no avail. German scholarship under the Nazis was isolated; the debate was quarantined. In addition, Nazism benefited from Bauer's thesis. After all, a church confused about its origins, whose doctrines were no more authentic than competing heresies, would pose little opposition to the national revival launched by the supremely confident Nazis. This stifled dissent. Oddly, Bauer's 1927 *Jesus der Galiläer* (Jesus the Galilean) played into the Aryan claim that Jesus wasn't racially Jewish. Forget about Jesus as King David's greater son and heir of the Davidic Covenant. Susannah Heschel, *The Aryan Jesus: Christian Theologians and the Bible in Nazi Germany*, 2010: "Thanks to the work of Walter Bauer situating Jesus in Galilee, Grundmann could easily... claim that Galilee had been populated by Aryans who had been forcibly converted to Judaism...but who were not racially Jewish" (p.143). See Robert P. Erickson, *Theologians Under Hitler*, 1985; Doris L. Bergen, *Twisted Cross: The German Christian Movement in the Third Reich*, 1996; Anders Gerdmar, *Roots of Theological Antisemitism: German Biblical Interpretation and the Jews, from Herder and Semler to Kittel and Bultmann*, Leiden: Brill, 2008 at http://www.brill.com/roots-theological-anti-semitism.

44. Jeffrey Bingham, "Development and Diversity in Early Christianity," *Journal of the Evangelical Theological Society*, 49, 2006, pp. 45-66.

45. Thomas A. Robinson, *The Bauer Thesis Examined: The Geography of Heresy in the Early Christian Church. Studies in the Bible and Early Christianity* 11. Lewiston /Queenston: Edwin Mellen, 1988, pp. 28. Robinson's work was reviewed in the *Catholic Biblical*

Quarterly: "argues effectively that the crucial data from Revelation and Ignatius can be explained in quite different fashion.... In his book, Robinson has mounted a worthy challenge to Bauer's perspective."

46. Ibid, p. 204.

47. Ibid. Also Andreas J. Kostenberger and Michael J. Kruger, *The Heresy of Orthodoxy* survey the historical research on Bauer's thesis on pp. 41-54. An early English response was H.E.W. Turner's (1907-1995) *Patterns of Christian Truth*, 1954 pp. 37-94. See James McCue, "Orthodoxy and Heresy: Walter Bauer and the Valentinians, 151-52; A.E.C. Heron, "The Interpretation of Clement in Walter Bauer's Rechtglaubigkeit und Ketzerer im Altesten Christentum in Ekklesiastikos, *Pharos* 55, 1973, pp. 517-45; Frederick W. Norris, "Ignatius, Polycarp, and 1 Clement: Walter Bauer Reconsidered," in *Orthodoxy, Heresy and Schism in Early Christianity*, Studies in Early Christianity 4, ed., Everett Ferguson, New York: Garland, 1993, pp. 237-58.

48. Paul Treblico, "Christian Communities in Western Asia Minor into the Early Second Century: Ignatius and Others as Witnesses Against Bauer," *Journal of the Evangelical Theological Society*, 2006, 49, pp. 17-44, esp. p. 22.

49. Catholic, Protestant, Orthodox all agree that there was a distinction between true and false, right and wrong, correct and incorrect doctrine from the very beginning which leads to the more sophisticated statements in the later creeds. See Catholic, John Henry Newman: *An Essay on the Development of Christian Doctrine*, orig. 1845, rep. 2012; Lutheran to Eastern Orthodox, Jaroslav Pelikan, *The Christian Tradition: A History of the Development of Doctrine, Vol. 1: The Emergence of the Catholic Tradition (100-600)*, Chicago: University of Chicago Press, 1975; Anglican, H.E.W. Turner, *Pattern of Christian Truth: A Study in the Relations Between Orthodoxy and Heresy in the Early Church*, orig. 1954, rep. 2004.

50. Apparently, then current controversies over dating and authorship convinced him to ignore the NT books. Today's consensus on dating and authorship would have allowed him greater confidence. See Andreas J. Kostenberger and Michael J. Kruger, *The Heresy of Orthodoxy* p. 69.

51. I am taking these texts, for the most part, at face value although I refer to serious critical considerations as with the Pastorals and 2 Peter. See Mt 16:13-19; Mk 8:27-30; Lk 9:18-20; Jn 6:66-69; 1 John 4:1-3; 2 John 7; 1 Cor 12:1-3. When John's disciples must test the spirits, how do they do it? They ask a doctrinal question. "This is how you can recognize the Spirit of God: Every spirit that acknowledges that Jesus Christ has come in the flesh is from God, but every spirit that does not acknowledge Jesus is not from God. This is the spirit of the antichrist..."

52. Ross Douthat's review of Karen Armstrong's *The Case for God* distinguishes between liberal theology which is experience oriented and orthodox theology which, while not ignoring experience, insists that the truthfulness of the theological propositions themselves be retained. http://www.nytimes.com/2009/10/04/books/review/Douthat-t.html ?pagewanted=all.

53. Eph 2:20; 4:11-13; 1 Tim 3.

54. Acts 15.

55. Mt 10:1-4; Mk 3:123-15; 6:7-13; Lk 6:13; 9:1-2; Mat 28:18-20; Lk 24:45-48; Jn 14-17; 20:21-22; Acts 1:8.

56. "When you received the word of God which you heard from us, you accepted it not as the word of men but as it actually is, *the word of God*, which is at work in you who believe. See 1 Thes 2:13; Cf. 1 Cor 5:3; 15:1-5; 2 Cor. 10:11; Rom 1:1-17; Gal 2; 2 Thess 2:15; 3:14. As *Scripture* see 2 Peter 3:15-16 and Dt 25:4/1 Tim 5:18/Lk 10:7.

57. See John Dickson, *The Christ Files: How Historians Know What They Know About Jesus*, Grand Rapids: Zondervan, 2005, "Before the Gospels: Jesus in Oral Tradition." For early confessions, creeds, hymns and liturgical phrases see Phil 2:6-11; Col 1:15-20; 1 Cor 15:1-5, "Jesus is Messiah" Mk 8:29; Jn 11:27. "Jesus is Lord" 1 Cor 12:1; Rom 10:9; Phil 2-11; Col 2:6. "Jesus is the Son of God" Matt 14:33; Acts 8:37.

58. Even a late date for the Pastoral Epistles indicates that authoritative verbal norms were already well accepted and could be invoked without controversy. Nothing new was

being presented. See 1 Tim 1:10; 2 Tim 3:16; 1 Jn.4:2-3; 2 Tim 1:13-14; Titus 2:1; Cf. 2:2; 1 Tim 6:20; Titus 1:10-16.

59. Troublemakers and unfaithful teachers like Hymenaeus and Alexander the Coppersmith get called out by name. "All Asia has turned against me" (2 Tim. 1:15). Paul tells the Ephesian elders that "after my departure savage wolves will come in among you, not sparing the flock" (Acts 20:29). Cf. Mt 24:24; Mk 13:22; 2 Cor 11:13; 1 Tim 1:18-20; 2 Tim 4:14-15; 5:17; Titus 1:10-16.

60. "As for all who walk by this rule [*kanoni*] peace and mercy be upon them" (Gal 6:16). A generation later, Clement of Rome writes: "Wherefore let us leave empty and vain thoughts; and let us come unto the glorious and venerable rule of our holy calling" 1 Clement 7:2.

61. "The [Rule] included the basic and fundamental beliefs that, according to the proto-orthodox, all Christians were to subscribe to, as these had been taught by the apostles themselves." See Ehrman, *Lost Christianities*, p. 194.

62. Andreas J. Kostenberger and Michael J. Kruger, *The Heresy of Orthodoxy*, p. 234ff.

63. Lk 12:48 adapted from *The Message* by Eugene Peterson, Colorado Springs: NavPress, 2002.

64. Lk 2:52-53 adapted from *The Message* by Eugene Peterson, Colorado Springs: NavPress, 2002.

65. "Orthodoxy," as I am using it, refers, first, to the Person of Jesus Christ who is the universal source of life and truth and, by derivation and delegation, the community he established and guides. As the Word (Logos), Jesus is the presence of truth in any human endeavor. Human beings are obligated to embrace that truth wherever they find it. Second, however, orthodoxy refers to the authoritative definition or impulse that originally birthed or gave life to a movement or institution. To be orthodox is to be faithful to the original inspiration, power, or person who remains the source of life for the community. Fidelity leads to flourishing; infidelity leads to corrupting. In my approach, the Nation of Islam (NOI) minister will be faithful to the NOI but, when faced with contradictions internal to the NOI, will naturally seek guidance from Islam which is the life-giving mother. The contradiction is heightened, however, when the NOI minister finally grasps and feels the fact that the worldwide Islamic community rejects NOI as aberrant, i.e., unorthodox. In the last years of his life, Malcolm X resolved this contradiction by leaving the NOI and embracing more classical Islam. He never consciously addressed Jesus like the dispirited Peter: "Lord, to whom shall I go. You have the words of everlasting life" (Jn 6:68). He was responding to a new truth that had just become plausible as a result of going on the pilgrimage called the Haj. He found it life-giving and he was going to the place he found life. See *CCC* 761, 842-845; Acts 10:35; Rom 2:11; Gal 3:28; Eph 2:11-22. Cf. Vatican II, *Lumen Gentium* 9; 13; 16.

66. Elijah Muhammad, *Yakub (Jacob): The Father Of Mankind*, Phoenix: Secretarius MEMPS Publications, orig 1965, rep. 2008. Dorothy Blake Fardan, *Yakub and the Origins of White Supremacy*, Bensenville, IL: Lushena Books, 2001. Contrast this separatist vision with Henri De Lubac's vision in *Catholicism: Christ and the Common Destiny of Man*, San Francisco: Ignatius Press, orig. 1947, rep. 1988.

67. While in prison, Malcolm had turned to Elijah Muhammad like a prodigal son to a patient, loving father. The leader had elevated the young man to a prominence that generated jealousy among the inner circle. Malcolm had been fathered morally and spiritually by Elijah Muhammad during the very years Elijah Muhammad had been fathering a number of children in a decidedly immoral and unspiritual manner. Malcolm had been a straight arrow and now his spiritual father was bent.

68. The Haj is exclusively for Muslims. Non-Muslims may not even enter Mecca never mind complete the Haj.

69. *CCC*, 841-842:. "The Catholic Church recognizes in other religions that search, among shadows and images, for the God who is unknown yet near since he gives life and breath and all things and wants all men to be saved. Thus, the Church considers all goodness and truth found in these religions as 'a preparation for the Gospel and given by him who enlightens all men that they may at length have life" (*CCC*, 843, cf. Vatican II, *Nostra Aetate*,1).

70. Malcolm X, *The Autobiography of Malcolm X (as told to Alex Haley)*, New York: Ballantine Books, 1965, pp. 391-392. This is indeed a Catholic truth worthy of acceptance. "It is Catholic teaching that the grace of Christ operates, not only in the Christian communions, but also in the non-Christian world, in Jews and in Turks and in Japanese" (Karl Adam, *The Spirit of Catholicism*, Garden City, NY: Doubleday Image, 1954, p.177-178).

71. For the remarkable spiritual drama of this story see Bryan Massingale, "Vox Victimarum Vox Dei: Malcolm X as Neglected "Classic" for Catholic Theological Reflection," *The Catholic Theological Society of America Proceedings* 65, 2010, pp. 63-88 at http://epublications.marquette.edu/cgi/viewcontent.cgi?article=1010&context=theo_fac.

72. Karl Adam, *The Spirit of Catholicism*, Garden City, NY: Doubleday Image, 1954, p. 180.

73. Ibid, p. 185. Cf. 1 Cor 1:10; 14:33. See James Cardinal Gibbons (1834-1921), "The Unity of the Church" in *The Faith of Our Fathers*, Charlotte, NC: TAN Books, orig. 1876, rep. 1980 at http://www.cathcorn.org/foof/2.html.

74. Jn 15:5; Jn 10:11, 27.

Opponent #10
Christian Origins: Rejecting the New Testament Text

1. Jeanette Leardi, "Q&A with Bible Historian Bart Ehrman," in the *Dallas Morning News*, July 29, 2006, quoted by Timothy Paul Jones in *Misquoting Truth*, Downers Grove, IL: InterVarsity Press, 2007, p. 11.

2. Most relevant to his polemic against the reliability of the New Testament: *The Orthodox Corruption of Scripture*, New York: Oxford University Press, orig. 1996, rep. 2011; *Lost Christianities: The Battles for Scripture and the Faiths We Never Knew*, New York: Oxford University Press, 2003; *Misquoting Jesus: The Story Behind Who Changed the Bible and Why*, New York: HarperOne, 2005; *Jesus, Interrupted: Revealing the Hidden Contradictions in the Bible (And Why We Don't Know About Them)*, New York: HarperOne, 2009; *Forgery and Counterforgery: The Use of Literary Deceit in Early Christian Polemics*, New York: Oxford University Press, 2012.

3. Bart D. Ehrman, *Misquoting Jesus: The Story Behind Who Changed the Bible and Why*, New York: HarperOne, 2005, p. 10. I have heard Ehrman in debate. His use of "we don't even have..." is the most effective rhetorical device of the night.

4. Daniel B. Wallace & Bart D. Ehrman, a Debate: *Can We Trust the Text of the New Testament*, , Dallas Texas, October 1, 2011.

5. Craig Evans, *Fabricating Jesus: How Modern Scholars Distort the Gospels*, Downers Grove, IL: InterVarsity Press, 2006, p. 21.

6. See csntm.org.

7. Darrell L. Bock & Daniel B. Wallace, *Dethroning Jesus: Exposing Popular Culture's Quest to Unseat the Biblical Christ*, Nashville: Thomas Nelson, 2007, p. 48.

8. John Warwick Montgomery, *History and Christianity*, Downers Grove, IL: InterVarsity Press, 1971, p. 29.

9. In 1934, a tiny papyrus fragment of the Gospel of John, the size of a large postage stamp, became the oldest "manuscript" of the New Testament. This manuscript (P52) has generally been dated to ca. A.D. 125. It's discovery shattered then popular claims that John's gospel was a late second century production. In the Fall of 2011, during a debate with Bart Ehrman, Daniel Wallace referred to other second century New Testament manuscripts and now, one that dates to the first century according to one of the world's leading paleographers. "How do these manuscripts change what we believe the original New Testament to say? We will have to wait until they are published next year, but for now we can most likely say this: As with all the previously published New Testament papyri (127 of them, published in the last 116 years), not a single new *reading* has commended itself as authentic. Instead, the papyri function to confirm what New Testament scholars have already thought was the original wording or, in some cases, to confirm an alternate reading—but one that is already found in the manuscripts."

10. Ehrman, *Misquoting Jesus*, p. 15.

11. Ben Witherington III, "Misanalyzing Text Criticism- Bart Ehrman's Misquoting Jesus," See http://benwitherington.blogspot.com/2006/03/misanalyzing-text-criticism-bart-html, June 6, 2006. Also Gordon Fee, review of *The Orthodox Corruption of Scripture*, in *Critical Review of Books in Religion* 8:204; Daniel Wallace, "The Textual Reliability of the New Testament: A Dialogue between Daniel Wallace and Bart Ehrman" in *The Reliability of the New Testament*, ed., Robert Stewart, Minneapolis, Fortress Press, pp. 13-60.

12. Craig A. Evans, *Fabricating Jesus: How Modern Scholars Distort the Gospels*, Downers Grove, IL: InterVarsity Press, 2006,p. 27.

13. Ibid, p. 21, 27.

14. "[Ehrman's] evangelical faith died by way of a hardening of the categories; and his self-reported post-mortem stands as a warning to evangelicals, from whom he inherited some of that hardening of categories." Robert H. Gundry, "Post-mortem: Death by Hardening of the Categories," *Books and Culture*, September-October, 2006. See Craig Evans, *Fabricating Jesus: How Modern Scholars Distort the Gospels*, Downers Grove, IL: InterVarsity Press, 2006, pp. 19-33.

15. F.E. Peters, *The Harvest of Hellenism*, New York: Simon and Schuster, 1971, p. 50.

16. See *CCC*, 101-114 and Vatican II's *Dei Verbum*, 11: "To compose the sacred books, God chose certain men who, all the while he employed them in this task, made full use of their own faculties and powers so that, though he acted in them and by them, it was as true authors that they consigned to writing whatever he wanted written, and no more."

17. Standard works on textual criticism: Bruce M. Metzger, Bart D. Ehrman, *The Text of the New Testament: Its Transmission, Corruption, and Restoration*, 4th edition, 2005; David Allan Black, *New Testament Textual Criticism, a Concise Guide*, 1994; Daniel B. Wallace, *Revisiting the Corruption of the New Testament: Manuscript, Patristic, and Apocryphal Evidence*, 2011; Wallace's website http://csntm.org/; Timothy Seid's website "Interpreting Ancient Manuscripts" http://legacy.earlham.edu/~seidti/iam/interp_mss.html.

18. Two of the oldest manuscriptsPapyrus 75 and Codex Vaticanus have exceptionally strong agreement. They are among the most accurate manuscripts that exist today. P75 is about 125 years older than Codex Vaticanus *yet it is not an ancestor of Codex Vaticanus*. Instead, Vaticanus was copied from an earlier ancestor of P75. The combination of these two manuscripts in a particular reading must surely go back to the very beginning of the second century.

19. This information is widely available. See Bruce Metzger, *Chapters in the History of New Testament Textual Criticism*, Grand Rapids Eerdmans 1963, p. 144; F.F. Bruce, *The Books and the Parchments*, rev. ed. Westwood: Fleming H. Revell Co, 1963.

20. Daniel B. Wallace & Bart D. Ehrman, a Debate: *Can We Trust the Text of the New Testament*, October 1, 2011, Dallas Texas.

21. Fenton John Anthony Hort, and Brooke Foss Westcott, *The New Testament in the Original Greek*, "Introduction" by Hort, 1881, p. 561. Philip Comfort, *Encountering the Manuscripts: An Introduction to New Testament Paleography & Textual Criticism*, Nashville, 2005, p. 100). Even Ehrman's "Doktorvater" (Teacher/Father), his mentor, the late Bruce M. Metzger, then dean of New Testament textual studies, admits "the general validity of their critical principles and procedures is widely acknowledged by scholars today."

22. Bruce Metzger and Bart Ehrman, *The Text for the New Testament: Its Transmission, Corruption, and Restorations*, 4th edition. Oxford: Oxford University Press. 2005, p. 126. It is always possible that Ehrman has changed his mind and this statement represents an earlier position.

23. Bart Ehrman, *Misquoting Jesus: The Story Behind Who Changed the Bible and Why*, San Francisco: HarperSanFrancisco, 2005, p. 90.

24. Bart Ehrman, *Misquoting Jesus*, 2005, p. 55.

25. Greek is a highly inflected language with sixteen different ways of saying "Jesus loves Paul." Nevertheless, their English translation would be exactly the same. They

still count them as textual variants if the order of words differ or the use of synonyms varies in any way, even if the meaning is unaffected. See Lee Strobel, *The Case for the Real Jesus: A Journalist Investigates Current Attacks on the Identity of Christ*, Grand Rapids: Zondervan, 2009, p. 87.

26. Albert Pietersma and Frederik Wisse, "How Reliable is the Text of the Bible?" in *The International Bible Commentary: A Catholic and Ecumenical Commentary for the Twenty-First Century*, Wm. Farmer, ed., Collegeville, MN: Liturgical Press, 1998, p. 196.

27. Ibid., p. 88.

28. See Jaroslav Pelikan *Whose Bible Is It? A Short History of the Scriptures*, Penguin Books Ltd, 2005, p. 156. Cf. Bruce M. Metzger, *A Textual Commentary of the Greek New Testament*, Peabody, MA: Hendrickson Publishers, orig. 1993, rep.2005, p. 648.

29. The standard story that Erasmus did not include it in his first two editions but felt forced to include it in the third because of a promise he made has recently been challenged by a major Erasmian specialist. The argument is not over its authenticity. This was settled for almost every textual scholar long ago. It was a medieval insertion. Erasmus' motives for reinserting it, however, are unclear. See Michael Maynard, *A History of the Debate over 1 John 5:7-8: a Tracing of the Longevity of the Comma Johanneum, with Evaluations of Arguments Against its Authenticity*, Comma Publications, 1995. He reports his correspondence with Erasmian specialist Henk de Jonge, Dean of the Faculty of Theology at Rijksuniversiteit in Leiden, Netherlands.

30. *NIV Study Bible*, Grand Rapids: Zondervan, orig. 1985, p. 1611.

31. Ehrman complains that where there are significant intentional changes they tend to favor a more "orthodox" rather than "unorthodox" understanding of Christ. In general, this is true. But his colleagues generally believe he has overstated the case. Gordon Fee, another leading expert on textual criticism, exegesis, and translation, appreciatively reviewed Ehrman's more scholarly, earlier work, *The Orthodox Corruption of Scripture*. He concludes: "Unfortunately, Ehrman too often turns mere possibility into probability, and probability into certainty, where other equally viable reasons for corruption exist." Gordon Fee, Review of *The Orthodox Corruption of Scripture*, by Bart D. Ehrman, in *Critical Review of Books in Religion*, Volume 8, 1995, p. 204.

32. Raymond Brown, et al, *The New Jerome Biblical Commentary*, Englewood Cliffs, NJ: Prentice-Hall, orig. 1968, rep. 1990, p. 1109. In 1707 John Mill published the first modern critical edition of the New Testament and observed that even with all the variant readings: "No cardinal or essential doctrine is altered by any textual variant that has plausibility of going back to the original." Likewise historian Philip Schaff in *Companion to the Greek Testament and the English Version*, rev. ed., New York: Harper Brothers, 1883, p. 177. When the monumental Revised Standard Version was introduced as the first serious challenger to the King James Version in 1946, the editors could say with supreme confidence: "It will be obvious to the careful reader that still in 1946, as in 1881 and 1901[*publication dates for earlier versions and revisions*], no doctrine of the Christian faith has been affected by the revision, for the simple reason that, out of the thousands of variant readings in the manuscripts, none has turned up thus far that requires a revision of Christian doctrine." Given the explosion in manuscript recovery and analysis over the last two hundred years, this is remarkable. See F.C. Grant, "An Introduction to the *Revised Standard Version* of the New Testament," 1946, p.42.

33. Bart Ehrman, *Misquoting Jesus: The Story Behind Who Changed the Bible and Why*, San Francisco: HarperSanFrancisco, 2005, pp. 252- 253.

34. Philip Schaff, *Companion to the Greek Testament and the English Version*, rev. ed., New York: Harper Brothers, 1883, p. 177.

35. J. Ed Komoszewski, M. James Sawyer, Daniel B. Wallace, *Reinventing Jesus: How Contemporary Skeptics Miss the Real Jesus and Mislead Popular Culture*, Grand Rapids: Kregel, 2006, p. 73

36. Albert Pietersma and Frederik Wisse, "How Reliable is the Text of the Bible?" in *The International Bible Commentary: A Catholic and Ecumenical Commentary for the Twenty-First Century*, Wm. Farmer, ed., Collegeville, MN: Liturgical Press, 1998, p. 196.

Opponent #11
Christian Origins: Reinventing the New Testament Canon

1. Revisionists like Bauer must explain away the overwhelming prima facie evidence in the New Testament that orthodoxy preceded heresy and unity preceded diversity. To do this he posits self-appointed authorities commonly called "the proto-orthodox" who selected the books of the NT [the *canon*] to prop up their own authority. This cynical view isn't driven by evidence. What group or individual could have manipulated history in this manner against competing Christian voices and in violation of the central Christian ethic of love?

2. See John 2:24, 25; Jer17:9; Dt 31:21; Is 11:3; 1 Kgs 8:39; Prov 4:23.

3. The Western literary *canon*, for instance, refers to authors like Homer, Shakespeare, Dante, Cervantes, Dostoevsky, etc., that represent, in some way, the "best" literature. Catholics possess a Code of *Canon* Law, which contains the decrees, dogmas, and disciplines that govern the internal life and structure of the Catholic Church. While groups fight over what to include in the canon most everyone acknowledges the inevitability of communities adopting canons in order to transmit them to the next generation.

4. The Scriptural "canon" forms like a gestating embryo. Like a fetus that develops and reveals its innate features over the course of the pregnancy, the canon grows while its innate qualities become better defined and more recognizable over a few centuries. Just like the fetus whose humanity is present from the beginning, the canon's authority is present embryonically from the beginning. The earliest Jesus movement, like Jesus himself, relied on a particular written canon, the Old Testament whose authority was well settled even as its boundaries weren't fully finalized. So too in the formation of the New Testament canon. For example, the *Acts of Paul*, a late 2nd century document, refers to a 3rd letter to the Corinthians. Ephraim, the Syrian deacon, accepted this as Pauline. For awhile it enjoyed some popularity among the Armenians. While there was a question about the number of letters Paul had written to the Corinthians, there was no question about the authority of the undisputed Corinthian correspondence. It was holy writ. See Raymond F. Collins, *The Birth of the New Testament*, New York: Crossroad, 1993, p. 197. In another instance, a bishop permitted the reading of the *Acts of Peter* in his church until he finally read it himself. He then forbade its use for the liturgy.

5. "The Bible, as we know it today, was collated by ... Constantine the Great... [He] commissioned and financed a new Bible, which omitted those gospels that spoke of Christ's human traits and embellished those gospels that made Him godlike." Dan Brown, *Da Vinci Code*, p. 231, 234.

6. Pseudepigraphic works are those whose real author falsely attributes his writings to some more authoritative or noted person. It also includes works that don't claim any particular authorship but which readers attribute to an author that is later found to have been a false attribution. For a fuller explanation, see Richard Bauckham, "Pseudo-Apostolic Letters," *Journal of Biblical Literature*, Vol. 107, No. 3, September 1988, pp.469–494. Also http://virtualreligion.net/iho/pseudepig.html. Are pseudoepigrapha outright forgeries? This continues to be debated. Bart Ehrman in *Forgery and Counterforgery* (2012) answers pretty fiercely, "Yes." He is, however, criticized for prematurely ending the discussion. A preliminary evangelical Protestant critique of Ehrman's *Forgery and Counterforgery* can be found in the Dec 2012 and Jan 2013 Tekton E-Block Online Journal http://www.tektonics .org/ezine/eblockback/index.html.

7. Darrell Bock, *Breaking the Da Vinci Code*, Nashville: Thomas Nelson Publishers, 2004, p. 64.

8. C.S. Lewis refers to this situation in his "Rejoinder to Dr. Pittenger" in *God in the Dock*.

9. There is a new respect for the canonical gospels as eyewitness testimony. A very brief but astute popular piece is John Dickson, *The Christ Files: How Historians Know What They Know About Jesus*, Grand Rapids: Zondervan, 2005. For a more academic approach:

- Richard Bauckham's *Jesus and the Eyewitnesses: The Gospels as Eyewitness Testimony*, Grand Rapids: Eerdmans, 2006;
- Dale Allison, Jr., *Constructing Jesus: Memory, Imagination, and History*, Grand Rapids: Baker Academic, 2010;
- C. Stephen Evans, *The Historical Christ and the Jesus of Faith: The Incarnational Narrative as History*, New York: Oxford University Press, 1996;
- James D.G. Dunn, *Jesus Remembered: Christianity in the Making*, Grand Rapids: Eerdmans, 2003;
- Catholic New Testament scholar John P. Meier has produced the five volume *A Marginal Jew: Rethinking the Historical Jesus*, New York: Doubleday, Anchor, 1991-2010. As with the massive volumes of Raymond Brown on *The Birth of the Messiah: A Commentary on the Infancy Narratives in the Gospels of Matthew and Luke* and *The Death of the Messiah: From Gethsemane to the Grave* there is a tremendous amount of helpful material for discerning readers. It is not always clear where the boundaries between science and faith, reason and revelation, dogma and speculation lie.
- For the non-biblical material dealing with Jesus the most respected is Robert E. Van Voorst's *Jesus Outside the New Testament: An Introduction to the Ancient Evidence*, Grand Rapids: Eerdmans, 2000. More popular works by Josh McDowell *He Walked among Us: Evidence for the Historical Jesus* as well as Gary Habermas, *The Historical Jesus: Ancient Evidence for the Life of Christ*, will be just as helpful as Van Voorst to most readers.

10. Not all of the NT apocrypha come from Nag Hammadi. Those that do, however, are largely Gnostic documents. The key tenet of Gnosticism (Greek, gnosis means knowledge) is, presumably, that salvation comes through secret knowledge, an epiphany of self-discovery, perhaps even the discovery of one's own divinity. Sometimes salvation is the liberation of the divine spark embedded in an evil material body. Karen King and others deny thate "Gnosticism" is a very helpful term. See her *What is Gnosticism?* On the self in Gnostic salvation see: *The Coptic Gospel of Thomas* (saying 1), in Bart Ehrman, *Lost Scriptures: Books That Did Not Make It Into The New Testament*, New York: Oxford University Press, 2003, 20.

11. Does Bart Ehrman's *The Orthodox Corruption of Scripture* show deliberate changes to the text for reasons of theological bias? Ehrman finds instances of it but nothing that would amount to a systematic program of altering all the biblical manuscripts. Nor has his work persuaded his colleagues even as they are grateful to have the list of changes that he has discovered. See NT scholar Gordon Fee's review of *The Orthodox Corruption of Scripture* in *Critical Review of Books in Religion* 8:204.

12. By Eusebius' time most canonical issues were settled but the status of James, 2 & 3 John, 2 Peter, Jude & the Apocalypse was still in doubt. *The state of the debate, however, hadn't changed much since the second century.* Cf. David Dungan, *Constantine's Bible: Politics and the Making of the New Testament*, Minneapolis: Fortress Press, 2007, p. 122.

13. Before the reign of Constantine, the church suffered great persecution under Emperor Diocletian. The bishops, priests and deacons weren't about to jettison their cherished Gospels for an imperial illusion. If Constantine had tried such a thing, the writings of the church fathers would reflect it. Ambrose, Augustine and their colleagues were not shy about confronting the civil authorities. Although they complain about superficial conversions and lax lifestyles, no one mentions an attempt by Constantine to alter any of our Gospels.

14. C.S. Lewis in his "Rejoinder to Dr. Pittenger" in *God in the Dock* addresses Christ's divinity in the Synoptic Gospels (Mt, Mk, Lk). Although not as frequently as John's Gospel, the Synoptics reveal Christ's divinity clearly. Christ's forgiving of the sins of others that hadn't been committed against his earthly person only makes sense if we understand that he is the God who is the offended party in all sinful encounters. Only God can forgive such sin, see Mark 2.

15. Bart Ehrman interviewed by Deborah Caldwell in *BeliefNet* n.d. http://www.beliefnet.com/Faiths/Christianity/2005/06/Unpacking-The-Code.aspx#ixzz20Ytpk3A7.

See also the more extensive Bart D. Ehrman, *Truth and Fiction in The Da Vinci Code: A Historian Reveals What We Really Know about Jesus, Mary Magdalene, and Constantine*, New York: Oxford University Press, 2006.

16. Henry Y. Gamble, *The New Testament Canon: Its Making and Meaning*, Philadelphia: Fortress Press, 1985, p. 12.

17. The Old/New distinction is anachronistic at this point in time but the logic of this distinction will make itself felt by the end of the second century.

18. Lee M. McDonald, *The Formation of the Christian Biblical Canon*, Peabody, MA: Hendrickson, 1995, p. 142.

19. Confer 1 Cor 5:3; 2 Cor 10:11; 2 Thess 2:15; 3:14.

20. James Barr, *Holy Scripture: Canon, Authority and Criticism*, Philadelphia: Westminster, 1983, p. 12.

21. The covenant is more than an agreement. The canonical writings are more than a history. The pattern goes like this:

• God acts to redeem and the story and remembrance of his mighty acts *provokes right belief.*

• The written stipulations of the covenant *prescribe right behavior* (e.g., the Ten Commandments). right conduct flows from Thanksgiving. This becomes a moral habit and disposition. We, thus, form character consistent with God's character as expressed in that act of redemption. The Hebrews, for instance, are to welcome strangers because they were strangers in Egypt and through God's deliverance from bondage they are to be known for their hospitality to the alien and the enslaved.

• The Tabernacle, priesthood, sacrificial system *prescribe right worship.* In right worship, we participate in liturgies. These liturgies re-present these past saving events and allow us to enter into them right now as though they were still alive and present with us.

These covenant prescribed and reinforcing activities become "canonical." They establish the standard, the rule, the measure which the community and its leaders use to keep alive and render plausible the metanarrative (big story) of God's redemption.

22. Michael J. Kruger, *Canon Revisited: Establishing the Origins and Authority of the New Testament Books*, Wheaton, IL: Crossway, 2012, 169-170.

23. Jesus has no intention of relaxing the demands of the law. The righteousness of his followers must exceed that of the Scribes and the Pharisees. "Not a jot or tittle will disappear until everything is fulfilled (Mt 5:17-20). See Mt 5:21, 27, 31, 33, 38, 43 for Jesus contrasts with the Pharisaic interpretation of the Mosaic law. The contrasts he sets up are clearly not between his teaching and Old Testament law since in 5:17-20 he reaffirmed the enduring validity of that law in exhaustive detail.

24. See Scott Hahn, *Letter and Spirit: From Written Text to Living Word in the Liturgy*, New York: Doubleday, 2005. Cf. his journal of biblical theology, *Letter and Spirit*. On Israel's understanding of "works of law" and "faith apart from works" see James D.G. Dunn's comments on "works of law" (Rom 3:20, 28) in his *Word Biblical Commentary: Volume 38A, Romans 1-8*, 1988. St. Jerome interpreted "works of law" as the unfruitful observances of the ceremonial laws of Moses, i.e., sabbaths, dietary laws, and circumcision. These markers of Jewish identity are obsolete and meaningless for the baptized who share in Christ's universal mission to the world. Cf. N.T. Wright, *Paul: In Fresh Perspective,* 2009.

25. Peter Jensen, *The Revelation of God*, Downers Grove, IL: InterVarsity Press, 2002, p. 81.

26. 2 Cor 3:6.

27. Francois Bovan, "The Canonical Structure of the New Testament: The Gospel and the Apostle" in *International Bible Commentary*, Collegeville, MN: Liturgical Press, 1998, p. 212.

28. 2 Tim 3:16.

29. The distinction between "Old" and "New" Testament is anachronistic at this point. The early Christians saw the Christ event as the climax of Israel's salvation history,

not the watershed event for a new religion. The later split between synagogue and church, the delay of the Lord's return insured that Christianity would grow up as a distinctly new religion. Jesus' reference to "New" Covenant, however, is in terms of Jeremiah 31:31 meaning a renewed rather than a brand, spanking new covenant. "The first unambiguous attestation of Old Testament and 'New Testament' as names of the two parts of the Christian Bible occurs almost simultaneously in Clement of Alexandria and Tertullian of Carthage" (Oskar Skarsaune, "Justin and His Bible" in Sara Parvis and Paul Foster, eds., *Justin Martyr and His Worlds*, Minneapolis: Fortress Press, 2007, p.54).

30. 1 Cor 7:14.

31. 1 Thess 2.

32. 2 Pet 3:16; Paul's authority is a subject of much discussion in his letters. See Gal 1:2; 1 Thess 2:13; 1 Cor 7:12. Even if one joins those who deny Petrine authorship and grants pseudonymity and late dating, the letter is still relatively early (80-140) to see such a straightforward acknowledgement of Paul's inspired writings. In other words, even if the writer is wrong, his argument shows that the mind of the early Church wasn't shocked by the apostles bringing forth new scripture. For a defense of 2 Peter see E.M.B. Green, *2 Peter Reconsidered*, London: Tyndale, 1960, http://www.biblicalstudies.org.uk/ pdf/2peter_green.pdf; Michael J. Kruger, "The Authenticity of 2 Peter," *Journal of the Evangelical Theological Society*, 1999, 42.4, p.645-671. Charles Bigg, *The Epistles of St Peter and St Jude*, in the *International Critical Commentary*; "Epistles of Saint Peter" in Catholic Encyclopedia, 1913 at http://en.wikisource.org/wiki/Catholic_Encyclopedia_(1913)/ Epistles_of_Saint_Peter. Michael Green admits that "No book of the canon is so poorly attested among the Fathers' but he also notes that 'no excluded book has nearly such weight of backing as 2 Peter." See Michael Green *Second Peter and Jude*, Tyndale New Testament Commentary, Downers Grove, IL: InterVarsity Press, orig.1968, rep. 2009, p. 13.

33. See Stanley E. Porter, "When and How Was the Pauline Canon Compiled? An Assessment of Theories," in *the Pauline Canon*, ed S.E. Porter Leiden: Brill, 2004, 95-127. See also D. Trobish *Paul's Letter Collection: Tracing the Origins* Minneapolis: Fortress, 1994.

34. Eph 2:20.

35. 2 Pet 3:2.

36. Augustine, c. 418 A.D., in *Against the Adversaries of the Law and the Prophets*, 1.20.39 in J.P. Migne, ed., *Patroligia Latina* 42:626, Paris, 1841-1855 as quoted in The Father William Most Collection, Bible, III (Canon) at http://www.catholicculture.org/ culture/library/most/getwork.cfm?worknum=199.

37. This quote is a composite I've drawn from many commentators. E.g., "Before Marcion, no canon of the New Testament existed and probably no one thought of one." Arthur J. Bellinzoni, "The Gospel of Luke in the Second Century C.E." in Richard P. Thompson, et al, ed., *Literary Studies in Luke-Acts: Essays in Honor of Joseph B. Tyson*, Macon, GA: Mercer University Press, 1998, p.63. Elaine Pagels, like her mentor Helmut Koester, Belinzoni and many others, exaggerates the importance of the conflict with Marcion for the formation of the New Testament canon. More than a hundred years after Christ's crucifixion, "some Christians, perhaps in Rome, attempted to consolidate their groups against the demands of a fellow Christian named Marcion, whom they regarded as a false teacher, by introducing formal statements of belief into worship." Pagels, *Beyond Belief*, p. 6, seems to honestly believe that there were no formal statements of belief in Christian worship until after Marcion. Yet New Testament scholars have identified Philippians 2:5-11; Colossians 1:15-20; 1 Timothy 3:16 as texts drawn, in all likelihood, from local liturgies. See below endnote 40, John Barton, "Marcion Revisited" in McDonald and Sanders, *The Canon Debate*, 2002, p. 354.

38. Helmut Koester, *Introduction to the New Testament, vol 2: History and Literature of Early Christianity*, Philadelphia: Fortress Press, 1982, p. 10 emphasis added. Cf. Elaine Pagels, *Beyond Belief: The Secret Gospel of Thomas*, New York: Random House, 2005, pp. 114-142.

39. Lee M. McDonald, *The Formation of the Christian Biblical Canon*: Revised & Expanded, Peabody, MA: Hendrickson, 1995, p. 154.

40. "Marcion, we may conclude, was important for two reasons. He rejected the Old Testament as the document of an alien religion; and he taught that Jesus had come to save humankind from the control of the evil Creator to whom the Old Testament witnesses. These are precisely the two aspects of his work on which patristic condemnations, from Tertullian onwards, focus. In the process he denied the validity of allegorical interpretation of the Old Testament, which he saw as a means of accommodating it to Christian belief; this too is picked up by Tertullian. *In short, Marcion was not a major influence on the formation of the New Testament; he was simply a Marcionite.*" John Barton, "Marcion Revisited" in Lee Martin McDonald, James A. Sanders, eds., *The Canon Debate*, 2002, p. 354.

41. 2 Tim 3:16.

42. Consult Paul's discussion of the charismata in 1 Cor 12-14.

43. Eusebius, *Ecclesiastical History*, 4.23. 12.

44. Eusebius, *Ecclesiastical History*, 6.20.3

45. Ehrman agrees that these criteria were used by the proto-orthodox. He considers the proto-orthodox to be the minority and therefore not truly representative of the Church. Bart D. Ehrman, *Lost Christianities:Christian Scriptures and the Battles Over Authentication*, Course Outline, vol. 2, Chantilly, Virginia: The Teaching Company. 2002, p. 37.

46. The Jesus Seminar makes the argument that the *Gospel of Thomas* is a first century production. This is a minority position. Most scholars believe that one third of the Gospel of Thomas can possibly be related to *Matthew, Mark, Luke* and *John*. The vast majority of scholars, including Ehrman place it in the second century at least twenty years after the *Gospel of John*. "Most interpreters place its writing in the second century, understanding that many of its oral traditions are much older" (Robert E. von Voorst, *Jesus Outside the New Testament: An Introduction to the Ancient Evidence*, Grand Rapids: Eerdmans, 2000, p. 189. The *Gospel of Thomas* is not a gospel or a proclamation of good news because there is no narrative, only a collection of sayings. The theology of the *Gospel of Thomas* is often contrary to the New Testament books.

47. F.F. Bruce, "Canon," in *Dictionary of Jesus and the Gospels*, Joel B. Green, Scot McKnight and I. Howard Marshall, eds., Downers Grove, Illinois: InterVarsity Press, 1992, p. 95-96.

48. See Oskar Skarsaune, "Justin and His Bible" in Sara Parvis and Paul Foster, eds., *Justin Martyr and His Worlds*, Minneapolis: Fortress Press, 2007, p.54. He is drawing on the respected work of David Trobisch, *Paul's Letter Collection: Tracing the Origins*, Minneapolis: Fortress Press, 1994.

49. *Muratorian Canon, 74.* Tertullian offers a similar reason for rejecting it. See *De pudicitia* (On modesty) chapter 10.

50. F.F. Bruce, "Canon," in *Dictionary of Jesus and the Gospels*, Joel B. Green, Scot McKnight and I. Howard Marshall, eds., Downers Grove, Illinois: InterVarsity Press, 1992, p. 96.

51. Origen, *Homily on Joshua*, 7.1. Bruce Metzger discusses this early complete NT list in *Canon of the New Testament: Its Origin, Development, and Significance*, Oxford: Clarendon, 1987, p. 39.

52. Andreas J. Kostenberger and Michael J. Kruger, *The Heresy of Orthodoxy: How Contemporary Culture's Fascination with Diversity Has Reshaped Our Understanding of Early Christianity*, Wheaton, IL: Crossway, 2010, p. 172.

53. Bruce Metzger, *The Canon of the New Testament: Its Origin, Development, and Significance*, Oxford: Clarendon, 1987, p. 254.

Opponent #12
Evolutionism: The New Cosmic Religion

1. Ray Kurzweil, *The Singularity is Near: When Humans Transcend Biology*, New York: Viking, 2005, p. 374. Kurzweil's novel understanding of spirituality requires careful analysis to avoid caricature. See William Dembski, "Kurzweil's Impoverished Spirituality" in Jay W. Richards, ed., *Are We Spiritual Machines? Ray Kurzweil vs. the Critics of Strong A.I.*, Seattle: Discovery Institute Press, 2002, 98-115. Kurzweil replies in the same volume.

2. E. O. Wilson, *On Human Nature*, Cambridge: Harvard University Press, 1978, p 201-202. Quoted in September 1986 Editorial, *Zygon*, vol. 21, no. 3; http://www .zygonjournal.org/editorial_9_86.html.

3. Ray Kurzweil, *The Singularity is Near: When Humans Transcend Biology*, New York: Viking, 2005, p. 374.

4. Ray Kurzweil, "Prologue" in *The Singularity Is Near: When Humans Transcend Biology*, New York: Penguin, 2006.

5. The Internet Speculative Fiction Database http://www.isfdb.org/cgi-bin/index .cgi. is most helpful in researching and identifying themes, works, and personalities. I am using science fiction in a very broad way.

6. William Kilpatrick, *Why Johnny Can't Tell Right from Wrong: And What We Can Do About It*, New York: Simon and Schuster, 1993, pp. 138-141; Cf. William Kilpatrick, Gregory Wolfe, Suzanne M. Wolfe and Robert Coles, *Books That Build Character: A Guide to Teaching Your Child Moral Values Through Stories*, New York: Simon & Schuster Touchstone, 1994.

7. Jèmeljan Hakemulder, *The Moral Laboratory: Experiments Examining the Effects of Reading Literature on Social Perception and Moral Self-Concept*, Amsterdam: John Benjamins Co., 2000.

8. Jonathan Gottschall, *The Storytelling Animal: How Stories Make Us Human*, New York: Houghton Mifflin, 2012.

9. Muriel Rukeyser, poem *Speed of Darkness*, New York: Random House, 1968.

10. Gabriel McKee, *The Gospel According to Science Fiction: From the Twilight Zone to the Final Frontier*, Philadelphia: Westminster/John Knox, 2007, p. 1 begins with this point.

11. Campbell and Moyers discuss Lucas' use of hero mythology in Bill Moyers & Joseph Campbell, *Joseph Campbell and the Power of Myth*, PBS series, 1988.

12. Bill Moyers, "Of Myth and Men," *Time*, April 26, 1999, p. 90.

13. http://blog.beliefnet.com/cityofbrass/2012/05/islam-and-star-wars-day-allah -is-the-force.html.

14. http://www.aish.com/atr/Star_Wars_Jewish_Themes.html?catid=909399

15. For a strong conservative Protestant critique, see Norman Geisler's 1983 *The Religion of the Force*. For a Catholic review of Episode III, *Revenge of the SITH* see http:// old.usccb.org/movies/s/starwarsepisodeiiirevengeofthesith.shtml. Also Steven Greydanus offers astute reviews as a Catholic http://catholic.net/index.php?option=dedestaca& origen=3&id=3230. See his decentfilms.com.

16. Thomas Disch, *On SFll* Ann Arbor, University of Michigan Press, David Sam05 p. 22.

17. It is the first of the "mad scientist" themed SF works. Francis Godwin's *The Man in the Moone* (1638) is sometimes called the first SF in English. Precursors of SF can already be seen in the 16th century.

18. John Milton, *Paradise Lost*, X, 743-745.

19. Eric S. Rabkin, "Science Fiction and Religion" in *Masterpieces of the Imaginative Mind: Literature's Most Fantastic Works*, lecture 19, Chantilly VA: Teaching Company, transcript Vol. 2 p. 94.

20. Stephanie Schwam and Jay Cocks, *The Making of 2001: A Space Odyssey*, New York: Modern Library, 2000 p. 163.

21. See Den of Geek, "How Philip K Dick transformed Hollywood" at http://www .themodernword.com/scriptorium/dick.html#Anchor-PRELUDE-49575.

22. Robert Sawyer, The Future is Already Here," speech at the Library of Congress, November 10, 1999, http://www.sfwriter.com/lecture1.htm.

23. The "warfare" model was seriously challenged in 1934 when Michael Beresford Foster (1903–1959)· from Oxford University's Christ Church published in *Mind* (1934-1936. Sociologist Robert Merton also attacked the warfare story but differently. In 1926, philosopher Alfred North Whitehead credited the medieval mind's insistence on the rationality of God as a contribution not an obstacle.

24. Journalist, SF and fantasy writer, Sandra Meisel discusses SF and Catholicism at www.ignatiusinsight.com/features2005/smiesel_sfintervw1_mar05.asp.

25. Pearce's work is very accessible and includes studies of Shakespeare, Lewis and Tolkien, Oscar Wilde, Roy Campbell, Alexander Solzhenitsyn, Hillaire Belloc, G.K. Chesterton, the Bloomsbury group, Virginia Woolf.

26. For a current example see Dean Koontz, *77 Shadow Street*, New York: 2012.

27. See Baylor University Professor of Literature, Ralph Wood in Justin Taylor's "P.D. James and The Children of Men" at http://thegospelcoalition.org/blogs/justintaylor/2006/12/10/pd-james-and-children-of-men/.

28. David Langford, "On Anthony Boucher" http://www.ansible.co.uk/writing/boucher.html.

29. Billee J. Stallings and Joan J. Evans, *Murray Leinster: The Life and Works*, Jefferson, NC: McFarland 2011, p. 52.

30. http://www.ignatiusinsight.com/features2005/tpowers_intvw_sept05.asp.

31. Bruce L. Edwards, "Walker Percy: An American Apologists" in *The C.S. Lewis Review* website, Oct 13, 2008 at http://www.cslewisreview.org/2008/10/walker-percy-an-american-apologist/. See also Walker Percy Project University of North Carolina http://www.ibiblio.org/wpercy/.

32. See Paul Elie, *The Life You Save May Be Your Own*, New York: Farrar, Straus, Giroux, 2005).

33. Arthur C. Clarke, C.S. Lewis, *From Narnia to a Space Odyssey: The War of Ideas Between Arthur C. Clarke and C.S. Lewis*, I Books, 2003.

34. C.S. Lewis, "Letter to Sister Penelope," July 9, 1939, in *Letters of C.S. Lewis*, London: Geoffrey Bles, 1966, p. 167.

35. James A. Herrick, *Scientific Mythologies*, Downers Grove, IL: InterVarsity Press, 2008, p. 22.

36. See Joseph Pearce , *Bilbo's Journey: Discovering the Hidden Meaning in The Hobbit* , Belmont Abbey, NC: St. Benedict Press, 2012. Tolkien's stature and influence as a writer far exceeds his original expectations. In the *New York Times*, poet and literary critic W.H Auden compared Tolkien's *Lord of the Rings* with *Paradise Lost*. See "At the End of the Quest, Victory" at http://www.nytimes.com/1956/01/22/books/tolkien-king.html. The Toronto Star reported that Tolkien's trilogy, *The Lord of the Ring* with sales of 150 million, was the second bestselling novel of all time. In 2009, Tolkien was #5 among "Top-Earning Dead Celebrities" just behind Yves St. Laurent, Rodgers and Hammerstein, Michael Jackson and Elvis Presley and just ahead of Charles Schulz (*Peanuts*), John Lennon, Dr. Seuss, Albert Einstein and Michael Crichton. See http://www.forbes.com/2009/10/27/top-earning-dead-celebrities-list-dead-celebs-09-entertainment_land.html?boxes=listschannelinsidelists. And, in a BBC survey, it was judged England's "best loved book" while Amazon.com customers voted it their favorite "book of the millennium."

37. Robert Sawyer, The Future is Already Here," speech at the Library of Congress, November 10, 1999, http://www.sfwriter.com/lecture1.htm.

38. Peter Berger, *The Desecularization of the World: Resurgent Religion and World Politics*, Grand Rapids: Eerdmans, 1999, p. 2; Cf. John Micklethwait and Adrian Wooldridge, *God is Back: How Global Revival of Faith is Changing the World*, New York: Penguin Press, 2009; Jose Casanova, *Public Religions in the Modern World*, Chicago: University of Chicago Press, 1994; Scott M. Thomas, *The Global Resurgence of Religion and the Transformation of International Relations: The Struggle for the Soul of the Twenty-First Century*, New York: Palgrave Macmillan, 2005; Monica Duffy Toft, ed., *God's Century: Resurgent Religion and Global Politics*, New York: W.W. Norton, 2011.

39. Julian S. Huxley, *Religion Without Revelation*, New York: New Thinkers Library, orig. 1928, reprint 1957. It was warmly reviewed in the *Eugenics Review*, April, 1958. 50:1, pp. 67–68 by Herbert Brewer. Along the same lines and from the same period is Charles Francis Potter's, *Humanism: A New Religion*, New York: Simon and Schuster, 1930.

40. Julian S. Huxley, "Introduction" to Pierre Teilhard de Chardin, *The Phenomenon of Man*, New York: Harper, 1955. Fr. Teilhard, a Jesuit priest and paleontologist, wrote

this book in the 1930s but it could not be published until 1955. He had been "silenced" to some degree by the doctrinal authorities of the Church who found him then and still do today, an unreliable teacher of Catholic doctrine.

41. John Dewey, *A Common Faith*, New Haven: Yale University Press, 1947, p. 21; a brief summary available at www.rationalists.org/resources/downloads/common_faith.doc.

42. David Sloan Wilson, *Darwin's Cathedral: Evolution, Religion, and the Nature of Society*, Chicago: University of Chicago Press, 2002.

43. He "proposes that religion — with all its institutional, emotional and prescriptive trappings — ranks as a kind of mega-adaptation: a trait that evolved because it conferred advantages on those who bore it." See Natalie Angier, "A Conversation With David Sloan Wilson: The Origin of Religions, From a Distinctly Darwinian View," *New York Times*, December 24, 2002. http://www.nytimes.com/2002/12/24/science/conversation-with-david-sloan-wilson-origin-religions-distinctly-darwinian-view.html?pagewanted=all&src=pm.

44. In 1864, Pope Pius IX's *Syllabus of Errors* rearticulated the Church's condemnation of the atheistic ideology of religious naturalism which reappeared from ancient times as a false, surrogate religion. *He did not condemn the scientific study of religion* which examines how religious ideas, practices and communities originate and influence human behavior. In short, the scientific study of religion explores how psychology, sociology, biology, and all disciplines of human knowledge interface with religious ideas and practices. See http://www.papalencyclicals.net/Pius09/p9syll.htm

45. James Herrick, *Scientific Mythologies: How Science and Science Fiction Forge New Religious Beliefs*, Downers Grove, IL: InterVarsity Press, 2008, p. 27.

46. Space prohibits dealing with some major SF themes like extraterrestrials, space travel and colonizing of other planets.

47. Mary Midgley, "Evolution as Religion: A Comparison of Prophecies" in *Zygon: A Journal of Science and Religion*, Vol 22, No. 2, June 1987, pp. 179-194. See also the book *Evolution as a Religion: Strange Hopes and Stranger Fears*, London: Routledge, 2002; Also, *Science as Salvation: A Modern Myth and its Meaning*, London: Routledge, 1994.

48. C.S. Lewis, "Funeral of a Great Myth" in *Christian Reflections*, Grand Rapids: Eerdmans, orig., 1967, rep. 1971, p. 83. Lewis also gives examples of pre-Darwin "Developmentalism" or "Evolutionism." Cf. Michael Ruse, "Is Evolution a Secular Religion?" *Science*, March 7, 2003 Vol. 299 no. 5612 pp. 1523-1524, and even Darwin himself who objected to the religious or mythic use of biological evolution. Darwin was well aware that various types of evolution and "evolutionism" preceded his *Origin*. He gets around to acknowledging it in the third edition (late 1860) in a list of thirty names. See Rebecca Scott, *Darwin's Ghost: The Secret History of Evolution*, New York: Spiegel & Grau, 2012, pp. 3-19.

49. Brian Swimme , *The Universe Story: From the Primordial Flaring Forth to the Ecozoic Era — A Celebration of the Unfolding of the Cosmos*, New York: HarperOne, 1994.

50. "Great Story" is the phrase describing "evolutionary Christianity." See http://thegreatstory.org/ec-leaders.html or evolutionarychristianity.com. Michael Dowd, *Thank God for Evolution: How the Marriage of Science and Religion Will Transform Your Life and Our World*, New York: Plume, 2009.

51. Loyal D. Rue and Edward Osborne Wilson, *Everybody's Story: Wising Up to the Epic of Evolution*, Albany: State University of New York, 2000.

52. Michael Ruse, "Saving Darwinism from the Darwinians," *National Post*, May 13, 2000, p. B-3. Cf. Thomas Nagel, *Mind and Cosmos: Why the Materialist Neo-Darwinian Conception of Nature Is Almost Certainly False*, New York: Oxford University Press, 2012.

53. Marilyn Ferguson, *The Aquarian Conspiracy. Personal and Social Transformation in Our Time*, New York: Tarcher, orig. 1980, rep. 2009, pp. 483-487.

54. Here "Omega man" has no relation to the 1971 film by the same name. William Day, *Genesis on Planet Earth: Search for Life's Beginning*, New Haven: Yale University Press, 1985, pp. 290-299. See Cardinal Schonborn, *Chance or Purpose*, San Francisco: Ignatius Press, 2007; International Theological Commission has also published *Communion and Stewardship: Human Persons Created in the Image of God* on July 23rd 2004. It is

available at http://www.vatican.va/roman_curia/congregations/cfaith/cti_documents/rc_
con_cfaith_doc_20040723_communion-stewardship_en.html.

55. William Day, *Genesis on Planet Earth: Search for Life's Beginning* (The Bio-origins
series), New Haven: Yale University Press, 1985, pp. 290-299.

OPPONENT #13
Myth of Humanity 3.0: Human Enhancement Through Technology

1. Adapted from H.G. Wells, *The Island of Dr. Moreau*, New York: Bantam Books,
1994.

2. The role of love and morality have recently been reconsidered as necessary comple-
ments to intelligence. See Julian Savulescu & Anders Sandberg, "Neuroenhancement of
Love and Marriage: The Chemicals Between Us," *Neuroethics*, 2008, 1, pp. 31–44; Ing-
mar Persson and Julian Savulescu, *Unfit for the Future: The Need for Moral Enhancement*,
New York: Oxford University Press, 2012. For a popular look see Kyle Munkittrick,
"Captain America Gets Enhancement Right," *Discover Magazine*, July 23, 2011 at http://
blogs.discovermagazine.com/sciencenotfiction/.

3. Francis Fukuyama, "The World's Most Dangerous Ideas: Transhumanism," *Foreign Policy*, 144, Sept 1, 2004, pp. 42-44 at http://www.foreignpolicy.com/
articles/2004/09/01/transhumanism. Cf., *Our Posthuman Future: Consequences of the
Biotechnology Revolution*, New York: Farrar, Straus and Giroux, 2002.

4. Op cit, p. 42 at http://www.foreignpolicy.com/articles/2004/09/01/transhumanism.
Jürgen Habermas argues in *The Future of Human Nature* (2003) that we do not have the
right to impose our choice to alter human nature on other humans which is what we would
do by altering an embryo's genetic material. This unilateral choice to alter human nature
violates the other's moral autonomy. Habermas' concerns inform chapters by Norman
Daniels, Eric T. Juengst, Ryuichi Ida, C.A. J. Coady and others in Julan Savulescu and
Nick Bostrom, *Human Enhancement*, New York: Oxford University Press, 2009.

5. This is a 2010 *Bibliography on Transhumanism and Religion* by self-declared agno-
skeptic Eric Steinhardt, Associate Professor of Philosophy at William Patterson University. Available at http://www.ericsteinhart.com/articles/transreligionlist.pdf.

6. Ronald Bailey, "Transhumanism: The Most Dangerous Idea?"*Reason*, Feb. 8,
2006. Libertarian Transhumanists, like Bailey, assert a right to human enhancement
and regard any attempt to limit or suppress this right as a violation of civil liberties. Bailey
is also an economic libertarians and denies that the poor unenhanced have any moral
claim on government to insure equal enhancement for all. Pauline Borsook's 2000 book
Cyberselfish: A Critical Romp Through the Terribly Libertarian Culture of High-Tech skewers
these anarchic and libertarian Transhumanists. James Hughes, who has led the World
Transhumanist Association (now Humanity+) proposes a social democratic Transhumanism in *Citizen Cyborg: Why Democratic Societies Must Respond to the Redesigned Human
of the Future* (2004).

7. Nick Bostrom, "A History of Transhumanist Thought" in *Journal of Evolution and
Technology*. http://www.nickbostrom.com/papers/history, 2005.

8. Julian Savulescu & Anders Sandberg, "Neuroenhancement of Love and Marriage:
The Chemicals Between Us," *Neuroethics*, 2008, 1, pp. 31–44.

9. Humanity+: http://humanityplus.org/learn/philosophy/transhumanist-declaration/
transhumanism-declaration-2002.

10. John Sutherland, "The ideas interview: Nick Bostrom," *The Guardian*, May 9, 2006.

11. Quoted in Bernard M. Daly, "Transhumanism," *America*, October 25, 2004.

12. David Hume, *Enquiries Concerning Human Understanding and Concerning the
Principles of Morals*, L.A. Selby-Bigge and P.H. Nidditch, eds., 3rd ed., Oxford: Clarendon Press, orig 1751, rep 1975, p. 409.

13. See Todd T.W. Daly, "Chasing Methuselah: Transhumanism and Christian
Theosis in Critical Perspective" in Ronald Cole-Turner, *Transhumanism and Transcendence*,
Washington D.C.: Georgetown University Press, 2011.

14. See Todd T.W. Daly, "Chasing Methuselah: Transhumanism and Christian *Theosis* in Critical Perspective" in Ronald Cole-Turner, *Transhumanism and Transcendence*, Washington D.C.: Georgetown University Press, 2011, p. 133.

15. This is a 7 minute piece in which various thinkers react to our culture's bland acceptance of death. http://hplusmagazine.com/2010/01/21/immortalists-short-film-jason -silva/.

16. Nick Bostrom, "In Defense of Posthuman Dignity," *Bioethics* 19, 2005, pp. 202-14.

17. "Nanotechnology is the understanding and control of matter at the nanoscale, at dimensions between approximately 1 and 100 nanometers, where unique phenomena enable novel applications" (National Nanotechnology Initiative). http://www.nano.gov/.

18. Simon Young, *Designer Evolution: A Transhumanist Manifesto*, Amherst, NY: Prometheus Books, 2006, pp. 11-15; Ray Kurzweil, *The Singularity Is Near: When Humans Transcend Biology*, New York: Penguin, 2006, p. 9, 233, 387.

19. Maxwell J. Mehlman, *The Price of Perfection: Individualism and Society in the Era of Biomedical Enhancement*, Baltimore: Johns Hopkins University Press, 2009, p. 8.

20. Modafinil is used for narcolepsy and excessive sleepiness in the day because of sleep apnea.

21. Julian Savulescu and Nick Bostrom, eds., *Human Enhancement*, New York: Oxford, 2009, p. 2.

22. Michael Sandel, *The Case Against Perfection: Ethics in the Age of Genetic Engineering*, Cambridge: Belknap Press of Harvard University, 2009, p. 2.

23. Sandel, ibid. See Gina Kolata, "$50,000 Offered to Tall, Smart Egg Donor," *New York Times*, March 3, 1999, p. A10. *Will parents be legally or, at least, ethically, obligated to provide enhancement to their unborn? The irony cannot be lost on a society that permits easy abortion. Could it be that a parent is not obligated to protect the life of the unborn but is obligated to provide enhanced intelligence, blond hair or upper body strength? On the one hand, the unborn child has no moral status beyond that of a rat, pig or carrot and can be eliminated at the choice of the mother. On the other that unborn child has such undeniable moral status that she can impose an obligation on the parents to provide physical and psychological enhancements. To kill or to groom, that is the question?* See John Harris, "Enhancements are a Moral Obligation" in Julian Savulescu and Nick Bostrom, eds., *Human Enhancement*, New York, Oxford University Press, 2009, pp. 131-154; Nick Bostrom, Rebecca Roache, "Ethical Issues in Human Enhancement" in *New Waves in Applied Ethics*, eds. Jesper Ryberg, Thomas Petersen & Clark Wolf, New York: Palgrave Macmillan, 2008, pp. 120-152 at http:// www.nickbostrom.com/ethics/human-enhancement.html.

24. The Theology of the Body (TOB) as taught by John Paul II represents a true development in the field of Christian anthropology. Sexuality is not a bad place to begin dealing with TOB but we shouldn't forget that our bodies are for more than sexual expression. To get started read Mary Healy, *Men And Women Are From Eden: A Study Guide to John Paul II's Theology of the Body*, Cincinnati: St. Anthony Messenger, 2005; Gregory Popcak, *Holy Sex!: A Catholic Guide to Toe-Curling, Mind-Blowing, Infallible Loving*, New York: Crossroads, 2008; Patrick Coffin, *Sex au Naturel: What It Is and Why It's Good for Your Marriage*, Christopher West, *Good News About Sex and Marriage: Answers to Your Honest Questions About Catholic Teaching*, Cincinnati: Servant Books, 2004 revised; John Paul II and Michael Waldstein, *Man and Woman He Created Them: A Theology Of The Body*, Boston: Pauline Books and Media, 2006; Karol Woytyla, *Love and Responsibility*, San Francisco: Ignatius Press, Polish orig. 1960, Eng orig. 1981., rep. 1993. *Humanae Vitae*, Encyclical of Pope Paul VI on the Regulation of Birth, 1968; *Donum Vitae*, Instruction on Respect for Human Life in Its Origin and on the Dignity of Procreation, 1987; *Evangelium Vitae*, Encyclical of Pope John Paul II, 1995. *Instruction Dignitas Personae on Certain Bioethical Questions*, Congregation for the Doctrine of the Faith, 2008.

25. John Haas' "Begotten Not Made: A Catholic View of Reproductive Technology" is an excellent brief introduction. http://old.usccb.org/prolife/programs/rlp/98rlphaa .shtml. See also William E. May, *Catholic Bioethics and Gift of Human Life*, Huntington, IN: Our Sunday Visitor, 2008; Janet E. Smith and Christopher Kaczor, *Life Issues, Medical Choices: Questions and Answers for Catholics*, Cincinnati: Servant Books, 2007. A recent

scholarly overview is Nicanor Pier Giorgio Austriaco, O.P., *Biomedicine & Beatitude: An Introduction to Catholic Bioethics*, Washington D.C.: Catholic University of America, 2011.

26. This hostile environment is no argument against Catholics participating in the Transhumanist movement in order to help it affirm authentic human flourishing. Two nationally known Catholic priests participated in the American Eugenics movement trying to emphasize those aspects of the movement which made for better families. Once the movement became committed to compulsory sterilization, they resigned. Christine Rosen spends considerable time following their work in *Preaching Eugenics: Religious Leaders and the American Eugenics Movement*, New York: Oxford University Press, 2004.

27. Bernard Daly "Transhumanism," *America*, October 25, 2004 notes that Ti said without comment from any other conference participant that "transhumanism is somewhat a product of secular humanism, which blindly rejects God, dehumanizes us into animals, claims that no objective statements can be made about morality (except the one just made), and ignores that we are intrinsically valuable because we are made in the image and likeness of God."

28. In the summer 2004 *National Catholic Bioethics Quarterly*, Ti Toth-Fejel wrote that, for instance, "nanotechnology is only a tool and can be used for good or evil..." Catholicism and Transhumanism do have a few areas of common ground. See James Hughes, "The compatibility of religious and transhumanist views of metaphysics, suffering, virtue and transcendence in an enhanced future," in *The Global Spiral* 8:2, May 2007 at http://www.metanexus.net/Magazine/tabid/68/id/9930/Default.aspx. Hughes claims that Transhumanism is more compatible with religious traditions outside the Abrahamic faiths of Judaism, Christianity, or Islam. As a former Buddhist monk, Hughes is deeply formed by the Eastern worldview. See also Darrell Jackson, "Constructing futures: Outlining a transhumanist version of the future and the challenge to Christian theology of its proposed uses of new and future developments in technology" in *The Journal of Faith and Science Exchange* 4, 2000, pp. 49-65 at http://digilib.bu.edu/journals/ojs/index.php/jfse/article/view/76. Also Eric Steinhart, "Teilhard de Chardin and Transhumanism," *Journal of Evolution and Technology*, Vol. 20, Issue 1, December 2008, pp. 1-22 at http://jetpress.org/v20/steinhart.htm.

29. Quoted in Bernard M. Daly, "Transhumanism," *America*, October 25, 2004. Daly reporting on the Transhumanist, *TransVision 2004* conference at the University of Toronto attended by 150 scientists, philosophers and engineers.

30. Simon Young, *Designer Evolution: A Transhumanist Manifesto*, Amherst, NY: Prometheus Books, 2006, p. 326. Cf. James Hughes, Report on the 2005 survey of the members of the WTA at http://transhumanism.org/resources/survey2005.pdf, 2005.

31. The Loebner prize is a monetary reward created in 1991 to encourage creation of chatbots that could converse convincingly as humans as determined by a credentialed judge.

32. Rebecca Taylor, Marymeetsdolly, "Transhumanism: Taking the Place of Our Creator" at http://www.marymeetsdolly.com/blog/index.php?/archives/1250 -Transhumanism-Taking-the-Place-of-Our-Creator.html.

33. Kyle Munkittrick, "Captain America Gets Enhancement Right," *Discover Magazine*, July 23, 2011, http://blogs.discovermagazine.com/sciencenotfiction/.

34. Larry Page, the founder and CEO of Google, helped establish Singularity University. Also on the team was Peter Thiel, a former CEO of PayPal. Andrew Hessel, a former research operations manager at Amgen and Sergey Brin, a co-founder of Google are also involved. See Ashlee Vance, "Merely Human? That's So Yesterday," *New York Times*, June 12, 2010.

35. Ray Kurzweil, *The Singularity Is Near: When Humans Transcend Biology*, New York: Penguin, 2006. The first use of "singularity" in this context was in a 1993 research paper called "The Coming Technological Singularity: How to Survive in the Post-Human Era." by Vernor Vinge, a science fiction writer, computer scientist, and math professor.

36. Jay W. Richards, ed., *Are We Spiritual Machines? Ray Kurzweil vs. the Critics of Strong A.I.*, Seattle: Discovery Institute Press, 2002; Ray Kurzweil, *The Age of Spiritual Machines: When Computers Exceed Human Intelligence*, New York: Viking, 1999.

37. George Gilder and Jay W. Richards, "Introduction" in Jay W. Richards, ed., *Are We Spiritual Machines? Ray Kurzweil vs. the Critics of Strong A.I.*, Seattle: Discovery Institute Press, 2002.

38. Lev Grossman, "2045: The Year Man Becomes Immortal." *TIME* magazine, Feb. 10, 2011 at http://www.time.com/time/magazine/article/0,9171,2048299,00.html #ixzz2Cq782ira.

39. "The Coming Technological Singularity" was presented by retired San Diego State University Mathematics professor and SF writer Vernor Vinge at the VISION-21 Symposium sponsored by NASA Lewis Research Center and the Ohio Aerospace Institute, March 30-31, 1993. In the Winter 1993 issue of *Whole Earth Review* he wrote, "Within thirty years, we will have the technological means to create superhuman intelligence. Shortly after, the human era will be ended." He was the first to use "Singularity" to describe this phenomenon.

40. Ray Kurzweil, *The Singularity Is Near: When Humans Transcend Biology*, New York: Penguin, 2006, p. 9.

41. Ibid. Cf. James J. Hughes, "The Compatibility Religious and Transhumanist Views," *Global Spiral*, 2007, www.metanexus.net/magazine/tabid/68/id/9930/Default. aspx. Cf. *Citizen Cyborg: Why Democratic Societies Must Respond to the Redesigned Human of the Future*, Cambridge, MA: Westview Press, 2004. See Ray Kurzweil, *The Age of Spiritual Machines: When Computers Exceed Human Intelligence*, New York: Viking, 1999.

42. Miguel Nicolelis, *Beyond Boundaries: The New Neuroscience of Connecting Brains with Machines and How it will Change Our Lives*, New York: Times Books, 2011.

43. Miguel Nicolelis, *Beyond Boundaries*, New York: Times Books, 2011, Kindle Location 3094 of 6908.

44. Ibid.

45. Jean-Dominique Bauby, *The Diving Bell and the Butterfly: A Memoir of Life in Death*, New York: Vintage, 1997 A movie of the same name was released in 2007.

46. Ray Kurzweil, *The Singularity Is Near: When Humans Transcend Biology*, New York: Penguin, 2006, p. 233.

47. Ray Kurzweil, *The Singularity is Near*, op cit, p. 387.

48. Kyle Munkittrick, "The Geek Rapture and Other Musings of William Gibson," *Discover Magazine*, http://blogs.discovermagazine.com/sciencenotfiction/. Cyberpunk SF novelists Neal Stephenson (b. 1959-) and Bruce Sterling (b. 1954-) have also voiced skepticism. See *The Singularity: Your Future as a Black Hole* at http://longnow.org/ seminars/02004/jun/11/the-singularity-your-future-as-a-black-hole/#. Other AI champions skeptical about "The Singularity" include cognitive scientist/atheist philosopher Daniel Dennett (b. 1942-), MIT professor of robotics Rodney Brooks (b. 1954-) and Yale computer scientist David Gelernter (b. 1954-).

49. The psychological phenomenon called "denial" grows from a spiritual/moral root. In *Genesis* 3:4, the serpent blatantly denies the truth of God's pronouncment in 2:17. The original human sin follows. The most fundamental denial is our refusal to accept our creaturely limitations. This human rebellion against reality is found in Gen 2-3, Rom 1:18-32, esp. 24, 28; 3:21; Jude 7-10; Ps. 81:12; Eph 4:19; 1 Pet 4:3. Exhibit A. the documentary film *Transcendent Man: The Life and Ideas of Ray Kurzweil* (2009), opens with the music of Philip Glass. Darkly and smoothly rolling like the waves of the ocean, the music continues as old Polaroids of Kurzweil's now deceased father form nostalgic collages. Kurzweil's grim voice muses over the visual display: "I do have a recurring dream.. that has to do with exploring this endless successions of rooms that are empty... and dark from one to the next... then feeling hopelessly abandoned and lonely and unable to find anyone else... That's a pretty good description of death... Death is supposed to be a finale but its actually a loss of everyone you care about... I do have fantasies sometimes about dying, about what people must feel like when they are dying or what I would feel like when I am dying.... It's such a profoundly sad, lonely feeling... that I really can't bear it." The music then climaxes with an abrupt cut off and then a grinning Kurzweil pops up center screen and goes glib and goofy: "*So I go back to thinking about how I'm not going to die.*" Just as Westerners receive reincarnation as a way of "not having to say you're

dead" so too, they receive the promises of Transhumanism as another way of denying the certain judgment of death. Cf. the most celebrated analysis of man's refusal to accept one's mortality, the 1974 Pulitzer Prize winning *Denial of Death* and its extension in the unfinished posthumous *Escape From Evil* by Ernst Becker (1924-1974).

50. Francis Fukuyama, *Our Posthuman Future: Consequences of the Biotechnology Revolution* , New York: Farrar, Straus and Giroux, 2002.

51. Francis Fukuyama, op cit, p. 218.

52. "Feeble-minded" was an official designation under the broad category of mental deficiency used in the 19th and into the 20th century. "Idiocy" was the most deficient; "imbecility" was a mid category. "Feeble-minded" was the highest functioning mentally deficient person. Michael Crichton, "Why Politicized Science is Dangerous," excerpted from *State of Fear*, http://www.crichton-official.com/essay-stateoffear -whypoliticizedscienceisdangerous.html.

53. See Christine Rosen, *Preaching Eugenics: Religious Leaders and the American Eugenics Movement*, New York: Oxford University Press, 2004.

54. Paul A. Lombardo, *Three Generations, No Imbeciles: Eugenics, the Supreme Court, and Buck v. Bell*, Baltimore: Johns Hopkins University Press, 2010.

55. Buck v. Bell, 1927.

56. Edwin Black, *War Against the Weak: Eugenics and America's Campaign to Create a Master Race*, expanded edition, New York: Four Walls, Eight Windows, 2012; Stefan Kuhl, *The Nazi Connection: Eugenics, American Racism, and German National Socialism*, New York: Oxford University Press, 1994; Rebecca Messall, "The Long Road of Eugenics: From Rockefeller to Roe v. Wade," *The Human Life Review*, Fall 2004, Vol. 30, Issue 4, pp. 33–74.

57. See G.K. Chesterton, *Eugenics and other Evils*, London: Cassell and Company, LTD, 1917/1922; Christine Rosen, *Preaching Eugenics: Religious Leaders and the American Eugenics Movement*, New York: Oxford University Press, 2004. See Assumption College, Worcester, MA: "Eugenics in the Culture Wars of the 1920s: Some Approaches to Studying a Neglected Topic" at http://www1.assumption.edu/ahc/1920s/eugenics/klan .html & http://www1.assumption.edu/ahc/1920s/eugenics/default.html.

58. Michael Crichton, adapted from *State of Fear*, http://www.crichton-official.com/ essay-stateoffear-whypoliticizedscienceisdangerous.html.

59. See "Transhumanist FAQ: What is Transhumanism?" at http://humanityplus .org/philosophy/transhumanist-faq/.

60. Envisioning ourselves as "between" species and a determination to take control of our evolutionary future marks the serious Transhumanist. Nick Bostrom, "TranshumanistValues," www.nickbostrom.com/ethics/values.html.

61. Given their intense focus and mission of providing "remedial catechesis" and restoring Catholic identity within the Catholic Church in America, many Catholics are oftentimes understandably ignorant of the vast number of allies we have among unbaptized men and women of good will. Gregory Wolfe has drawn our attention to *The New Religious Humanists*, New York: Free Press, 1997. Wolfe's focus was on those in the humanities but many of those I'm calling "Prudentialists" are drawn from the sciences.

62. Michael Sandel develops this in *A Case Against Perfection*, chapter 5, "Mastery and Gift," pp. 85-100.

63. Gerald McKenny, "Transcendence, Technological Enhancement, and Christian Theology" in Ronald Cole-Turner, *Transhumanism and Transcendence: Christian Hope in an Age of Technological Enhancement*, Washington D.C.: Georgetown University Press, 2011, p. 178-179.

64. Michael Sandel, *A Case Against Perfection*, p. 85.

65. If a technological elite determines the future of the race what would "life together" mean? Even atheist Jürgen Habermas argues in *The Future of Human Nature* (2003) that we do not have the right to impose our alterations of human nature on other humans. This represents a fundamental breach in human solidarity. Isn't that what we are doing, however, if we alter an embryo's genetic material? This will invite many experiments. Should we blend human and non-human traits and create human-animal chimeras? What about

abolishing deafness, blindness or other handicaps that we are told are no longer "handicaps or disabilities"? How would LGBTQIA advocates feel about a eugenics protocol eliminating same sex attraction or any sexual ambiguity or gender confusion? Will AI enable us to disconnect" bodies" from consciousness. Virtual reality would, then, become our reality and guarantee that none of these other changes would be "physically" permanent.

66. Many will recognize in this new salvation offered by Transhumanism, an adaptation of the ancient heresy of Pelagianism so successfully attacked by St. Augustine.

67. "[Materialism] has neuroscience in a chokehold and has had it there since the nineteenth century." Jeffrey M. Schwartz and Sharon Begley, *The Mind and the Brain: Neuroplasticity and the Power of Mental Force*, New York: Regan Books, 2002, p. 25. For a reply to the materialist challenge, see C. Brugger, "Aquinas on the Immateriality of Intellect: A Non-materialist reply to Materialist Objections," *The National Catholic Bioethics Quarterly*, vol. 8, no. 1, Spring 2008, pp. 103-119.

68. For a rigorous refutation of an instrumentalist view of human beings, Brugger recommends Patrick Lee and Robert P. George, *Body-Self Dualism in Contemporary Ethics and Politics*, Cambridge: Cambridge University Press, 2007.

Part Four / Abusers of Power and Wealth

OPPONENT #14
Caesar Redivivus: Better Living Through Secularized Government

1. Leszek Kolakowski, *Modernity on Endless Trial*, Chicago: University of Chicago Press, 1990, p. 179.

2. Gary Scott Smith, *Faith and the Presidency from George Washington to George W. Bush*, New York: Oxford University Press, 2009; Michael and Jana Novak, *Washington's God: Religion, Liberty, and the Father of Our Country*, 2007; Darrin Grinder, *The Presidents & Their Faith: From George Washington to Barack Obama*, 2012. Grove City College political scientist Paul Kengor demonstrates the persistent importance of religious faith in the life of those who enter public service. See his *God and Ronald Reagan: A Spiritual Life* (2005); *God and George W. Bush: A Spiritual Life* (2005) *and God and Hillary Clinton: A Spiritual Life* (2007). President Obama, after the December 14, 2012 massacre of 20 elementary school children in Newtown, Connecticut, shared the platform in an interfaith service with a dozen different clergy in which America's current Chief Executive quoted the New Testament with an effectiveness and believability that matched George Washington, if not Abraham Lincoln.

3. *O'Reilly Factor*, November 29, 2012.

4. John F. Kennedy, speech at The American University, Washington, D.C., June 10, 1963.

5. To a more or less degree, this humanistic perspective is represented in the late Western tradition by Karl Marx (1818-1883), Herbert Spencer (1820-1903), John Dewey (1859-1952), Julian Huxley (1887-1975), and the Humanist Manifesto of 1933. More recently, this frame of mind is represented by people like Paul Kurtz (1925-2012), E.O. Wilson (b. 1929-), Jurgen Habermas (b. 1929), Richard Dawkins (b. 1941-), A.C. Grayling (b. 1949-), David Sloan Wilson (b. 1949-), Luc Ferry (b. 1951, Niall Ferguson (b. 1964-), Sam Harris (b. 1967-), Ayaan Hirsi Ali (b. 1969-), Samantha Power (b. 1970-), and Steven Pinker (b. 1954-).

6. An icon of political liberalism, he was central to "a number of overlapping movements interested in laying out a social theory to underwrite political transformation." Robert Westbrook, *John Dewey and American Democracy*, Ithaca, NY: Cornell University Press, 1991, p. xv, 317-318, 433-434; See also Ryan Alan, *John Dewey And The High Tide Of American Liberalism*, 1997; William Andrew Paringer, *John Dewey and the Paradox of Liberal Reform*, 1990.

7. Hilda M. Neatby, *So Little for the Mind*, Toronto: Clarke Irwin & Co. Ltd., 1953, pp.22-23. She's playing off Aquinas' practice in the *Summa Theologia* of citing Aristotle as "the philosopher."

8. Melvin L. Rogers, *The Undiscovered Dewey: Religion, Morality, and the Ethos of Democracy*, New York: Columbia University Press, 2009, p. 27; Cf. Steven C. Rockefeller's sympathetic *John Dewey: Religious Faith and Democratic Humanism*, New York: Columbia University Press, 1991, p. 222.

9. Steven C. Rockefeller, ibid.

10. In spite of Dewey's appreciation for the intellectual shift suggested by Darwinism, he continues to hold a more Newtonian than Darwinian view of rationality and Enlightenment confidence in progress. See Melvin Rogers, *The Undiscovered Dewey*, p. 3.

11. John Dewey, "The Influence of Darwinism on Philosophy" *Popular Science Monthly*, July, 1909 and reprinted in John Dewey, *The Influence of Darwin on Philosophy*, New York: Henry Holt, 1910. See also http://members.door.net/arisbe/menu/library/aboutcsp/Dewey/Darwin.htm.

12. His movement out of Christianity seemed to parallel his move from Hegelian idealism to the newly developing Pragmatism. See Melvin L. Rogers, *The Undiscovered Dewey*, p. 8. Dewey did, however, continue to engage theologians like Reinhold Niebuhr. See Richard John Neuhaus, "The Real John Dewey," *First Things*, Jan 1992. On Dewey's religious history see Steven C. Rockefeller's *John Dewey: Religious Faith and Democratic Humanism*, New York: Columbia University Press, 1991, pp 317 ff. and David Hildebrand, *Dewey*, Oxford: One World, 2008, pp.183-206. For a severe but intelligent Christian critique from Gordon H. Clark (1902-1985), the former chair of Butler University's philosophy department and a thoroughgoing Calvinist see *Dewey*, Philadelphia: Presbyterian and Reformed Publishing, 1974.

13. For a brief critique of secular liberalism from the standpoint of historic Christianity see Francis J. Beckwith, *Politics for Christians: Statecraft as Soulcraft*, Downers Grove, IL: InterVarsity Press, 2010 pp. 119-143. Beckwith is, arguably, the best single volume to orient a Christian to political science.

14. Avery Cardinal Dulles, "John Paul II and the New Evangelization" in *Church and Society: The Laurence J. McGinley Lectures, 1988-2007*, New York: Fordham University Press, 2008, p. 116.

15. Carl Becker, *The Heavenly City of the Eighteenth Century Philosophers*, New Haven: Yale University Press, orig. 1932, rep 2005, p. xi. Becker claims Enlightenment thinkers took the attributes of the Christian God and located them in "nature" and "natural law." In this way, Becker concludes that the Enlightenment just substituted a new deity for the existing deity, and thus should be more correctly considered an example of medieval, rather than modern philosophy. Peter Gay's much quoted June 1957 critique in the *Political Science Quarterly* has not buried Becker's thesis which continues being studied 80 years after publication. http://userpages.umbc.edu/~jamie/html/on__the_heavenly_city_of_eight.html.

16. See the classic study by Norman Cohn, *The Pursuit of the Millennium: Revolutionary Millenarians and Mystical Anarchists of the Middle Ages*, New York: Oxford University Press, 1970.

17. The Catholic Church, in contrast, teaches that this is a deception of the Antichrist (*CCC*, 675).

18. James Block, *A Nation of Agents: The American Path to a Modern Self and Society*, Cambridge, MA: Harvard University Press, 2002, p. 334.

19. Paul Tillich (1886-1965) is the best-known exponent of faith as "ultimate concern." See Paul Tillich, *Dynamics of Faith*, New York: Harper, 1957, pp. 1, 2. Tillich claims even atheists have "ultimate concern" p. 52.

20. See Benjamin Wiker and Jonathan Witt's *A Meaningful World: How the Arts and Sciences Reveal the Genius of Nature*, Downers Grove, IL: InterVarsity Press, 2006 for the inevitability of finding pattern, design, and meaning in our experience of the world. See Viktor Frankl's *Man's Search for Meaning* in many editions. Five years in Nazi camps, he discovers that survival is not a matter of physical fitness as much as existential purpose. "Our generation is realistic, for we have come to know man as he really is," Frankl writes. "After all, man is that being who invented the gas chambers of Auschwitz; however, he is also that being who entered those gas chambers upright, with the Lord's Prayer or the Shema Yisrael on his lips."

21. Lesslie Newbigin, *Foolishness to the Greeks: The Gospel and Western Civilization*, Grand Rapids: Eerdmans, 1986, p. 132.

22. Francis J. Beckwith, *Politics for Christians: Statecraft as Soulcraft*, Downers Grove, IL: InterVarsity Press, 2010 pp. 151ff.

23. John Dewey, "The Future of Liberalism," an address presented at the 24th annual meeting of the American Philosophical Association, Eastern Division, New York University, December 28, 1934 quoted in Allan Wolfe, *The Future of Liberalism*, New York: Alfred A. Knopf, 2009.

24. Wesley J. Smith, "Peter Singer Falls for Immortality Quest," *National Review Online*, Dec. 11, 2012. www.nationalreview.com/human-esceptionalism/335337/peter-singer-falls-immortality.

25. Ashlee Vance, "Merely Human? That's So Yesterday," *New York Times*, June 12, 2010.

26. The first use of "Transhumanism" goes back to the 1930s and is attributed to Julian Huxley. In 1957, Huxley, the grandson of Darwin's "bulldog" Thomas Huxley and first director of UNESCO, reprised it: "I believe in *transhumanism*. Once there are enough people who can truly say that, the human species will be on the threshold of a new kind of existence, as different from ours as ours is from that of Peking man. It will at last be consciously fulfilling its real destiny" in Julian Huxley, "Transhumanism," *New Bottles for New Wine: Essays*, London: Chatto & Windus, 1957, pp. 13-17.

27. Robert Westbrook, *John Dewey and American Democracy*, Ithaca, NY: Cornell University Press, 1991, p. xv, 317-318, 433-434.

28. Melvin L. Rogers, *The Undiscovered Dewey: Religion, Morality, and the Ethos of Democracy*, New York: Columbia University Press, 2009, p. 2.

29. The Catholic faith does not specify any particular political system as best. Freedom and equality, however, are central to the Christian drama of redemption. Christians have largely embraced liberal democracies for four reasons: 1. Liberty to worship, 2. The people have some mechanism to hold governments accountable, 3. Participation in their own government through voting, forming of political parties, running for office, etc., 4. It seems consistent with a Christian understanding of the human person who is free to pursue excellence and virtue and do so through compliance with the natural or moral law. Francis J. Beckwith, *Politics for Christians: Statecraft as Soulcraft*, Downers Grove, IL: InterVarsity Press, 2010, p. 59.

30. See Patrick Deenen, *Democratic Faith*, Princeton, NJ: Princeton University Press, 2005. Journalist Ken Myers' interview of Deenen is available at http://www.marshillaudio.org/.

31. 1 Jn 3:3; *CCC*, 163.

32. Ronald Cole Turner, *Transhumanism and Transcendence: Christian Hope in an Age of Technological Enhancement*, Washington DC: Georgetown University Press, 2011, pp. 194-195.

33. Friedrich Nietzsche, *The Will to Power*, Section 960, 1885-1886, http://www.yuga.com/Cgi/Pag.dll?Pag=110.

34. See Phyllis Schlafly and George Neumayr, *No Higher Power: Obama's War on Religious Freedom*, Washington, D.C.: Regnery, 2012; Still engaging is Richard John Neuhaus' *The Naked Public Square: Religion and Democracy in America*, Grand Rapids: Eerdmans, 1988.

35. Allan Wolfe, *The Future of Liberalism*, New York: Alfred A. Knopf, 2009, p. 183.

36. This view of freedom has less to do with America's founders who envisioned a republic of virtue than with John Stuart Mill's *On Liberty* (1859) where we read: "the only purpose for which power can be rightfully exercised over any member of a civilized community, against his will, is to prevent harm to others." http://www.utilitarianism.com/ol/one.html. Mill has taken a limiting principle for doubtful moral situations and elevated it into the supreme principle. For the Catholic the supreme principle is that "good should be done and evil avoided." John Paul II addressed this "harm principle" in *Evangelium Vitae*.

37. Cass Sunstein, *The Second Bill of Rights: FDR's Unfinished Revolution — And Why We Need It More Than Ever*, New York: Basic Books, 2006.

38. FDR (1882-1945) said: "I ask Congress to explore the means for implementing the economic bill of rights- for it is definitely the responsibility of the congress to do it." Such thoughts weren't new with the New Deal. Montesquieu (1689-1755) wrote: "The alms given to a naked man in the street do not fulfill the obligations of the state, which owes to every citizen a certain subsistence, a proper nourishment, convenient clothing and a kind of life not incompatible with health."

39. Cass R. Sunstein, *After the Rights Revolution: Reconceiving the Regulatory State*, Cambridge, MA: Harvard University Press, 1993. Cass Sunstein has served as President Obama's regulatory czar.

40. I like to remind people that Bill Clinton nine times used the phrase *The New Covenant* in his acceptance speech but it found no echoes among the increasingly secularized Democrats. I suspect Christians within the party thought it overreached to the borderline of sacrilege.

41. Quoted in George F. Will, "Obama: the real radical," *Washington Post*, September 5, 2012.

42. Turners $1 billion gift created the United Nations Foundation which now exists to broaden support for UN initiatives. Turner chairs its board. The annual report cover letter for the Bill and Melinda Gates Foundation lists four initiatives, all of which greatly enhance governmental organizations. http://www.gatesfoundation.org/nr/public/media/annualreports/annualreport04/letter/.

43. Richard John Neuhaus, *The Naked Public Square*, Grand Rapids: Eerdmans, 1984, p. 154.

44. Maryanne Walsh, "Memo to HHS: Show Me the Data," blog, November 7, 2011 at http://usccbmedia.blogspot.com/2011/11/memo-to-hhs-show-me-data.html.

45. This led to an unnecessary interruption of services to victims. The USCCB continue to work on reconciliation hopeful that this is but a temporary snafu.

46. The American Freedom Law Center represents Ms. Dixon. We are learning that employment in government agencies strip us of certain protections. In addition, diversity is limited to gender and skin pigment but doesn't include diverse points of view. See http://www.americanfreedomlawcenter.org/cases/23/crystal-dixon-v-university-of-toledo.html.

47. Kathy Shaidle, "Coercively 'Tolerant'" http://www.catholicculture.org/culture/library/view.cfm?recnum=8600.

48. In 1 Cor 6:1-8 (reflecting on Deut 1:9-17; 16:18-29) St. Paul warns that since unbelievers lack the Spirit of God, they are unfit to judge between those who have received Christ's Spirit since this Spirit is the spirit of reconciliation, peace and contentment and teaches us to suffer injustice, quickly reconcile and offer forgiveness abundantly to one another. Such self-government had marked Israel who had judged herself with her own appointed judges from within the covenant people. He simply assumed that the Church would apply and follow that pattern.

49. See Robert Barron, *Catholicism: A Journey to the Heart of the Faith*, New York: Doubleday Image, 2011, pp. 28-35.

50. Lesslie Newbigin, *Foolishness to the Greeks: The Gospel and Western Civilization*, Grand Rapids: Eerdmans, 1986, pp. 131-132.

51. Seyoon Kim, *Christ and Caesar: The Gospel and the Roman Empire*, Grand Rapids: Eerdmans, 2008; Richard J. Cassidy, *Jesus, Politics, and Society*, 1978; *Paul in Chains: Roman Imprisonment and the Letters of Paul*, 2001; N.T. Wright, "Paul's Gospel and Caesar's Empire" in *Paul and Politics: Eccklesia, Israel, Imperium, Interpretation*, ed., Richard A. Horseley, pop. 160-183, 2000.

52. Christopher Bryan, *Render to Caesar: Jesus, the Early Church, and the Roman Superpower*, New York: Oxford University Press, 2005; Neil Elliot, "The Anti-Imperial Message of the Cross," in *Paul and Empire: Religion and Power in Roman Imperial Society*, ed., R.A. Horsley, pp. 167-183; James S. McLaren, "Jews and the Imperial Cult: From Augustus to Domitian in *Journal for the Study of the New Testament* 27, 2005, pp. 257-278; John Howard Yoder, *The Politics of Jesus: Vicit Agnus Noster*, 1994.

53. David Aikman, *One Nation Without God: The Battle for Christianity in an Age of*

Unbelief, Grand Rapids: Baker Books, 2012, p. 165. See also *Jesus in Beijing: How Christianity Is Transforming China And Changing the Global Balance of Power,* Washington DC: Regnery, 2006. Aikman was formerly TIME's Senior Foreign Correspondent.

54. Jean Bethke Elshtain offers a lengthy analysis of political sovereignty in *Sovereignty: God, State, and Self,* New York: Basic Books, 2008.

55. "France Monitoring Traditionalist Catholics for 'Religious Pathology,' " *Catholic News Agency,* Dec 13, 2012.

56. Neil Postman, *Amusing Ourselves to Death: Public Discourse in the Age of Show Business,* New York: Penguin Books, 1985, pp. xix, xx.

57. Neil Postman, *Amusing Ourselves to Death,* pp. 155-156. Mark Halperin's *The Way to Win: Taking the White House in 2008,* New York: Random House, 2006 describes this reality in political campaigns. See especially his description of "The Freak Show."

58. An expression used to describe how rulers can gain public approval through pandering to the indulgences of their constituency who no longer care about civic values or virtues and seek only to satisfy themselves.

59. Mark Robertson, "Time Spent On Web and Mobile Video To Triple By 2013," ReelSEO Marketing Guide, http://www.reelseo.com/mobile-web-video-consumption-2013/#ixzz2EQ J8BdBo.

60. Office of National Drug Control Policy, "Prescription Drug Abuse" at http://www.whitehouse.gov/ondcp/prescription-drug-abuse.

61. Is the public even capable of governing itself? This argument was opened up in 1922 by Walter Lippmann and John Dewey. Lippman took the negative, Dewey the positive. First, Lippman's *Public Opinion* (1922) — Dewey's review in *The New Republic* (1922) — Lippmann's *The Phantom Public* (1925) — Dewey's The *Public and Its Problems* (1927). Cf. "The 'Lippmann-Dewey Debate' and the Invention of Walter Lippmann as an Anti-Democrat 1986-1996" by Michael Schudson in *International Journal of Communication* 2, 2008, 1031-1042.

62. Edward S. Herman, Noam Chomsky, *Manufacturing Consent: The Political Economy of the Mass Media,* New York: Pantheon Books, 1988, 2002.

63. Phil 3:19.

64. Pew Forum on Religion and Public Life, http://projects.pewforum.org/2012-presidential-election-candidate-religious-groups/#for-obama.

65. Many Christians accept evolution as a biological theory explaining the history of the human body's formation. At some point, in some way, however, God acted to form an ensouled person.

66. 1 Pt 2:9.

67. Pew Forum on Religion and Public Life, http://projects.pewforum.org/2012-presidential-election-candidate-religious-groups/#for-obama.

68. See Deal W. Hudson and Matt Smith, "Applying the Principles: Prudential Judgment" in *Issues for Catholic Voters, 2012 Edition,* Catholic Advocate. Available as Amazon ebook.

69. USCCB, *Forming Consciences for Faithful Citizenship,* Part I, 34.

70. Bishop Paprocki's column *Catholic Times* Sept 23, 2012. http://ct.dio.org/bishops-column/59-think-and-pray-about-your-vote-in-upcoming-election/video.html http://www.ncregister.com/daily-news/bishop-paprocki-warns-of-intrinsic-evils-in-democratic-platform/.

71. Paul A. Lombardo, *Three Generations, No Imbeciles: Eugenics, the Supreme Court, and Buck v. Bell,* Baltimore: Johns Hopkins University Press, 2010; Edwin Black, *War Against the Weak: Eugenics and America's Campaign to Create a Master Race,* expanded edition, New York: Four Walls Eight Windows, 2012; G.K. Chesterton, *Eugenics and other Evils,* London: Cassell and Company, LTD, 1917 orig. rep. 1922.

72. Julie Sullivan, "State will admit sterilization past," *Portland Oregonian,* November 15, 2002. It now appears that the United States led the way in compulsory sterilization programs for the purpose of eugenics. The state of Indiana was not the first to introduce such laws (Michigan had in 1897) but was the first to pass one which it did in 1907. In the end, over 65,000 individuals were sterilized in 33 states under state com-

pulsory sterilization programs in the United States. The last forced sterilization was in Oregon in 1981.

73. Christine Rosen, *Preaching Eugenics: Religious Leaders and the American Eugenics Movement*, New York: Oxford University Press, 2004; For today's cooperation between Catholics and evangelical Protestants see Deal W. Hudson, *Onward, Christian Soldiers: The Growing Political Power of Catholics and Evangelicals in the United States*, New York: Simon & Schuster, 2008.

74. Richard John Neuhaus, *The Naked Public Square*, Grand Rapids: Eerdmans, 1984, p. 155.

75. Thomas Hobbes (1588–1679) published *Leviathan or The Matter, Forme and Power of a Common Wealth Ecclesiasticall and Civil*, commonly referred to as *Leviathan* (1651) taken from the biblical sea monster Leviathan in Job 41 and Isaiah 27. It is one of the great European books on statecraft alongside Machiavelli's *The Prince*, Locke's *Second Treatise on Civil Government*, Montesquieu's *The Spirit of the Laws*, and Rousseau's *Social Contract*. Hobbes wrote it during the chaos and bloodshed of the English Civil War (1642-1651). It is the most compelling argument for governance by an absolute ruler.

76. Ernest Marshall Howse, *Saints in Politics: The 'Clapham Sect' and the Growth of Freedom*, London: Allen & Unwin, 1973; Stephen Tomkins, *The Clapham Sect: How Wilberforce's Circle Transformed Britain*, London: Lion UK, 2010.

77. Quoted in Garth Lean, *God's Politician*, Colorado Springs: Helmers & Howard, 1987, p. 69.

78. Greg Koukl, http://www.str.org/site/News2?page=NewsArticle&id=5265. In a book yet to be absorbed by Christian activists, James Davison Hunter in *To Change the World: The Irony, Tragedy, and Possibility of Christianity in the Late Modern World*, New York: Oxford, 2010 challenges the assumption that increased individual conversions necessarily leads to changed culture. For those concerned about the cultural consequences of the gospel, this is essential if we are to sharpen our thinking.

79. See John Lewis Gaddis, *The Cold War: A New History*, New York: Penguin, 2006.

80. Richard John Neuhaus, *The Naked Public Square*, Grand Rapids: Eerdmans, 1984, p. 155.

OPPONENT #15
Consumerism: Branding the Heart

1. David Brooks, *Bobos in Paradise: The New Upper Class and How They Got There*, New York: Simon & Schuster, 2000, p. 61.

2. Rodney Clapp, "Why the Devil takes VISA: A Christian Response to the Triumph of Consumerism," *Christianity Today*, October 7, 1996.

3. John Paul II, Encyclical Letter *Sollicitudo Rei Socialis* [On Social Concern], December 30, 1987.

4. Petra Nemcova and Jane Scovell, *Love Always, Petra: A Story of Courage and the Discovery of Life's Hidden Gifts*, New York: Warner Books, 2005, pp. 1-2.

5. According to the U.S. Geological Survey. See *National Geographic News*, January 7, 2005 at http://news.nationalgeographic.com/news/2004/12/1227_041226_tsunami.html.

6. She appeared in many other issues of SI and worked with Benetton, Max Factor, Victoria's Secret and dozens of others.

7. Petra, baptized Catholic, grew up in a spiritually indifferent household excepting her prayerful, Mass attending grandmother. Petra admires her and is pleased to know someone is praying for her. Petra, herself, tells us that she does pray as well as sends "positive energy." Why? "I do believe that there is a greater power, and that we often lose track of this. Sometimes we think we are more powerful than anything, which is foolish. We should respect the greater power or energy or God, whatever we choose to call it. In my childhood the only 'power, 'communism', was not so good." See Petra Nemkova, *Love Always, Petra*, pp. 23- 24.

8. Mt 6:24-25; 16:26; Cf. Mk 8:36-37.

9. Reported in John De Graaf, et al, *Affluenza: The All Consuming Epidemic*, 2nd edition, San Francisco: Berrett-Koehler Publishers, 2005, p. xv. See http://www.huffingtonpost .com/petra-nemcova/restoring-the-lives-of-ch_b_399537.html.

10. Petra (b. 1979-) is still young and successful enough to host Carlos Slim (b. 1940), momentarily the world's richest man, and famed vocalist Marc Anthony (b. 1968-) at her philanthropic dinners. See http://www.happyheartsfund.org/.

11. "Conspicuous consumption" comes from Norwegian-American economist Thorstein Veblen (1857-1929) whose *The Theory of the Leisure Class* (1899) was tremendously influential.

12. The word "consumerism" first appears in the OED (1915) as "advocacy of the rights and interests of consumers." Its present usage as a criticism of American commercial culture can be traced to the term "conspicuous consumption" around the turn of the 20th century.

13. John Paul II, Encyclical *Centismimus Annus*, May 1, 1991, #36. See "World Day of Peace Message," January 1, 1990; Encyclical *Centismimus Annus*, May 1, 1991, # 37, 49, 41; Encyclical *Redemptor Hominis*, #16; Encyclical *Sollicitudo Rei Socialis* [On Social Concern], December 30, 1987 #28.

14. For instance, Benedict XVI, Encyclical *Caritas in Veritate*, June 29, 2009, #34; Benedict XVI and Woodeene Koenig-Bricker, *Ten Commandments for the Environment: Pope Benedict XVI Speaks Out for Creation and Justice*, 2009. See paragraphs 47, 260, 310, 331-376, 462-486, 554-560 of the *Compendium of the Social Doctrine of the Church*, Pontifical Council for Justice and Peace, 2003.

15. April Lane Benson, ed., *I Shop Therefore I Am: Compulsive Buying and the Search for Self*, New York: Jason Aronson, 2000; April Lane Benson, *To Buy or Not to Buy: Why We Overshop and How to Stop* (2008); Adrienne Baker, ed., *Serious Shopping: Essays in Psychothereapy and Consumerism*, 2000.

16. Jonathan Porrit's loathsome ideology holds that contraception, abortion and family planning will ease global warming and that people with more than two children are irresponsible spongers. How, in the long run, he hopes to provide for the well-being of the human by encouraging practices that imply human beings are not desirable as goods, is a sign of blindness that comes from denial of God's goodness manifested through his created order.

17. Jonathan Porrit, "Consumerism" *Big Ideas* http://www.mymultiplesclerosis .co.uk/big-ideas/consumerism.html. See Thomas Frank, *The Conquest of Cool: Business Culture, Counterculture, and the Rise of Hip Consumerism*, 1998. Frank shows how consumerism's seductive power turned the beat and hippie counter cultures into today's dominant commercial pop culture. Think of Nike using the song "Revolution" to sell sneakers, or Coca-Cola using replicas of Ken Kesey's LSD-fueled bus to peddle Fruitopia as two small examples.

18. Rabbi Jonathan Sacks, Lecture "Has Europe Lost Its Soul?" delivered at The Pontifical Gregorian University, Rome, December 12, 2011. http://www.chiefrabbi .org/2011/12/12/has-europe-lost-its-soul-transcript-of-lecture-delivered-at-the -pontifical-gregorian-university-rome/.

19. John Paul II, Encyclical *Centismimus Annus*, May 1, 1991, #36.

20. Neuromarketing is the field which examines how to stimulate consumer senses, emotions, sensorimotor and cognitive faculties, including heart and breathing rates. MRI, polygraph, EEG and other technologies are currently employed to gain data. Google, CBS, Frito-Lay have been early leaders in the field according to Natasha Singer. "Making Ads that Whisper to the Brain," *The New York Times*, November 3, 2010 at http://www.nytimes.com/2010/11/14/business/14stream.html.

21. Quoted in Sky Jethani, *The Divine Commodity: Discovering a Faith Beyond Consumer Christianity*, Grand Rapids: Zondervan, 2009, p. 50.

22. D.G. Myers & E. Diener, "The Pursuit of Happiness," *Scientific American*, May, 1996, pp. 70-72.

23. Quoted in Sky Jethani, *The Divine Commodity*, 2009, p. 50.

24. Daniel Boorstin, *The Image: A Guide to Pseudo-events in America*, New York: Atheneum, orig 1961, 1980, p.45-47.

25. Ron Sider, *Rich Christians in an Age of Hunger*, Downers Grove, IL: InterVarsity Press, 5th edition, 2005 xiv.

26. http://www.goodreads.com/quotes/tag/consumerism.

27. The goods of the earth are universally destined, i.e., they exist for all God's children. The Church is also absolutely clear on the sanctity of private property. See the Pontifical Council for Justice and Peace, *Compendium of the Social Doctrine of the Church*, 2003, paragraphs 171-184, 206, 482, 582.

28. John Paul II, "World Day of Peace Message," #15, January 1, 1990.

29. James B. Twitchell, *Shopping for God: How Christianity Went from In Your Heart to In Your Face* (2007); *Branded Nation: The Marketing of Megachurch, College Inc., and Museumworld* (2004); *Twenty Ads that Shook the World, The Century's Most Groundbreaking Advertising and How it Changes Us All* (2001); *Lead Us Not Into Temptation: The Triumph of American Materialism* (2000); *Adcult USA: The Triumph of Advertising in America* (1997).

30. James B. Twitchell, *Twenty Ads that Shook the World*, 2000, p. 1.

31. Yumiko Ono, "Marketers Seek the 'Naked' Truth in Consumer Psyches," *Wall Street Journal*, May 390, 1997, B1.

32. Bob Garfield interviewed in PBS Frontline, *The Persuaders*, directed by Barak Goodman and Rachel Dretzin, written by Barak Goodman & Douglas Rushkoff, WGBH Educational Foundation, 2004.

33. We notice only eighty and react to only twelve. James B. Twitchell, *Twenty Ads that Shook the World*, 2000, p. 2.

34. *Didache*, #4 in *Early Christian Writings: The Apostolic Fathers*, Andrew Louth & Maxwell Staniforth, trans. New York: Penguin, rev. 2008, pp. 192-193.

35. Rodney Clapp, "Why the Devil takes VISA: A Christian response to the triumph of consumerism," *Christianity Today*, October 7, 1996.

36. Today we define "usury" as excessive interest. This was not always so. The presumption had been against loans with any interest. The most recent relatively complete papal discussion of usury is Pope Benedict XIV's encyclical of 1745, *Vix pervenit*. He does find instances where interest on a loan is licit. "One cannot condone the sin of usury by arguing that the gain is not great or excessive, but rather moderate or small; neither can it be condoned by arguing that the borrower is rich; nor even by arguing that the money borrowed is not left idle, but is spent usefully..." For good reasons we can't consider, this doesn't threaten papal infallibility. The Vatican itself invests money in interest bearing loans.

37. Raymond de Roover, "The Concept of the Just Price: Theory and Economic Policy," *Journal of Economic History*, 18:418-434. Albert the Great (1206-1280) commenting on the *Sentences* of Peter Lombard proposed that the just price to charge for something is not what it cost, but what "goods are worth according to the estimation of the market at the time of sale." Thomas Aquinas (1225-1274) asks "Whether a man may justly sell a thing for more than it is worth?" See Arthur Eli Monroe, *Early Economic Thought: Selections from Economic Literature Prior to Adam Smith*, New York: Gordon Press, 1975.

38. Kenneth Clark, *Civilisation: A Personal View*, New York: Harper & Row, 1969, p. 330.

39. In 1311, the Cathedral Church of the Blessed Virgin Mary of Lincoln (the Lincoln Cathedral) replaced the Great Pyramid of Giza as the world's tallest building. Churches continued to hold the number one position until the Washington Monument in 1884. The early age of skyscrapers (1880-1900) doesn't challenge the dominance of churches. The first decade of the 20th century, however, begins to see secular skyscrapers regularly rising above churches and cathedrals.

40. The Empire State Building (mixed offices) and the Bank of America Tower are second and third in New York.

41. The second-, third- and fourth-tallest buildings in Chicago are the Trump International Hotel & Tower, the Aon Center and the John Hancock Center, respectively.

42. Church buildings do not need 80 plus floors for liturgical purpose. But religious communities could cooperate with church agencies. schools, including life-long adult catechesis, associations of the lay faithful, organizations promoting the corporal works of mercy, Mutual Aid Societies and Christian credit unions and insurance companies. Regarding height: church towers, spires and the minarets of mosques are often significant.

43. John Paul II, Encyclical, *Centesimus Annus*, May 1, 1991, #36. Cf. Richard John Neuhaus, *Doing Well and Doing Good*, New York: Random House, 1992, p. 51. This was Neuhaus's commentary on *Centisimus Annus*.

44. Quoted in Lauren Tyler Wright, *Giving - The Sacred Art: Creating a Lifestyle of Generousity*, Woodstock,VT: Skylight Path Press, 2008, p. 87.

45. My thanks to Skye Jethani for this phrase. See his insightful and finely written book *The Divine Commodity*.

46. Barton, the son of a preacher, did his best to "corporatize" Christianity. He portrayed Jesus as a corporate executive in *The Man Nobody Knows*. He regularly drew on his religious upbringing for inspirational messages. In 1923, Barton told GM president Pierre du Pont that the role of advertising was to help corporations find their soul. 'I like to think of advertising as something big, something splendid, something which goes deep down into an institution and gets hold of the soul of it... Institutions have souls, just as men and nations have souls."

47. Three Marlboro men – Wayne McLaren, David McLean and Dick Hammer- died of lung cancer, thus earning Marlboro cigarettes, specifically Marlboro Reds, the nickname "Cowboy killers." Lilo McLean, wife of David McLean, sued Philip Morris, which makes Marlboro cigarettes, along with Liggett Group, R.J. Reynolds, the American Tobacco Company and Brown and Williamson in her federal lawsuit. See "Wife of Marlboro Man suing Tobacco Companies" *Associated Press* Saturday, September 14, 1996. After developing lung cancer in 1990, Wayne McLaren became an anti-smoking crusader citing his 30-year smoking habit as the cause of his cancer. During the time of McLaren's anti-smoking activism, Philip Morris denied that McLaren ever appeared in a Marlboro ad. In 1976, a British documentary *Death In the West*, about the cigarette industry centered around the myth of the Marlboro Man. Philip Morris sued the filmmakers and in a 1979 secret settlement all copies were destroyed.

48. Rick Telander, "Your Sneakers or Your Life," *Sports Illustrated*, May 14, 1990.

49. Skye Jethani, *The Divine Commodity: Discovering a Faith Beyond Consumer Christianity*, Grand Rapids: Zondervan, 2009, pp. 47-48.

50. Quoted in Mercer Schudardt, "Swooshtika," *Regeneration Quarterly*, July 1, 1997.

51. Rick Telender, "Your Sneakers or Your Life," *Sports Illustrated*, May 14, 1990.

52. Skye Jethani, *The Divine Commodity: Discovering a Faith Beyond Consumer Christianity*, Grand Rapids: Zondervan, 2009, p. 51.

53. Naomi Klein in PBS Frontline, *The Persuaders*, directed by Barak Goodman and Rachel Dretzin, written by Barak Goodman & Douglas Rushkoff, WGBH Educational Foundation, 2004.

54. Naomi Klein interview Jan 24, 2004, by Douglas Rushkoff for PBS Frontline, *The Persuaders*, directed by Barak Goodman and Rachel Dretzin, WGBH Educational Foundation, 2004. See Naomi Klein, *No Logo*, New York: Picador, 1999.

55. PBS Frontline, *The Persuaders*, directed by Barak Goodman and Rachel Dretzin, written by Barak Goodman & Douglas Rushkoff, WGBH Educational Foundation, 2004.

56. Douglas Atkin interview for PBS Frontline, *The Persuaders*.

57. Ibid.

58. Walter Brueggemann, *Journey to the Common Good*, Louisville: Westminster/ John Knox, 2010, p. 26.

59. Abraham Joshua Heschel quoted in Jerome Segal, *Graceful Simplicity*, New York: Henry Holt, 1999, p. 167.

60. Benedict XVI, Encyclical, *Caritas in Veritate*, June 29, 2009, #34. See John Paul II, Apostolic Letter, *Dies Domini*, July 5, 1998.

61. L. Shannon Jung *Sharing Food: Christian Pratices for Enjoyment*, Minneapolis: Fortress, 2006, p. 161.

62. See James 1:2-18.

63. Matt 26:39; Lk 22:42.

64. Cf. Hebrews 12:2.

65. Mt 13:44ff.

66. C.S. Lewis, *The Weight of Glory* and Other Addresses, New York: HarperOne, orig. 1949, rep. 2000, p. 26.

67. Psalm 42:1-2.

68. Psalm 63:1.

69. Psalm 37:4.

70. Psalm 36:8.

71. Quoted in Rodney Clapp, "Why the Devil takes VISA: A Christian response to the triumph of consumerism," *Christianity Today*, October 7, 1996.

72. Eugene LaVerdiere, *The Eucharist in the New Testament and the Early Church*, Collegeville, MN: Liturgical Press 1996, pp. 1-2.

73. 1 Tim 4:4-5.

74. Laura Hartman, author of *The Christian Consumer*, interview by Caryn Rivadeneira, "Black Friday, Cyber Monday and the Christian Consumer," *Christianity Today*, Nov 27, 2011. Political activists want to combat consumerism without reference to spirituality. Hartman urges otherwise. "We have to go beyond fair trade. We have to go beyond organic. We don't only have to consume as if we are concerned citizens—which we should be. We should also consume as if we are believing, practicing Christians, which means that we consume in faith. God's power is even bigger than the big concerns that come with our consumption."

75. Eph 5:20.

76. Phil 4:6,7.

77. Col 2:6,7.

78. Col 3: 15,17.

79. Col 4:2.

80. I am grateful to the late evangelical apologist Francis A. Schaeffer (1912-1984) for many of these verses and thoughts regarding thanksgiving. See his *True Spirituality*, Carol Stream, IL: Tyndale, especially chapter one, orig. 1971, rep. 2001.

81. 1 Thess 5:18-19.

82. John 15:26, 27; Cf. 14:15-31; 16:1-15.

83. 1 Cor 15:17, 19, 32.

84. I have a suspicion that professional philosophers and logicians would find fault with the formulation but I think she is saying that to see something as it truly is, is to participate in God's knowledge of the thing.

85. Titus 2:10.

86. For the theology behind this point see John Saward, *The Beauty of Holiness and the Holiness of Beauty: Art, Sanctity & the Truth of Catholicism*, San Francisco: Ignatius Press, 1997.

KRESTA
in the afternoon
hosted by
Al Kresta
BUILD THE CHURCH.
BLESS THE NATION.
for conversations
of consequence
visit avemariaradio.net